HISTORICAL GEOGRAPHY

Through the Gates of Space and Time

Robin A. Butlin

Professor of Geography, Loughborough University of Technology

Edward Arnold

A division of Hodder & Stoughton

LONDON NEW YORK MELBOURNE AUCKLAND

© 1993 R.A. Butlin

First published in Great Britain 1993

Distributed in the USA by Routledge, Chapman and Hall, Inc.,
29 West 35th Street, New York, NY 1001

British Library Cataloguing in Publication Data
Available on request.

ISBN 0 340 48969 3

Whilst the advice and information in this book is believed to be true
and accurate at the date of going to press, neither the author nor the
publisher can accept any legal responsibility or liability for any errors
or omissions that may be made.
Typeset in 10 on 11pt Sabon by Wearset, Boldon, Tyne and Wear.
Printed and bound in Great Britain for Edward Arnold, a division of
Hodder and Stoughton Limited, Mill Road, Dunton Green,
Sevenoaks, Kent TN13 2YA by Biddles Ltd, Guildford and King's
Lynn.

For Norma, Catherine, Ian and Richard; for my father, Rowland Butlin; and for Martin and Sam.

'. . . that seductive and composite science, historical geography, which opens for us the gates of space and time' (Y.-M. Goblet, 1955).

Contents

Preface

This book is a celebration, critique, and demonstration of historical geography. Historical geography is the study of the geographies of past times, involving the imaginative reconstruction of a wide range of phenomena and processes central to our geographical understanding of the dynamism of human affairs, such as change in the evaluation and uses of human and natural resources, in the form and functions of human settlements and built environments, in the advances in the amount and forms of geographical knowledge, and in the exercising of power and control over territories and peoples. The data and information sources on which such reconstructions are based are extensive, from pre-census and census population data to paintings and written accounts, official and personal, of place-located experiences and processes. They are not sources uniquely employed by historical geographers, but are examined, repaired, analysed, and deconstructed with reference to senses and ideologies of space and place. Historical geography has been an important aspect of the study of geography in academic institutions since at least the second half of the nineteenth century, though in Europe the explicit use of the concept and term can be traced back directly to at least the seventeenth century. The character and emphases of the subject have changed over time, reflecting the changing ideologies, individual and more general contexts and practices of scholars, societies, and institutions. Historical geography in its proto-modern form evolved as a branch of history, that is as an ancillary subject, providing in essence background geographical or environmental information to the study of the chronology and major political and social experiences of peoples, states, empires, frontiers, and civilizations.

Although changes took place in the late nineteenth and early twentieth centuries in the contents of works which included 'historical geography' in their title, it was not until the 1920s and 1930s that a 'modern' form of historical geography began to emerge, which reflected among other things the growing presence of geography departments in the universities and other institutions of western and central Europe and North America. Thus, in Britain historical geography developed in the 1920s and 1930s as an active and distinctive subject, interest in which was initiated by a relatively small group of scholars, some of whom were trained in subjects other than geography. Even at that point there was interesting variety: there was no single definition or tradition, and significant debate took place on the nature of the subject. Different and changing traditions and contexts of and for historical geography developed elsewhere, in the United States, Germany and France, for example, and these traditions continue, with varied degrees of modification, to the present day, so that there are variations in character within individual countries and culture areas. Within Britain, for example, there are different schools and traditions: one can speak, perhaps in the past tense, of what might be termed a 'metropolitan' classical tradition, usually thought to be epitomized by the work influenced by Darby, strongly influenced by the materials and the methods of academic history. This contrasts with the Aberystwyth 'school', associated with the work of Fleure and Bowen, more European and anthropological in its traditions, having particular interest in the peoples of the Celtic West, and with no strong overt attachment to theoretical and methodological statement. In France and Germany, much historical geographical study has been practised by geographers working within the tradition of human (anthropogeographical) geography, with strong emphasis on the historical evolution of landscape. These traditions are widespread elsewhere in continental Europe and in Scandinavia, reflecting the influence of early French and German geographical thought. Within the United States and Canada, both types of tradition are found, as they are in Australia and New Zealand. In Japan there is a strong tradition in historical geography, with an attendant emphasis on landscape.

The significance of this rich variety of traditions should not be lost: although historical geography and an historically sensitive human or cultural geography focus essentially on historical aspects of the geographies of the past, the emphasis varies from one such tradition or perspective to another. There is more than one way of uncovering the geography of the past, more than one route to this end, and claims to the superiority of any one approach, together with attempts to encapsulate this myriad of approaches into a single definition or ideological framework, must therefore be viewed with caution, if not suspicion.

The history of historical geography is outlined in the first three chapters of the book, which comprise the first ever history of the subdiscipline. These historiographical chapters are strategically important in their own right, for they allow an assessment to be made of the place of historical geography in the history of geographical thought, and the reasons for the coming and going of particular research topics. They serve more than antiquarian interest by tracing the major ideas that have inspired and structured the evolution of historical geography down to the present, and therefore provide an appropriate historical entrée to questions of theory, method, and the writing of thematic narrative accounts of processes of change, which are considered and exemplified in the remaining chapters.

An important point to emphasize at the outset is the dynamic nature of the subject: its methodologies and theories have never been static for long, and in those locations where older traditions have been retained because of a reluctance to accept and review new concepts and methods, the subject has been conspicuously weakened and its intellectual potential has been realized by disciplines other than geography. It is the dynamic nature of historical geography which makes it such a challenging, exciting, rewarding and greatly enjoyable subject, hence its continued significant presence in curricula and research agenda and inventories.

Much of the excitement generated by historical geography at the present day, therefore, reflects a willingness on the part of an influential number of its practitioners to evaluate new techniques and methodologies, and to incorporate them, where appropriate, into their teaching and research. Equally, there is a general willingness to re-evaluate traditional and long-used methods and approaches, and to incorporate the best of them into research programmes. The undoubted advancement of the subject is reflective of a blend of constant re-evaluation and periodic revolution. Another associated and significant characteristic within recent times is a willingness to incorporate methodologies and ideologies from other disciplines, notably such social sciences as social anthropology, sociology, and social and economic history.

It is increasingly being recognized that the geographies of the past are not simply objects preserved in time waiting to be excavated by the diligent scholar. There are, in fact, many different versions of past geographical experiences and events, whose recovery is as dependent on the inclinations, intuitions, enthusiasms, imagination and expertise of the individual scholar as on the rigorous pursuit, testing and analysis of key pieces of evidence. This trend in historical geography reflects major epistemological changes in the humanities and social sciences, and is in part a reaction against the narrow, supposedly objective and scientific, methods of analysis associated with the 'quantitative revolution' in the 1960s and 1970s. A range of methods and theories is now being employed, with varied success, by historical geographers, which places greater emphasis on the reading, narrative description, and interpretation of the past, and this in turn has required the use of a wider range of evidence, well beyond the statistical sources which traditionally have been central to historical geography. Just as in the nineteenth and early twentieth centuries historical geography reflected the broader influences on geography and indeed on everyday life, such as colonialism and the disputes and debates on the scientific and theological implications of theories of evolution, so in more recent times has historical geography become engaged in the consideration of such issues as the historical geography of capitalism, of deprivation and poverty, of power, social concern, protest, and Utopian ideals. As historical geographers, we reflect the concerns of the times in which we live, and interpret and reinterpret the geographies of the past accordingly, though wherever possible we also attempt to view the past through the perceptions of those who lived in the past: to understand, however hazily, their own views of place and time.

One important and greatly encouraging feature of contemporary historical geography is the wide range of information that is communicated through the medium of specialist groups of scholars and an increasing number of journals and specialist monograph series, in addition to the participation of specialist historical geographers in the activities and publications of more broadly based local, national and international geographical societies and institutions. The congresses of the International Geographical Union have included sections on historical geography since the late nineteenth century, and many national geographical societies whose members are primarily professional geographers include specialist groups in this field. The important *Journal of Historical Geography* was founded in 1975, and there are others with similar titles published in the United States, Japan, former Czechoslovakia, and the Netherlands.

It can be said with confidence, therefore, that historical geography continues to be an active, exciting and challenging art. Harris encapsulates this excitement in his essay on the historical mind and the practice of geography: 'There is an immensely rich tradition of scholarship that has a good deal to do with what I have described here as the historical mind, which is open to life as it is, which draws inspiration from both science and art, which depends on the considered judgement of the individual scholar, and which never has constrained the most eccentric brilliance' (Harris 1978, 136).

The purpose of this book is to portray aspects of this fascinating subject, by the exposition and interpretation of some key themes in the past and at the present. It attempts to combine theoretical exegeses of a mode of thought, through extensive review of the relevant literature, with useful and up-to-date surveys of rural, urban, industrial and commercial processes and their effects. The selection of these themes and their interpretation is a personal one, and covers both areas of consensus and of disagreement and debate. The book reflects the personal views and enthusiasms of a scholar working within British and European traditions, and who has some familiarity with the main thrusts in historical geography in North America, Australia, and New Zealand. The view of historical geography from within, for example, an African, Russian, Chinese or Latin American tradition would undoubtedly be different: works offering these and other new perspectives would be eagerly anticipated.

The writing of this comprehensive and ambitious book would not have been possible without the support over a much longer period of time than just the time of its writing of a large number of people, whose influence on and encouragement of my work and thinking has been profound. Richard Lawton taught me the skills of historical geography at Liverpool over 30 years ago, and I am deeply grateful for his friendship and professional encouragement since then. The late Brian Harley, whom I also met at Liverpool when he was first appointed to a lectureship there, was a consistent source of intellectual stimulus, factual information, and exemplar of sound scholarly practice. Colleagues in the geography departments at the University of Keele (then the University College of North Staffordshire), University College, Dublin, the University of Nebraska, Queen Mary College, University of London, and more recently Loughborough University of Technology, have directly and indirectly contributed to the contexts of my thinking through their own research and through discussion. In the recent past my colleagues at Loughborough, where I have been privileged to play a part in the development of a young and vibrant department, have allowed me liberal access to their own reference collections and to their ideas. The crafting and production of the book has owed much to the remarkably perceptive insights and critical comments of Mike Heffernan, who read the penultimate draft of the text, to Geoff Petts, who made valuable comments on a draft of Chapter 5, to the logistical and secretarial support of Jeanne Preston, Jacki Bowyer, Ruth Austin, Val Pheby and Gwyneth Barnwell, and the cartographers Ann Tarver, Erika Milwain and Peter Robinson, and to the unlimited help from staff of the University Library at Loughborough and the unseen but greatly appreciated staff at the British Library's Lending Division at Boston Spa. I am grateful to Charles Withers for allowing me to consult his forthcoming paper on the *Encyclopédie*. My thinking about and practice of the historical geographer's craft has been greatly influenced by many individual friends and scholars with whom I have not shared an institutional base. They include: Alan Baker, who also kindly commented on the structure of this book, Bob Dodgshon, Derek Gregory, Glanville Jones, Tony Phillips, Hugh Prince, John Langton, the late Clifford Darby, John Andrews, Harold Fox, Graeme Whittington, Bruce Proudfoot, Malcolm Wagstaff, Michael Williams, Roger Kain, Harald Uhlig, Hans-Jürgen Nitz, the late Ingeborg Leister, Hermann Grees, Paul Claval, Pierre Flatrès, Brian Blouet, Joe Powell, Bob Newcomb, Cole Harris, Leslie Hewes, Donald Meinig, Jehoshuah Ben-Arieh and Ruth Kark. There are many more practising historical human geographers and historians, part of the visible and invisible colleges of scholars, whose work has been of seminal importance to me. Grants from the Leverhulme Trust, the British Academy, and the Economic and Social Research Council supported research used in Chapters 1–7.

Successive editors at Edward Arnold—John Wallace, Susan Sampford, and Laura McKelvie—have shown astonishing patience, and I am very grateful to them for their consistently confident view that one day the long-awaited manuscript would materialize.

Most of all I owe an enormous debt of gratitude to my wife Norma and our children Catherine, Ian, and Richard, for their unfailing support and encouragement, and for helping me to put the frequently intense preoccupations of an academic into more sensible and realistic perspectives.

Robin A. Butlin
Loughborough
June 1992

Acknowledgements

I wish to acknowledge the permission kindly given by the following to base the maps and diagrams indicated on their published and unpublished work: Leicestershire County Council Libraries and Information Service, Coalville Brench (Fig. 1.2); Nottingham University Library (Fig. 1.3); Professor C.W.J. Withers (Fig. 1.7); Dr A. Charlesworth (Fig. 3.1); The Trustees of the Ulster Folk and Transport Museum (Fig. 3.2); Dr G. Kearns (Fig. 3.3); Harcourt Brace Jovanovich (Fig. 4.2); Professor R.C. Harris and the University of Toronto Press for plate 17 from *Historical Atlas of Canada*, vol. 1, edited by R. Cole Harris © University of Toronto Press, reprinted by permission of University of Toronto Press incorporated (Fig. 5.2); Dr C.N. Roberts (Fig. 5.3); Professor M.L. Parry (Fig. 5.4); Dr J. Grove (Fig. 5.5); Professor A. Verhulst (Figs 5.6 and 5.7); Mrs K.M. Davies, the editors of *A New History of Ireland*, and Oxford University Press (Fig. 5.8); Dr S. Barends, Dr A.J. Haartsen, Dr J. Renes and Dr T. Stol (Fig. 6.1); (Fig. 6.2) taken from a reproduction of a map published by Harry Margary, Lympne Castle, near Hythe, Kent; Dr P.J. Jarvis and The Institute of British Geographers (Fig. 6.4); Dr R.L. Heathcote (Fig. 7.1); Longman Group UK Ltd (Fig. 7.2); Dr J.M. Powell (Fig. 7.4); Professor C.T. Smith (Fig. 8.1); Professor H. Uhlig (Fig. 8.3); Professor K.-E. Frandsen (Fig. 8.4); Professor S. Helmfrid (Figs 8.5 and 8.6); Professor H.-J. Nitz (Fig. 8.7); Professor J.M. Wagstaff (Fig. 9.2); C. Sargent, 'The Latin American City' in Blouet, B.W. and Blouet, O. (eds), *Latin America: An Introductory Survey* copyright 1982 by John Wiley & Sons, Inc; reprinted by permission of John Wiley and Sons, Inc; (Fig. 9.4); Dr C.W. Chalklin (Fig. 9.6); The Department of Geography, University of Birmingham, and Mrs H. Thorpe (Fig. 9.7); The Bildarchiv Preussischer Kulturbesitz; (Figs 10.3 and 10.4); Longman Group UK (Fig. 10.5).

1

Contexts and Histories of Historical Geography
(*c.* 1700–1920)

Introduction

At the outset a particular difficulty of the historiography of historical geography needs to be addressed. This is a problem of identity: the question of the significance of the use of the term 'historical geography' in the titles of publications, sometimes quite minor works which adopt a very limited view of geography, as opposed to those not so titled but which use an approach of historical geography which is more in tune with its modern identity. This is not just a question of labels, for a reading of the historiography of historical geography can be affected significantly if only works which include the term in their title are considered. It is possible, for example, to see a decline of the subdiscipline from the apparent diminution of articles and books using the term 'historical geography' in France in the first half of the twentieth century, but against this, it is equally possible to contend that much historical geography was being published by historical journals, such as the *Annales* (see Chapter 2), in that period, and which embraced basic concepts such as regionality and the relations between society and space through time, thereby suggesting a period of strength and vigour.

Historical geography is characterized in this book as the study of the geographies of past times, through the imaginative reconstruction of phenomena and processes central to our geographical understanding of the dynamism of human activities within a broadly conceived spatial context, such as change in the evaluation and uses of human and natural resources, in the form and functions of human settlements and built environments, in the advances in the amount and forms of geographical knowledge, and in the exercising of power and control over territories and peoples. Such a definition admits to the historiography of the subdiscipline both types of work referred to, albeit to different degrees, and underlines the need to understand their contexts, with the choice of examples clearly a matter of personal preference. It is a valid exercise to attempt to understand what was meant by the term 'historical geography' at particular times in the past, but it is not the sole objective of its historiography.

The problem does, however, point towards a wider question: the changing nature of the relationships between history and geography, and their effects on the different forms of historical geography. Darby (1953) sets the context:

> The theme of the relations of geography and history is a well-worn one. It has engaged the attention of man since he first began to examine the nature of human society on the face of the earth. The classical philosophers speculated upon the connection between peoples and their environments, and the histories of Herodotus and Thucydides are impregnated with geographical descriptions and considerations. Throughout the Middle Ages, this speculation fell into abeyance, but, with the revival of the Renaissance, it sprang to life once more. There is a much quoted sentence from Peter Lelyn's *Microcosmus* which runs: 'Historie without geographie like a dead carkasse hath neither life nor motion at all', but what we do not so often hear is the beginning of the quotation: 'Geographie without historie hath life and motion but at randome, and unstable' (Darby 1953, 1).

Historical geography is considered here mainly in origin and early development as a European, multi-facetted and complex hybrid discipline, the product of differing fusions of geographical and historical traditions which themselves are illustrative of broader European intellectual, moral and political preoccupations (Fig. 1.1). History and geography have generally been regarded as separate traditions, the one focusing on narratives of people and events through time, the other on space, maps, and environmental influences, though the service that the one can render to the other has long been acknowledged. The location of historical geography within and between the complex intellectual arenas of both traditions is, however, neither simple or unproblematic, and a variety of different historical geographies has developed in different periods and places, reflecting different intellectual, political, and moral contexts. This is an important consideration, especially as far as the developments of the nineteenth and early twentieth centuries are concerned, when attempts to establish geography in the universities were sometimes frustrated by the unsympathetic attitudes of historians, who felt either that geography was little more than a basic gazetteer or inventory, or that its perceived links with political affairs such as nationalism and colonialism made it a subject to be treated with suspicion.

In the Beginning: Scriptural Historical Geography

In Europe, the concept and practice of historical geography in the seventeenth and early eighteenth centuries, was closely associated with scriptural or biblical geographies of the Old and New Testaments. This theme, as will be shown, continued to figure in historical geography throughout the nineteenth and the early twentieth centuries.

Probably the earliest example of this type of geography is the biblical toponymy titled *Onomastikon*, compiled early in the fourth century AD by Eusebius, Bishop of Caesarea. This type of biblical or sacred geography continued through the medieval to the early modern period (and some examples can be found in modern theological literature), often including maps of the Holy Land. Impetus was given to this work by the emphasis of the Reformation on the authority of the Bible, and a renewed interest in its

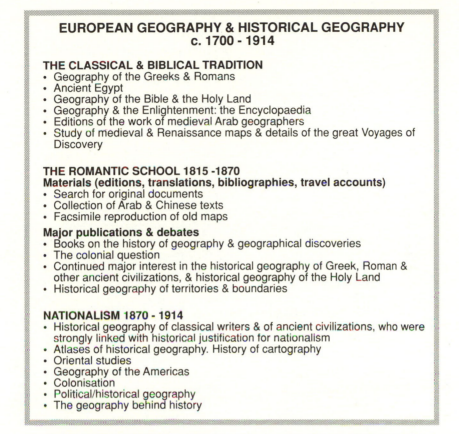

EUROPEAN GEOGRAPHY & HISTORICAL GEOGRAPHY
c. 1700 - 1914

THE CLASSICAL & BIBLICAL TRADITION
• Geography of the Greeks & Romans
• Ancient Egypt
• Geography of the Bible & the Holy Land
• Geography & the Enlightenment: the Encyclopaedia
• Editions of the work of medieval Arab geographers
• Study of medieval & Renaissance maps & details of the great Voyages of
  Discovery

THE ROMANTIC SCHOOL 1815 -1870
Materials (editions, translations, bibliographies, travel accounts)
• Search for original documents
• Collection of Arab & Chinese texts
• Facsimile reproduction of old maps
Major publications & debates
• Books on the history of geography & geographical discoveries
• The colonial question
• Continued major interest in the historical geography of Greek, Roman &
  other ancient civilizations, & historical geography of the Holy Land
• Historical geography of territories & boundaries

NATIONALISM 1870 - 1914
• Historical geography of classical writers & of ancient civilizations, who were
  strongly linked with historical justification for nationalism
• Atlases of historical geography. History of cartography
• Oriental studies
• Geography of the Americas
• Colonisation
• Political/historical geography
• The geography behind history

Source; N. Broc (1979) 'Histoire et historiens de la géographie. Notes bio-bibliographiques
(milieu du XVIIIe siècle - 1914)

Fig. 1.1 *Outline of major themes in human and historical geography in Europe, c. 1700–1914*

detailed topographical and geographical contexts, giving rise to attempts to
accommodate revealed knowledge and the authority of the Bible with the
empirical knowledge and authority of the new scientific theories. Much of this
work was Protestant, but it also had major consequences for Catholic
thinking, reflected in the types of geography advocated by the Jesuits, for
example, for teaching in their colleges. Dainville, in his important study of
geography as taught by Jesuits in sixteenth- and seventeenth-century France
(Dainville, 1940), has shown how the appeal of the Reformation to the
exclusive authority of the Bible generated great interest in its contents,
including the many places of which it speaks, and many cartographers,
including Mercator and Finé, launched their careers with chorographies and
maps of the Holy Land. The Jesuits, as Dainville shows, did not lag behind this
new enthusiasm for sacred geography, and detailed prescriptions were made
for the teaching of the subject.

In the early years of the eighteenth century Edward Wells (1667–1727), a
former student of geography and divinity at Oxford and a clergyman of the
Church of England, published four volumes on the 'historical geography' of

the Old and New Testaments. In his *Historical Geography of the New Testament* (1708) and his three-volume *Historical Geography of the Old Testament* (1710, 1711, 1712) he incorporated an amalgam of theological and geographical ideologies and perspectives to provide a geographical context for the events and teachings of the Bible. He had not visited the Holy Land himself, and his historical geographies of the Old and New Testaments were based on his own analysis of the contents of the Bible and a wide range of secondary sources, including the accounts from the classical Greek and Roman geographers to seventeenth- and early eighteenth-century maps and accounts of travel, together with contemporary biblical and theological treatises. There were many similar European accounts of the 'sacred geography' of the Holy Land produced in the seventeenth and eighteenth centuries, and they reveal prevalent and changing ideas in western Christian understanding of the interrelationships between people, environment, and divine purpose (Desreumaux and Schmidt, 1988). Wells' consciousness of this tradition of sacred geography is clear from the chapter 'Of the Sacred or Bible Geography' (Chapter 15) in his *A Treatise of Antient and Present Geography* (1701; see Fig. 1.2), and also from his prefatory remarks to, and arrangement of, the two works on the historical geography of the Old and New Testaments (Butlin, 1992). These European sacred geographies from the seventeenth and eighteenth centuries, though similar in purpose, were produced from within different traditions. Most, like Wells and Samuel Bochart (the French author of a book, *Geographia sacra seu Phalag et Chanaan*, published in 1646 and concerned with the genealogies of the Canaanites and the Phoenicians; see Fig. 1.3), reflected an essentially late medieval system of geographical knowledge and historical chronology, were in tension with the new science of the seventeenth century, and adhered to strictly literal interpretations of such biblical questions as the (assumed) repeopling of the earth by the sons of Noah after the Great Flood.

Attempts to explain the topography and sites of biblical geography continued into the nineteenth century, but against a changing intellectual and theological climate, and the outstanding work is that of the Scottish clergyman and academic George Adam Smith: his book *The Historical Geography of the Holy Land* was first published in 1894 (Butlin, 1988). For Smith historical geography had a particular meaning and purpose, clearly indicated in the preface to the first edition:

> There are many ways of writing a geography of Palestine, and of illustrating the history by the Land, but some are wearisome and some vain. They do not give a vision of the Land as a whole, nor help you to hear through it the sound of running history. What is needed by the reader or teacher of the Bible is some idea of the outlines of Palestine — its shape and disposition; its plains, passes and mountains; its rains, winds and temperatures; its colours, lights and shapes. Students of the Bible desire to see a background and to feel an atmosphere; to discover from 'the lie of the land' why the history took certain lines and the prophecy and the gospel were expressed in certain styles; to learn what geography has to contribute to questions of biblical criticism; and above all, to discern between what physical nature contributed to the religious development of Israel, and what was the product of moral and spiritual forces. On this last point the geography of the Holy Land reaches its highest point of interest (Smith, 1894; 1966, 11).

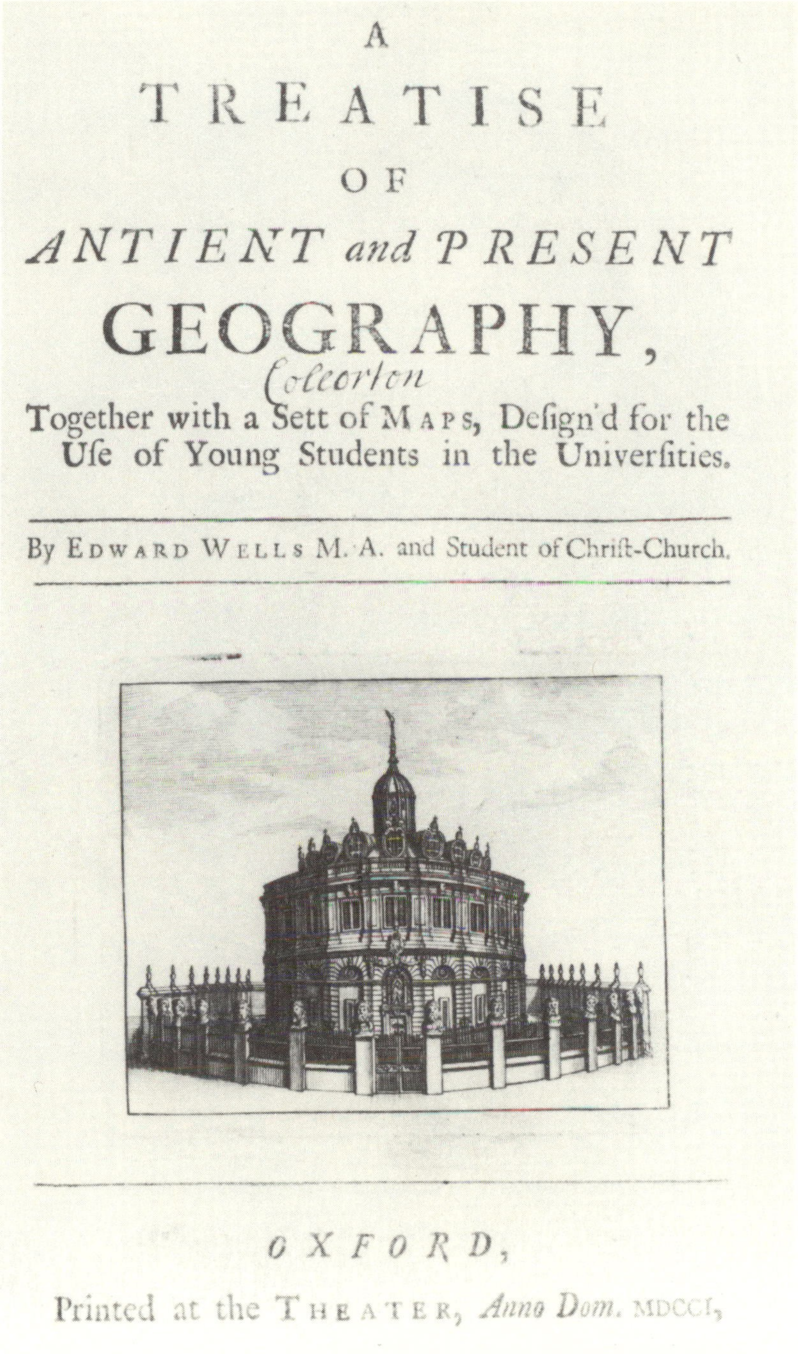

A

TREATISE

OF

ANTIENT and PRESENT

GEOGRAPHY,

Coleorton

Together with a Sett of MAPS, Defign'd for the
Ufe of Young Students in the Univerfities.

By EDWARD WELLS M. A. and Student of Chrift-Church.

OXFORD,

Printed at the THEATER, *Anno Dom.* MDCCI,

Fig. 1.2 *Frontispiece of Wells'* A Treatise of Antient and Present Geography *(1701). This text, by the author of* An Historical Geography of the New Testament *and* An Historical Geography of the Old Testament, *comprises a comparative study of the geography of the ancient and 'modern' world, by themes and by regions, and contains a chapter on 'sacred geography'. From a copy in Coleorton Public Library, Leicestershire*

Fig. 1.3 *Samuel Bochart (1599–1667), orientalist and pastor of the French Reformed Church. Author of* Geographia sacra seu Phaleg et Chanaan *(1674 with later editions to 1712), from which this portrait is taken. This is one of the influential early modern works dealing with the geographical background to the Bible. From a copy in Nottingham University Library*

The Historical Geography of the Holy Land was a guide and study aid to the relevant aspects of the geography and the history of the Holy Land, for biblical scholars and students, through the medium of first-hand description, the incorporation of up-to-date scientific, textual and archaeological publications from European, Hebrew and Arabic sources, and the use of modern critical techniques. *The Historical Geography of the Holy Land* contains, in addition to some very powerful and evocative descriptive prose of scenery and landscapes, important digests of up-to-date scientific description and explanation, including details of daily fluctuations in temperatures and wind direction, and the tectonic history of the Rift Valley. This is an important book whose intellectual context reflects wider currents of nineteenth- and early twentieth-century thought, including some of the theories and descriptions of the German geographer Ritter, the new discoveries coming from archaeological excavations, and the new biblical criticism from Germany. Smith was a priest and academic teacher of Old Testament exegesis, but was in contact with the new scientific geography of the late nineteenth century through the newly founded Scottish Geographical Society and through the geographical section of the British Association for the Advancement of Science. He published two other major works in a similar tradition of historical geography: *Jerusalem* (1907–08) and *The Atlas of the Historical Geography of the Holy Land*, a collaborative work with the Edinburgh cartographer John Bartholomew, the first edition being published in 1915.

The Historical Geography of Classical Civilizations

One of the common denominators of European historical geography in the nineteenth century was the study of the geography of early civilizations, including conspicuously the classical civilizations of Greece and Rome. This was a continuation of a tradition which had begun in the eighteenth century, and had been closely linked to studies of the history of geographical thought and the history of maps and mapping. An added factor was the importance of the recovery of the constitutional and republican ideals of classical civilizations, especially Rome, as models for the new nationalisms and colonial ambitions of European states in the nineteenth century.

This kind of historical geography seems to have been very strong in Germany. Gabrielle Schwarz has written of this interest in her brief account of the life and work of the German geographer Partsch (1851–1925). Referring to Partsch's publications on the ancient classical world, she states that 'this element in his work shows the connection between geography and classical studies which was prevalent in Britain, as well as in Germany, in the last decades of the nineteenth century, indeed to such an extent that in German historical geography not only the conceptions of the classical world were apparent but from the early years of the twentieth century an historical approach was also applied to other and later periods' (Schwarz, 1986, 127). Partsch published *The Limits of the Ancient Classical World* in 1916, *The River Bi-furcation in the Argonaut Myth* in 1919, and had edited Neumann's *Physical Geography of Greece* (1885). He had strong enthusiasm for physical geography, and was to combine his interests in studies of the geography of parts of modern Greece, moving from an anthropogeographic to a cultural geography perspective in the last years of the nineteenth century (Schwarz, 1986, 127).

Curtius was an historian, taught by Ritter, whose work was influential on this type of historical geography, and exemplified notably his book on the

Pelopponesos (1851/52). Curtius figures strongly in Mertz's *A History of European Thought in the Nineteenth Century*, especially the section on historical geography, in which the 'foundation of a new branch of research on the borderland of natural and political history, the geography of ancient and modern Greece' (Mertz, 1904, 294) is attributed to Curtius, though for Mertz historical geography seems almost synonymous with archaeology. This research into the historical and cultural geography of classical civilizations continues well into the twentieth century, reflected, for example, in the publications of Alfred Phillipson (1864–1955), notably his major study of the Byzantine Empire, *Das Byzantinische Reich als Geographische Erscheinung* (1939) and his book on the Mediterranean, *Das Mittelmeergebiet* (1904).

This theme was particularly well developed in Britain by a group of scholars which included Zimmern, Myres, Ramsey, and others. *The Greek Commonwealth*, written by Zimmern, a lecturer in ancient history at Oxford, was first published in 1911, and its preface indicates Zimmern's prime purpose, which was a study of fifth-century Athens and its environs, with particular emphasis on geography and economic conditions: 'It is now generally admitted that neither an individual nor a nation can be properly understood without a knowledge of their surroundings and means of support — in other words, of their geographical and economic conditions. This doctrine, obvious though it seems today, was somewhat slow in winning acceptance in connexion with the study of ancient Greece' (Zimmern, 1911, 5). He implies that the incorporation of the modern sciences into the study of ancient history was somewhat slower in Britain than in continental Europe, and confirms this with an acknowledgement to the use he makes in connection with the first part of the book on the geography of the Mediterranean by the German geographer Phillipson: *Das Mittelmeergebiet*. The first four chapters deal respectively with the Mediterranean area, the sea, the climate, and the soil, and the second and third sections deal with politics and economics. The book is illustrated with maps, including a general reconstruction of the vegetation and land use of Attica, and in very many respects has a modern geographical flavour about it.

In his report of 1885 to the Royal Geographical Society, Keltie, in his account of the teaching of geography at Oxford, states: 'Classical geography is expected in the Literae Humaniores School, but classical geography in this country is an extremely meagre affair' (Keltie, 1885, 104). Work of this kind is additionally to be found in Bunbury's *History of Ancient Geography among the Greeks and Romans, from the Earliest Ages till the Fall of the Roman Empire* (1879), and Smith's *Dictionary of Greek and Roman Geography* (1870). A fascinating book produced in this context is Tozer's *A History of Ancient Geography*, first published in 1897 and revised in a second edition in 1935. Following closely in the tradition of Bunbury's *History of Ancient Geography . . .*, it seeks to examine the progress of geography 'from its early dawn in the Homeric period to its fullest extension in the Augustan age' (Tozer, 1935, v). It deals essentially with the varied aspects of geographical thought and description to be found in the works of the great classical writers of Greece and Rome, including Homer, Hecataeus (Fig. 1.4), Herodotus (Fig. 1.5), Aristotle, Strabo (Fig. 1.6) and Ptolemy, and there are a number of interesting observations by Tozer himself on what was considered to be the late nineteenth- and early twentieth-century view of historical geography. In the introductory chapter, therefore, he divides geography into four sections:

Fig. 1.4 *The world according to Hecataeus of Miletus (c. 520 BC), based on his* Periodos or General Survey. *Source: reconstruction by Tozer (1935, 70–1).*

mathematical, physical, descriptive or political, and historical geography. Historical geography

> regards the earth from the point of view of its effect on human society and the progressive development of the race. With this object it considers the modifying influence on national character which has been produced by the aspect of the country, by the facilities or impediments which it presents in respect of communications with other peoples, and by the occupations which it naturally fosters. And it also points out the effect which geographical features have produced, both in determining campaigns and battles, which have been the turning-points of the world's history, and in fixing beforehand the power which particular countries have exercised at certain periods (Tozer, 1935, 3).

The best examples of this type of reflection are to be found, in Tozer's view, after the time of the Roman conquest of Greece, in the writings of Aristotle, Polybius and Ephorus, for example. Strabo's work is also dominated in his view by a strong emphasis on historical geography. Thus, 'Among these

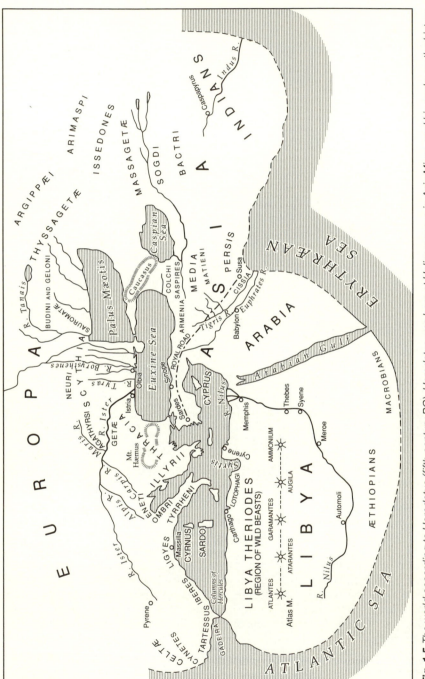

Fig. 1.5 *The world according to Herodotus (fifth century BC). Herodotus was born at Halicarnassus in Asia Minor, and his works on the history of the war between Greece and Persia, and his accounts of travel and his geographical knowledge are represented in this reconstruction of his perception of the earth. Source: Tozer (1935, 74–5). His geographical writings continued to be a source of information for historical geographers until the seventeenth and eighteenth centuries*

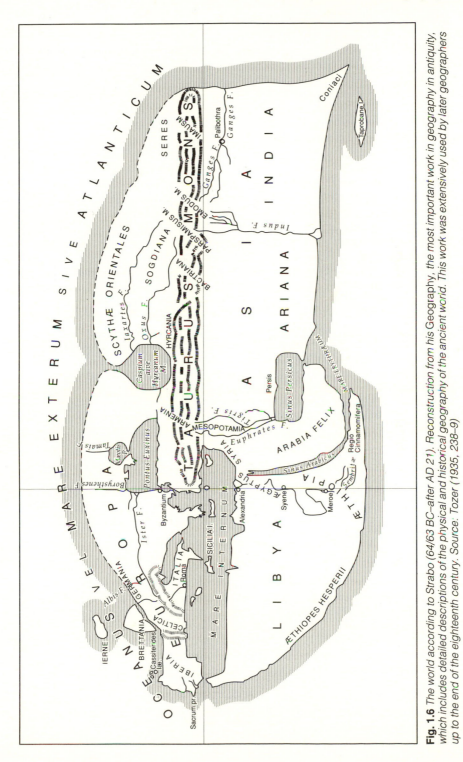

Fig. 1.6 *The world according to Strabo (64/63 BC–after AD 21). Reconstruction from his Geography, the most important work in geography in antiquity, which includes detailed descriptions of the physical and historical geography of the ancient world. This work was extensively used by later geographers up to the end of the eighteenth century. Source: Tozer (1935, 238–9)*

various departments of geographical study the one which predominates in Strabo's work is undoubtedly the historical. Not only does he everywhere introduce the history of a country side by side with its geography, but he illustrates the one by the other, and endeavours to point out the intimate connexion that existed between the two' (Tozer, 1935, 246). Tozer is primarily concerned with the geography behind ancient history, and with a concept far removed from that of the present day, but the frequency of his use and discussion of the term 'historical geography' clearly indicates the importance in his time of this type of connotation.

The classical traditions which strongly influenced the practice of historical geography in nineteenth-century France comprised in fact an amalgam of the classical tradition of the eighteenth century and the so-called 'Romantic school' of the nineteenth. The classical tradition, centred in the eighteenth century around the Académie des Inscriptions et Belles Lettres, focused on the geography of the classical world of Greece, Rome, and Egypt, together with work on medieval texts and the maps and accounts of the voyages of discovery of the Renaissance. In some respects this tradition carried over into what has been described as the 'Romantic school', strongly influential in the period 1815–70, one of whose main thrusts was the intense and critical scrutiny of original sources, both French and foreign. New institutions in this period were the École des Langues Orientales, founded in Paris in 1795, and the Société Géographique de Paris, founded in 1821, and which inaugurated its published series *Recueil de Voyages et de Mémoires* with a manuscript of the travels of Marco Polo. Renewed interest was shown in the literature of Arabic, Chinese and Scandinavian texts, in Greek and Latin geographical accounts, to which may be added the study and reproduction of old maps. The context of historical geography at this time has been clearly indicated in Broc's major study of the history of geography, for example in his account of the inaugural lecture by the Hellenist historian and geographer Joseph-Daniel Guignaut (1794–1876) at the Sorbonne in 1835, in which the topics of his future courses of lectures were to be: 'la géographie fabuleuse et mythique [jusqu'en 500 avant Jésus-Christ]; la géographie historique et positive—(500–300 av. Jésus-Christ)' (Broc, 1979, 83).

Geographical History

A somewhat different but overlapping tradition, also labelled 'historical geography' was the study of the history and geography of changes in the territorial possessions and boundaries of states, empires, and royal houses and administrations. The earliest example may be a French text, published in Paris in 1697 and written by the Abbé Louis de Courcillon de Danegeau: *Nouvelle métode de géografie historique pour aprendre facilement et retenir . . . la géografie moderne et l'anciene, l'histoire moderne et l'anciene, le gouvernement des états, les interets des princes, leurs généologies . . . .* A parallel though later view is to be found in Diderot and d'Alembert's *Encyclopédie, ou Dictionnaire raisonée des sciences, des arts, et des métiers, par une société des gens des lettres* published in 17 volumes between 1751 and 1765. Historical geography appears with the other five branches of geography listed in volume VII: 'Géographie naturelle, géographie civile ou politique, géographie sacrée, géographie ecclesiastique and géographie physique'. Historical geography in this context has close links with three other types of geography listed, namely civil or political geography, sacred geography, and ecclesiastical geography. Historical geography seems to be an amalgam of the geography behind history and commercial geography, a notion also encountered in the work of the contemporary French geographer Buache. Buache's *Essai de Géographie Physique* of 1752 defines historical geography in terms of the history of human habitation of the earth, changing political and territorial geography, and changes in the nature of geographical thought through time. This traditional definition of historical geography as including the history of geographical thought is worth noting, as it resurfaces in the early and late twentieth century. In broader terms geography itself was seen as part of a grouping of subjects around mathematics and physics, including chronology and cosmography. Geography is represented on several branches of the tree of knowledge or 'Illustrated system of human knowledge' which is used in the prospectus for the *Encyclopédie*, and this tree (see Fig. 1.7) is thought to be a copy (with modifications, including the treatment of religion) of the tree of knowledge which is part of Bacon's *The Advancement of Learning*, first published in 1605 (Furbank, 1992, 37). This Enlightenment perspective seems to have regarded geography in its various aspects as both a humanistic subject and an applied science, with historical geography very much associated with classical humanism. In France it was closely associated with the Académie des Inscriptions, especially with the scholar Fréret, who held the opinion that geography and chronology were inter-linked as the 'two eyes of history', and he and his contemporaries were much concerned with the relationships between ancient and modern geography (Broc, 1974a, 257–8).

During the period of the Third Republic, the essential characteristics of French historical geography reflected changes in approaches to history, including the move away from the Romantic approach to a more positivist, critical and objective perspective, but linked also to an intensification of nationalist and colonialist concerns, ambitions and fears, which at times overpowered objectivity in an obsessive way. The German influence, both in geography and history, was very important, and contributed to the more critical scrutiny of historical evidence. The later years of the nineteenth century witnessed the flowering of academic geography in higher education in France, especially in the 1890s, when the number of chairs in geography increased rapidly, so that by 1900 there were few universities which did not possess a chair. Before 1870 there had only been a handful of chairs in, or partly in, geography. A chair of geography was created in 1812 at the Sorbonne (a conversion from a chair in history and modern geography) whose holder, Himly (1823–1906), was the only full-titled Professor of Geography in all the French faculties, though the geographical interest was maintained at the Collège de France by Levasseur, at the École Normale by Desjardins, and at St Cyr by Lavallée and Dussieux. Another important feature was the increase in the number of geographical societies, especially in the 1880s and 1890s, and which had been responsible for a broadening of awareness of geography by the general public, as well as stimulating and supporting French colonial endeavours. In France there was an increasing concern with the portrayal of French scholarship through participation in international conferences and organizations, and a continuing desire for the centralization of control of potentially

COSMOGRAPHY
*Description of the Earth, or science
which teaches the construction,
form, arrangement and relations of
all the component parts of the
Universe. It is divided into
'Uranography', Hydrology and
Geography.*

GEOGRAPHY
*Or the description of the terrestrial part of the globe, that
is to say of the dry part. The Earth is distributed in
relation to the aqueous part of the interior Earth, or
Mediterranean part and the exterior Earth, the maritime
or coastal part.*
Geography can be considered under three different ages:
*1 Ancient Geography, which is the description of the
Earth related to the knowledge which the ancient scholars
had up to the fall of the Roman Empire.*
*2 Geography of the Middle Ages since the fall of the
Roman Empire to the revival of the Arts/Humanities.*
*3 Modern Geography, which is the actual description of
the Earth since the revival of the Arts to the present.*
*Geography can be divided into the following parts:
Natural, Historical, Civil and Political, Sacred,
Ecclesiastical and Physical.*

Natural Geography
*Refers to the divisions which Nature has effected on
the surface of the globe, such as seas, mountains,
rivers, isthmuses etc; and to the colours of different
people, their languages etc.*

Historical Geography
*With reference for a country or a city,
historical geography presents the different
revolutions, the princes to which they have
been subject, the changing commerce in which
they have been engaged, the battles, sieges,
peace treaties - in a word all that pertains to
the history of a country.*

Civil or Political Geography
*The description of types of sovereignty by
reference to civil and political administration.*

Sacred Geography
*For the purpose of studying the countries
mentioned in the Scriptures and in
Ecclesiastical history.*

Ecclesiastical Geography
*The division of ecclesiastical jurisdiction between
patriarchies, primacies, dioceses, archdeaconries,
deaneries etc.*

Physical Geography
*Considers the terrestrial globe, not so much by the form of the
surface as by that which makes up its substance.*

Fig. 1.7 *Extract (translated) from the tree of knowledge in the* Essai d'une distribution
généalogique des sciences et des arts principaux *in the Supplement, vol. II, of Diderot, D. and
D'Alembert, J. (eds),* Encyclopédie, ou dictionnaire raisonné des sciences, des arts, et des
métiers *(1780)*

dangerous regionalist organizations, including the 'sociétés savantes'. Within historical geography some of the main preoccupations were with the geography of classical civilizations, the geography of administrative and territorial boundaries, and the geography of the Renaissance and later voyages of discovery, together with the related history of cartography.

In Britain the links between history and geography in the nineteenth century were strong, with history dominant and leading to the concept of historical geography as the study of the geographical background to history. The relations were, at academic level, quite productive though this had not, by the late nineteenth century, helped geography forward to a separate existence in the universities. Historical geography was largely written and taught by historians, mainly at Oxford, with an emphasis on the geography behind history. The context and types of work in historical geography in the nineteenth and early twentieth centuries have been described in outline by Baker (1952). In essence, the type of historical geography advocated and practised was the geographical context of historical events, principally though not exclusively the historical contexts of ancient civilizations, with the map and the atlas as important aids in analysis and description. This is what Darby (1953, 1) calls the 'geography behind history', or what contemporaries called the 'relations of geography and history'. It was different from the classical historical geography developed in this country from the 1930s onwards. Given the late development of academic geography in institutional form, it is not surprising that one of the parents of historical geography was history. It is a little more surprising, perhaps, that the other parent was physical geography. The key figures in historical geography in the nineteenth century were mainly clerical academics from Oxford. Baker (1952) suggests that the key figure in the early nineteenth century was Arnold, elected to the Regius Chair of Modern History in 1841 a year before his death, who trained with the geologist Buckland and was influenced by German historian Niehbuhr. His Oxford lectures revealed strong currents of historical geographical thinking and his *Extracts from Travelling Journals* indicate a highly talented gift for geographical description. Stanley, a man who heard Arnold's Oxford lectures, continued this important link between history and historical geography.

Stanley held the chair of ecclesiastical history at Oxford from 1856 to 1863. Baker, in his essay on the history of geography in Oxford, says that 'Stanley, first as a fellow of University College, and later as professor of ecclesiastical history ... became the recognized leader of the new geographers, and long afterwards it was said of him that he had done more than any living man to promote the intelligent study of historical geography' (Baker, 1963a, 123). Stanley's most important work from our point of view was his *Sinai and Palestine. In Connection with their History* (1856).

Freeman was Regius Professor of Modern History at Oxford, and he played an important role in the advancement of historical geography, notably through his book *The Historical Geography of Europe* (1881), whose purpose was

to trace out the extent of territory which the different states and nations of Europe and the neighbouring lands have held at different times in the world's history, to mark the different boundaries which the same country has had, and the different meanings in which the same name has been used .... Historical geography, in this sense, differs from physical geography which regards the natural features of the earth's surface. It differs also from studies like ethnology and comparative philology. . . . But, though it is distinct from these studies, it makes much use of them (Freeman, 1881, 1–2).

Freeman made the distinction between geography as a branch of history (via books of geographical information and maps) and as a help to history, in which the first-hand experience of historically significant places, through extensive travel, is crucial, illuminating the type of historical geography which he wrote.

Examples of this new realistic geographical history cited by Darby (1962) are Michelet's *Histoire de France* (1833), Curtius's *Peloponnesos* (1851), and Stanley's *Sinai and Palestine* (1856). The new history of the mid-nineteenth century reflected debates and speculations on the nature and methods of history itself: Buckle in his *History of Civilization in England* (1857–61) attempted a more scientific history by reference to 'mental and physical laws' which influence human behaviour, these included climate, food, soil, and nature (Darby, 1962, 152). The best of the historical geography produced by these historians was characterized by a sound geographical imagination and sense of place, often accompanied by good maps, and sometimes whole atlases. Darby has suggested that as the nineteenth century progressed, the old preoccupation of historians with political relations and incidents decreased, and they 'became increasingly preoccupied with other aspects of human endeavour. These new interests reflected wider changes in the intellectual climate and of economic circumstances of the time. . . . Men were asking new questions not only about their own age but also about the past. Economics, anthropology, sociology, philology, law, and geography were being called into the service of Clio, and a new approach was fortified after the appearance of Darwin's *Origin of Species* in 1859', producing what some thought to be a new, genetic, or realistic history, so that 'as the study of history became more realistic, it became more geographical. Perhaps it would be more accurate to say that the writings of many historians showed an increasing awareness of the fact that the drama of man and society takes place upon the earth and is not unaffected by it' (Darby, 1962, 152). Against this positive incorporation of a geographical dimension into historical studies at this time, Darby sets the growing problem of extreme statements of the role of geography in human affairs, leading to over-enthusiastic determinism and environmentalism, themes that were influential for a time in both Europe and the United States. The analysis of history of the relations between history and geography in Europe can be traced back to the lectures of Kant in Königsberg from 1756 to 1796 (and even before this), which set a basis for discussion of geography as a setting and scene for historical events, so that 'the changes of history result in "completely new geographies": geography is the study of places as they have been, and are being, transformed by the hand of man' (Darby, 1962, 156).

During the period of the Third Republic, the essential characteristics of French historical geography reflected changes in approaches to history, including the move away from the Romantic approach to a more positivist, critical and objective perspective, but linked also to an intensification of nationalist and colonialist concerns, ambitions and fears, which at times overpowered objectivity in an obsessive way. The German influence, both in geography and history, was very important, and contributed to the more critical scrutiny of historical evidence. An interesting feature of the development of French historical geography at this time, and reflective, in some respects, of new ideologies for geography as a renovating force was the publication for the first time in 1886 of the *Bulletin de Géographie Historique et Descriptive*, the annual publication of a committee of that name. The broader context of its origin has significant bearing on the ideological connections of nineteenth-century French geography and, indeed, science in general. Its progenitor was the Comité des Travaux Historiques et Scientifiques, founded in 1834 by Guizot, and whose ostensible purpose was to publish documents from national and local archives (Fox, 1980).

The committee was possessed of a strong patriotic fervour, and in addition to the reviews of publications of provincial societies, of foreign geographical journals, and of national congresses, the committee increasingly encouraged publication in the *Bulletin* of articles on voyages of discovery of the fifteenth, sixteenth, and seventeenth centuries, especially those which stressed the early role of France in discoveries in the New World, and of articles on the geographical justification of French colonial aspirations and achievements.

Another major thrust, particularly encouraged by the secretary of the committee, Hamy, was what Broc has called 'une véritable chasse aux documents les plus divers' (Broc, 1970, 23) throughout France, pertinent to the historical geography of France and to the history of geography, and which resulted in the publication of some important works. Although it might be contended that much of the work which was published in the *Bulletin* related to the history of geography as well as to historical geography, there is no doubt that these were seen as related and important subjects by those who used the term 'historical geography' in their research at the time.

It is difficult to argue, however, that the *Bulletin* itself was an influential medium for communication of ideas in historical geography, for as Berdoulay has indicated it was not sold commercially and the ministry decided on its distribution, which was not widespread (Berdoulay, 1981, 150). In many respects it was surpassed by the *Annales de Géographie*, founded in 1891. A measure of the change at the turn of the century is the nature of the contents of the *Bulletin* in 1891 and 1913: Berdoulay has drawn attention to the fact that in 1891 about two-thirds of the articles published in the *Bulletin* were in the older tradition of historical geography, the remainder being accounts of scientific explorations, whereas in 1913, the last year in which the old title was used, although more than half the articles were on historical geography, the rest comprised accounts of explorations, physical geography, and regional studies, reflecting a change in the membership of the committee, which now included Vidal de la Blache, de Margerie, Gallois, Raveneau and Schrader (Berdoulay, 1981, 159).

In France one of the critical aspects of the history of historical geography in the early decades of the twentieth centry was the development of a more comprehensive, historically sensitized, human geography, what Dion chose to call a 'retrogressive human geography', and a distancing of this new approach, under the initiatives of de la Blache and his school, from the older type of French historical geography identified by the work of Longnon and Himly. One indicator was the change in the title of the *Bulletin de Géographie Historique et Descriptive* to the more simply styled *Bulletin de Géographie* in

1913, though in fact the contents of the *Bulletin* did not change markedly in style.

Two Figures in French Historical Geography in the Nineteenth Century: Himly and Longnon

Two influential figures in French historical geography in the nineteenth century were Louis-Auguste Himly (1823–1906) and Auguste-Honoré Longnon (1844–1911). Himly was born in Strasbourg and completed studies in literature and theology in Germany. He heard Ranke, the major German historian, lecture in Berlin, and became interested in medieval history. He received further historical training in the critical use of historical sources at the École des Chartes, graduated in history and geography in 1845, and received his doctorate in 1849. Berdoulay (1977, 43) suggests that 'It was therefore through history that Himly approached geography. As early as 1852, in charge of a university course in history, he taught the territorial formation of the European states. He came to specialize in geography only because of a contingency of his career, when he replaced Guigniaut at the Sorbonne. . . . He was not a member of the Société de Géographie until 1859, and moreover he never hid the fact that he had "always preferred history"'. He was appointed to a chair of geography at the Sorbonne in 1862.

The general assessment of Himly's influence on the nature of historical geography in France is that it was, not surprisingly, cautious, traditional and conservative. Broc describes Himly in rather uncomplimentary terms as a man with the profile of a retired officer who had occupied the chair of geography at the Sorbonne (until he was replaced in 1899 by Vidal de la Blache), and who was, although an excellent specialist, a convinced adversary of modern geography (Broc, 1970, 25), and others have inferred that he was totally ignorant of the methods of modern geography.

It is clear that Himly's influence was very strong, particularly through his insistence that the majority of doctoral theses in geography at the Sorbonne be in historical geography, especially in the historical geography of classical civilizations and the history of geography. There is, therefore, in some sense a paradox attached to Himly, whose liberalism and ideology secured him an influential position at the Sorbonne which enabled him to advance the intellectual modernization of that institution, especially in his capacity as Dean, while apparently taking an orthodox line over historical geography. One of his major publications appeared in 1876: *L'Histoire de la Formation Territoriale des États de l'Europe Centrale*, a work in two volumes which provides a geographical base for the history of central Europe. He also contributed scholarly notes and reviews to the *Bulletin de Géographie Historique et Descriptive*, and other journals.

Longnon was another central figure in French historical geography in the nineteenth century. He was born in Paris in 1844 into an artisan family, and on leaving school at the age of 12 worked as a shoemaker for 13 years, after which the unrelenting efforts at study to which he dedicated all his spare time allowed him to enter the École Pratique des Hautes Études as a student in the history and philology section. He was appointed as an assistant in the imperial archives in 1870 and became archivist in 1871. He was also, in 1879, appointed tutor in the historical geography of France at the École Pratique des Hautes Études.

Longnon was an active member of the Commission de Géographie Historique de l'Ancienne France. This committee was a successor to an earlier committee—the Commission de la Topographie des Gaules—and was established in 1880, as part of the constellation of scholarly working groups attached to the recently created Comité des Travaux Historiques et Scientifiques. A report on its activities by Longnon in 1882 indicates a very broad brief for the Commission de Géographie Historique, treating in theory with the geography of France from very early times to the modern period, though in practice he indicates that the terminal date accepted was that of the Middle Ages. The type of work commissioned and carried out included lists of place-names, and maps of many aspects of archaeology and topography. One major map under way was that of Gaul during the pro-consulship of Caesar.

In 1892 he was elected to a chair in the historical geography of France at the Collège de France, his chair replacing that in the history and moral philosophy of France formerly held by Maury. His major publications included *Livre des vassaux du comté de Champagne et de Brie, 1192–1222* (1869), *Géographie de la Gaule au VIe siècle* (1878), *Paris pendant la domination anglaise, 1420–1456* (1878), *Atlas historique de la France, depuis César jusqu'à nos jours* (1884–89), and the *Dictionnaire topographique du département de la Marne* (1891), together with many contributions to historical periodicals including the *Bulletin de la Societé de l'histoire de Paris et de l'île de France*, which he edited from 1875. His *Géographie de la Gaule au VIe siècle*, which was dedicated to Maury (whom he succeeded to a chair at the College de France), gives an idea of his concept of historical geography. The three parts of the work deal respectively with: the geographical terms and language of the sixth century; the political geography of Gaul; and the description of the topography of Gaul by Gregory of Tours.

Longnon's influence on French historical geography was to a degree constrained by his appointment at the Collège de France, where he did not teach students or supervise doctoral theses, though it may be said that he was, through his influence on key committees, influential in promoting the older style of historical geography.

Historical Geography in Latin America

While various types of historical geography were developing in Europe in the nineteenth and early twentieth century, there are indications that a form of the subject, associated (as partly was the case in France) with national pride and independence was developing in the newly independent states in Latin America. The evidence to date is rather thin, but in an article on the origins and development of the Sociedad Geografica of Lima in Peru, founded in 1888, Cabrera shows the contexts to be: first, the need to re-establish the national identity and pride of Peru after its defeat by Chile in the Saltpetre War of 1879–33; second, to emulate the scientific roles of the geographical societies in Europe, by launching studies of Peru in relation to its needs and resources. One fascinating outcome was the establishment of principal objectives, which included the study 'de la *Geografía General Descriptiva del Perú* . . . . De la

Historia Natural del Perú .... De las *Razas, Etnografía, Arqueología y Geografía Histórica del Peru*' (Cabrera, 1992, 149). Parallel studies of the Instituto Histórico e Geográfico of Brazil, founded in 1838 in Rio de Janeiro by members of the political and administrative élite of the country (de Figueiroa, 1992), and of the Instituto Nacional de Geografía y Estadistica in Mexico in 1833 in the period of the First Federal Republic (Benitez, 1992), give little direct indication of a concern with historical geography to the same ends as those assumed for Peru. The Brazilian institute, however, was clearly founded at an important stage in the establishment of a policy of centralization and, with the need to create a greater sense and symbolism of national identity, it modelled itself on the Paris Institut Historique, linking history and geography in the understanding of the natural history of the country. Further research may yet reveal a more widespread interest in historical geography in these and other Latin American countries at this time.

Historical Geography and Colonialism

In the later nineteenth century one of the common areas of interest in historical geography and the history of geographical thought in Europe was the history of colonialism and imperialism, especially though not exclusively those aspects of national claims to territory overseas which could be supported by historical events and records (real and imagined). This area of investigation followed on from earlier geographical and historical researches into the history of voyages of discovery and exploration. In Britain examples of publications on the historical geography of colonialism include George's *Historical Geography of the British Empire* (1904), and a series of books, edited by Lucas, with the general titles *Historical Geography of the British Colonies* and *Historical Geography of the British Dominions* according to the areas included. Lucas's series was produced between 1887 and 1924, and was primarily an historical account of the different colonies and colonial regions. Given the pace of colonial and imperial change from the late nineteenth to the early twentieth century, there were frequent revisions of the regional volumes. The major part of the series comprised seven regional volumes, covering the Mediterranean and Eastern Colonies, the West Indian Colonies, West Africa, South and East Africa, Canada, Australasia, and India.

George's *Historical Geography of the British Empire* was first published in 1904, and had reached a seventh edition by 1924. In his preface he indicates the purpose of the book: 'My object in writing this little book has been to present a general survey of the British Empire as a whole, with the historical conditions, at least so far as they depend on geography, which have contributed to produce the present state of things' (George, 1924, v). Distinctive characteristics of this book include the high quality of narrative and the soundness of the geographical and historical information, doubtless questionable in matters of detail by late twentieth-century scholars, but nonetheless impressive. The third is the ethnocentric perspective adopted. Of the Maoris of New Zealand: 'Though far higher in the scale than any other natives of the southern hemisphere, and having among them many individuals who rise to a high level of education and intelligence, they seem unable, as a race, to assimilate civilization. Like the red men of North America, though at a slower rate, the Maoris are apparently destined at no very distant date to disappear' (George, 1924, 198).

The works mentioned above have little to do with historical geography in its modern sense, and are mainly colonial histories with material included on economic and mercantile matters and the nature of the inhabitants of those areas and the labour systems.

The connection between geography and colonialism in all the colonial powers of Europe, and conspicuously so in Britain, France, Germany, the Netherlands, Belgium and Italy, is important yet complex, and is reflected in many publications, some of them bearing the phrase 'historical geography'.

The relationship between geography and colonialism in France is analysed by Said in his influential book *Orientalism*:

> Geography was essentially the material underpinning for knowledge about the Orient. All the latent and unchanging characteristics of the Orient stood upon, were rooted in, its geography . . . . The cosmopolitanism of geography was, in Curzon's mind, its universal importance to the whole of the West, whose relationship to the rest of the world was one of frank covetousness. . . . By the end of the nineteenth century, political and intellectual circumstances coincided sufficiently in France to make geography, and geographical speculation (in both senses of that word), an attractive national pastime (Said, 1978, 217–18).

The development of new energies and enthusiasms for geography in France can be dated from the time of the Franco-Prussian War, the French defeat leading to critical re-examination of the system of education which some blamed for the French overthrow, with education becoming a very important issue after 1871. The energies of government and of geographical societies were in 1870–71, therefore, much given to the promotion and publication of works on colonial geography, frequently in its historical aspects, partly to rectify and ensure against a repetition of the defeat by the Prussians, with their supposedly superior geographical knowledge, and partly to secure a wider territorial base to compete with their European rivals, especially Britain and Germany. In this latter aspect there were really two subheadings, the civilizing mission of French culture when spread abroad as a key to the survival of France as a major power, and the economic arguments, familiar in all other colonial countries in the late nineteenth century, of the necessity to tie to France colonies which would supply raw materials, labour, and provide markets for French produce. Initial French colonial expansion was carried out in 1830 in Algeria, continued in Algeria in the 1840s and West Africa in the 1850s and 1860s, though with relatively little support from within France. The major and more supported colonial thrust came in the 1890s when many colonialist societies came into being under the general heading of the Parti Colonial, some related to a particular country or region such as French Africa, French Asia, Morocco, and reflected a process supported within metropolitan France. The geographical involvement is mainly to be seen through the activities of the Société de Géographie de Paris (founded in 1821), where there was initially strong support, but subsequently fracture, partly by commercial interests, resulting in the foundation of separate societies of commercial geography in Paris and the main provincial cities such as Lyon and Bordeaux, and partly through opposition to colonialism from within the society. The society's journal contains many articles on colonialism, often in its historical aspects.

In a comparison of the relations between geography and colonialism, the differing chronology, ideological bases and actual geographical extent of colonial aspirations and achievements of the three colonial powers under consideration must be clearly borne in mind. Germany differs in many respects from Britain and France: national unification was not achieved until 1871; there was no long tradition of overseas colonization and control; the extent of colonial conquest in the nineteenth and early twentieth centuries was very modest, and the contribution to the German economy was little more than marginal. That is not to say, of course, that colonialism as an ideal and as a prospect was not important: throughout the late nineteenth and early twentieth centuries arguments for and against overseas investment and territorial control occupied politicians, commercial traders, bankers, and scientists, and led to the formation of special-interest societies, some specifically for the advancement of colonial trade and settlement, others having such items high on their agendas, and many of which paralleled in purpose and achievement similar organizations in France and Britain. Geographical societies, both the more scientific and later the more commercial geographical societies, and individual scholars promoted the cause, and articles and books on the historical and contemporary geography of the German colonies were produced.

Historical Geography and Geographical Institutions

While much of the development of what variously was regarded as historical geography can be most readily identified at the national level, though frequently with regard to extranational scholarly influences, there were some interesting activities and attempts to further the international study of this broad field. Of particular significance are the various sections of International Geographical Congress meetings, starting in 1871, which related to aspects of historical geography.

The International Geographical Congresses, whose meetings continue to the present, for the most part included sections on historical geography or more generally labelled sections which have contained papers and discussions on the subject. The first ever international geographical congress was held in Antwerp in 1871, and subsequent congresses prior to the Second World War were held in Paris (1875), Venice (1881), Paris (1889), Bern (1891), London (1895), Berlin (1899), Washington DC (1904), Geneva (1908), Rome (1913), Cairo (1925), Cambridge (1928), Paris (1931), Warsaw (1934), and Amsterdam (1938). The number of specialist sections varied from congress to congress, there being only four in 1871 and 14 in 1908. Sections on historical geography, either individually or in association with the history of geography and other aspects of geography were part of the formal structure of most of the congresses. Thus, at the Paris conference of 1875 there were six sections or groups, the fourth group being the 'Groupe Historique', comprising historical geography and the history of geography, ethnography, and philology. The 1881 Venice congress had eight sections, the fifth group being historical geography and the history of geography. Most congresses followed this pattern, the exceptions being Bern in 1891 which had no separate sections, London (1895), whose only historical section was that on the history of cartography, and the Cambridge meeting of 1928 which had a very broadly based historical section, though papers were given by some of the founders of modern historical geography in Britain such as Taylor and Baker. The nature of topics dealt with in the historical geography sections prior to the Cambridge meeting tended to revolve around the history of cartography, voyages of exploration and discovery, the reconstruction of past geographies from various classical and medieval sources, the history of the names of places, changes in political boundaries and territories, and the production of historical atlases.

2

The Beginnings of Modern Historical Geography
(*c.* 1920–50)

Historical Geography in Britain

Historical geography was the subject of debate in the first three decades of the twentieth century, and an indication of the way in which the fledgling science of geography was beginning to exercise its conceptual wings and its growing independence. By the late 1920s there is clear evidence of the emergence of an historical geography of a recognizably 'modern' kind. This was in part the outcome, in Britain, of the individual and collective work of a number of historical geographers, including Darby, Gilbert, Baker, Taylor, Bowen, and others, trained sometimes in other disciplines, whose published work comprises what may be termed 'classical' historical geography. This in some respects was a new and specialist generation of historical geographers, but an important element of continuity from older traditions of the historical element within a broader human geography are provided in the ideas and writings of such major and influential scholars as Mackinder and Roxby. Mackinder, the great advocate of a 'new geography' in the late nineteenth and early twentieth centuries, incorporated specific sections on historical geography in his major works, including his famous paper on 'The scope and methods of geography', delivered to the Royal Geographical Society in January 1877 (and with a section on the historical geography of south-east England), and in his influential book *Britain and the British Seas* (1902) in which his chapter on historical geography deals with the ethnographic and demographic distributions as a basis for historical development of administrative and political organization (Kearns, 1985a, 71–3).

Mackinder's broader role as an advocate for a new type of geography is important, for, as Kearns has indicated, while he had a background in the hard sciences, '. . . it was also fortunate that he managed to retain this grounding in the physical sciences while also persuading historical scholars that geography had a separate and valuable contribution to make to the humanities in general. Several of these historians, such as Myres, developed cordial and supportive relations with geography' (Kearns, 1985a, 80). The close link between political and historical geography is well exemplified in Mackinder's works and in pieces by others on topics of then current importance, seen in historico-geographical contexts. An early example is W.R. Kermack's study (1919) of the historical geography of the Dardanelles which affords continuity with even earlier work in historical geography through its citation of, for example, Ramsey's *The Historical Geography of Asia Minor* (1890) and with other contemporary concerns with the historical geography of statecraft and war, evidenced, for example, in Vaughan Cornish's 'Notes on the historical and physical geography of the theatres of war' (1915), concerned with geographical aspects of the First World War. Cornish in later, more peaceful times produced a series of studies of the historical geography of capital cities (Cornish, 1923). Roxby, trained as an historian at Oxford, but strongly influenced by the regional interests of Herbertson and of the French regional school, incorporated perspectives from historical geography into, for example, his regional studies of East Anglia (Roxby, 1909–10).

An early debate on the nature of historical geography took place at the annual meeting of the Geographical Association in 1921, the reported discussants being Fairgrieve and Myres. Fairgrieve indicates that in his view there seem to be three different ideas about the nature of historical geography, one that it is the history of geographical discovery, another that it is concerned solely with the effects of geographical conditions on history, and the third that it is a common field for history and geography. In his view, 'Historical geography deals with the discussion of how present conditions, the modern world, are the outcome of past happenings' (Fairgrieve, 1921, 41). The context of the discussion appears to have been the relations of geography and history in the school curriculum, and the relative stages in the curriculum which should be emphasized. J.L. Myres' contribution included the statement that 'the function of historical geography is to ensure that the present is apprehended as a stage in a continuous process, and that that process, as far as man is concerned, is a process of adjustment between man's needs and aspirations on one side, and the geographical factors which limit or permit his realization of desires and ideals' (Myres, 1921, 42).

A few years later Jones, in his inaugural lecture at the London School of Economics and Political Science, 'Geography and the university' (Jones, 1925), having announced at the outset that 'Modern geography, as a school and university study, has arrived. There is no need to push at an open door' (Jones, 1925, 241), outlined the study of geography as the study of the relationship between people and environment, employing a selection of historical and physical facts. After citing the growth of the city of St Louis in Missouri as an example of the interrelationship between geographical site and changing historical circumstances, he makes the interesting observation, repeated in later years by those more clearly recognized as specialist historical geographers, that 'If geography has come to mean a study of man's interrelation with his physical environment, then all geography is historical geography, just as all subjects of study are a part of history, or at least have their historical aspect' (Jones, 1925, 250–1).

The programmatic debates continued in the 1930s. In 1932 a discussion of 'What is historical geography?' took place in London, with Myres in the chair (Morris *et al.*, 1932). Some contributions tend to lean towards the influence of geography on history type of approach. Hence, Fawcett's 'Historical geography is essentially that part of geography in which we are studying the influence of historical events on geographical facts. But the description and investigation of such events is history' (Morris *et al.*, 1932, 39–45), making a distinction between historical geography and geographical history. Perhaps the most often cited contribution was that of Taylor: 'The application of the adjective "historical" to the noun "geography" strictly speaking merely carries the geographer's studies back into the past: his subject matter remains the same' (Morris *et al.*, 1932, 42). She went on, however, to suggest the use of the term 'retrospective geography', in order to facilitate the incorporation of the history of geography and of geographical discovery. Gilbert suggested that there were at least five different definitions of historical geography, and that 'Historical geography should combine the methods of modern regional geography with those of historical criticism' (Morris *et al.*, 1932, 43). He developed and emphasized his views in a longer contribution, published in the same year in the *Scottish Geographical Magazine*, claiming that the term 'historical geography' lacked precision and an objective, which served to 'obscure the existence of a true historical geography' (Gilbert, 1932, 129). Having examined various conceptions of historical geography, notably those of historical geography as an account of changes in frontiers and boundaries, as the history of geographical exploration and discovery, as the history of geography as a science, and as a history of the influence of the geographical environment on the course of history, he concludes with a firm definition of historical geography. That definition is: 'The real function of historical geography is to reconstruct the regional geography of the past. Historical geography should confine itself to a descriptive geographical account of a region as it was at a given past period, and should not endeavour to make the explanation of historical events its main objective. . . . Historical geography combines the methods of regional geography with those of historical criticism . . . it is obvious that persons who attempt this work should be trained in methods of historical as well as geographical research' (Gilbert, 1932, 132). In 1933 East gave his view of the subject: 'The task of the historical geographer is thus succinctly defined: from a mass of data which he can collect from archaeology and history, from old and new maps, plans and charts, and from studies of present-day geography, he has judiciously to reconstruct and to present "period pictures" of human activities and distributions in relation to their physical milieu' (East, 1933, 282).

Not all of this extensive debate and review can be seen as the laying of entirely sure foundations for future developments in historical geography. The view that the history of geographical thought and the history of voyages of exploration and discovery, for example, should be excluded from its programmes of research and teaching produced an unnecessarily narrow conception, which was strongly influential from the 1930s to the 1970s, at least in Britain. In addition, the events of the First World War and the growing geopolitical distortions of the fascist states in Europe in the 1920s and 1930s seemed to reduce the political component of historical geography for all but a few early and later practitioners (such as East and Pounds), so that in Britain focus was on an 'innocent' past recovered from documentary sources, though there was probably an indirect element of patriotism in this focus on the British (most frequently the English) past.

Historical geographers in Britain were not merely debating the contents of their subject, they were also demonstrating its stimulus and practice, and the nature of the substantive articles and books published reflect the particular interests and training of the individuals involved. Some of the earliest and most important contributions came from the 'Aberystwyth school' of historically sensitive human geography, whose publications (notably by Fleure and Bowen) reflected the influence of archaeology and French human geography and in which the term 'historical geography' was used if not debated. An early example of this type of approach, though produced in Liverpool rather than Wales, was Fitzgerald's short booklet *The Historical Geography of Early Ireland* (1925). In 1932, Bowen published an article 'Early Christianity in the British Isles. A study in historical geography', the first of a large number of publications that examined the geography of Celtic saints and settlements (Bowen, 1932). Peake and Fleure's collaborative series, *The Corridors of Time*, published in nine volumes between 1927 and 1936, were influential works reflecting this school of thought. In a different, perhaps more metropolitan tradition, East's *An Historical Geography of Europe* was published in 1935, a work described by its author as 'an attempt to apply in a particular case the modern conception of historical geography' (East, 1935, vii), and which dealt in three sections with the geography of settlement in Europe, the political geography of Europe, and the economic geography of Europe, from the time of the Roman Empire onwards.

Additional and important works of the 1930s included E.W. Gilbert's *The Exploration of Western America, 1800–1850: an Historical Geography* (1933), Eva G.R. Taylor's studies of *Tudor Geography, 1485–1583* (1930) and of *Late Tudor and Early Stuart Geography, 1583–1650* (1934), J.N.L. Baker's studies of The Geography of Daniel Defoe, in the *Scottish Geographical Magazine* (1931) and his *A History of Geographical Discovery and Exploration* (1931), together with the early published papers of H.C. Darby, especially two on 'The role of the Fenland in English history' (1931) and 'The medieval sea state' (1932), which evidence the influence of the strong tradition in English academic history, dating back to the mid-nineteenth century, of the study of the geography behind history. The work of Taylor merits attention: she was one of the few women geographers in England in the inter-war period, having been appointed to a full-time lectureship in geography at Birkbeck College, University of London, at a mature age, and she worked initially in the field of the history of geographical thought from 1485. In 1930 she published her work on *Tudor Geography 1485–1583*, followed in 1934 by *Late Tudor and Early Stuart Geography 1583–1650*, both books looking at the background of geographical thought and of nautical theory to the voyages of discovery, and the work of Dee, Hakluyt and Purchas (Campbell, 1987, 48–9). She was the only woman contributor to Darby's *An Historical Geography of England before AD 1800* (1936), with two chapters respectively on 'Leland's England' and 'Camden's England'. She taught historical geography at Birkbeck College, and was elected to the chair of geography in 1930, adding thereafter to her work on the history of geographical thought contributions to the Royal Commission on the Distribution of Industrial Population (the Barlow Report) and to a campaign for the production of a national atlas of Britain (Campbell, 1987, 50–1).

Work in this 'classical' phase of historical geography, associated indelibly in England with the work of Darby and a small band of pioneer scholars, may be seen in the context of attempts to establish historical geography as a credible academic pursuit and at a time of concern about overstatements of the

influences of the geographical environment. The work produced was experimental, of meticulously high standards of scholarship, and apparently successful in its achievements, if judged by the longevity of the texts produced and the
favourable light in which they were reviewed. Darby (1983, 423), refers to the
'ferment' of the 'new geography' in Britain in the 1920s and 1930s, with which
'came the rise of historical geography as a *self-conscious* discipline. We "new
geographers" realised that every past had once been a present. There was a
high degree of unanimity among us. We had something of the dogmatic
fervour of new converts to a faith, heightened by the fact that the position of
geography was not all that well established in our universities'. Pragmatic
attempts at new methodologies were made in *An Historical Geography of
England before AD 1800* (1936), using cross-sectional reconstructions of the
geography of past periods, with sources of material and the problems discussed
determining the methodologies, which were extremely varied. Darby, the
editor of the book, describes how he pondered over the possibility of writing a
philosophical introduction, but came to the conclusion 'that the time was not
yet ripe' (Darby, 1983, 423). While the methodology of historical geography
was advanced by that volume, theory was not: a somewhat puzzling feature in
view of the amount of contemporary writing on the theory of history. The
outcome, as Baker (1984a, 17) has indicated was that 'Darby's search for a
method in historical geography discovered a diversity of problems, of courses,
of approaches and techniques. His principal finding was an experimental and
pragmatic scholarship. Its limitations were recognized by Darby himself . . .'
One of the limitations of the classical approach to the past was that which
involved essentially horizontal 'cross-sections' of history, which were somewhat static and did not give a sense of dynamism to the past. This was the style
adopted in *An Historical Geography of England before AD 1800* (1936), and
modified in the later *A New Historical Geography of England* (1973) to a
combination of cross-sections or time-slices and 'vertical' narrative sections.

It is many respects *An Historical Geography of England before AD 1800* is
an epitome of 'classical' historical geography in Britain, its main characteristics
being the use of cross-sections as technical approaches to the management of
time-periods and themes, expert knowledge of source materials and their
limitations, an extensive use of distribution maps at a variety of scales, and a
liberal though unspecified practical interpretation of the functions of historical
geography, together with a very high standard of narrative and analytical
writing.

Although *An Historical Geography of England before AD 1800* was written
to meet 'the increasing importance of the subject [historical geography] in
university studies' (Darby, 1936, vii) it also reflected the debate on the nature
of historical geography. In its consideration of 'period picture' and evolutionary accounts of particular phases of development or specific topics or
sources, it was, as Darby recalls, a methodological compromise. By the time
Darby came to edit *A New Historical Geography of England* (Darby, 1973)
not only was the range of original research on which it could be based (and the
number of specialist practitioners of historical geography) greatly increased,
but Darby's ideas on the necessity to integrate studies of particular periods
with linking narratives which systematically explored processes of change over
the intervening phases had crystallized into a marriage of 'horizontal' and
'vertical' approaches to the writing of historical geography (Fig. 2.1).

'AN HISTORICAL GEOGRAPHY OF ENGLAND BEFORE AD 1800' H.C. Darby (ed.) 1936	'A NEW HISTORICAL GEOGRAPHY OF ENGLAND' H.C. Darby (ed.) 1973
I. Introductory Background: Prehistoric South Britain	1. The Anglo - Scandinavian Foundations
II. The Human Geography of Roman Britain	2. Domesday England
III. The Anglo-Saxon Settlement	3. Changes in the Early Middle Ages
IV. The Scandinavian Settlement	4. England *circa* 1334
V. The Economic Geography of England, AD 1000 - 1250	5. Changes in the Later Middle Ages
VI. Fourteenth - Century England	6. England *circa* 1600
VII. Medieval Foreign Trade: Western Ports	7. The Age of the Improver: 1600 - 1800
VIII. Medieval Foreign Trade: Eastern Ports	8. England *circa* 1800
IX. Leland's England	9. Changes in the Early Railway Age: 1800 - 1850
X. Camden's England	10. England *circa* 1850
XI. England in the Seventeenth Century	11. The Changing Face of England 1850 - *circa* 1900
XII. The Draining of the Fens, AD 1600 - 1800	12. England *circa* 1900
XIII. England in the Eighteenth Century	
XIV. The Growth of London, AD 1660 - 1800	

Fig. 2.1 *Contents of the two versions of the books edited by Darby on the historical geography of England, illustrating contrasting approaches in 1936 and 1973*

There were additionally some more unusual works among the articles and books of the early twentieth century, one of which was Carrier's *Historical Geography of England and Wales (South Britain)*, published in 1925, and subdivided into four sections: the first on 'The Races of Britain'; the second and third on 'The Middle Ages'; and the fourth on 'The Modern Period'. A rather idiosyncratic work, but the general themes of the book are important and, to later generations, familiar: the evolution of the geographical aspects of the social, economic and administrative changes in England and Wales, which anticipate many of the major studies by historical geographers of the same themes in this and later decades. Thus, Section II ('The Middle Ages [I]'), has separate chapters on: 'Ecclesiastical influence upon the geography of England'; 'Territorial divisions: shire-making; Community divisions: hundred, village, borough, parish'; 'The influence of geography upon medieval warfare'; and 'The battle of land and sea: disappearance of forest and fen'. The work is unreferenced, and although one general impression is that of a very basic textbook, it could conceivably be seen as a work ahead of its time, highlighting the major themes which would engage historical geographers in Britain and elsewhere for a long time to come.

Historical Geography in France

There was through the first half of the twentieth century a decline in the number of articles in historical geography published in the major geographical journal, *Annales de Géographie*. This decline in a separately identified historical geography was paralleled by the rise of the *Annales* school of economic and social history, under the influence of the historians Bloch and Febvre, and the continuing geographical sensitivity of narrative and local and regional history. The *Annales* school was that associated initially with the journal *Annales d'Histoire Économique et Sociale*, first published in 1929, which subsequently became the famous *Annales: Économies, Sociétés, Civilisations* in 1946, having been renamed *Annales d'Histoire Sociale* in 1939, and *Mélanges d'Histoire Sociale* between 1942 and 1944 (Fink, 1991, 130). The main interests of the *Annales* school were in the social, behavioural, material and structural aspects and analysis of history. The relationship between French geography and the *Annales* school of history has been reviewed by Baker (1984a), who points to the parallel strengthening of the geographical element in the historical studies by the 'Annalistes' and the accelerating sense of history incorporated into the new French human geography initiated by Vidal de la Blache and his followers (who also stressed—as much for pressing political as scientific geographical reasons—the importance of regional characteristics and analyses). A key point to be made, however, is that notwithstanding the lack of a clear historical geography label, the *Annales* tradition was an historical geography tradition, in that the 'Annalistes' did overtly and consciously seek a fusion of history and geography, reflecting broader international, national and regional contexts of Strasbourg, where the journal was based, after the First World War.

There was, however, some measure of continuity in France with the older style of historical geography. Mirot's *Manuel de Géographie Historique de la France* which was published in Paris in 1929, and may be seen in part, as C. Jullian indicates in his preface to the first edition, as an attempt to revive a secular tradition which had been almost lost for about half a century, though it was also a political historical geography of France (Fig. 2.2). Mirot's book emphasizes the contexts of the territorial ecclesiastical and administrative evolution of France, thus mirroring one type of work characteristic of the nineteenth century. This was not a matter of chance: Mirot was a former pupil of Longnon, and subsequently a member of the French school at Rome and curator in the French national archives.

The *Bulletin du Comité Français de Géographie Historique et d'Histoire de la Géographie*, 1935, 1936, 1938

In May 1935 there appeared the first of three numbers of a new but very short-lived journal, the *Bulletin du Comité Français de Géographie Historique et d'Histoire de la Géographie*. The reason for the foundation of this bulletin was that there was no national organization in France for the study of historical geography and the history of geography, which had declined in importance, for example, at the Sorbonne.

The first number of the *Bulletin* was published in May 1935, and contained an interesting and important article by Goblet, entitled 'Géographie historique

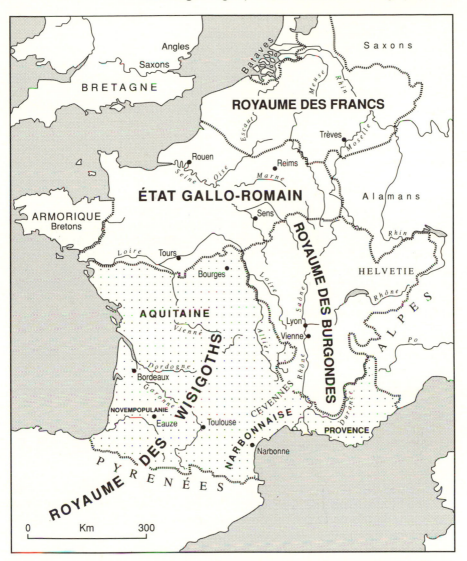

Fig. 2.2 *Gaul in AD 482. Based on: Mirot,* Manuel de Géographie Historique de la France, *(1929). A good example of the interest of French historical geographers in the nineteenth and early twentieth centuries in the evolution of the kingdoms and administrative divisions of historic France*

et histoire de la géographie' (1935), in which he reviews the associations between geography and history, and stakes a claim for historical geography as a separate branch of geography. Goblet was a political geographer, who had undertaken a major study of the transformation of the political geography of Ireland in the seventeenth century through the Down Survey maps and anthropogeographic essays of Petty (based on a major collection in the Bibliothèque Nationale in Paris) (Butlin, 1990a; Parker, 1991). He contended that although geography was frequently regarded as an auxiliary science to history, the reverse was the case. The term 'historical geography', he saw partly as comprising the study of the administrative geographies of past times, but in a broader sense as a series of complete geographical tableaux of past times. He suggested that there is no basic difference between modern or contemporary historical geography, except that historical geography is primarily concerned with the past, but the methods and approaches are essentially the same. His definition of the goals of historical geography bears close resemblance of many of those expressed in Britain in the early 1930s, and is a progressive view of historical geography compatible with the new human geography of Vidal de la Blache and his successors.

The *Bulletin* of which the third and last number appeared in May 1938, provides an interesting short chapter in the history of historical geography in France. Although it cannot be seen as a symbol of an avant-garde view of the subject, judging by the large number of military officers and the small number of names of 'progressive' geographers numbered among its members, and its failure to attract the types of contribution envisaged by Goblet, it appears that his aims were firmly geared to the stimulation of a new interest in historical geography and the history of geography. Historical geography in France henceforth was more bound up with an historically sensitive human geography, at least until the late twentieth century, whereas in Britain a clearer separate identity was made and preserved by many practitioners.

Historical Geography in Germany

Although there are parallels in the history of historical geography in Germany and other European countries, there are also differences, notably the lesser emphasis on historical geography as a separate branch of human geography or 'anthropogeographie'. The strong links with history as a discipline are, however, similar to those in France and Britain, for example. Fehn, in a short introduction to a more general article on historical geography, has suggested that before 1882 (a year which he thinks marks the beginning of modern German historical geography), historical geography was, as elsewhere, largely practised by historians and dealt with such topics as historical topography, the history of political and administrative boundaries, the geography of classical civilizations, the study of the 'geographical factor' in history, the history of cartography and the production of historical maps and atlases, the study of changing conditions of physical geography, and of past regions and their human habitation (Fehn, 1975). Interesting insights into the contexts within which historical geography was researched and taught are afforded by the lists of lecture courses given in the major German universities in the nineteenth century as, for example, in Schröder's (1977) study of the history of geography in the University of Tübingen.

The nature of what was titled 'historical geography' in Germany, particularly in the nineteenth century, was therefore very complex, not least because of the very different backgrounds (geography, history, archaeology) and institutional contexts from and in which individual scholars worked. The foundation of the Central Commission for German Regional Studies in 1882, according to Fehn (1975) does, however, herald the beginning of 'modern' German historical geography.

In the early twentieth century Kötzsche, an expert regional historian, published a paper on 'Sources and basic concepts of the historical geography of Germany and its neighbours' (1906), in which he claimed that the role of historical geography was to observe the earth's surface and its elements as a domain of human habitation through periods of historical development.

Hettner, an important geographical theorist of the early twentieth century, commented (Hettner, 1922) on the position of historical geography within the framework of university geography, and saw historical geography as the geographical study of past times, which placed it as a separate study between geography and history, and one which was able to provide substantial assistance to studies of contemporary geography as well as to historical studies. He complains, however, that in reality its important potential contribution is not being realized, with energies being devoted primarily to work of a descriptive and history of state boundaries type, instead of going forward to promote comprehensive regional studies. The main thrusts of historical geography in Germany in the first half of the twentieth century were, in fact, partly those of a study aid to cultural and cultural landscape research and to the history of cartography.

Cultural landscape research in the pre-Second World War period was closely related to the understanding of the present-day landscape, and its purpose was outlined by Mager's writing on historical geography and the genesis of cultural landscapes (Lenz and Fricker, 1969), for Mager felt that without the association with the present it was difficult to speak of historical geography. In contrast, the view of the historian Curschmann, who was an active participant in historical geography sections of international congresses in the early part of the century, was that historical geography was a 'new branch on the large historical studies tree', and his own work was primarily devoted to the production of historical atlases of individual territories and landscapes (Curschmann, 1916; Fehn, 1976).

The major formative and seminal works in German historical geography are varied and wide-ranging. There is perhaps a stronger sense of continuity of method in Germany than, say, in France and Britain. The influence of Ritter in drawing the attention of historians to the relations of geography to the course of human affairs, was a continuing and important one.

As with other European countries, historical geography in its formative years reflects the insights and enthusiasms of individual scholars, some, at least initially, working outside the universities and institutes of higher education. An all-round scholar-pioneer was Gradmann (1865–1950), a parish priest who started work on the biogeography of the Swabian Alp region, where he discovered vegetational indicators of prehistoric settlement sequences, and who then extended his interest to historical cultural landscape studies. He established a typology of two main types of genetic cultural landscapes, each with a specific ecological basis and set of closely correlated geographical and historical elements. The two elements were the largely treeless steppe-heath areas, associated with early Neolithic settlement (Fig. 2.3), and the forested areas: this 'steppenheide' theory received much discussion. He ultimately became professor of geography at the University of Tübingen, and his best known major work is his *Süddeutschland*, published in 1931. Another major scholar was Schlüter (1872–1952). Schlüter was one of the first historical geographers to have been trained as a geographer: he had written his doctoral

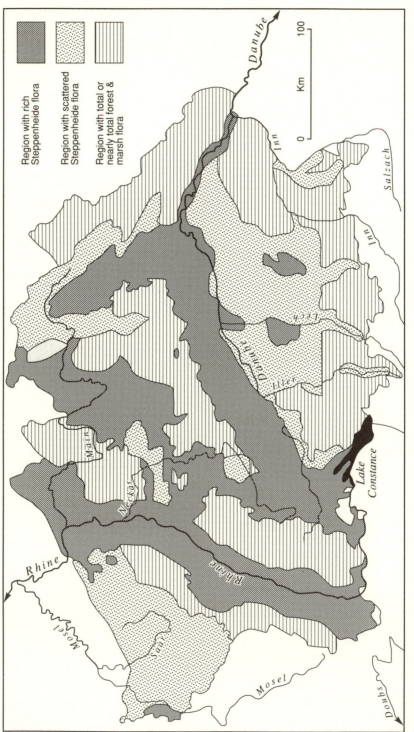

Fig. 2.3 *The regions of largely treeless steppenheide (steppe/heathland) flora in southern Germany, associated with early Neolithic settlement: based on the reconstruction by the German geographer Gradmann in Süddeutschland (1931, 67)*

dissertation on the settlement of the Unstrut Valley, followed by a major thesis in 1903 on the settlements of north-east Thuringia. His interests included the geography of settlement in central Europe, and his publications included an atlas of middle Germany, and his best-known and monumental study of the history of settlement in central Europe *Die Siedlungsräume Mitteleuropas in frühgeschichtlicher Zeit*, published in three volumes, 1952–58, and focused on a remarkable map which reconstructed the distribution of forests in central Europe at the beginning of the major age of clearance in the early Middle Ages (Dickinson, 1969, 126–36). An interesting point here is that in both Germany and France, and via Germany to the United States, the rural landscape or 'landschaft' and its evolution was bound up closely to ideas of nationhood and territory, giving interesting political and ideological dimensions to historical geography.

Historical Geography in the United States

The history of development of historical geography in North America follows a very different pattern from that of Europe, partly because of the roots of academic geography having been in geology rather than, as in Europe, substantially in history, partly because of the strong tradition of cultural geography, and partly because of the relative lateness of development of geography in the universities. As far as historical geography is concerned, however, the pattern of research of the 1920s and 1930s, as elsewhere, was conditioned by a small group of highly influential individual scholars, conspicuously Harlan Barrows, Ralph Brown, and Carl Sauer.

The institutional context of early professionalised geography in the United States is relevant to our understanding of the nature of historical geography at the time (Dunbar, 1981, 74–6). Beckinsale has indicated that geography was introduced at Harvard in 1841, at Princeton in 1854, Cornell and Wisconsin in 1868, and at Yale by 1875, though not as a separate subject in another department (Beckinsale, 1981, 108). The first major separate department of geography was that of the University of California (1898), and the first department to offer the Ph.D. in geography was Chicago (in 1903), and remained the only one to do so until 1923 (Dunbar, 1981, 74–6; Rugg, 1981, 183). The institutions in which historical geography was most conspicuously developed were the departments of geography at the universities of Chicago, California (Berkeley), and Minnesota. Historical geography was as much, of course, a personal view as an institutionally influenced view of the geography of the past, and thus it is important to recognize, as Clark (1954, 81) has done, the importance for historical geography of the work of Marsh (in *Man and Nature, or Physical Geography as Modified by Human Action*, 1894) and Shaler (*Nature and Man in America*, 1891, and *Man and the Earth*, 1905), at a time when academic geography was little developed in the United States.

The influential figure at Chicago was Barrows (1877–1960), whose impact on historical geography has been evaluated by Koelsch (1962; 1969). The course initiated by Barrows in Chicago in 1904 was entitled 'Influence of geography on American history' (later changed to 'Historical geography of the United States'), and its purpose was to provide 'A study of the geographic conditions which have influenced the course of American history' (Koelsch,

1969, 634), strongly influenced by the work of the historian of the American frontier, Turner, and the geographer Semple, a colleague at Chicago and author of the book *American History and its Geographic Conditions*, published in 1903. Semple's ideas on the influence of the geographical environment on geographical and historical change, strongly and obviously influenced by Ratzel, had a significant effect on the initial development of Barrows' ideas on human and historical geography, as also did those of Brigham, but by the early 1920s, as Koelsch has indicated, his ideas had shifted from a geographical influence perspective to that of geography as human ecology (Koelsch, 1969, 637), a phrase used as the title of his presidential address to the Association of American Geographers in December of 1922 (Barrows, 1923). Barrows' thesis incorporated such more recent influences as his government service in the First World War, and later during the period of the New Deal an increasing orientation towards an ecological perspective, and the ideas on historical geography of his Chicago colleague Towers (Koelsch, 1969, 638).

Barrows' course of lectures at Chicago had a very strong regional element. The course was influential in at least two ways: it was very well attended and seems to have encouraged students to progress into further work on the subject, and it also, as Koelsch has suggested, helped 'American geography to make its shift from a search for "geographical influence" to more rewarding questions associated with the area studies tradition and with alternative formulations of the man–land tradition' (Koelsch, 1969, 650). Merrens (1965, 538) takes a pessimistic view of the contribution of historical geography in the United States in the first quarter of the twentieth century, seeing an unhelpful concern with environmental determinism and lack of use of primary-source materials, coupled with the failure of the briefly attempted debates between historians and geographers.

In Merrens' analysis (1965) there was thought to be a change in historical geography in the United States in the 1920s and 1930s, involving a diminution of interest in the man–land tradition and environmental determinism and an increasing involvement with spatial and area studies traditions, together with the beginning of another trait—the intensive investigation of primary sources: the former reflected in the work of Brown and the latter in the population studies of Friis, including *A Series of Population Maps of the Colonies and the United States* (Friis, 1940a, b). The further reading or interpretation of the emphases of historical and geographers generally in the United States at this time need intensive investigation, though strong statements have been made by Mitchell and Groves (1987) and Earle (1992) that this was a period when the historically sensitive part of geography was forced to retreat in the face of what Earle (1992, 14) regards as a powerful geographical mainstream from the Midwest.

This circumstance notwithstanding, a major figure in historical geography in this period was Brown (1898–1948), trained at the University of Pennsylvania and at the University of Wisconsin, and who, after an initial period (1925–29) at the University of Colorado, spent the rest of his professional career at the University of Minnesota. As with Barrows, in the 1920s, when geography was acquiring a stronger emphasis on human habitation and environmental relations, Brown taught and wrote on human adjustments to environment, with developing interests in past American regions and in the influence of beliefs and images on the history of settlement and change (Miles, 1982). A more deliberate orientation to historical geography came in the 1930s, historical geography being for Brown the regional geography of the past. His two major books, *Mirror for Americans* (1943) and *Historical Geography of the United States* (1948), were seen by Clark (1954, 83) as 'a monument to . . . the coming of age of historical geography', and by Meinig as 'the first substantial modern products of [the] field' (Meinig, 1978b, 1187). *Mirror for Americans* was an attempt to write the past geography or 'likeness' of an area (the subtitle was *Likeness of the Eastern Seaboard, 1810*) as it might have been written by an imaginary author of the time (Thomas P. Keystone), using only materials and information that would have then been available, and eschewing the use of later documentary and statistical evidence. Darby has described this book as 'a magnificent tour de force and an intellectual exercise that throws light upon some of the problems involved in the creation of the "historic present". It is, moreover, a work of great charm that must delight all who read it' (Darby, 1962, 131). *Historical Geography of the United States* is a work of great stature and literary merit. In his introduction Brown indicates his view of historical geography: 'This interpretation of the functions of historical geography, which has long been defined but rarely exemplified as simply "the geography of the past", depends on original, eyewitness accounts and contemporary maps. The availability of such material has mainly prescribed the space and time limits of this regional study. In general, regions are considered at the earliest period for which there is reliable and adequate source material. . . . This is a survey of the character of American regions in earlier times' (Brown, 1948, iii–iv). The six sections of the book are: 'The colonization period'; 'The Atlantic seaboard at the opening of the nineteenth century'; 'The Ohio River and lower Great Lakes regions, to 1830'; 'The new northwest, 1820–1870'; 'The Great Plains and bordering regions, to 1870'; and 'From the Rocky Mountains to the Pacific Coast, to 1870' (see Fig. 2.4).

Although it is possible to query the terminal date of the time covered in the book (1870) and the variation in regional coverage within it, the *Historical Geography of the United States* is a pioneer work which has still not, of its kind, been superceded, and which still pays careful reading and scrutiny. It contains evidence of the hallmarks of Brown's scholarship, especially the use of a wide range of documentary, published, and cartographic evidence, allied to an extensive field knowledge, and in some respects may be seen as a contemporary parallel to the new type of historical geography being developed in Britain. His work reflected a change of direction from the earlier authorities such as Semple and Brigham (whose *Geographical Influences in American History*, a regionally based study of the influence of physiographic regions on American history had been published in 1903). Brown was familiar with Barrows' work, and used it with students, but his own work differed in its greater emphasis on regions and in the priority given to a wide range of documentary evidence (though Barrows' work was by no means entirely based on secondary sources). In addition, Lowther has suggested that Brown's two books are in effect good examples within historical geography of an approximation to the idealist methodology of Collingwood, in so far as 'In writing of the geography of that time and place [in this instance the geography of the eastern seaboard of the United States in the year 1810] only as it appeared in terms of contemporary knowledge and ideas, Brown was to a large extent

'HISTORICAL GEOGRAPHY OF THE UNITED STATES'
Ralph. H. Brown (1948)

PART ONE: THE COLONISATION PERIOD

1. Early Geography: Fact and Fancy

2. Taking Possession of the Land

3. Making Land and Sea Productive

4. Filling Up the Land: French and English Settlements

5. Filling Up the Land: Spanish Settlements in Florida and the Far West

PART TWO: THE ATLANTIC SEABOARD AT THE OPENING OF THE NINETEENTH
CENTURY

6. The Land: A General View

7. The Sea: Its Industries and Commerce

8. Regional Studies: The South

9. Regional Studies: The North

10. Frontiers of the Seaboard States and the St. Lawrence Valley

PART THREE: THE OHIO RIVER AND LOWER GREAT LAKES REGIONS, TO 1830

11. A General View of the Land

12. People in the Land: The State of Ohio

13. People in the Land: Down-river Country

14. Travel and Trade on the Ohio River and Canals to the Great Lakes

15. Detroit and Southeastern Michigan

PART FOUR: THE NEW NORTHWEST, 1820-1870

16. The Upper Lakes Country: Fur Trade, Mining Industries, and Forest Exploitation

17. From Mining to Farming in Southern Wisconsin

18. Minnesota: Territory and State

19. The United States in 1870

PART FIVE: THE GREAT PLAINS AND BORDERING REGIONS, TO 1870

20. The Great Plains Region: What It Was, and What It Was Thought to be

21. Passage Across the Plains: Routes of Trade and Migration

22. Settlement in the Central and Northern Plains

23. Texas: Farming Frontier and Cattle Kingdom

24. Gold in the Hills and Water on the Plains: Colorado

PART SIX: FROM THE ROCKY MOUNTAINS TO THE PACIFIC COAST, TO 1870

25. The Oregon Country; Inland Empire and Coastal Valleys

26. The Great Basin and the Arid Southwest

27. Report on California: I.San Francisco and Its Hinterland

28. Report on California: II. Southern Valleys and Sierras

29. Regional Settlement: A Panorama

Fig. 2.4 *The approach to periodization and regionalizations of the historical geography of the United States from Brown's* Historical Geography of the United States *(1948)*

rethinking the thoughts of the past', idealism reflecting the view that 'The ideas of a society are as necessary to a study of its geography as they are to a study of its history' (Lowther, 1959, 34–5).

It is interesting to compare Brown's view of historical geography with that of another great American contemporary, Sauer (1889–1975). His parents were German, and he spent some time at school in southern Germany. Sauer was strongly influenced by German geography of the late nineteenth and twentieth centuries, which he seems to have discovered in the early 1920s and which, it is thought, provided him 'with the intellectual material and ideas for the formulation of the more rigorous and humane geography for which he had been searching', and in which 'he also found some reflection of his own, perforce rejected, cultural identity' (Williams, 1983, 4). Such major authorities as Ratzel, Schlüter and Hahn were of major significance in his thinking and writing, at least until the early 1940s. Sauer's highly individualist and iconoclastic style and approach contrasts markedly with that of Brown. Miles has suggested, for example, that whereas Brown studied the America of the European settlers, Sauer studied that of the Indians; while Brown had close affinities with history and historians, Sauer's were with anthropology and anthropologists such as Kroeber; Brown felt that a genetic approach was not essential, and Sauer clearly did (Miles, 1982, 82–4). Sauer's views of historical geography were both negative and positive: although steeped in the ideas of anthropogeography of Ratzel, for example, he rejected the version of them incorporated in Semple's work, and he was also less than sympathetic to the historical geography of Barrows. He was more sympathetic to the work of Brown, whom he described as the 'most active worker in the field of historical geography' (Williams, 1983, 18). His view of the relevance of a genetic approach to landscape was reflected in his view of historical geography given in his major paper 'The morphology of landscape' (1925): 'Historical geography may be considered as the series of changes which the cultural landscapes have undergone and therefore involves the reconstruction of past landscapes' (1925; 1963, 345). Similar sentiments regarding the importance of a genetic approach to the study of human occupation were voiced in Whittlesey's paper on 'Sequent occupance' (1929, 162–5) incorporating the notion of the backward and forward temporal links of human settlements in a cultural continuum (see Chapter 8).

In his later paper 'Foreword to historical geography' (1941), Sauer complained of the neglect of historical geography in North America, and drew attention to the strong intellectual heritage, especially from Germany, of historically and regionally sensitive studies in human geography:

> The historical geographer must therefore be a regional specialist, for he must not only know the region as it appears today; he must know its lineaments so well that he can find in it the traces of the past, and he must know its qualities so well that he can see it as it was under past situations. . . . Historical regional studies of the kind indicated are in the best and oldest geographic tradition. Cluverius, in the seventeenth century, did some extraordinarily acute reconstructions of Germany and Italy, skilfully uniting knowledge of the classics and knowledge of the land. Humboldt's *Essay on New Spain* is still the classic of the historical geography of Mexico (Sauer, 1963, Leighly (ed.) 362–3).

He also instances the work of Meitzen in Germany, and says that 'the influence of Fleure and Taylor is evident in the studies of the younger English geographers', and suggests that 'it is about time that we in this country become actively conscious of this, the great tradition in human geography' (Sauer 1941; 1963, 362–3). Although his interest in methodological statements declined thereafter, Sauer's teaching, graduate supervision, and publication has left a major mark in the fields of cultural and historical geography, in the form of the Berkeley/Sauerian school of thought, associated very much with studies, based on extensive field knowledge, of early cultures and landscapes, especially of regions of Latin America, and with studies of the spread of plant and animal domestication.

Jakle (1971) has characterized developments in historical geography in the United States in the 1940s and beyond in the following terms. From the late 1940s there was a further development of the use of general models in historical geography, including the regionalization and chorological tradition developed in the work of Clark, especially his study of Prince Edward Island (1959), and Clark and his students' work involving a synchronic, cross-sectional approach. Parallel developments, exemplified in later chapters, include improvements in historiographic techniques, concerns with geographical change through time within the larger body of human and cultural geography, and a general drift towards model-building.

The history of the development of historical geography in Canada is more recent than in the United States, though there is obviously overlap and mutual influence, as there is also with France in Quebec. Robinson (1967) has summarized the history of the teaching of geography in Canada in the following terms: 'At the turn of the century geography was probably stronger in the schools in most provinces than it was in most states [of the United States] but in both countries it seemed to be mainly an uninspired collection of facts about particular places in the world. There was no leadership from Canadian universities to improve the quality of geography nor to change its content or philosophy' (Robinson, 1967, 217). The teaching of geography in the University of Montreal had begun in 1910, with a period of intensification as a result of the arrival of French-trained geographers in the 1920s and 1930s. In Ontario, geography had been taught in Toronto since 1906, though the main period of growth really began in Toronto, Western Ontario and McMaster in the 1920s. Of particular significance for historical geography was the work of the economic historian Innes, who also taught economic geography at Toronto in the 1920s. His major work *The Fur Trade of Canada* (1931) was a major influence. Harris has argued that Innis was one of the initiators of the 'Laurentian' interpretation of the history of Canada: 'Canada, Innes argued, grew out of the westward arc of the St Lawrence–Great Lakes system, the rivers of the west, and the Canadian Shield, that is out of the territory of the fur trade. This "Laurentian" interpretation, bolstering as it did a sense of nationhood, and falling on the intellectual background of social Darwinism and environmentalism, dominated historical scholarship in Canada for thirty years' (Harris, 1967, 235). The major development of historical geography in Canada, however, came after the Second World War.

Historical Geography in Australasia and Asia

The foundations of historical geography in Australia and New Zealand are to be found at a very much later date than those countries considered so far. The dates of establishment of the major geographical journals are an indicator: *The Australian Geographer* was established in 1928, and *The New Zealand Geographer* in 1945. The institutional history of geography in Australia and New Zealand shows that it was very much later into the academic field than in many other countries. Heathcote and McCaskill have indicated that although the first post in geography in Australia (the associate professorship of Griffith Taylor at the University of Sydney) was established in 1920, other posts did not follow until the 1950s, when there was a rapid expansion in the subject (Heathcote and McCaskill, 1972). In New Zealand the subject was first established in 1937, at the University of Canterbury, with Jobberns as the first head of department. Jobberns was an admirer of the Sauer school of cultural geography at Berkeley, and appointed as visiting lecturers two Berkeley graduates, Robert Bowman and Andrew Clark, and a few years later Kenneth Cumberland was appointed to a post in the department. These developments were strongly influential in the subsequent course of historical geography in the country (Heathcote and McCaskill, 1972, 154). There was rapid development of geography in New Zealand in the 1940s. Prior to 1945, there was, not surprisingly, little historical geography published or practised in either country. In Australia, some important work on settlement, especially in relation to climatic limits, was undertaken by Griffith Taylor, though the majority of the work in the field was by historians and economic historians. Roberts' *History of Australian Land Settlement, 1788–1920* (1924) and his *The Squatting Age in Australia, 1835–1847* (1935) were important historical works which began to touch upon more overtly geographical matters such as patterns of land settlement, as also did Price's *The Foundation and Settlement of South Australia, 1829–1845* (1924), and C. Fenner's work on population change in South Australia in the nineteenth and early twentieth centuries. Chapter Two, 'The historical survey of settlement,' of Wadham and Wood's *Land Utilisation in Australia* (1939) has been described as 'the first continental-wide venture in historical geography in Australia' (Heathcote and McCaskill, 1972, 148).

The early form of historical geography in New Zealand was that of an emphasis on processes of rural change through time, the outstanding example of which was Guthrie-Smith's *Tutira, the Story of a New Zealand Sheep Station* (1921), by the man who was part-owner of the station from 1882 to 1940. This book 'is the sort of historical geography that could not have been written from documents, but only from the observations of an intelligent participant in change that took place over half a century' (Heathcote and McCaskill, 1972, 158).

The history of historical geography in other Pacific and in Asian countries is as yet insufficiently documented, but seems to have emanated from cultural traditions very different from those of western Europe, though not in practice unaffected by them, with particular influence having come from Germany. The history of historical geography in Japan has been outlined, for example, by Senda (1982): 'In the Meiji era (1868–1912) modern geography came to provide a scientific framework for traditional studies of regions and landscapes. At first, historical geography was an ancillary method serving the science of history. In 1899 the discipline gained independent professional status when many historians under the leadership of Kida, Professor of Japanese History at Kyoto University, founded the Society of Japanese Historical Geography, whose monthly bulletin of historical geography was published from 1899–1923' (Senda, 1982, 171). Major works in historical geography followed the establishment of a geographical institute within the history department in Kyoto, including a *Historical Geography of China*, published in two volumes in 1928 and 1929 by Ogawa, its first professor. Other scholars of note in the 1920s and 1930s were Fujita, Yonekura, and Komaki. Komaki published *A Study of Prehistoric Geography* in 1937, using the cross-sectional method to explain geographical patterns, and evidencing the strong influence of the German geographers, Schlüter, Passarge and Hettner. A different 'antecedent' approach was that of Uchida, who 'regarded historical geography as a means of tracing the antecedents of the geography of the present time' (Senda, 1982, 172).

Institutions and Historical Geography: the International Committee for Historical Sciences and the International Geographical Congresses

One of the interesting 'institutional' features of the dialogue between historians and geographers in the first half of the twentieth century was the establishment, under the aegis of the International Committee of Historical Science, of the Committee of Historical Geography. The context of the foundation of this committee can be traced through the *Bulletin of the International Committee of Historical Sciences*, the first volume of which was published in 1926. A series of international historical congresses had been held in Rome (1903), Berlin (1908), London (1913) and Brussels (1923). At the Brussels congress, arrangements were put in hand for the organization of congresses on a regular basis, whose purposes included the production of an annual historical bibliography and comparative studies of the organization of historical teaching and research in different countries. At the Oslo congress of 1928, a special session on 'géographie historique' was held (part of a section on 'auxiliary sciences'), at which papers were given on the theme of historical cartography and historical atlases. Following this initiative, Belgian historians decided to organize an international congress of historical geography in 1930, held in Brussels, with Pirenne, the Belgian historian, as President, and Quicke as Secretary. Its main theme was the history of cartography and historical atlases, a principal focus (of local and national significance) was the work of the cartographer Ortelius, but a number of important papers pointed the way to changes in historical geography, and it was attended by a number of historical geographers who were to be influential in changing the direction of the subject in the 1930s and after. The first major section dealt with progress in historical geography in Germany, France and Spain, intermingled with progress reports on the production of national historical atlases. Subsequent sessions dealt with aspects of political geography, rural and urban geography, ecclesiastical geography, means of communication, linguistic geography, physical geography, and topographic history. The latter two sections contained some interesting papers, including those by Darby on 'The role of the Fenland in English history', Pergameni on 'Different conceptions of historical geography', and by Taylor on 'The influence of the great Flemish cosmographers of the XVIth century upon the contemporary voyages'.

Although the Brussels conference contained perhaps only the seeds of a new historical geography rather than fully matured plants, it does seem to have marked a turning-point in the subject, certainly for example in Britain and in Belgium itself (Quicke, 1931; Darby, 1979; Verhulst, 1980). As far as the International Geographical Congresses were concerned, historical geography figured as a special session at most of them, sometimes in isolation, sometimes in conjunction with, for example, the history of geography (as at the Rome congress of 1913). A new formal organization, the International Geographical Union, was established in 1922, and under its aegis the international congresses continued. The Cairo meeting of 1925 had a combined historical geography and history of geography session, the Cambridge meeting of 1928 had a separate historical geography session, as also did the Paris congress of 1931, the Warsaw congress of 1934 and the Amsterdam congress of 1938.

3

Historical Geography in the Second Half of the Twentieth Century

Introduction

This chapter takes the narrative from *c*. 1950 to the last decade of the twentieth century, a period of both continuity and change, the balance between the two varying enormously from one country and tradition to another. Some possible avenues for exploration for the future are also considered.

Much interest has been generated within and beyond historical geography in the later twentieth century by a fairly clear movement away from the narrow interpretations of its scope as a means of reconstructing a non-politicized and acultural past towards the questioning and investigation of a number of historical geographies of a greater variety of pasts by adopting a wider range of theoretically informed perspectives, with an increasing discourse with cultural, political and ideological questions and contexts.

The role of historical geography within geography as a whole and human geography in particular, has remained a vibrant one, irrespective of the changes in human geography and the major directions of research which historical geographers have followed. The notion that in the period of the quantitative revolution in geography in the late 1960s and 1970s historical geographers for the most part found themselves on the periphery of the discipline waiting for a return to a more central position cannot be supported (Gregory, 1981a), for the productivity rate remained very high. The advance of human geography has been spearheaded by some critically important work by historical geographers, showing that historical geography is at the frontier of new perspectives in this field, a consequence of which has been an increased historical sensitivity of human geography, together with an acceleration of cognition of and debate with other social sciences. The extent to which this trend has encouraged a belief that historical geography should be encouraged to lose a distinctive identity and return simply as an historical dimension to human geography is an important and debatable question.

In a review of the potential revival of a greater degree of 'historicity' in human geography, Driver (1988) examines four different senses of the use of historical perspective in human geography: the legacy of the past; evolution;

agency and the making of history; and the grounding of theory in context. He demonstrates the complexity and partial incompatibility of different claims for historical approaches in human geography, concluding that 'any division between a non-historical human geography, oriented to the present, and an historical geography oriented to the past can no longer be sustained' (Driver, 1988, 504). This is a strong claim, whose merits are clear, but it does make a somewhat arbitrary distinction which is not always borne out in the practice of historical and human geography, nor should such an argument, related primarily to matters of stress and emphasis rather than absolutes, be conceded as a strong case for the abandoning of a distinct identity for historical geography, in whatever traditions and contexts it be defined: the subject and the term have too important and varied connotations in present practice and in the histories of geography and history as academic disciplines and in the practice of scholarship for this to happen. This does not deny the need for historical geographers constantly to re-evaluate and redefine where necessary the contents of their main goals of research and teaching.

The Relations between Geography and History

As has been shown in Chapters 1 and 2, historical geography in its various forms has long been inextricably associated with history, most often in a very positive way. There are those who feel that a gap developed, however, from the early decades of the twentieth century, when much that was good in, for example, French historical geography of the traditional kind, was largely rejected in favour of a new, historically sensitized human geography, and the adoption of a geographically sensitive approach to social history by the members of the *Annales* school, though there is, as already suggested, a different way of reading that situation. This legacy continued to pose problems for historical geographers such as Boyer, who in an article on traditional and new forms of historical geography ascribed what he considered to be the 'marginalization' of French historical geography from the 1930s and especially in the post-war period to the particular histories of historical and geographical science in France, and to the rigidity of French university structures as he thought they affected the production of research theses in the field of historical geography (Boyer, 1978). The position is understandable if only a narrow labelling of historical geography in France is accepted. The adoption of a more functionalist approach to human geography in many countries of western and northern Europe after the 1968 revolutions seemed to have created a gap between geography and history, and left historical geography to the historians, an experience shared, in somewhat different political contexts and from earlier dates, by former socialist states, including what was the Soviet Union. There are other reasons given for the apparent distancing of geography and history for part of the twentieth century. One of these is the contended misunderstanding of the much changed nature of geography in general and historical geography in particular, by historians. As Jakle (1971, 1085–6) has suggested:

> For historians, in general, the basic concepts of modern geography remain remote; indeed many historians continue to think in purely environmental

and deterministic terms when considering geographical factors in their work. Too many historians in treating geographical considerations narrow their focus to the physical environment and its influence on events, personalities, and the courses of history being narrated. This concentration reflects favourably on the intriguing but now dated arguments of such geographers as Ellen Churchill Semple and Ellsworth Huntington and such historians as Frederick Jackson Turner and Arnold Toynbee, all of whom were influenced to varying degrees by the notions of the German geographer Friedrich Ratzel. . . . While most historians reject strictly deterministic doctrines, many continue to focus exclusively on the physical environment as the sole substance of their geographical consideration . . . the reader of history is often left without a proper spatial frame of reference in which to place historical explanation.

Jakle cites a number of exceptions to these characteristics, and after an analysis of the changes experienced in the nature of modern geography, including historical geography, concludes optimistically with the hope that there would in the future be much more sharing of common ground, with historians paying more attention to spatial environmental contexts and geographers to the historical contexts of behavioural environments. This is a view which is enthusiastically shared by another American historical geographer Meinig who, for example, in a paper published in 1978 states that 'Geography and history are rooted in the basic stuff of human existence. As fields of study they are analogous, complementary, and interdependent. Their relationship is implied by such common terms as space and time, places and events—pairs that are fundamentally inseparable' (Meinig, 1978b, 1186).

Some of the earlier scholars working and writing in the field of historical geography in Britain reflect a productive relationship between history and geography: partly, no doubt, because they were either trained initially as historians or incorporated a substantial measure of historical study into their geographical training. An additional link with political geography is often evident. East's works, notably *An Historical Geography of Europe* (1935) and *The Geography Behind History* (1938) are good examples. The extensive work of Pounds in the field of historical geography shows a similar combination, and a commitment to the dissemination of this important mixture to a broad spectrum of the population. Hence, in the introduction to his *An Historical and Political Geography of Europe* (1947b), written for the use in advanced studies in schools, Pounds states that:

No attempt is made to define historical geography. The book contains much history that would be of use to geographers and perhaps some geography that historians would do well to know. Its purpose is, quite simply, to trace the influence of essentially geographical factors—the surface topography of the earth—on, first the course of European history and then on the intricacies of world politics. This does not represent the whole content of historical geography, as the writer conceives it. It is merely that part of it which, in his experience, has the greatest value both to the student of immature years and to the hypothetical man in the street (Pounds, 1947, 5).

In such works as these, the relations between geography and history are seen as naturally productive, subject to predictable qualifying cautionary remarks about the dangers of crude geographical determinism. This productive relationship is, on the whole, characteristic of the late twentieth century, and is to be applauded and encouraged, notwithstanding some of the cautionary views cited above. This relationship has more recently been further explored by Earle (1992), who reasserts a case for geographical history, in the sense of a focus on relationships between geography and history that have influenced human affairs and political events in the past, for he thinks the 'distinctions made between geographical history and historical geography have been overdrawn and excessively canonical . . . the perspective of historical geography, in the first instance, focuses upon those relationships which have shaped the evolution of place and landscape; geographical history, in contrast, focuses upon relationships which have shaped human affairs in the past' (Earle, 1992, 6). His attempt to classify much recent writing in historical geography as geographical history is unlikely, however, to be agreed or supported.

There is still much scope for detailed examination of the relationships, past and present, between historical geography and history, both in terms of similarities, differences, and emphases.

Changing Theory and Methodology

The general development of work on theory and methodology has varied in many countries. On the whole, greatest attention to theory, and perhaps methodology, seems to have been paid in the United Kingdom, Sweden, the United States and Canada, at least in respect of what might be termed 'western' historical geography. There have been interesting developments in the Netherlands, where a particular expertise has developed in the study of coastal change, linking historical materials such as old maps with geomorphological evidence. Within former socialist countries methodologies and theories of a somewhat different kind have influenced the nature of historical geography advocated and practised. In the last few spectacular years there have been changes to various forms of capitalism and in some cases to bewildering and dangerous forms of attempted ethnic and cultural self-expression, themselves remaking the maps of Europe and Asia, and raising vital questions about the role of the past, especially cultural heterogeneity, in shaping the present and future. The contexts of evaluation of progress in theory and methodology in historical geography obviously vary very widely: a notion which needs strong and repeated emphasis. Even a superficial reading of the contributions to the volume *Progress in Historical Geography* (Baker, 1972), notwithstanding the understandable underrepresentation of overviews from socialist, African and Asian countries, indicates the variety of appraisals of progress, and more recent overviews show this still to be the case. Studies of work in historical geography in France, for example, indicated a continued attachment to traditional sources and region-based analyses, with some significant measure of antipathy to more general types of theory. Caution must be exercised here, however, for in spite of Baker's reference to the 'limited amount of methodological debate within French historical geography', related to 'the relative absence of an explicitly reflective critique', claiming this to be a reflection of the limited way in which geography responded to the new *Annales* school of history in the 1920s and 1930s (Baker, 1984a, 14–15), it may equally be claimed that very good historical geography was practised by the 'Annalistes', but without the label. Nonetheless there is a strengthening of historical geography under its own name, partly because of questions about theory and methodology asked by French geographers, historians, and social scientists. Some recognition of the need for further development in theory and methodology was made by Claval (1981; 1984), and his own work has been a major contribution in this respect.

While the strong tradition of 'landschaftskunde' and a stress on environmental relations are to be found in modern studies of historical geography in Germany, there is an increasing interest in theory and methodology (Fehn, 1982), including the examination of the applicability of variants on the Wallerstein world-systems theory by a group led by Nitz at Göttingen (Nitz, 1984). The strong involvement of Swedish human geographers with theory and methodology has had a strong historical dimension, with the consequent production of important work in the fields of changing rural and urban communities, based on detailed examination of documentary and of field evidence.

Progress in historical geography in Japan seems at present to comprise an attempted accommodation of process studies with the construction of cross-sections, based on detailed records of landownership (Senda, 1982), and there is obviously a growing awareness in Japan of the methodological developments elsewhere. In the United States and Canada, progress in methodology and theory are largely related to refinements of the cultural historical traditions, established, *inter alia*, by Sauer and Clark, though major methodological and theoretical debates have developed around humanistic, idealist, structuralist and post-modernist approaches. Similar trends are evident in Australia and New Zealand (Powell, 1981; 1988; Wynn, 1977). The new environmentalist approach is very much evident in J.M. Powell's writings, and the flavour of the trend is captured in the introduction to his *An Historical Geography of Modern Australia* (1988, xii–xiv):

> So many geographers express the highest of humanitarian aspirations in their collective efforts to write the 'book of the bond' between nature and society. And, given the renewed self-doubt within academia and the current desire for rapprochements with the community at large, the Australian experience may repay a peculiarly interesting chapter in that daunting tome, because multi-layered forms of geographical reasoning have been equally well represented in sophisticated and commonsense environmental appraisals effecting prodigious landscape changes. Accordingly, designs in historical geography may essay the kinds of timely practical syntheses which colleagues in various branches of geography, and fellow-travellers in other subject areas, do not usually expect from such 'purist' endeavours.

It may well be argued that only partial perspectives are afforded by consideration of 'national' trends and schools of thought. In most countries momentum and change in historical geography occurs through the influences of individuals and groups. Hence, for example, Simms (1982) has listed various schools of influence in Britain, and a number of appraisals of the influence of individuals on traditions within the subject have been published (e.g. Harris, 1976; Slater and Jarvis, 1982; Gourou, 1982). It is essential, therefore, that measures of change and advancement in theory and methodology in historical geography be related to the cultural, historical and even political contexts of the research work evaluated. Though this chapter reflects what might be seen as a Western view and evaluation of significant changes in approach, a view from Africa, Asia or Latin America would almost certainly order the priorities for research and measures of progress in the subject in a very different way.

Continued Traditions from 'Classical' Historical Geography

There remains a strong tradition in historical geography originating in the 'classical' phase, which was characterized by Gregory (1981a), as a period with a strong commitment to historical study of landscape and to the mapping of historical data sources, with occasional ventures into the reconstructions of regional geographies of the past. While this type of work can easily be labelled 'empiricist' and 'positivist' such categorizations can be rather misleading.

Within these rather restricting and narrow terms of reference of traditional or classical historical geography—of an experimental and pragmatic scholarship, in which methodology is determined by problem and source but within which explicit theory plays a small part—some advances can be recognized, mainly of a methodological and procedural kind. Methodological progress has largely been evidenced by the use of new sources, the re-evaluation and refinements of known sources, and the employment of new analytical techniques. The extent to which the interpretation of sources of evidence remains a hallmark of historical geography is clearly indicated in Prince's review of historical geography (Prince, 1980). Here he draws our attention to the search by historical geographers for new sources of evidence and their re-evaluation of known sources. A notable single-source based study has been Darby's *Domesday England* (1977) the publication of which has been completed in the period under review. Hence, R.E. Glasscock's observation (1978, 395) that 'The Domesday geography has become a lynchpin of English historical geography. . . . In the last thirty years it has become the archetypal example of work based on a single source for a single year. *Domesday Book* . . . has lent itself to this kind of treatment and, in a sense, has produced its own methodology'. Glasscock counters the criticism of this type of study as merely source-based empiricism by pointing to the value of formal presentation of scarce (medieval) sources as a basis for detailed analytical study, and followed this route himself in his publication *The Lay Subsidy of 1334* (Glasscock, 1975). Despite the detailed work involved in these studies of *Domesday Book* Hamshere (1982, 105–6) could write that 'In many respects the rigorous statistical analysis of Domesday data is still in its infancy. Such is the complexity and mass of source material that generations of scholars have been employed merely in outlining the basic parameters of analysis'.

The use of computers has considerably aided the development of sophisticated analyses of large data sets. Outstanding examples from Britain are: the various works on the 1801 crop returns; the tithe files and awards of the nineteenth century; the data pertaining to parliamentary enclosures; probate inventories; the *Domesday Book* itself; and major works on the analysis of census and other population records. While much of the analysis of this type is justifiably concerned with the accuracy of data and the methodology of its employment—often in relation to other sources—broader issues are always raised which lead to discussion and debate. Thus, in Overton's analyses of probate inventories, for example, the technical difficulties of analysis and their solution are necessary and intermediate steps (the preliminary steps being the identification of problems) to the solution of important problems of agricultural change seen in broader historical and intellectual contexts, including those of an agricultural revolution or revolutions (Overton, 1977; 1984a, b; 1985). The derivation of accurate data bases from important sources as means rather than ends in themselves has been the important and commendable object of many works by historical geographers, including work by Turner on the 1801 crop return (Turner, 1981), by Turner and Chapman on the parliamentary enclosures (Turner, 1980; Chapman and Harris, 1982; Chapman 1987), by Kain and Prince on the tithe surveys (Kain 1984; 1986; Kain and Prince, 1985), by Lawton (1978) and others on the census returns, and the reconstruction of the population history of England by the Cambridge Group (Wrigley and Schofield, 1981). Data source evaluations and demonstrations of use of similar kinds are to be found in and for many countries other than Britain, many in relation to census data and to the historical geography of agriculture and land use, with particular reference to records of landownership and occupance, examples of which are given in Chapter 4.

Additional and much-worked sources of information of particular significance are cartographic sources and the evidence of the land and landscape, as interpreted by the use of field work (including excavation) air photography/ remote sensing, and documentary evidence. The history of cartography has become almost a separate discipline and is offering new vistas and methodologies in historical geography.

A proper evaluation of these types of research within conventional or classical traditions of historical geography requires both a critical assessment from within their own apparent terms of reference and also from within the broader context of the changing tendencies of history of geography. In their own self-admitted (or implicit) terms of reference, there are grounds for both dissatisfaction and satisfaction with progress.

Many of the conventional data-related and field-work related studies do assume a position of attempted 'objectivity' and a neutrality and passivity of place and space, take a seemingly linear/progressive approach to the past, and generally do not explicitly state either the role of theory or an ideological perspective of the past being reconstructed. In some respects this represents not only a failure to establish a reflexive critique which would result in alternative approaches being developed, but also a failure to follow up Darby's important statements of the problems of geographical explanation and the nature of the relations of geography and history (Darby, 1953; 1962).

Within the contexts of classical and neo-classical historical geography attempts have been made to incorporate 'behavioural' and 'phenomenological' approaches, but there has been considerable confusion in the use of these terms, for there is no necessary link between 'behavioural' approaches and a 'scientific', 'positivist' geography, and there is certainly no relationship between such a mode of geographical inquiry and 'phenomenology'. Phenomenological or behavioural methodologies are negations of positivism. Thus, Gregory (1976; 1978) and Billinge (1977) have argued that the 'behavioural' and 'phenomenological' stances which geographers have used have been total misnomers, in the sense that their essence of anti-positivism has been ignored or suppressed.

Attempts to modify a positivist approach in historical geography have been made, using theoretical realism, by Gregory in his book on the evolution of the woollen industry in the West Riding of Yorkshire (1982b). The essential features of this approach include: a concern with careful conceptions of structures and mechanisms (systems of social practice); an interpenetration of 'theoretical' and 'empirical' methods; and an emphasis on the significance of context and of time–space structures in relation to the operation and outcome of processes.

Space, Place, Time and Scale

As geographers deal with earth space, so historians have been traditionally seen as dealing with time as the common denominator of their discipline. Although it may be philosophically argued that time and space are integral manifestations (timeless space and spaceless time having been disregarded by scientific philosophy), the two separate constructs viewed in a Kantian sense have been traditionally used by geographers, at least, to define geography and history as separate disciplines. It is doubtful, however, that geography can continue its search for spatial understanding by ignoring the integral dictates of time and space as a natural unity; thus have geographers come to focus on the processes of spatial organization through time (Jakle, 1971, 1087).

Historical geography is essentially a geographical subject. Its excitements and intellectual possibilities and challenges largely derive from that fact, and it follows logically therefore that space, place, time and scale are critical components of the historical geographer's thinking and practice. The way in which historical geographers have thought about these components has, however, changed very much even in recent times, and the dynamics of this thinking are crucial to an understanding of past and present work. Having said this, it is important to dismiss any explicit or implicit notion that the properties and relations of time and space are the unique prerogative of geography in general, and thus also of subdisciplines such as human and historical geography.

Space

According to Johnston (1986, 443–4), human geography uses absolute, relative and relational concepts of space. In their introduction to a significant series of statements on the links between social relations and spatial structures, Gregory and Urry (1985, 3) argue, with considerable justification, that 'spatial structure is now seen not only as an arena in which social life unfolds, but rather as a medium through which social relations are produced and reproduced'. Space, in other words, is not simply a passive plane or field or stage upon which the dramatic and the undramatic aspects of human existence are enacted at a variety of scales, but a more pliable medium which is shaped and which shapes through interaction with different modes of social, economic, and cultural reproduction. Space is increasingly being treated both as an objective or scientific measure, for example, of area or pattern of distribution, and also as a subjective experience, involving images, perceptions and personal 'mental' maps, with different cultural traditions having widely different perceptions and understandings of space and of territory. Harvey is helpful on this subject: 'I think it important to challenge the idea of a single and objective sense of time or space, against which we can measure the diversity of human conceptions and perceptions. I shall not argue for a total dissolution of the objective–subjective distinction, but insist, rather, that we recognize the multiplicity of the objective qualities which space and time can express, and the role of human practices in their construction' (Harvey, 1989, 203). He goes on to suggest and demonstrate through a materialist perspective that concepts of time and place are created, and therefore to be understood by and through, material/actual cultural practices and experiences of time and space. The notion that different cultural experiences and different modes of production each have their own geography or spatial 'fix' is an important one, both for human geography and for historical geography. Two examples may help, concerned with medieval society and with industrializing society.

The social relations and spatial structures of medieval society, certainly in Europe, involved a complex set of social and hierarchical relations which mapped into and were reflected by a distinctive mode of production involving, *inter alia*, land, urban/rural linkages, and exchange. The complexity of this system and its spatial fix has been well outlined by Dodgshon (1987; 1990), who has considered the nature of feudalism as a source of spatial order. Thus: 'Feudalism generated a qualitatively distinct system of spatial order. An essential part of its character was the way in which the king used his lordship or superiority over all men and all land to create a control system that was both regulatory and exploitive in a territorial as well as a social sense. In effect, feudal relations were mapped into the landscape, their explicit geographical component being the part of the way the king both controlled and exploited his realm' (Dodgshon, 1990, 256).

The actual effect of these complex feudal relations, in England for example, was untidy, described by Dodgshon (1990, 256) as a 'patchwork landscape, with a community's right to cultivate land being confined to a core of assessed land represented by customary tenements', with fringes (larger in the north than the south and east) of non-assessed waste. The extent of feudal influence in Britain and in Europe was very uneven, so that even within one mode of production the interaction with and moulding of space was extremely complex. For the early medieval period the social production of space is also a very complex matter, and the evidence is of varied quality and quantity. In a series of major studies of multiple estate organization in England and Wales, Jones (1961; 1971; 1972; 1976; 1985) has documented the social organization of space from the time of the early kingdoms of the Saxon colonization of England from the fifth century to the later reorganization during the Scandinavian colonization, and that of the royal multiple estates of the contemporary petty kingdoms of Wales. The role of fortified places ('burhs') in the reconquest of England and the unification of the state is of importance in this context.

A different and possibly more dramatic example of the social modification of space is that through industrial capitalism, dealt with at greater length in Chapter 10. Capitalism proceeded apace from its early beginnings in about the sixteenth century and through the medium of price-fixing markets, the circulation of capital and commodities, the need and drive to produce surplus value by increasing the efficiency of credit and marketing systems, the control of labour and material resources, and the integration of the space economy at regional, national and global scales, effected what has been termed by Marx as an annihilation of space by time (Harvey, 1985a).

The process continues into late capitalism, but is everywhere apparent both in the surviving landscapes of nineteenth-century capitalism and in the related and extensive records of the capture of space by time in the interests of profit. That is not to say that there are not within these landscapes of the social production of space elements of altruistic interpretation, such as model villages and suburbs and a variety of philanthropic constructions and events, though even many of these have their patrician flavour.

Time in historical geography

Given the roots of historical geography in the academic study of history it is no surprise to find that the question of time in geography and historical geography was not very deeply explored until the beginnings of the rise of 'modern' geography. Thus, Ogilvie, writing as late as 1952 on the 'time-element' in geography, said that 'Because geography is concerned primarily with space rather than time, we are inclined to take the time-element inherent in our own discipline rather casually, except when deliberately studying the geography of a region as it was at a given historical period' (Ogilvie, 1952, 1). Although not specifically dealing with historical geography, he suggests the application of the methods of historical geography to the study of particular regions in order to analyse the stages of their development.

A more recent and sophisticated analysis of the links between historical geography and time is that by Prince (1978), whose main topics are: timing as a problem in geographical theory; time and space dimensions; time as change; development series; systems of change; spatial diffusion; fabricated history; theoretical unrealities; behavioural historical geography; perceived time; and antiquarianism.

Period in place: the periodization of change through time

The measurement, assessment, description and analysis of change in human experience through time is an essential ingredient of historical geography. Of particular importance is the question of periodicity, that is the judgement of the extent of major epochs in human affairs and the statistical analysis of trends in change through time. The judgemental aspect of particular slices of time is one which for the most part historical geographers take for granted: we accept and use convenient labels for parts of history such as the Middle Ages, the early modern period, the Industrial Revolution, without always defining our terms. Equally, time is sliced up into 'ages', e.g. of improvement, of statistical data sets like *Domesday Book*, of discoveries through exploration, of imperialism, of political revolution, or intervals of multiples or fractions of 100 years. This aspect of periodization, largely and often unquestioningly inherited from the long-hallowed traditions of use by historians, needs some debate in historical geography. In addition, however, the statistical analysis of trends from reasonable data is an important one. The nature and reliability of data is considered in Chapter 4, but the trends involved merit some brief consideration. An interesting problem is the distinction between short-term and long-term trends, and the nature of cycles, whether of production or population statistics or of weather patterns. These dynamics of change requires a methodology for the study of time series which has yet to be well developed in historical geography, even though well developed in economics and the physical sciences (Prince, 1971, 21). A time series is a sequence of values produced by regular observations or measurements of a fluctuating variable, such as temperature, prices of crops or other goods, or population size and composition, as measured by decennial censuses. A good example is Charlesworth's (1979) use of data on agricultural labourers' riots in 1830 in England to assist with a narrative and analysis of the timing and spread of the riots, primarily in south-east England (Fig. 3.1). The peaks of rioting shown on the graph indicate the issuing of a proclamation by the Whig Lord Melbourne against the rioters, followed by two circular letters to magistrates, instructing them to deal harshly with the rioters so that property would be defended.

An array of statistical tests can be applied to time-series data of good quality, including the running mean which smoothes time-series data, calculations of trends, testing for cyclical behaviour and for randomness, correlation tests for two time series, the logistical curve for organic time series, and tests for Poisson distribution (rare events) (Cole and King, 1968, 441). The determination of the nature of change, whether cyclical or logistical for example, is an interesting study in this context for the historical geographer,

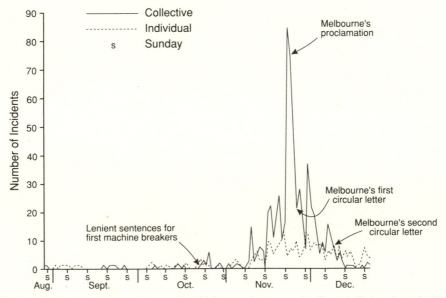

Fig. 3.1 *Time-series analysis of agricultural labourers' protests: the Captain Swing riots of 1830 in England. Source: Charlesworth (1979, 8)*

and a number of examples, including Whitehand's study (1972) of building cycles in Glasgow in the period 1864–1968 and their effects on the spatial patterning of the city, have been cited by Baker (1975). Such techniques as Fourier analysis and the use of the long-wave analysis models, such as that of Kondratieff, may be of some use, but the frequently imperfect data available do partly constrain their adoption, except for fairly recent periods. While the range of potential applications of statistical tests for time trends is wide, their use by historical geographers, as indicated above, is still remarkably limited, and seems to owe as much to methodological habit and preference as to the nature of the data used in research (Hamshere, 1987, 65).

Spatial diffusion

The diffusion or spread of a phenomenon, for example new agricultural techniques and crops or of a particular disease across space over the period or periods of time, is a fundamental problem and question frequently addressed by research in historical and cultural geography. Key aspects of such studies are the nature and utility of the evidence, the spatial and chronological paths and periodicities and rates of spread and the extent of non-adoption or non-exposure either through chance or deliberate avoidance. The types of diffusion that may be identified include expansion diffusion, where the phenomenon studied spreads from one place to another, but remains in some form in the place from which it spread, as with the spread of new crops in the agricultural revolution in England, as opposed to relocation diffusion where the phenomenon leaves the original source or 'hearth' area and moves on to new locations, as with instances of population migration. The means of spread or diffusion may be contagious, that is through direct contact, or hierarchical, through a hierarchy of classes or places, a process known as 'cascade diffusion' when only downwards from major to minor centres (Cliff, Haggett, Ord and Versey, 1981). Studies of cultural diffusion may be dated back to the origins of modern European geography in Germany in the early and mid-nineteenth century, including the work of Ratzel, but has been considerably advanced by the work in the twentieth century by geographers influenced by, among others, the research of Sauer at Berkeley in California on agricultual and cultural origins and dispersals, and by Hägerstrand at Lund in Sweden on innovation waves (Gregory, 1986b, 106–7). Hägerstrand's pioneer studies in the 1950s were concerned with the adoption of agricultural innovations in central Sweden and the refining of a four-stage model of contagious innovation diffusion: primary (the beginning, where the adoption of innovation is largely confined to a centre); a second or diffusion stage (where strong centrifugal diffusion develops); a third, condensing stage with similar rates of adoption in all regions; and a fourth, saturation stage in which the diffusion process slows. The four stages can be summed in a logistical S-shaped innovation diffusion curve (Hägerstrand, 1952). Two examples follow to illustrate the potential and actual value of spatial-diffusion models to the historical geographer: the spread of agricultural innovations and the spread of epidemics.

The spread of agricultural innovations
The spread of agricultural innovations and agricultural information has been extensively studied by historical geographers. Of particular interest has been

the testing of various hypotheses of an 'agricultural revolution' in England, variously dated at periods between the late sixteenth and mid-nineteenth century, through analysis of records of new crop and animal-breed adoptions and diffusions. Overton (1985) has studied the diffusion of root crops and grass substitutes in the counties of Norfolk and Suffolk in eastern England in the period 1580–1740, with particular reference to the spread of information of the new crops and the patterns of adoption or non-adoption. He demonstrates that literary evidence indicates that the starting period of diffusion of grass substitutes was the 1660s and that of turnips *c.* 1680–90, with both found in some parts of the two counties by the 1730s. Using data from 4000 farmers' probate inventories for the periods 1587–98, 1629–40 and 1660–1735, Overton shows a slow initial rate of adoption of root crops from the 1580s to the 1680s, followed by a rapid increase of adoption rate to about 50 per cent by 1710, with a similar chronology but lower percentage adoption rate for grasses (Overton, 1985, 211). Incentives to adoption included increases in farm size, the use of turnips to reclaim light land with sandy soils, the nitrification values of clover, and the possible attempt by farmers, in the climatic 'Little Ice Age' of the late seventeenth century, to cultivate new fodder crops as risk insurance against failure of the hay crops. Constraints on adoption included the complications of common property rights, including those of communal grazing and cultivation, and the nature of the physical environment.

The diffusion of an individual root-crop—the potato—in Europe in the seventeenth and eighteenth centuries had been studied by Denecke (1976), using a wide range of documentary sources, and showing a diffusion in three stages: first, via botanical gardens; secondly, through cultivation as a food plant in private gardens; thirdly, through cultivation as a field crop (see Fig. 3.2).

Clearly there are difficulties when modern diffusion theory is employed in studies of places and times for which data is scarce and inconsistent, but the engagement between the two is important and revealing. Walton has suggested caution to historical geographers tempted to follow the Hägerstrand idea of the importance of the adoption related to information flow and in turn to personal contact between farmers who are potential adopters, and suggests instead that 'explanations of the diffusion process have to allow for the fact that large numbers of landowners saw their contribution to "improvement" as a means of enhancing personal prestige and status. The information flows among the élite—the materials they read, societies they joined, the letters they wrote to each other—become important in determining how certain innovations first appeared in particular localities. Whether the innovations then spread any further depended largely on their appropriateness to the working farmer' (Walton, 1987, 142).

The spread of epidemics

Another area of the use of diffusion as a research target in historical geography has involved the study of the orgin and spread of diseases through epidemics. Where data, usually for modern periods and places, exist, the opportunity arises and has been taken to apply the stochastic Monte Carlo diffusion models of Hägerstrand and others. A good example is the study by Cliff, Haggett, Ord and Versey (1981) of the historical geography of a series of epidemics of

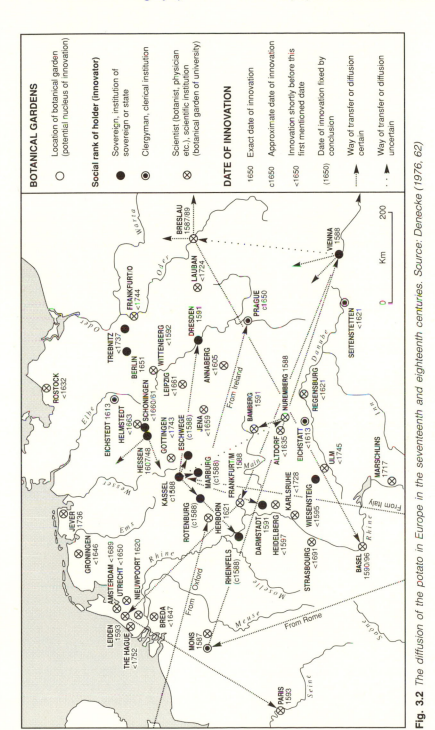

Fig. 3.2 *The diffusion of the potato in Europe in the seventeenth and eighteenth centuries. Source: Denecke (1976, 62)*

German measles, whooping cough, and influenza in Iceland in the period 1901–74. Having reviewed the nature and ingredients of Hägerstrand's and other later models of the diffusion of innovations, they concluded that wave-like behaviour of innovation is more likely in instances where there is increasingly rapid fall-off of contact probability between transmitter and receiver of information or a disease with increasing distance between the two, and noted the problems posed by the idiographic nature of most diffusion events, including epidemics, in the past. They then proceed to analyse an unique set of data for Iceland which, because of repetition of epidemics, enables calibration and testing.

Cliff, Haggett, Ord and Versey's choice of Iceland as a location for their study of epidemic diffusion was partly determined by the ability of the place and the data to satisfy basic conditions of replicability, stability over time and space, observability and isolation. Their findings were, in relation to successive measles epidemics in Iceland (16 major waves from 1896–1975) that: a combined hierarchical/contagious diffusion model was the most satisfactory; that it is difficult to predict the levels, times and places of epidemics and other diffused phenomena; that simple models are unsatisfactory, stochastic models better, but that even more sophisticated models are needed; and that early warning systems, the isolation of infected individuals and immunization were important defence measures. A later study concentrated on the epidemics of 1846, 1882, and 1904, and has interesting things to say about the speed of epidemics increasing from one to the next and about the varying conformity to a simple wave model of diffusion (Cliff, Haggett and Graham, 1983). It will be interesting to see more studies of this kind, which allow, given the quality of the data, an analysis over time of trends in health-related phenomena. The further one delves back in time, of course, the more difficult this exercise becomes, though this has not deterred or precluded major studies of the spread, for example, of the 'Black Death' or cholera in global or more local contexts. Jones (1981) has offered some interesting preliminary observations, in the context of a fascinating and imaginative study of the role of environments, economies and geopolitics in the comparative histories of early modern Europe and Asia, on the spread of human and animal diseases in Europe. He suggests that 'The predominant direction of spread of human and animal diseases has been out of the Orient, across Russia or the Near East, and into Europe. These were the routes taken by cattle plagues, the bubonic plague, and in the nineteenth century by cholera. The implication may be that the vast, densely packed and poor populations of Asia were the primary breeding grounds or reservoirs of organisms parasitic on man and his livestock' (Jones, 1981, 31). He also suggests that there were differences in time-pattern between Asian and European experiences of epidemics, and in patterns of resistance. Some large-scale modelling of these phenomena might be an interesting exercise. Heterogeneous data sources, such as those listed by Dobson (1987) for epidemic diseases in south-east England from 1601–1800 might be analysed using similar techniques to those of Overton (1985) in his studies of crop diffusion. Kearns' work (1985b) on the diffusion of cholera in nineteenth-century England offers good examples of diffusion studies in historical geography (see Fig. 3.3).

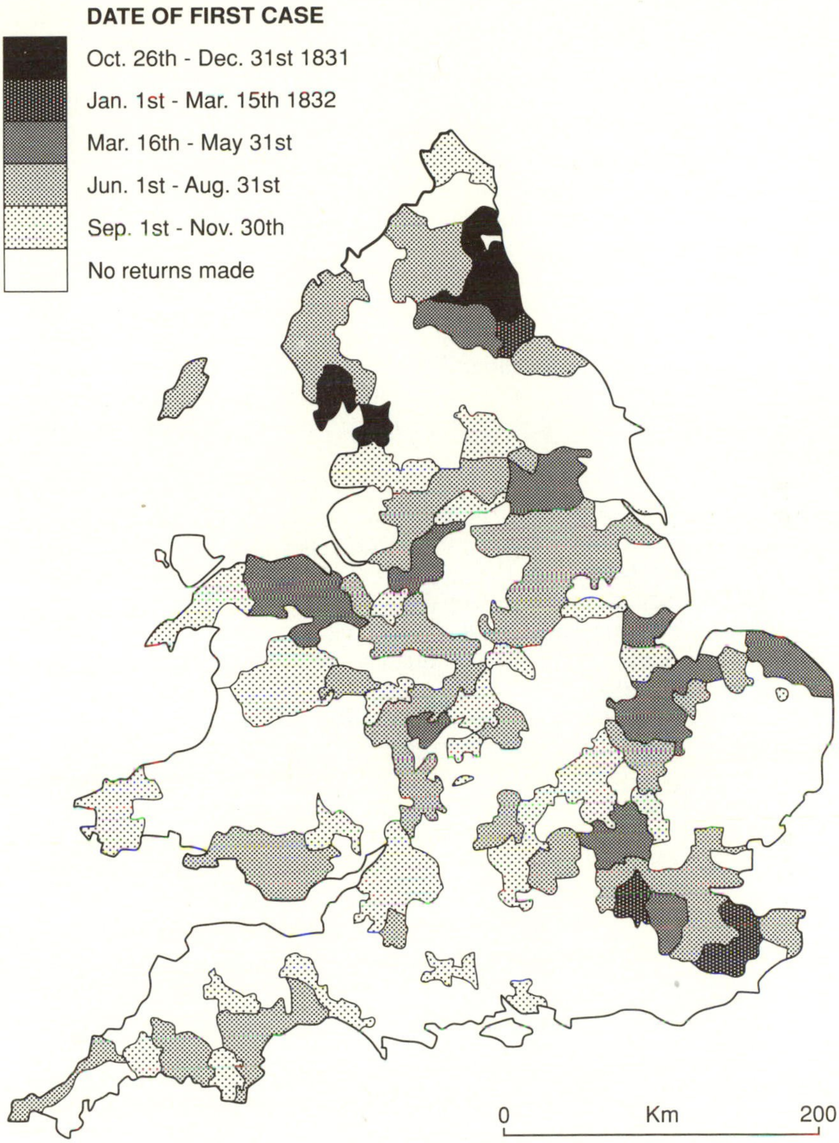

DATE OF FIRST CASE

Oct. 26th - Dec. 31st 1831

Jan. 1st - Mar. 15th 1832

Mar. 16th - May 31st

Jun. 1st - Aug. 31st

Sep. 1st - Nov. 30th

No returns made

0   Km   200

Fig. 3.3 *The diffusion of cholera in England in 1831–2. Source: Kearns (1985c, 64)*

Time-geography and the analysis of life-paths

One aspect of time which has increasingly been attracting the attention of human and historical geographers is the concept of 'time-geography', that is to say a set of concepts, first promoted in the 1960s and early 1970s, especially by the Swedish geographer Hägerstrand, which attempt to encompass and model personal and ultimately collective experiences in the contexts of time and space. The life experience or 'path' of an individual obviously has time and space components, and can be conceived therefore as a continuous path through time and space. Abstract space, when personalized through located experience, becomes place, and is inextricably interlocked with various measured and perceived senses of time. Time-geography includes, therefore, the study of life-path analyses at several different scales, and involves the mapping of the trajectories of individuals, usually by means of a demographic system of notation known as Lexis-Becker diagrams or dynamic diagrammatic maps, with the movement of individuals plotted against a vertical time-axis and a two-dimensional horizontal space-axis. The Hägerstrand theory and notation scheme allows for interactions between individual life-path trajectories at three different scales: the individual scale; the station scale (e.g. places of work or transaction); and the population or activity system scale, constrained, however, by such factors as capability of individuals, the capacity for, and length of, interaction with others (coupling constraints), and authority or steering constraints, that is restriction of activity on account of rules and regulations.

Pred has made several attempts to exemplify the time-geography, life-path approach. In a study of production time, family time and free time in cities of the United States in the nineteenth century, using a time-geographic perspective, he demonstrates that the emergence of factory and large-shop modes of production eroded the self-determination of time use and imposed an industrial time-discipline and radically altered the nature of the family in a variety of ways pertaining to its formulation of time-use strategies, including the use of free time (Pred, 1981).

In a later study of social and spatial transformation in southern Sweden in the period 1750–1850 Pred links time-geography and structuration theory into a theory of place as historically contingent process, by looking at pre- and post-enclosure village communities. While this is an interesting account of social and economic change in this region, it largely fails to engage in the level of micro-detail necessary for the more sophisticated analysis of changes in agrarian society demonstrated to advantage by the Hoppe and Langton (1986) study described below, and thus promises more than it actually achieves.

The methods have been, however, subject to strong criticism on grounds of their simplicity, and similarity to logical positivism, though others have read the method as a form of structuralism. A major objection has been the apparent reduction of the role of human agency (Gregory, 1986c, 486).

Broader criticism of the concept of time-geography has been made by Baker (1979; 1981), arguing that: time and space are not the sole concerns of geographers; excessive emphasis in time-geography on paths and projects makes for too much description and too little attention to process; time-geography tends to undervalue the social organization of space and time, and the role of groups as opposed to individuals, choices as well as constraints. Periods and places are more significant for the historical geographer than general concepts of space and time. Thrift and Pred responded to this critique by attempting to demonstrate that time-geography has greater flexibility in relation to the understanding of process, that the use of time-geography is compatible with a Marxian humanist ideology, and that time-geography, rather than trying to provide a general theory of structures, is trying to provide a theory of structuration (Thrift and Pred, 1981). Harvey has also pointed to some limitations of this approach: while agreeing that time-space biographies 'form a useful datum for considering the time-space dimension of social practices' (Harvey, 1989, 212–13), he feels that it does not answer broader questions relating to, for example, the dominance of certain social relations by others and the mode of assignment of meaning to places, spaces, history and time, suggesting that more appropriate ways of dealing with such problems are to be found in socio-psychological and phenomenological approaches to time and space.

Hoppe and Langton have pointed to a specific problem of time-geography, namely the 'wide gap between the ambitions expressed in the theoretical parts of time-geographical work . . . and what has actually been achieved in terms of empirical analysis' (Hoppe and Langton, 1986, 439). Following Gregory's notion of the importance of considering space as 'compositional' rather than 'contextual' (Gregory, 1985), they explore the Hägerstrandian notion of a 'station' by examining in detail agrarian society in the Hundred of Dahl on the shore of Lake Vättern in the plainland of central Sweden in the period 1810–1860 within a broader context of agrarian change in western Europe and in Sweden.

Scale

Historical geographers study problems of the past at different scales. These can range from global, as in studies of world systems such as that of Wallerstein (1974; 1980; 1989) through regions of continental or national scale, to small areas or 'parishes'. The scale involved has a number of important consequences. It directly affects the level of generalization and detail that is appropriate and that can be accommodated. A study of world systems of exchange and control, for example, would generally involve fairly sweeping generalizations, at least in terms of the initial statements of theory, which may then be backed up by more detailed regional or perhaps thematic studies. A study of an individual township or parish, on the other hand, would focus primarily on detail of various kinds, such as the families and their history and composition, nature of employment, agrarian and industrial structure, details of the physical environment and the built environment and so on. That is not to say that such a study should be simply descriptive, and nothing else: while careful and imaginative narrative description should be a very important part of historical geography, process and theory should be essential ingredients of studies at all scales, and the parochial study needs to be seen in broader contexts of process and theory. The study of a small rural region in upland Lancashire in Pennine England in the late eighteenth century must, for example, take into account trends in European and even global patterns of trade in addition to the essential detail of the local and regional production and exchange systems. This generalization is also true even for preliterate societies, even though the evidence for such reconstructions and interpretations is scarcer and more difficult to interpret.

The scale question is also bound up with the nature of processes of change. Different processes operate at different scales, and processes can vary through time, so the matter is an extremely complex one.

Alternative Approaches and Themes for Historical Geography

Increasing reaction against an explicit or tacit attachment to the theory and methodology of the natural sciences, on the grounds that they offer models which are unhelpful or harmful to the social sciences and humanities, has been well under way since the early 1970s. The rejection of inductive or hypothetico-deductive reasoning, related to the assumption that theory and explanation springs virtually unaided from supposedly neutral and unbiased 'facts' (and in the case of geography related to a Kantian/Newtonian view of space) was and is a widespread phenomenon in the social sciences and the humanities. The actual form of response has varied widely, one characteristic within human and historical geography being a turning to the philosophical and theoretical writings of scholars in other disciplines, notably social history, sociology, social psychology and politics. Much-favoured sources of inspiration include the unorthodox Marxism of Habermas and the Frankfurt school, the Marxist theory of the French philosopher Louis Althusser, the histories or 'archaeologies' of the human sciences by Michel Foucault, the works of the French *Annales* school of history, the challenging writings of E.P. Thompson and Raymond Williams, the development of new feminist critiques and gender perspectives, a revival of interest in region, community and locale, and some preliminary skirmishes with post-modernism.

The earlier of the new directions in historical geography were primarily concerned with Marxist, humanist, idealist, and structuralist/structurationist perspectives, with related preferences for orientation to regional geography, and a new form of environmentalist perspective. Views of space and spatial structure have changed, away from the scientistic geographical view of space as fixed entity which 'organizes' and influences societies and economies towards a conception of space as a flexible, socially transferable and organizationally manipulable entity, produced in the image of complex social and material production systems, the most potent of which is capitalism. Marxist theory involves complex attempts to understand society in a comprehensive way, placing particular emphasis on a materialist conception of history (historical materialism), that is one in which features and structures of a society are seen as the outcome of processes of historical development, closely linked to the prevailing socio-economic structure or modes of production. Human labour is an important component, and much of the understanding of the historical experience of human labour is the surplus value of that which it produces, that is by its appropriation to limited and largely privileged classes, notably and specifically under capitalism. Central to the Marxist theory is the distinctive mode of production labelled 'capitalism', with which is associated deprivation, commodification, proletarianization and immiseration of much of the populace that becomes bound up with it: the result of capitalism creating a world after its own image.

While there has been much debate on the nature, causes and chronology of the transition from the feudal to the capitalist mode of production, what perhaps is more important to geographical studies of the past is the fact that 'the creation of wage labour in an antagonistic class relation to capital fundamentally altered the way in which society produced and sought to satisfy its material needs, fundamentally altered the social relations with nature, and therefore fundamentally altered the geography of a given area' (Harvey, 1981,

209–10). Marxist theory, in its many and developing forms, though conceived in the mid-nineteenth century, does obviously offer an attractive and powerful analytic theory and method, with its particular emphasis on society, alienation, and freedom in a complex mesh of theory and historical materials. The theory offers a 'text' which is open to a variety of readings, and which will accommodate concepts of social structure and human agency.

Examples of the use of Marxist perspectives to aspects of historical geography include Dunford and Perrons' *The Arena of Capital* (1983), and Harvey's *The Limits to Capital* (1983), *The Urbanization of Capital* (1985a), and *Consciousness and the Urban Experience* (1985c), subtitled *Studies in the history and theory of capitalist urbanization*. *The Arena of Capital* offers a brave, if limited, attempt to read the historical geography of Britain through a particularly unyielding Marxist framework; *The Limits to Capital* is a mainly abstract work, though clear focus on substantive issues is provided by Harvey's *The Urbanization of Capital*.

In his study of *Consciousness and the Urban Experience*, Harvey has analysed the changing geography of Paris in the mid- and late nineteenth centuries from a modified Marxist perspective, based on circuits and crises of capitalism, and is concerned with the correction of approaches which involved 'capitalism *in* space without considering how space is produced and how the processes of production in space integrate into the capitalist dynamic and its contradictions. Historical materialism has to be upgraded, therefore, to historical–geographical materialism. The historical geography of capitalism has to be the object of our theorizing' (Harvey, 1985c, xiv).

Critiques of this work have not been slow in forthcoming. Dennis (1987; 1988) argues, as a minor criticism, that there is too much reliance on secondary, modern analyses and insufficient attention to contemporary data for the nineteenth century (to be found in the form of primary archival material), also that there is too close an adherence to a 'fundamentalist' Marxism. Harvey (1988, 306) in an overreactive reply, comments on the value of 'the intertwining of theory and historical materials' and seems to experience discomfort at his work being labelled 'historical geography', at least in its more conventional sense. Kearns (1991) is concerned at the reductionist tendency of this form of Marxism, particularly its neglect of cultural and ideological struggles. Many important debates have been stimulated by Harvey's work, debates which owe much to the powerful insights into theory and its crucial relevance to historical geography afforded by Marxist theory.

Humanistic theory, which has attracted the attention of historical geographers, has a broad base, and has close links with Marxism. It is a critical and radical philosophy in the sense of rejecting the apparent tenets of positivism and spatial science in geography (albeit that these were possibly unfairly equated with an uncritical conservative politics), though it has been allied to philosophies such as phenomenology, existentialism and idealism. There are deep and varied roots for the various forms of humanism, with modern western humanism owing much to its development in the Italian Renaissance of the fourteenth century, but differing from it because of greater emphasis on secular and transcendental meaning. For historical geographers, Harris offered advice on the application of the habits of 'the historical mind', to the practice of humanistic geography (Harris, 1978), this 'habit of mind' being an implicit rather than explicit methodology, exemplified by the work of Sauer and

Braudel, and amounting almost to a total cultural/historical geography, steeped in the land and experiential evidence of place in the past. This and other recommendations for historically focused studies of the role, awareness, value and meaning of human life and experiences in its cultural, political and social contexts can be readily accepted in principle. Exemplification of this type of approach is provided, *inter alia*, by Guelke's attempt to demonstrate an idealist approach to understanding the past. Guelke's consistent attempts to introduce an idealist alternative in human and historical geography (Guelke, 1974; 1975; 1982) have not been extensively supported or followed up. Relying on Collingwood's *Idea of History* (1946), he seeks to focus attention on the thoughts and actions of individuals in history, and from them to create and understand the theories behind the action. Problems arise from both the theoretical basis and its unusual logic and from the inadequacy of the attempted exemplification of this approach in his study of the Dutch settlement of the Cape Colony in the period 1652–1780.

A more promising line of inquiry has been opened by Gregory's (1981b; 1982a) advocacy of a structurationist approach in human and historical geography. Linked closely to the ideas of the Cambridge sociologist Giddens, the notion of structuration ties together the voluntarism characteristic of humanistic geography and the notion of constraining/facilitating structures or institutions pertinent to human experiences, such as systems of social practices and structures of social relations. Individuals and groups of 'actors' remain important, but are studied in a context of interaction with structures of social relations and systems of social practice, both consciously and unconsciously, thereby effecting transformation and themselves experiencing changes in view, action and reaction. This structurationist perspective examines the wide questions of structure and agency and the dialectic between action and structure in studies of situated human experiences, which involve the admittance of 'the existence of *unacknowledged* conditions and *unintended* consequences of action in this way demands a move towards structural explanation distanced from conventional empiricism' (Gregory, 1982a, 248).

It is important to note how this set of ideas emerges out of Marxism, and how it is symptomatic of the now very close reciprocal connections between social theory and human geography, for questions of time and space are central to structuration theory. Exploration and development of this complex structure can be seen in Gregory's *Regional Transformation and Industrial Revolution* (1982b). A key element, demonstrated in this work, is the significant revival of a theoretically informed narrative, but a persistent problem is that while the use of narrative to capture place is not generally difficult, its ability to convey spatial structure is more problematic, and this is central to structuration theory. Interestingly, with reference to this problem of narrative and spatial structure, de Certeau (1988, 115), writing of 'spatial stories', sees lived experiences of daily travel as spatial trajectories, which may be described by narrative structures that 'have the status of spatial syntaxes'. Narratives of lived experiences in space thus constitute space as a 'practiced place', for 'in relation to place, space is like the word when it is spoken, that is, when it is caught in the ambiguity of the actualization, transformed into a term dependent upon many different conventions, situated as the act of a present (or of a time), and modified by the transformation caused by successive contexts' (de Certeau, 1988, 117). The practice of narrative that also incorporates adequate theory is extremely difficult, but is preferable, perhaps, to analytical and descriptive accounts of aspects of the past that formally separate-out theory and practice as a matter of routine and course.

Post-modernism and historical geography

Post-modernism involves an explicit rejection of many of the tenets of modernism, the latter seen as a series of reflections and exemplifications of confident rational certainties of understanding and explanation of wide ranges of phenomena, characterized by philosophies and practices of reasoning that begin in the eighteenth century and reach their apogee in the early twentieth century. Post-modernism is posed in stark contrast to a modernism that was about progress as an almost inevitable linear process and experience, the dominance of new technologies and about scientific reasoning of causes and effects (evidenced perhaps in geography and historical geography through the search for and use of mechanistic explanations and metaphors and of general overarching theories or meta-narratives), and the adoption of a perspective of equating the passage of time with a reasonably steady 'improvement' in agriculture, industry, and standards of living. Post-modernism is more scep-tical of grand theory and, owing much to the critical theory of deconstruction—the linguistic movement associated with Derrida—which claims that written works derive not a single identity based on the intentions of the author but an infinite number of interpretations and understandings through individual and personal readings of the text, appears in simple terms to be a radical recognition and celebration of the potential for many differences of individual interpretaion and understanding of, for example, literary texts, places, environments and histories. Geographers and historians are beginning to take notice of the consequences of post-modernism (however defined) for their own scholarly practices, but with inevitably mixed views. Harvey, in a major analysis, *The Condition of Postmodernity* (1989), contends that post-modernists depict modernism in a gross and caricatured over-simplification, dismiss its material achievements too easily, and underestimate the degree of continuity between the two movements. In a very powerful statement, he contends that

> Postmodernist philosophers tell us not only to accept but even to revel in the fragmentations and the cacophony of voices through which the dilemmas of the modern world are understood. Obsessed with deconstructing and delegitimating every form of argument they encounter, they can end only in condemning their own validity claims to the point where nothing remains of any basis for reasoned action. Postmodernism has us accepting the reifica-tions and partitionings, actually celebrating the activity of masking and cover-up, all the fetishisms of locality, place, or social grouping, while denying the kind of meta-theory which can grasp the political–economic processes ... that are becoming ever more universalizing in their depth, intensity, reach and power over daily life (Harvey, 1989, 116–17).

This might cynically be construed as a passionate plea for the retention of Marxist meta-narrative theory (at a particular point in time when Marxist states with their command economies are rapidly disappearing and with them, at least for some, the credibility of Marxist theory), but the objections do have valid point and purpose. They are echoed in Driver's (1992) paper on the possibilities and potential hazards of the adoption of a critical perspective of the history of geographical knowledge, especially in his analysis of the problem of choosing histories and the confrontation, as he sees it, between conventional Marxism and post-structuralism, effecting an unhelpful polarity for contextual history, and an evasion of recognition of the mediating role of the historian in the narrating of history. One major problem of post-modernism, particularly deriving from the critical position of Foucault, is that it "ultimately leaves us no basis on which to choose or to act. It refuses to tell us what should be valued (a moral question) or what should be done (a political question). At its extreme, as others have shown (Fraser, 1989), it can disable the very idea of a critical project. In hailing the end of a particular history, it risks lending credence to clearly ideological pronouncements about 'The end of history' (Fukuyama, 1989), as if the failure of one orthodoxy amounted to the erasure of all other historical possibilities" (Driver, 1992, 36–7). Driver helpfully concludes: firstly, that Said's (1985; 1989; 1990) critical philosophical discourses may be of assistance and offer ways forward, being at once critical of the Enlightenment heritage of modern humanities and of the post-modern 'aesthetic response', while advocating an openness to alternative discourses (though it should be noted that Said often refers to himself as in the post-modern movement); secondly, that the writing of geographical history offers a range of choices, as does the writing of history, and that, following Habermas, critiques of the 'master narratives of the Enlightenment (including Orientalism) have the effect of vastly enlarging our vision of possible geographies and their histories' (Driver, 1992, 37), possibilities which surely offer exciting prospects and subjects for research in possible historical geographies and their histories? Parallel debates are now taking place within history (Stone, 1991; 1992; Joyce, 1991; Kelly, 1991; Spiegel, 1992), and there is a growing body of literature, including the work of Said, using post-modernist and orientalist perspectives.

An important feature of new writings in historical geography will now, more than ever, be the need to specify very carefully our assumptions and methodologies in readings of maps, descriptions, numerical data sources and other evidences from the past, and to allow not only for a multiplicity of perspectives, the 'celebration of differences', but also for an acknowledgement of important differences in the concepts of language as mediator of human perception of the inhabited and imagined worlds. This is well put by Spiegel (1992, 200): 'Just as there are multiple models of mediation, so there are various ways of viewing language: the fashionable, post-modern performative idea of language as constitutive of the world, hence inherently self-reflexive; or an instrumentalist or constative view of language, in which language is seen to describe and explicate as well as to "invent" reality. . . . This second concept of language is normally employed in scientific discourse or in any discipline concerned with purveying information about the world rather than with the construction of social meaning'. Post-modernist geographers would not make such a distinction, but the acceptance of at least the duality of perspectives argued for by Spiegel would, among other things, help to ensure that the new intellectual architectures envisaged are at least made from bricks which contain some straw, and not confined to stream-of-consciousness evaluations of the more malleable evidences and texts from and for the past.

Gender and historical geography

The overwhelming balance of writing on historical geography has been by men: that is a fact. The writing of historical geography would have been infinitely more interesting had this not been so: that is an opinion that is a reflection of broader contexts of underprivileging of women in society at large, and in institutions of learning in particular (Zelinsky, 1973b).

Views on the participation of women in geographical research and understanding have changed since then, but nowhere near sufficiently. The discernible increase in the number of women in academic institutions in very recent years, together with broader debates on greater equality of opportunities for all members of society, has led to the formulation and statement of many alternative and additional perspectives on a very wide range of aspects of life, social structure, and scholarship which is beginning radically to transform our ways of thinking and seeing. Great advances have been made through feminist and women's studies publications and groups, and slowly but surely these new perspectives are being experienced in the world of academic geography. As Kofman and Peake, writing of a 'gendered agenda for political geography' (1990, 314) indicate: 'Recent developments in gender issues in geography have moved beyond making women more visible in the use and organization of space to exploring the nature of gender relations, the construction of femininity and masculinity and the relationship between patriarchical and class structures in time and place'. As far as historical geography is concerned, the progress is too slow but nonetheless discernible. Rose and Ogborn (1988) have spelled out some of the problems and general issues and possibilities for a more gender-sensitive historical geography. They argue initially that through the neglect of women's and gender perspectives in research and writing, and through ignorance of feminism, historical geographers have either marginalized women in their narratives or ignored women to the point where they 'become hidden from geography as they were once "hidden from history". They disappear from the reconstructed past as if they had never been ... the neglect of gender as a major social structure means that historical geography is propagating an inaccurate understanding of the past ... the exclusion of women from historical geography is a political act. It demeans women's historical roles in society, the economy and the polity and so helps to sustain their present oppression' (Rose and Ogborn, 1988, 405). While the first part of this statement is undoubtedly generally agreed, the last must be disputed: seeing what is incontrovertibly an essential aspect of the past as having been neglected and the necessity of resolving to effect a greater balance in gender issues in the future is one thing, but surely the case is overstated for a past and present conspiracy to demean on the part of historical geographers? Rose and Ogborn suggest in more positive vein that historical geographers can learn from feminism, especially from feminist theory, history and praxis, and particularly through such concepts as patriarchy, as constructed and applied, for example, in studies of conflict over the use of women's paid labour between employers and trade unions (Foord and Gregson, 1986), in the structuring by (and presumably of) space of the social relations of gender, including voluntary and involuntary segregation, in locality studies, in the use of women for symbolic and material ends in the material landscape and the creation of their own landscapes by women. Some of these themes are presented and demonstrated in Kay's (1991) exegesis of and prospectus for women's and men's perspectives of the regional historical geography of the United States and Canada, with reference to the lived experiences of the frontier and pioneer settlements (see Chapter 8).

The scope for both feminist and gender perspectives is obviously enormous, and will involve searches for wider ranges of sources than hitherto, and for similarities and dissimilarities of specific gender experience across and between classes. What this must lead to will be the production of many, more sensitive, nuanced, and indeed realistic views of the life-worlds of the past within their many geographical contexts and constructs, and an enhancement of the richness of a range of disciplines, not least historical geography. We need to know more about not only the exploitation but also the dominance of women in production systems in the past, of the aspects of life and landscape which were of particular interest to women travellers, and how these did or did not contrast with the perspectives offered by male contemporaries, of the ways in which written evidences, of all kinds, of women's experiences were constrained by cultural and ideological factors (and in the case of published accounts by discriminatory editing), the roles played by women in individual and collective movements of protest and opposition to social inequalities and exploitation, and in the celebration of local and national experiences.

Historical geographies of communities

Another interesting field of historical geography attracting attention at present, and likely to continue to do so in the future, is concerned with the historical geography of communities.

The term and concept of 'community' is complex, and used in different senses, sometimes meaning a group of people who inhabit one place, some-times with the ecological inference (though not always explicit demonstration) of sets of interrelationships between individuals and groups inhabiting that place, sometimes as an ideal type or model of a section of population. The commonest connotation in an unexamined sense contains elements such as a specific geographical location and commonality of territory, social interaction, a sense of cohesion and common interest. Difficulties arise from this set of concepts, not least the problem of ecological fallacy, which implies a common sense of purpose simply because of geographical proximity, for there are too many historical and contemporary examples of tension and violent opposition and enmity within communities for this to be an unqualified and unexamined general assumption. The narration and analysis of communities in the past can derive much benefit from recent theories developed within the social sciences and social anthropology, which 'have emphasized the construction of social practices in time and space, the importance of day-to-day routine and unreflected practical consciousness to the generation and maintenance of social structures and through the multiple realms of communication, the cultural mediation of social practices' (Revill, 1989, 179).

The terms 'people's history' or 'history from the bottom up' have been used by social historians to describe this revived emphasis on the historical experiences of the majority of the population (as opposed to the history of the élite and the privileged), though the problematic is very much wider than this (Samuel, 1981; Wolf, 1982). Work by Lemon, especially his *The Best Poor*

Man's Country: A Geographical Study of Early Southeastern Pennsylvania (1972) pointed the way to a humanistic approach to the historical geography of communities and regions. More positivist work on 'social areas' within nineteenth-century cities has stimulated a reaction in the form of a more structural/humanist approach. Billinge's (1982) paper advocates an alternative approach to the study of historical communities which pays more attention to human agency, and focuses on class, community and institutions and exemplifies this possibility in a later study of the Manchester Literary and Philosophical Society (Billinge, 1984). This approach is gathering momentum, particularly in urban and industrial historical geography (see Chapters 10 and 11), and also in the study of rural communities, linked in the case of some Swedish-based work, to the concepts of time-geography. The Locknevi project, for example, an interdisciplinary research project looking at the rural society of Locknevi parish, in Småland, Sweden, has resulted in publications which interrogate archival and field evidence by use of various types of theory, including Marxist theory (Fogelvik, Gerger and Hoppe, 1981; Miller and Gerger, 1985). A combination of a theory of place as a historically contingent process, with structurationist theory and time-geography has been used by Pred (1985; 1986) in interesting regional and community-related studies of enclosures in Skåne, Sweden, in the eighteenth and nineteenth centuries.

It is clear that studies of the historical geography through the experiences of ordinary people, in complex urban and rural societies, have much to offer, and that further studies of such communities, of the rural and urban proletariat are needed. One particularly interesting and exciting development is the application of the idea of a 'people's historical geography' to work in Africa, and the 'task which confronts the historical geographer is to understand how (for example) South Africa's brutal landscapes were forged in subordination and struggle, and how the geography of privilege and deprivation has saturated the experience of both overlords and underlings in the society' (Crush, 1986a). If the Marxist/humanist/structurationist/post-modernist theories and methodologies are to be employed, however, they need considerable refinement beyond what, in the case of Marxist analysis, Thrift has called 'jumbo Marxism' (Thrift, 1983), and this can only be achieved by a reflexive engagement between theory and practice.

Regions in historical geography

The region, has always had a significant place in historical geography (however it is or has been conceived) and it will undoubtedly continue to be a key feature of the subdiscipline (Butlin, 1990c). It is an aspect of geographical study which has regularly come into and out of fashion, yet is of such importance that it does not go away for long. The practice of the historical mind, as Harris (1978) advises, is well effected by immersion in a region.

A wide range of types of regional description, classification and analysis classification at differing scales has been undertaken by historical geographers and historians. Brown's *Historical Geography of the United States* (1948) was constructed on both thematic and regional bases, the major 'regions' being the Atlantic seaboard, the Ohio River and Lower Great Lakes regions, the New North-west, the Great Plains and bordering regions, and the Rocky Mountains to the Pacific coast. A strong tradition of regional writing by historical geographers has been developed in the United States and Canada, evidenced by such works as: Meinig's *The Great Columbia Plain* (1968), *Southwest* (1971), and the regional sections of his *The Shaping of America* (1986); Merrens' *Colonial North Carolina* (1964); Mitchell's *Commercialism and Frontier: Perspectives on the Early Shenandoah Valley* (1977); and Clark's *Three Centuries and the Island* (1959), and *Acadia* (1968). British historical geographers and historians have on the whole given much time to the study of agrarian regions, as in the case of the agarian regions identified by Thirsk for England (Thirsk, 1987). The importance of the regional maps in the eighteenth- and early nineteenth-century county reports to the Board of Agriculture has been stressed by Darby (1954), and an example is given in Fig. 3.4, which shows both soil regions and mineral resource regions in a rapidly industrializing region of north-east England.

Later studies of major agricultural regions include the classic map of the agricultural regions of the United States from Paullin's *Atlas of the Historical Geography of the United States* (1932; see Fig. 3.5).

With the increase in enthusiasm for the processes of modernization and industrialization, however, more attention has been given to the regional characteristics and dynamics of labour processes, production systems, class structures and means and forms of cultural and political expression. These are themes in, for example, Gregory's *Regional Transformation and Industrial Revolution* (1982b), a study of the woollen industry of the West Riding of Yorkshire in the eighteenth and nineteenth centuries.

The French tradition of regional writing developed early in the twentieth century by the school of Vidal de la Blache is not particularly evident in the late twentieth century in the writing of regional studies, either in 'pure' historical geography or in historically sensitized studies of the conditions of contemporary regions. Dion's *Le Val de Loire* (1934), dating from the first half of the century, remains an outstanding example of historical regional writing. Many of the maps, however, in de Planhol's *Géographie Historique de la France* (1988) contain much information on the historic regions of France, and there are a number of sections (see Chapter 8) that deal with regional cultures and regionalisms. Clout's *Themes in the Historical Geography of France* (1977) also contains some interesting and important perspectives on French historic regions and regionalism.

One interesting medium for the portrayal of regional character and consciousness is the 'regional' novel, whose usefulness for the regional geographer was suggested by Gilbert (1960), characterized by Bentley (1966, 7) as 'a novel which, concentrating on a particular part, a particular region, of a nation, depicts the life of that region in such a way that the reader is conscious of the characteristics which are unique to that region and differentiate it from others . . .', a phenomenon that was much in evidence from 1840 to 1940. Darby (1948) employed regional novels in his work on Hardy's Wessex, regarding them as sources of reliable geographical evidence rather than texts to be deconstructed and examined through the internal life-worlds of the principal characters. Barrell (1982) approaches the Hardy novels from the points of view of the 'geographies' of the characters and the narrators in *Tess of the d'Urbervilles* and *The Return of the Native*, the former characterized by a circular, 'primal' vision of geography, the latter linear and more wholly visual, more concerned with geology, cartography and the picturesque.

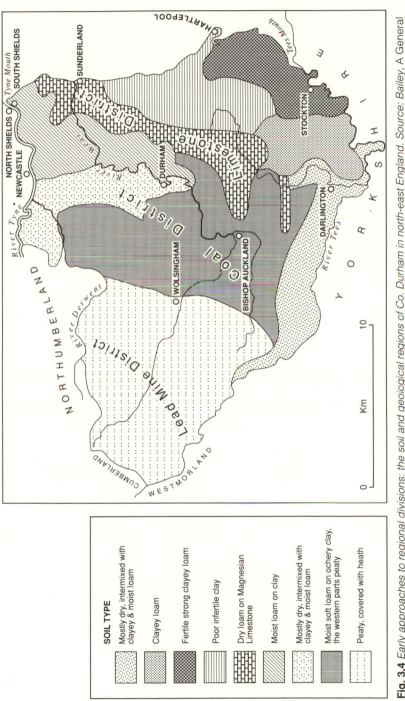

Fig. 3.4 *Early approaches to regional divisions: the soil and geological regions of Co. Durham in north-east England. Source: Bailey, A General View of the Agriculture of Durham (1810)*

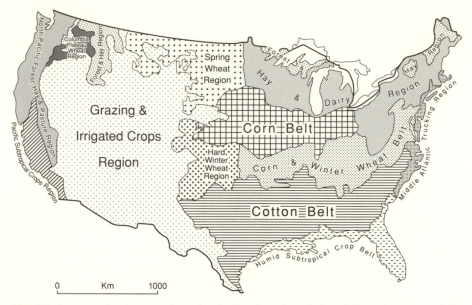

Fig. 3.5 *An example of economic regionalization from the mid-twentieth century: map of the agricultural regions of the United States in 1924. Source: Paullin,* Atlas of the Historical Geography of the United States *(1932, Plate 142)*

There clearly exists a need first both to recover the regional consciousnesses of the past, and second to produce our own contemporary comparative regional schemas of the past for the purposes of analysis and interpretation. The first attempts to fathom and interpret the ideas and place perception of those who in the past have exhibited regional sensitivity in their schemes and writings or have drawn up and attempted to implement schemes of regional division for purposes of scientific description or improvement of social, economic and political administration. The second, and probably more important, involves the need to attempt to construct regions and regional systems *de novo* from adequate theoretical bases, and employs such criteria and elements as language, religion, class, popular culture and politics, the interaction of social processes at local, national and international scales, together with such resources as land, industrial raw materials and transport systems. The construction of the regional geographies of the past need not be constrained by the lack of ready-made systems of regionalization: the real challenge for geographer and historian is that of informed and innovative invention of schemes by means of which spatial patterns of the past may be better understood.

4

Sources of Evidence and Data in Historical Geography

Introduction

A very large part of historical geography is and has been concerned with the use of historical data sets of varying scales and degrees of completeness and accuracy as bases for the reconstruction of a wide range of aspects of the geographies of the past. Such data sets have rarely if ever been produced with the geographer in mind. They derive mainly from the needs of local and national administration to have records and inventories, for example, of population, taxation, landownership and land use, and legal changes in property rights and management, including drainage. The end product is a massive range of census data, maps of many kinds, reports on exploration and land potential, ecclesiastical records, a multiplicity of fiscal documents, records of local and national courts, and a whole range of documents produced by individuals which have fortunately survived in private archives. All these, of course, relate to historic times and literate societies. For the reconstruction of the geographies of human habitations in both prehistoric time and preliterate societies (the two not necessarily always coincident), different sorts of evidence have to be used, including a major range of types of field evidence.

The evidence of relict features of the past is also extensive, and a central theme of historical geography in its more modern form has been the investigation and analysis of surviving relics of past societies and economies. In this respect the use of modern remote sensing techniques, notably aerial photography, has been a benefit to research in historical geography.

The essential problems of data use and provision for the historical geographer are not entirely different from those of the historian, but with the added challenge and difficulty of the need to have a priority for data that can be used to indicate spatial perspectives. Primary and secondary sources are of importance, but historical geographers, especially in Britain, have had a strong inclination and habit of preferring to use primary sources, from archives for example. What constitutes a 'primary source' is an interesting question for discussion, for much material even in its apparently raw (unprinted) documentary form has been extensively worked and recast, such as the *Domesday Book* of 1086, enclosure awards, tithe commutation awards, land register documents and so on. There is nothing particularly sacrosanct about the nature of 'primary' as opposed to 'secondary' data or information, for both need careful scrutiny and verification, though it must be said that often the circumstances and atmosphere in which documentary material is consulted (national and local record repositories) can add a sense of historical context and atmosphere of both positive and negative kinds.

A potent series of criticisms about the use of primary sources has been made by Harley (1982, 262) namely that: 'there is no properly developed tradition within historical geography of editing original documents as a research or teaching activity', and that 'some historical geography is coy in the critical description of evidence'. These limitations are explained by the tendency of historical geographers in the past towards excessive polarization of theoretical and empirical approaches, and by the relatively late date of development of historical geography, whose short period of genesis was prematurely terminated—before full reign could be allowed to the scholarly evaluation of data sources—by the advent of scientism in human geography. Harley's view is that the development of new methodologies for the scholarly evaluation and employment of evidence in historical geography, with particular reference to the language and contexts of that evidence, is of vital importance.

The tradition within historical geography of setting high and critical standards of use of primary data sources is one which obviously has to be maintained and advanced, but only within a carefully thought out and constructed interactive theoretical framework. In *Geographical Interpretations of Historical Sources*, Baker, Hamshere and Langton (1970, 19) state that

> Empirical analysis has always been overwhelmingly prevalent in English historical geography, and there is no reason to believe that this will not continue to be the case . . . the logical conclusion of empirical analysis is the inductive derivation of theoretical principles. One of the major current objectives of human geography is the foundation and testing of formal hypotheses, the anticipated culmination of which is the establishment of dynamic theories of location. The contribution of historical geography to this end is potentially massive, especially if, as seems likely, the systems concept is to provide a framework for the analysis of dynamism.

If, however, the analysis is conducted on an empiricist basis, the assumption is made that theories and observations are independent, and that conventional hypothesis-testing methodologies can be used. If this assumed independence is not accepted, then such methodologies cannot be used. The significance of systems theory for the explanation of dynamic processes of change was developed by Langton (1972), who stressed that it was essentially an empirical method (though it may be argued that this is true of systems analysis but not of systems theory). General systems theory, however, has not been extensively used by historical geographers in spite of its attractiveness in relation to the complexity of the problems which they have sought to analyse, which could not be solved by use of essentially closed-system models to which linear techniques were applied.

A related historiographical point is the concept of historical geography as part of a spatial science, and mainly concerned with the analysis of spatial structure, which did prove attractive to a number of practitioners for a limited period of the 1970s and 1980s. Some attempts, some more successful than others, were made to apply a variety of mathematical modelling and analytical techniques to historical geography, including graph theory, nearest-neighbour analysis, central-place theory, the rank-size rule and location theory. Examples have been listed by Gregory (1981a) who also contended that this was an abdication of the multidimensional richness of traditional historical geography and its reduction to an uninteresting unidimensional character.

Availability, accuracy and interpretation are three key aspects of data use. Availability is a major problem, both of information and data for single points in time and over periods of time. Where sources are available, how representative are they both in spatial and temporal terms? Baker, Hamshere and Langton (1970) outlined some of these difficulties in their preface to a series of studies of geographical interpretations of historical sources, including: spatial sampling; the tendency for records of rural and urban and industrial ownership and production to reflect only the experience of the privileged owner-classes and thus reflect only part of the experience of a whole society at particular times; changes in the areal units for which data were collected; and changes in systems of dates, weights and land measures. Such problems are not entirely without solution, of course, for gaps in data series may occasionally be filled by careful extrapolation or by the use of alternative sources.

Accuracy

The establishment of the relative accuracy and reliability of data and information sources, in addition to their 'meaning' in the broadest possible sense, is an important process for the historical geographer. As Harley has indicated, historical geography does not have a tradition of editing historical documents, and substantive publications frequently lack a critical analysis of sources, concluding that 'Historical geography lacks a proper philosophy of sources and fails to bring to them—as evidence *qua* evidence—those conceptual insights which are otherwise an integral part of approaches to the past' (Harley, 1982, 263), giving as reasons the tendency to separate rather than integrate theoretical and empirical approaches and the relative newness of historical geography as a traditional scholarly subject, the latter having encouraged a chase into the past with untested theories developed in a particular positivist phase of human geography. Harley recommends the adoption of models and theories that will increase our understanding and interpretation of evidence, including coding models (the source of evidence being the code) and the reconstruction of the contemporary contexts of sources, from linguistics, for the purpose of static, genetic and dynamic studies, such models for relevant evidence being one part of the research approach of the historical geographer, the other relating to the major problem under scrutiny. More specifically relating to the accuracy and reliability of evidence, a range of critical tests can be applied, ranging from physical tests to establish or verify the age of the paper and ink on and with which old maps have been drawn to statistical tests for large data sets. There is and can be no limit to the range of evidence available to the historical geographer, and greater imagination and ingenuity in the identification of new problems will inevitably lead to the use of a greater range and more imaginative use of sources. While it would be impossible even to outline here all the types of data set used by historical geographers, a selection of data types is presented to give an impression of the kinds of material available and of some of the problems and possibilities of use.

Population Data

Prehistoric demography and palaeodemography

While the major part of the research carried out on the history and geography of past populations has been based on written records of one kind or another, it has been possible to recover some aspects of early population by reference to the actual remains of humans and the artifacts and structures which they produced. The techniques and methods involved are particularly useful for the study of preliterate societies, though there is sometimes overlap between the material remnant evidence and early written evidence, including inscriptions. Indirect evidence is provided by study of the numbers and sizes of houses from a particular early period, for example, which can be multiplied by an appropriate multiplier to arrive at an estimate of former population, and this can be related also to data from household utensils for storage, cooking and serving, whose volume may reflect the changing size of household over time.

Palaeodemographic techniques involve the study of skeletal remains in order to assess and analyse vital and broader rates of change in population size and structure, a task beset with many difficulties, including that of identification of age and the determination of the extent to which the buried population is representative of the community with which it was associated. As Willigan and Lynch (1982, 45) indicate, 'In order to learn about the underlying patterns of mortality from skeletal remains, palaeodemographers have had increasing recourse to life-table and stable or stationary population models. However, the incidence of short-lived demographic crises is one historical feature that may cause the age and sex structure of skeletal populations to deviate sharply from these models, and to render the task of determining underlying populations of mortality nearly impossible'.

Demographic information before the nineteenth century

The numbering of the population of an administrative region or state, at a very wide range of scales, has been an integral part of resource and control strategies in many regions of the world from late prehistoric and early historic times. The purpose has not always been simply that of a population count: frequently taxation and the extraction of levies of many kinds has been the root cause, and the data provided, though inevitably imperfect, indirect, and distorted, particularly because of exemptions and evasions, has been an important source of information for historical geographers and historical demographers.

The general position regarding pre-census population data has been well expressed by Woods (1979, 8):

> While there is evidence to suggest that there were early censuses in China in the second millenium BC, in the Kandu Empire from the sixth century BC, and in early Egypt, little survives from these times which could be regarded

as a full population census by present-day standards. Up until the beginning of the nineteenth century in western Europe and the USA, earlier in Scandinavia and later in central and eastern Europe, it is necessary to rely on a series of scattered and indifferent sources in order to make even rough approximations of the number of people in an area.

Nonetheless the widely scattered data sources have been extensively and productively used, and a highly selective group of examples follows to give some indication of the types and problems of interpretation involved.

For the medieval and early modern period in England there is a considerable range of sources from which aspects of population geography, and related questions such as wealth and poverty, can be reconstructed. These include the major Domesday survey of 1086, a series of Poll Taxes from 1377, data from the Hundred Rolls of 1279, Lay Subsidies of the fourteenth and early sixteenth centuries, the Hearth Taxes of the late seventeenth century, the Communicant Returns of 1603, and the 'Compton' census of 1676 (a return by parish priests of the number of their parishioners), most of which have been used to estimate national and regional population totals and aspects of population distributions and densities, using, in cases where data is given on a head-of-household basis, an estimated multiplier reflecting the size of family. Using the data from the extensive but complex Domesday survey of 1086, Darby calculated the total population recorded as 275,000, but as these were principally heads of households, a multiplier of five was used to estimate the total population for the whole of England, excluding the largely unrecorded northern counties, of 1.5 million. The mapped data indicates strong regional variation in population density, ranging from high densities in East Anglia and the coastlands of Sussex and Kent, and low densities in such areas as the Weald, the Fenland, the Breckland, the New Forest, Dartmoor and Exmoor (Darby, 1973b, 45–6). Although the Lay Subsidies (taxes on movable goods payable to the Crown) offer little help with estimation of population totals, they have been extensively used to assess the geographical distribution of wealth. Glasscock's studies (1973; 1975) of the 1334 Lay Subsidy, allowing for the omission of the county palatinates and the border counties with Scotland and the distortions introduced by evasions of tax payment, conventional valuation, corrupt officials and lawful exemptions from tax payment, provide interesting indicators of the variations in assessed wealth, showing a poorer north and west of England contrasting with a richer south and east.

Extensive work has been undertaken on the basis of a particular key source of information on births, marriages and deaths: the parish register. The civil registration of these events only started in England and Wales in 1837–38, in Scotland in 1855 and in Ireland in 1864, but the parish registers, comprising records of births, marriages and deaths compiled by parish priests of the established church date back to 1538 in England, when they were instituted by Cromwell, though they are sparse before 1558, and are more abundant from the beginning of the seventeenth century. They date from 1552 in Scotland, becoming more frequent by the end of the seventeenth century, though there are far fewer of them than have survived for England. There are major problems with their use, including variation in accuracy through time, the exclusion of data for the non-established churches, clandestine marriages, and birth–baptism shortfalls through very early infant mortality (Finlay, 1981).

The principal techniques used to analyse the registers are aggregative analysis and the calculation of demographic rates. Aggregative analysis involves the tabulation on a monthly or annual basis of the frequency of births, marriages, and deaths, which enables correlation, for example, with economic fluctuations including poor and good harvests and other aspects of seasonality, plague mortality and other forms of mortality crisis, and gender ratios in communities. The analytical techniques that enable demographic rates to be calculated from this data source include time-series analysis through inverse projection to derive measures of population size and age structure via age distribution and series of births and deaths, backward projections to derive population trends from corrected data from parish registers, and family reconstitution—the grouping together of all the vital events experienced by a particular family (Finlay, 1981). All of these techniques have been employed in the major study of English population change in the period from 1541 to 1871 by Wrigley and Schofield (1981), employing parish register data from a sample of 404 parishes. Considerable modification of the sample material was necessary to compensate for the high percentage of large parishes and small percentage of small parishes, changes through the period covered baptismal practices, the growth of religious non-conformity after 1700, and the inclusion of the total events for London to provide a national data set (Smith, 1990).

Similar data series exist for other countries in Europe. For the medieval and early modern periods, data sources include the population data in Abbot Irmion's polyptique of *c.* 810(a survey of the lands of the Parisian monastery of Saint-Germain des Prés); the 1328 Hearth Survey list of 33 territorial units in France; Hearth Tax surveys of the Low Countries, northern France and the Duchy of Burgundy, and in Zurich and Basel in Switzerland in the late fourteenth and the fifteenth centuries and urban-specific counts of population such as the 1431 count of the men of Nuremberg fit for military service (Pounds, 1974, 125–7). Italian 'stati d'anime', lists of souls, that is of individual communicants, compiled at parish level, are extant mainly from the seventeenth century, and are important sources of nominative and sometimes household data for the seventeenth and eighteenth centuries (Willigan and Lynch, 1982, 86–7). French parish registers of baptisms, marriages and burials go back to the fifteenth century, the result of instructions by some bishops to parish priests to keep such data, but the first Crown edict dates from 1539 and applied only to births and some deaths, being extended by the Edict of Blois to include marriages, with royal legislation on compulsory registration of deaths dating from 1667, though papal decree had specified this requirement from 1614 (Henry, 1965, 436–7). Parish registers are poor before 1670, were unevenly kept from 1670 to 1737, and are accurate from 1737, though there are regional exceptions to this generalization. From 1806, with the introduction of the État Civil, information on births, marriages and deaths was returned on a commune basis for the whole of France. An early census was that taken on the basis of returns requested by the Duc de Beauvillier from the Intendants of the provinces at the end of the seventeenth century, and there were some partial censuses between 1660 and 1700.

Outside Europe the sources of information for derivation of pre-census population characteristics are obviously wide and varied. The 'relaciones geográficas' for the Spanish colonial territories in Central and South America, available from the early sixteenth to the mid-nineteenth century, include estimates of population, Indian and Spanish, counts of congregations and communicants for dioceses, and accounts of epidemics (Gerhard, 1972). Specialist studies of population migration in colonial Spanish America (Robinson, 1990) have used such sources as the *Visita General* by Viceroy Toledo of 1575, and the *Numeración General* of Viceroy Palata of 1683–86, the latter used by Evans in an analysis of migration processes in Upper Peru in the seventeenth century and planned as a modern type of census, envisaging the listing of each Indian by name, age, civil status and family, and place of origin (Evans, 1990). Large empires such as that of China, or the Ottoman Empire which dominated much of the Middle East and the Mediterranean lands in the high and late Middle Ages, had complex and extensive administrative systems which frequently produced direct or indirect data which can be used for population assessment. For China early census data is available, *inter alia*, from the year AD 2, at the end of the Han dynasty, for AD 157 to AD 609, for the late tenth century and for the Ming period from the fourteenth to the mid-seventeenth centuries (Tuan, 1970). The Ottoman Empire had a very sophisticated system of central and provincial administration and record keeping, and extensive records exist of various taxes paid, some specifically levied from Christians and Jews, which offer possibilities for the reconstruction of many aspects of the historical geography of population.

The above comprise no more than a brief set of examples of the types of source available for the study of population before the advent of censuses in the late eighteenth and the nineteenth centuries. Although their specific nature varies from place to place, the commonest sources are population registers, parish registers, genealogies, tax records, and early (and usually limited) counts of population. Their usefulness depends on the project of research in hand, and the range of techniques available for the repair, calibration and correlation of the data which they contain.

Census data

The practice of counting the number of inhabitants of a country on a regular basis is in Europe essentially a product of the late eighteenth and nineteenth centuries, and is strongly related to the growing power of the state, with one means of assessing strategies for economic and military development being the gathering of appropriate sets of statistics, of which the census was a key feature.

The earliest comprehensive census was that taken for Iceland in 1703, followed by that for Sweden/Finland, begun in 1749 and involving forms requiring details of births, marriages, deaths, age structure and the causes of death. Further important data was derived from the registration of births, marriages and deaths, made compulsory in Sweden/Finland in 1686 and in Norway (for baptism and burial) in 1735 (Mead, 1981, 104, 114). The first national census for Norway was in 1769. Some of these censuses were based on data from continuous registration rather than period counts, and the systematic and regular counting of national populations in Europe dates from the nineteenth century. The first French census dates from 1801 and censuses were subsequently conducted at five-year intervals until after 1945. Germany's national censuses date from the year of the creation of the German state (1871), those of Austria–Hungary from the 1880s, and of Spain from 1857,

and Italian censuses from 1861, though it was not until the early twentieth
century that most European countries had regular censuses (Woods, 1979,
16–17). Population counts in the territories subject to European settlement in
the eighteenth and nineteenth centuries vary in chronology and development,
reflecting the different phases and areas settled over time. Census counts began
in the United States in 1790, following on from more restricted population
enumerations in the colonial period, which are summarized, for example, in
the census volumes for 1850 and 1909. A map based on the 1790 census,
showing the population distribution of part of the eastern seaboard of the
United States is shown in Fig. 4.1. There are, however, deficiencies in the data,
partly because of the wide areas over which the population was spread, the

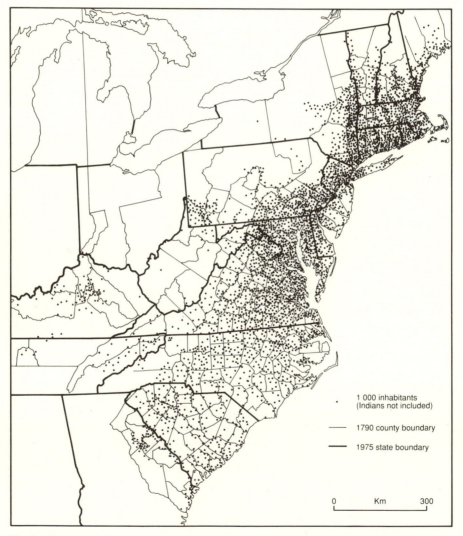

Fig. 4.1 *Population of the eastern seaboard of the United States, 1790. Source: Paullin,* Atlas of
the Historical Geography of the United States *(1932); and Cappon (1976, 65)*

large numbers of immigrants and of internal migration, and regional differences in efficacy of enumeration (Potter, 1965, 633).

In Canada, the first national census came shortly after confederation, and was taken in 1871, but data are included for earlier years, sometimes inevitably in limited form. Thus, the fourth volume of that census contains summaries for earlier years: there are, for the areas of Atlantic Canada, for example, 16 listings for Nova Scotia for 1671–1861, 10 for Newfoundland for 1687–1869; eight for New Brunswick for 1695–1861; and five for Prince Edward Island for the period 1728–1861 (Hamilton, 1974, 60). In Australia the first major census of population was in 1851, though there were earlier counts of smaller early-settled areas, largely in the form of data from musters, but these omit the aboriginal population and inevitably some of the settlers, so that by 1800 it is estimated that only 1 or 2 per cent of the actual population had been recorded, though by 1900 the figure had reached 95 per cent (Caldwell, 1987, 23).

In other regions of the world the commencement of the taking of national censuses was on the whole much later. In Africa, censuses tend to date from the early twentieth century, and large areas are still without reliable data. For the most part reliable statistics for population are first available only from the late colonial period, including censuses, registration of births and deaths, and migration data. Estimates of the population of the countries of East Africa, for example, are available for 1902 (Kenya, Uganda, mainland Tanzania and Zambia) and slightly earlier (1895) for the island of Zanzibar and for Malawi, and census counts date from 1911 and 1921, but the first complete census was not taken until 1948 (Datoo, 1979, 47). Parts of North and South Africa are exceptions to this generalization. French data for the former being available from the mid-nineteenth century, and data from early-settled provinces of South Africa, notably Cape Province, from 1865. Censuses began in some countries of Latin America in the middle and late nineteenth century, dating for example from 1869 in Argentina and 1872 in Brazil. In India the first major census, following earlier incomplete attempts, was in 1881, and in China in 1920. Major Russian censuses began in the late nineteenth century, though there is earlier data for specific towns and regions (Woods, 1979, 18–19).

The first census for England, Wales and Scotland was conducted on 10 March 1801, and decennial censuses have been taken, with rare exceptions, ever since, in the first year of each decade. The first effective census for Ireland was not conducted until 1821 (an earlier attempt in 1814–15 being aborted before completion). These censuses provided essentially numbers of people, but did not of themselves provide data on the detailed dynamics of population change, that is of the vital events of births, marriages, and deaths. Civil registration of births, marriages and deaths began in England and Wales in 1837–38, in Scotland in 1855 and in Ireland in 1864. Prior to these dates information on baptisms, marriages and burials was largely derived from the records of the established church, as indicated earlier.

The purpose of the 1801 census of Great Britain was to obtain a figure for the number of persons, families and houses, together with a general idea of the balance of occupations of the populace, and also to ascertain the extent of increase or decrease of the population. Questions concerning the numbers of people in each enumerated place were put by house-to-house enquiry by enumerators. Questions concerned with baptisms and burials in the years

1700, 1710, 1720, 1740, 1750, 1760, 1770, 1780, and each subsequent year to 1800, and with marriages in the period 1754–1800, were addressed to the clergy, whose responsibility in England it had been since 1538 to keep parish registers. In Scotland all the questions were to be answered by the local schoolmaster or other fit person. The results of the census were first published in the form of two *Abstracts*, the *Enumeration Abstract* in two parts (England and Wales, 1801, Scotland, 1802) and the *Parish Register Abstract* (1801).

For the censuses of 1811, 1821 and 1831, changes were introduced, including those concerning the nature of uninhabited houses, the family as a unit for evaluation of occupation, age characteristics, and the nature of the parish register abstract returns. The early censuses, though useful, are beset by difficulties of accuracy and reliability, which reflect in part the methods of data collection, which was essentially oral. The overseers of the poor (substantial householders or schoolmasters who were variously responsible for the collection of the basic household data) visited each household between 10 March and 30 April 1801, and wrote down the response of the householders on a form provided. One consequence was the underestimation of the population of England and Wales by 5 per cent for 1801, and by 3 per cent for 1811. Major changes were introduced from 1841, and it is from this date that the census data becomes much more reliable and useful than it had been before. Each householder now received an individual census schedule which had to be completed for the night of the date specified. These were collected by the enumerators and copied into the enumerators' books, which became the basis of the published census statistics, and which also provide very detailed and useful sources for the reconstruction of the historical population geography for the dates and years of the census. They have been used in detailed studies of regional, rural and urban societies in nineteenth-century Britain (Tranter, 1985, 10; Mills and Pearce, 1989). The data available from the successive censuses varies from 1801 to the present day, and for the earlier censuses presents considerable problems of use, including: the changing administrative units on which the collection of census data was based (with the consequence that very detailed demographic work is only possible from 1851, the year when registration districts and counties were created); the actual timing of the census; and the reliability of the returns made from households and individuals, and of the census enumerators themselves. The main uses of census data for Britain have been for studies of changing population totals and densities at many different scales, from local to national; of patterns of population movement (details of which are available in the censuses from 1851); of occupational and social structures; and when necessarily used in conjunction with other sources, such as the data of births, marriages and deaths, the complex dynamic processes of population change (Lawton, 1987; 1990; Woods, 1979).

The greatest intensity of research and published work on census data by historical geographers has, not surprisingly, been for those regions with the longest and most complete data, that is for Scandinavia, western Europe and the United States and Canada. Similar work has been produced for countries with more recent detailed censuses which have a high degree of accuracy, such as Australia, New Zealand and Japan, but the problems attendant on the population data from many parts of Africa, for example, make very detailed historical studies difficult if not impossible. The first census of India was carried out in 1881, and Gosal (1984, 204) suggests that 'Among the countries of the developing world India is one of the most fortunate in having a well-developed census system for a long period, making it possible to examine its population in spatial–temporal dimensions. The data for most characteristics of population have been available by districts (equivalent to a county in the West) for almost the entire hundred-year period', though even here major difficulties are presented by the lack of data for vital rates.

Parliamentary Papers and Official Surveys and Reports

A valuable source of evidence for demographic, social and economic changes in many regions and countries of the world is the massive amount of official material deriving from surveys and reports on such matters as landownership, land use and agricultural potential, unemployment and poverty, and the spread and decline of particular industries. Within countries settled by British colonists and under various degrees of control from Britain, and indeed within Britain itself, a particularly important source of information comprises the parliamentary papers, including the Royal Commissions and the published volumes of Special Committees of Enquiry of the House of Commons and of Lords, which, generally speaking, were special enquiries into topics deemed at the time to be important and deserving of intense scrutiny, that scrutiny often being based on specially compiled sets of statistical data, and frequently also containing verbatim reports of the evidence of expert and involved witnesses. Their range is enormous: major items for the nineteenth century include agriculture, trade depression, the coal trade, mining accidents, transport and communications, posts and telegraphs, industrial relations, children's employment, factories, textiles, trade, the Poor Law, planning, sanitation, water supply, the police and civil disorder, transportation to the colonies, the native inhabitants of Australia and Canada, Africa, Australia, Canada and its boundary, the East India Company, New Zealand, the West Indies, emigration, famine, population, and the slave trade.

A very large volume of the material for Britain itself deals with the state of agriculture and with agricultural depression and distress, the Select Committees of 1821, 1822, 1833, 1836 and 1837, dealing with agricultural distress, and of 1844, dealing with enclosures. The accounts and papers within the parliamentary papers also contain important material, including the assessments to Income Tax, Schedule A, for which details are published for all parishes in England and Wales for the years 1818, 1844 and 1860, providing data for the constructions of rents per acre (Grigg, 1967, 79–80).

In addition to these published reports and papers of the British Parliament, there is a massive amount of supplementary material which has enabled reconstructions of major aspects of agrarian, industrial and urban life to be undertaken. Limited data on crop returns are available from Home Office enquiries during the period of the Napoleonic Wars for the years 1793, 1795 and 1801, the last year's statistics deriving from a requirement that clergy send to their diocese details of the acreages under wheat, barley, oats, rye, turnips, rape, peas, beans and potatoes. From 1866 the Board of Agriculture gathered and published a wide range of data on agricultural land use including the area of land under different crops, and the types and numbers of livestock. Two major sources of information extensively used by historical geographers and historians are the parliamentary enclosure acts and awards (the acts being published in the parliamentary Blue Books), and the data from the activities of the Tithe Redemption Commission. The rapid advance of agrarian capitalism in the eighteenth and nineteenth centuries effected a transformation from medieval systems of agrarian management to a more modern system based in individual ownership of property and the use of new crops and rotations, many of which had been introduced in the sixteenth and seventeenth centuries but whose widespread adoption came later. The legal procedure to transfer land from communal management and use-rights to individual ownership was the parliamentary private Act of Enclosure, followed by the General Acts of the early nineteenth century. The extent of activity and data generated may be symbolized by the number of Acts for Enclosure in England in the period 1730–1844, summarized by Turner (1984), as 5265 Acts, of which 3093 were concerned with open field arable, and 2172 with common land and waste. Although much of the early pioneer work on enclosure in England and Wales was based on statistical digests from the parliamentary papers, more recent work has been based on sampling, for large-scale studies (Chapman, 1987) and detailed analysis in the case of smaller-scale studies, of the award documents which contain details, including maps, of the state of landowner-ship and management in a parish before and after enclosure, and the recommendations of the enclosure commissioners who were legally charged with carrying out the reallocation of land, farmsteads and roads. The Tithe Commutation Act of 1836 provided for the commutation to a money rent of the tithe or tenth of the main annual agricultural produce in a parish that was payable to the church. The commutation was carried out by tithe commis-sioners, whose enquiries to 14,829 tithe districts in England and Wales resulted in the tithe files, one for each district, the analysis of which has been the basis of extensive studies of mid-nineteenth century agricultural geog-raphy. Of particular importance is the data for parishes where the tithes were either commuted by compulsory award or by voluntary agreement, data contained in printed report forms for 'arable' and 'pastoral' counties and in the tithe awards, which contain maps of land use and tithe liability.

Royal Commissions and the Factory Inspectors' Reports, together with reports of select committees, such as the House of Lords Select Committee of 1828 on the state of the wool trade, and the 1836 return on employment in cotton, wool, worsted, flax and silk factories of the United Kingdom, in addition to the extensive analysis of census data, have been important bases for investigation of question of urban and industrial development.

Historical geographers have made extensive use of these published papers and official statistical sources. Coppock (1956; 1984) has outlined the potential for and problems of use of the Board of Agriculture returns from 1866; the 1801 crop returns have been extensively mapped and analysed (Henderson, 1952), as have the tithe surveys, files, and awards (Kain, 1984; Kain and Prince, 1985; Kain, 1986). Extensive use of the parliamentary papers, in combination with estate records, newspapers, periodicals and directories, is made in Phillips' (1989) major study of the underdraining of farmland in England during the nineteenth century. Problems posed by the advance of steam-powered machinery and the dissolution of traditional work practices in the hosiery industry in the mid-nineteenth century were evidenced in high unemployment among the traditional framework knitters, working in a domestic system, leading to a major depression and high rates of unemployment and a parliamentary enquiry into this industry. The resulting report of 1845, the *Report of the commissioner appointed to enquire into the condition of the framework knitters*, provided fine-grained statistical detail for the year 1844 about the condition of framework knitting in various parts of Britain, with particular concentration on the East Midlands of England. This information was the basis of the study by Smith (1963) of the economic geography of the hosiery industry in Britain in the mid-nineteenth century, including a series of maps constructed from the data provided in the report. Parliamentary enquiries also figure in studies of the textile industries, such as Rodgers' (1960) analysis of the Lancashire textile industry in 1840, which uses as a mapping basis the statistical surveys incorporated in the 1838 returns to Parliament of the Factory Inspectors under the legislation of the Factory Act of 1833, and in Gregory's (1982b) study of the woollen industry of the West Riding of Yorkshire.

A wide range of official surveys and statistical data from the late eighteenth century onwards is available from, *inter alia*, many of the countries of western and northern Europe, North America, Australia and New Zealand, South Africa, and Japan. In France, the information from the 'ancien cadastre parcellaire' (Clout and Sutton, 1969) a detailed ground survey of every commune, (resulting from a law of 1807, a survey completed for the whole of metropolitan France by 1850, and revised thereafter) has been combined with statistical data for agricultural production (such as the evaluations of land revenues resulting from legislation of 1850 and 1879) and other aspects of land use to produce detailed national and regional analyses of French agriculture and rural life. Clout and Phillips (1972) incorporated information from the 'ancien cadastre', agricultural enquiries from 1793–94 and 1814, the decennial agricultural censuses (*Statistique agricole de la France*) from 1852, 1862 and 1882 into their study of the use of fertilizers in French agriculture in the nineteenth century, and similar sources are employed in Sutton's (1984) work on the reclamation of wasteland in France in the eighteenth and nineteenth centuries and in Clout's (1980; 1977b) statistical overview and assessment of the agriculture of France in the eighteenth and nineteenth centuries. Inevitably much of the information contained in official surveys and statistical sources for lands which experienced intensifying European settlement in the eighteenth and nineteenth centuries dealt directly with land allocation and assessment of land potential, though they covered a very wide range of topics. Christopher (1988, 10–11) points to the massive bureaucratic systems associated with colonial rule, especially in the British Empire: 'The administration sought to order society and to change it. In order to do so it required information. Colonial governments undertook a vast accumulation of material on many aspects of colonial life and lands. . . . The random reports of the early colonial period gave way to the systematic annual report of colonial administrations, notably the Blue Books and their successor Statistical Registers inaugurated in 1822. Similarly censuses were taken which by 1891 were intended to be regular and on an Empire-wide basis'. Of particular importance are the commissions of enquiry initiated by both British and individual colonial governments, together with the correspondences between the metropolitan and colonial governments.

A vast range of data sources provide evidence for the allocation of land for farms and settlements from the public domain and from crown lands in the case of the British colonies. In the United States in the late eighteenth-century revolutionary period and during the nineteenth century a philosophy of a new republic, and its westward expansion, founded on small family farms was adopted by early presidents such as Jefferson. A varied array of land allocation systems can be identified before 1812, including those involving settlement companies, such as the Ohio Company of Associates, which promoted the settlement of Ohio west of the Seven Ranges by purchasing at very low price 1.5 million acres of land from the Federal government, with each shareholder being allocated one full section of land (640 acres), parts of other sections, and one-third of an acre for a house site (Brown, 1948, 215). During the nineteenth century the major agent of land disposal continued to be the Federal government. Hence

> Uncle Sam's acres were numerous and far flung by 1815. The business of surveying, sectioning, advertising, selling and collecting the proceeds constituted the largest single area of economic activity in the country and the major obligation of the Federal government. . . . After the individual states claiming the trans-Allegheny region had surrendered their rights, the public domain of the United States amounted to more than 200,000,000 acres. This was increased to a billion acres by the Louisiana purchase and the acquisition of Florida, Texas, Oregon, and California. No problem so continuously absorbed the attention of Congress for the next century as that of the management, sale, and donation of this great empire (Gates, 1960, 51).

The Ohio Enabling Act of 1802, the Bounty Land Acts which allocated land to encourage enlistment and to reward war veterans of the war of 1812, the Homestead Act of 1862, the Timber Culture Act of 1873, and the Desert Land Act of 1877, were some of the more important means of allocating the public domain and encouraging the westward spread of settlement. Not all land was allocated in this way, large tracts also being routed via speculators and the railroad companies, who sold in turn to settlers. The land survey and layout system, initiated by the Ordinance of Ascertaining the Mode of Disposal of Lands in the Western Territory in 1785 and the Act Providing for the Sale of the Lands of the United States in the Territory Northwest of the River Ohio in 1796, introduced the township, range, and range system, the township being a square or rectangle of 36 square miles, subdivided into quarter sections of 640 acres and other units which are multiples of 40 acres, laid out in relation to lines of latitude and longitude by surveyors, thus creating the very common and familiar geometric chequerboard patterns in the landscape (Johnson, 1957; 1975). The Federal records for settlement of the public domain are substantial. Initial responsibility for land sale was given to district land offices, and in 1812 the central office was given the status of a bureau when the Congress established the General Land Office within the Treasury, responsible for administration of the public domain and, from 1836, for the work of surveying and mapping. The public land records comprise identification records, including field notes and plans of the survey, status records which record ownership, case records which record the history of each action taken in relation to a particular plot of land, and control records, copies of patents, and proclamation orders (Smith, 1975, 291). The cartographic contents are particularly valuable, and were first extensively used by Schafer (1921–22) in his studies of the agricultural settlement of Wisconsin. In some parts of the United States there were problems in confirming land grants when territorial authority changed, so that when California was ceded to the United States by Mexico, an enormous amount of time and trouble was taken by the US General Land Office to check and confirm the grants (Brown, 1948, 510–11), which are shown, with their irregular outlines, in Fig. 4.2.

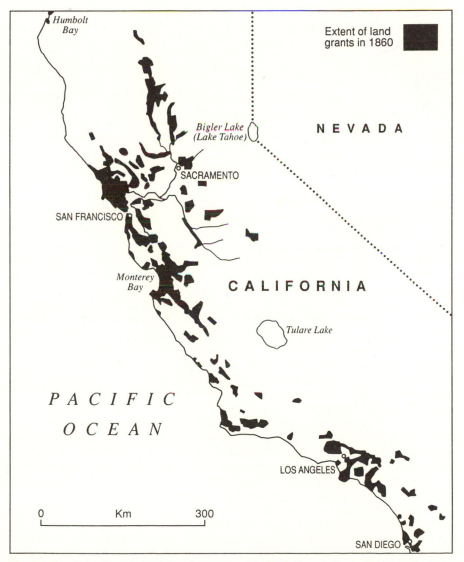

Fig. 4.2 *Private land grants in California, surveyed in 1860. Source: Brown (1948, 511)*

Data-processing Methodologies

One of the most important technical advances in historical geography from the 1970s onwards has been the possibility, through the rapid extension and increased availability of powerful computing facilities and desk-top computers, of launching significant assaults on the major data sets of the nineteenth and twentieth centuries in particular, though the data from earlier periods has also been processed. Though the number of large-scale projects realized hitherto is small, the potential for use is almost unlimited, including the possibilities for mapping of processed historical data. Among the large-scale studies for England are those of the Cambridge Group for the History of Population and Social Structure, especially the reconstruction of the population history of England by Wrigley and Schofield (1981) based on a sample of 404 parishes, using parish register data, Kain's computer-produced maps incorporated in his atlas of tithe file statistical data from the mid-nineteenth century (1986), and Chapman's studies of the amount and extent of parliamentary enclosure in England (Chapman, 1987). In addition to the computer processing and storing of statistical and quasi-statistical data, the storage of full texts is of major importance, and opens the way for a wide variety of statistical and content analyses. The computerizing of the text of the *Domesday Book*, containing over a million words, has presented interesting possibilities and major problems (Palmer, 1986), and the possibilities for mapping the data are even greater than the 800 maps produced by more conventional means in the seven volumes of the monumental *Domesday Geographies* produced by Darby and his collaborators between 1952 and 1977. At a smaller, regional scale, Overton (1977; 1984a) has demonstrated the potential and the usefulness of computer mapping of an interesting source of information for the agrarian economy and society of early modern England: the probate inventory, a list compiled for probate purposes at the death of a farmer, giving details of crops, livestock and equipment. The purpose of the data collection from the inventories was to trace and explain the diffusion of cropping innovations in East Anglia from the sixteenth to the early eighteenth century, and the mapping was carried out on the basis of allocation to squares in an arbitrary grid system superimposed on the area of study. Alternative procedures also employed are contoured surfaces and point symbols.

The technology of data processing and storage is changing at a very rapid rate, not simply in relation to the power and sophistication of computers, but in the widening of the ranges of additional technology. For the historical geographer one of the restrictions for archive-related study in the past has been the obvious necessity of having to travel in order to work on archive material at source. While this necessity will never be eliminated, the new technologies are facilitating 'distant' use of important sources. Microfilm was one of the earlier steps in this direction, but the increasing use of the Compact Disc Read Only Memory system (CD-ROM) for data storage, providing the equivalent of 250,000 pages of A4 text on a single 12 cm disc and offering major advances in the retrieval and processing of data with appropriate software, is an important indicator of progress. Data from the tithe surveys of England and Wales following the Tithe Commutation Act of 1836 are now published in this form, based on Kain's (1986) atlas and index of the tithe files. Census data, for example the British 1881 census, are available in this form, as also are state and county data from the United States decennial censuses of the eighteenth, nineteenth and twentieth centuries. Newspapers, and a range of other data sources are now being marketed in this form by commercial enterprises (Colson, Middleton and Wardley, 1992). On-line data sets, and data archives such as the British Economic and Social Research Council's for historical and contemporary data, and access to specialist bibliographies and to the catalogues of individual academic and specialist libraries, will also transform the study of historical geography and economic and social history.

Software packages for mainframe and personal computers have long been part of the technical weaponry of the historical and human geographer working on large data sets. The application of statistical tests and processes, such as variance and regression analysis, significance tests, and numerical taxonomies, together with the application of space–time modelling concepts including time-series analysis, has been extensively facilitated by computer software packages, and new developments include complex data base management systems (DBMS), a form of information management which permits complex mapping and hypothesis testing (Colson, Middleton and Wardley, 1992). Automated cartography, very much part of the intensive development of Geographical Information Systems (GIS), also offers major possibilities for historical geographers, though it has to be said that in this field, as in the wider field of computer applications for historical statistical data, the literature in the appropriate journals is still surprisingly scarce, reflecting not only the difficulties of unevenness of historical data but perhaps also the caution of historical geographers to move into these new methodologies.

Field Evidence

While much of the research undertaken by historical geographers has had its roots in libraries and archives, part of its excitement is the linkage which can be made between the written sources and the field evidence of the places researched and studied. The nature of field investigation can, of course, vary. On the one hand there is the necessity for intelligent and sensitive perambulation of the area under investigation, informed for some by prior reading of documents and published accounts, for others, at least initially, by a more informal osmotic experience of the region and its landscapes. Investigation and experience of a study area or region in an informal way is still one of the most rewarding aspects of research in historical geography, with aspects and facets of landscape spontaneously posing interesting questions for investigation, which may then be followed up in a more formal and structured way. As historical geography moves to broader theoretical and methodological perspectives and techniques, so an ever-widening series of questions needs to be posed and answered, in relation to field evidence and the nature of landscape and other aspects of the discipline.

The range of possibilities for the incorporation of fieldwork, field evidence and field experience is almost endless. Much valuable study has been and is being undertaken of relict features of the landscape, some obvious from the ground, others initially visible only through remote sensing via air photographs and satellite imagery. Relict features, or the remains of the material cultures of people and settlements in the immediate or the remote past, when mapped and analysed with painstaking care and appropriate degree of reservation about the explanatory potential of the evidence available, can shed much light on the dynamics of change in the past, or on stability. Deserted medieval and early modern settlements have been a particularly favoured object of investigation in Europe, involving the combination of field mapping and excavation of sites with the available documentary evidence and the use of appropriate explanatory theories and models. The changing features of the farming-related aspects of rural landscapes are common denominators of the field investigations by historical geographers and by historians, including: the analysis of remaining open-field systems in Europe, Latin America and China, for example; the extensive review and classification of types of vernacular architecture, including farm buildings, the nature of field shapes and boundaries; the extent of former agricultural terraces and irrigation systems; and changes in the extent of woodland and forest, together with aspects of their systems of management. In the urban and industrial contexts, the highly specialized understanding of changing industrial technology, partly through relict features of production, resource and transportation systems, allows for insights into the processes of development of industries at many different scales, and the fascinating problem of the rise and demise of particular industries through time. Urban as well as industrial 'archaeology' provides much evidence for description, analysis and explanation, through both material structures such as surviving house types across many social spectra, institutions such as schools, prisons, recreational facilities, wholesaling and retailing establishments, railway stations, libraries, public bath houses, churches and temples.

The intellectual dangers and difficulties of field work include those of over-simplistic interpretation, especially through assuming that similarity of form indicates similarity of age and function, and an over-reliance on the field evidence alone without further checking and interpretation through other available means of evidence. The further back in time the investigation goes the greater the difficulty of identification and interpretation. The well-developed techniques, backed up by highly sophisticated scientific analyses of human and other material remains, now employed by archaeologists, are frequently used by geographers investigating changing societies and economies in the distant past, and the increasing tendency for historical geographers to work in interdisciplinary teams on such projects is to be applauded.

Maps as Evidence

One of the many rewarding experiences in the practice of historical geography is an intense involvement with maps, including historical maps and maps drawn for the purpose of display and analysis of research findings. But maps are more than sources of hard evidence and means of representation of information of a factual kind. They are also codes of meaning, of senses of place and landscape and their portrayal, of past perceptions and ideologies of power and control, of the technical limitations of land measurement and survey, and, in many instances, including that of older maps of 'distant' places, of geographical and cultural ignorance or bias. The language of maps, including the form of reproduction of the names of places, is an important and interesting object for investigation, as is the symbolic representation of topography. The older the map, the more necessary does it become to contextualize and decode its meanings and its symbolism in addition to assessing its accuracy as a portrayal, subject to the limitations of technology of surveying and map reproduction, of landscapes and places in the past. While in the late twentieth century we are accustomed to the use of highly accurate maps at a wide range of scales, and indeed to remotely sensed images of the earth as a whole from satellite imagery, many of the maps used by historical geographers, for example from late sixteenth- and early seventeenth-century England or from seventeenth-century Palestine, were not based on original survey, but represent a point of evolution of a whole genealogy of maps, the basic information for which may pre-date the actual map under consideration by more than a hundred years. They also represent very different notions of space and territory from those current today.

An essential skill required by the historical geographer, therefore, is that of what has been called the 'deconstructing' of maps and map evidence, especially in two senses, one scientific, the other cultural, though the distance between the two may be small or even at times illusory. The basis of this idea comes from a series of publications by Harley (1988a,b; 1989a,b,c), in which the distinction between two sets of epistemological 'rules' of cartographic history is clearly stated and developed: 'One set may be defined as governing the technical production of maps and are made explicit in the cartographic writings and treatises of the period. The other set relates to the cultural production of maps. These must be understood in a broader historical context than either scientific procedure or technique. They are, moreover, rules that are usually ignored by cartographers so that they form a hidden aspect of their discourse' (Harley, 1989c, 4).

The main outlines of the history of mapping have been well established for some time, and current research on the history of cartography (Harley and Woodward, 1987) is filling in many of the gaps. The origins of world maps lie in prehistory, such as the early circular Babylonian maps of Mesopotamia showing the territories of Babylonia and Syria and other places surrounded by the Persian Gulf and with Babylon at the centre. This 'ethnocentric' tendency—of showing the known world of the originators of the map, with their own centres of civilization or the centre of their religious beliefs, such as Mecca or Jerusalem, at the centre—continued up to the time of the European Renaissance, via the world maps of the Greeks, the Chinese, the Arabic and Christian maps of the medieval period. The early maps of the Greeks had some measure of scientific accuracy through systems of coordinates, such as the world map of Ptolemy produced in the second century AD, but this largely disappeared in the so-called 'Dark Ages' of western European civilization until the appearance initially in the fourteenth century of the Portolan navigation charts of the Mediterranean and the subsequent burst of geographical and cartographic information and production associated with the new ages and voyages of discovery, initially by the Portuguese, from the early fifteenth century onwards. Although it seems that scientific geography declined in the West, it developed and was sustained in China, with a grid system produced in about AD 100 and with extension of mapping technique progressing through the T'ang and Sung dynasties. In the Mongol period accurate maps were made.

The Chinese produced the first relief maps, initially on wood (Ronan, 1983, 166).

From the Renaissance onwards, maps, because of the developments in printing and the production of paper, and gradual improvements in surveying instruments and techniques, occupy an increasingly significant role in administration at many different scales and in the dissemination of geographical knowledge. The history of cartography and the problems and opportunities for the analysis of maps for the period from the Renaissance onwards, especially up to the late eighteenth century, indicate the continuing need to see maps as both products of ideology and culture and of scientific knowledge. An interesting indication of the former is to be found in maps which have close links with religious belief, such as maps printed in Bibles and maps of the Holy Land. The question of the origins and genealogies of maps and illustrations of the Holy Land of this period, including maps from Bibles, is a fascinating subject, on which interesting work has been, and continues to be, undertaken (Delano Smith, 1987; 1990). Delano Smith has shown, for example, that 'the story of maps in Bibles is the story of the Reformation in general. In particular, it concerns the religious convictions of leading reformers such as Martin Luther and John Calvin and their followers. Each of the maps involved bear witness to a complex web of contracts which would have been at times covert, dangerous, even fanatical. Most of the books in which these maps first appeared offended the authorities, and many were outlawed and burned, thus accounting for the rarity of some of these early editions' (Delano Smith, 1987, 2). Although the first printed Bible with illustrations dates from 1455 (illustrated manuscript Bibles are much older, of course), the first map in a printed Bible dates from 1525. Both printed maps and illustrations in Bibles were created to mirror and complement the symbolism and imagery of the written text. The themes of pictures and maps were consistent over long periods of time, and embrace common themes, including the location of the Garden of Eden and the territories of the tribes of Israel. Maps dealing with religious themes accelerated in production with the invention of printing and with the increasing emphasis on the authority of the Bible at the Reformation, and many such maps were produced both within and outside Bibles through the seventeenth, eighteenth and nineteenth centuries.

Maps abound of the territories colonized by Britain and other European powers from the fifteenth century onwards, some giving only the barest of outlines, others, being associated with formal grants of land and permission to trade, give details of land allocations and settlements, such as the 1635 map of Bermuda drawn by W. and J. Blaeu (Fig. 4.3), showing division into the land allocations and territories of Bermuda, which was colonized in 1612 by charter of the Virginia Company, and over which the British Crown took control in 1684.

Estate maps

The mapping of the extent and make-up of landed estates in both old and new worlds is of particular interest to the historical geographer, as is the progress made in the mapping of urban areas. The history of estate mapping in Britain is fairly well known. Estate maps in England actually date, though in very small number, from about the early fourteenth century, but increase in number after

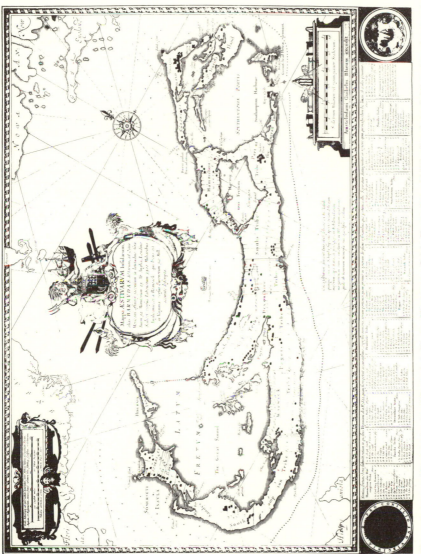

Fig. 4.3 *Map of Bermuda, by W. and J. Blaeu (Theatrum Orbis Terrarum, 1635) showing division into the land allocations and territories of Bermuda, which was colonized in 1612 by charter of the Virginia Company, and the British Crown took control in 1684*

1550 as a result of major improvements in the techniques of land surveying, and the increased need for maps to facilitate the disposal and sale of church lands because of the dissolution of the monasteries, the beginnings of change from open-field to enclosed-field farming systems, various other forms of land improvement including drainage, and major changes in landownership during the periods of the Commonwealth and the Restoration in the seventeenth century (Harley, 1972, 23). Many of the early estate surveyors became famous for county and national maps, such as Norden, and Saxton. The high point of estate mapping was in the period from 1700 to 1850, largely on account of the dramatic changes occurring in the countryside and the town through the general impact of growing capitalist relations of production and such specific processes as the consolidation of strips and the enclosure of open fields, the leasing of land, and land improvement through various kinds of reclamation of fen and heath. The estate maps are most often at quite large scales, between about 1:6336 and 1:1600, and indicate landownership, land use, and some-times land quality, often by employment of colour shading or various kinds of symbol. Together with the terriers or written details which accompany them, such estate maps have been a major source of evidence for studies by historical geographers and others of changes in the English countryside in the late medieval and early modern periods. Where sequences of detailed maps are available, the evolution of rural settlements and related economies can be built up in great detail, as in the case of several major studies of the famous open-field village of Laxton in Nottinghamshire (Orwin and Orwin, 1938; Beckett, 1989), and in Yates' (1960) study of the parishes of South Harting and Rogate in north-west Sussex, using, *inter alia*, maps from 1632, 1652 and 1694.

The history of production of estate maps in Scotland, Ireland and Wales has a somewhat different chronology from that of England, especially before the eighteenth century. Ireland was the subject of various attempts at colonial 'plantation' by settlers, on land appropriated from the Irish inhabitants by the English Crown, in the sixteenth and seventeenth centuries, and a number of surveys of the planted lands provide some basic information on topography and land use, though the number and quality of estate maps as such is low and poor for Ireland in this period. Some impressions of landscape and human modification thereof is to be had from such sources as the maps drawn for the Leix and Offaly plantation of 1556 and the Munster plantation of 1586, the Barthelet maps for the military campaigns in Ulster, the plantation maps of Ulster in the early seventeenth century, the Strafford survey of Connaught of 636–40, and the maps of Sir William Petty's Down Survey of 1654–59. (Andrews, 1961; 1962; 1985). The estates of Ireland were extensively mapped in the eighteenth and the nineteenth century, both for the purposes of land management and of land sales (Andrews, 1985). The Scottish experience involved a similar combination of mapping and survey for military and control purposes and the provision of map data for estate management. Early topographic maps similar to those produced in England by Speed were produced for Scotland by Pont in the late sixteenth century, and edited and republished in the seventeenth century. There are no extensive estate surveys in Scotland until the eighteenth century: in the early years English surveyors were employed by the large landowners, but later in the century an indigenous tradition of surveying developed as estates were improved and reorganized, and large numbers of estate maps and plans for the eighteenth and nineteenth centuries are extant (Whyte and Whyte, 1981). A major cartographic information source for the mid-eighteenth century is the Military Survey of Scotland, undertaken from 1747 to 1755, and the consequent Roy map, named after William Roy, the surveyor who undertook its production. The surveying started in the Highlands in the aftermath of the 1745 rebellion, for the specific purpose of providing a cartographic information basis for the establishment of military forts and posts and the building of roads, but ultimately covered the whole of mainland Scotland. The scale of the map is approximately 1:36,000, and includes in variable detail settlements, place-names, land use, woodland and relief. Its accuracy is greater in respect of some features than others, and there are problems of omissions, leading to the statement by Whittington and Gibson (1986, 61) that it 'is at one of the most intriguing and at the same time infuriating documents available to the researcher into Scotland's past landscapes'. The Highland clearances in the nineteenth century were the cause of production of maps, albeit of doubtful accuracy.

Welsh estate maps also increased in number during the second half of the eighteenth century.

Estate and cadastral maps are common for most European countries in the period from the sixteenth century onwards. Sweden has a wealth of cadastral maps for this period, especially as a result of the extensive surveys of the seventeenth century. Baigent (1990) has outlined the history of Swedish cadastral mapping in the period 1628–1700, related to the foundation of the national survey board at the time of Gustav II and a period of consolidation at home and expansion abroad. The purpose of the surveys initiated in 1628 was to examine the country's potential for development and improvement. Two types of maps, 'geographical' and 'geometrical', were produced, the former small-scale topographic and the latter large-scale cadastral maps. This mapping tradition continued in Sweden into the eighteenth and nineteenth centuries, connected with, for example, the reorganization of village lands through a series of enclosure movements.

The mapping of France

The history of topographic and cadastral mapping in France is an important part of the assessment of the availability and utility of maps as data sources for the historical geography of that country. The origins of 'modern' cartography in France dates from the seventeenth century, particularly on account of the interest of Louis XIV, who came to power in 1661, and his minister Jean-Baptiste Colbert, who initiated a survey of France in 1663 which required the production, among other things, of geodetic maps. The advancement of mapping techniques in France was effected by the foundation in 1666 of the Académie Royale des Sciences, which was asked in 1668 to facilitate the production of accurate maps for Colbert's survey, and by the formation of military and civil associations of 'ingénieurs géographes' (Crone, 1978, 85), though the production of national and local maps had made little progress by the time of Colbert's death in 1683. The establishment of accurate meridians and the detailed mapping of the whole of France, took time, and was largely carried out by the Cassini family, who completed the triangulation and first national map survey of France in 1744, and a second major survey was completed in 1788. The first survey resulted in a map of France of 18 sheets, the second, more detailed survey, in a map of 118 sheets at a scale of 1:86,400 (Konvitz, 1987, 16). The details of human settlement and occupation are more satisfactory than the unsophisticated topographic detail.

The broader context of mapping in France in the seventeenth and eighteenth centuries is interesting, for it demonstrates the changing perception of space and its control. Sahlins (1990) has shown that from the seventeenth century onwards there were in France changing ideas of territory and its delimitation, starting with an imagined bounded and unified national space in the seventeenth century, characterized by jurisdictional sovereignty rather than coherent territory, and often delimited by natural boundaries such as rivers and mountains, even sometimes invented for the purpose:

> Mountain ranges and sometimes rivers duplicated, if they did not determine, the shape of dotted or dashed lines that distinguish both provinces and states. Such was the case among the many seventeenth-century map-makers, including Nicolas Sanson (1600–1667), 'the government's first official cartographer', and a highly successful publisher of commercial atlases. Sanson's cartography of state was not devoid of scientific techniques or contributions to the history of map-making. Yet, seduced by the idea of natural limits . . . he invented mountain ranges forming political boundaries where in fact there were none (Sahlins, 1990, 1428).

The notion of the importance of natural boundaries was enhanced in the eighteenth-century context of classical humanism the importance of using the boundaries of ancient Gaul, and reflected in the Cassini surveys of the late seventeenth and early eighteenth centuries, in which the mountain ranges of the south and east were important. There was a change of outlook in the later eighteenth and nineteenth centuries:

> In the eighteenth century, the image of natural boundaries lost its bellicose and historical resonance as the idea became part of an enlightened programme of political reform, itself brought on by the international weakness of France. The French Revolution preserved the Enlightenment interpretation while politicizing natural frontiers and created—in the context of France's expansionist Rhineland policy—a political programme and an ideological doctrine. Finally, in the nineteenth century, the idea was reinterpreted as a symbol of national unity reconciling the principles of monarchy and republic, and was widely diffused among a growing middle-class reading public, especially as it regained a militaristic connotation between the two world wars (Sahlins, 1990, 1450–1).

Maps and surveys of Latin America

The Spanish and Portuguese colonization of Central and South America has yielded a wealth of evidence for the geographical contexts of that colonization, including the very detailed *Relaciones Geográficas* or *Relaciones de Indias*, reports to the Spanish Crown, dating from the late sixteenth century, resulting from edicts for the answering of very specific questionnaires which were designed to to assist in the development of policy for government of these remote colonies (Edwards, 1975), as well as a range of maps of estates and newly planted towns. The *Relaciones Geográficas* derive from the needs of the

Spanish Crown to find a way of assimilating the new colonial territories into the Spanish imperial system and provide for both change and continuity from and with indigenous social and production systems, and therefore the need for detailed information about these areas, and it was obtained by frequent questionnaires and inquiries, often addressed to the more educated members of communities. The earliest examples are the regional surveys commissioned by Cortés in 1522–23, and these were followed by descriptions of provinces required by the Crown from the priors of Dominican and Franciscan mon-asteries, the *Suma de Visitas* of 1548–50, the responses to a very complex questionnaire of 1604 sent to civil magistrates, individual descriptions of mid-seventeenth century, and major surveys of the eighteenth century resulting from royal 'cedulas' (edicts) of 19 July 1741 and of 20 October 1776 (the *Relaciones Topográficas*), for example (Gerhard, 1972). The information in these sources varies, of course, but the most detailed contain information on topography, geology, climate, flora and fauna, history, population size, native customs, languages and dress, rural and urban settlement characteristics, religion, economy and communications. They have to be treated critically, of course, and compared with other sources wherever possible to attempt a determination of their accuracy and reliability. The meanings of individual technical descriptive words need to be more fully understood (Robinson, 1972). The *Relaciones* have been used by geographers and historians in the reconstruction of the geography of the Spanish Empire in Central and South America (Cline, 1964; Gerhard, 1972; Edwards, 1975; Donkin, 1985), but very much more work on this type of data source remains to be done.

The Widening of the Ranges of Evidence used by Historical Geographers

One of the most interesting and encouraging aspects of historical geography at present is the indication of a significant extension of types of evidence used in relation to the reconstruction of the past, this feature reflecting a more liberal and imaginative approach to and the asking of a wider range of questions about the past. Evidence from newspapers, personal diaries, travel accounts, literacy and educational records, paintings, poetry, oral evidence, records of trade unions and agricultural societies and cooperatives, business records, farm accounts, architectural styles and landscape designs, and increasing emphasis on gender perspectives, indicate interesting possibilities for further research and study, both from a qualitative and a quantitative perspective.

5

The Reconstruction of Physical Environments

Introduction

The reconstruction of the physical and ecological environments within which successive phases of human occupance took place, and which were subject to major phases of modification by, for example, woodland and forest clearing, changes in drainage, and the establishment of settlements and networks of communications, is a long tradition in the field of historical geography. Of particular importance in the pioneering phase of historical geography in the earlier part of the twentieth century was the reconstruction of prehistoric environments, a reflection in part of the practice of historical geography in relatively recently colonized territories and of a close connection with archaeology and anthropology. This tradition of reconstruction of early environments has continued, and is closely linked with scientific expertise in both archaeology and anthropology and various aspects of physical geography and environmental science.

The broad conceptual and methodological context within which such work has been carried out is that of a clear notion of a strong symbiotic relation between human occupancy and environmental change. Three main aspects will be emphasized here: firstly, the reconstruction of prehistoric, primitive landscapes, or 'urlandschaften'; secondly, the various ways in which natural environments have been modified through human action; and thirdly, the way in which perceptions of environment have conditioned that human action. Each of these aspects is not confined to studies by historical geographers: there is much of value to be found in the work of physical geographers, archaeologists, historians, ethnologists and anthropologists, and environmental scientists.

'Urlandschaften'

The term 'urlandschaft' is a German word meaning primitive or prehistoric landscape, and entered into the geographical literature partly through the work of the German geographer, Gradmann (1865–1950). Gradmann worked within the late nineteenth century German tradition of the science of landscape studies, which often involved a sequence of topics followed in specific regional studies, starting with the physical environment and then proceeding to the various sequences of human settlement and economic activity. His two major studies were his work on the original plant geography of the Swabian Alps of south Germany (Gradmann 1898; 1901), from which came his 'steppenheide' theory about the relationships between vegetation types and Neolithic colonization (see Chapter 2). He also published a survey of the 'urlandschaft' of Palestine (Gradmann, 1934). Parallel later work of this kind, though related to a particular cultural perspective of the geography of early human habitation, is to be found extensively in the work of Sauer, the American geographer. From a German family in Missouri, and schooled in Württemberg near the Schwarzwald in southern Germany, Sauer, who was more fully cognisant than most of his contemporaries of the important work by German human geographers, especially the anthropogeographic work of Ratzel, on the analysis of historic changes in landscape, had particularly admired and defended Gradmann's work *Süddeutschland* (1931), and was very much interested in the work of anthropologists, botanists, geologists and archaeologists (Williams, 1983, 4, 7). He saw what he described as the cultural landscape as having been constructed from the natural landscape, and it was the early interface between human habitation and natural landscape, particularly vegetation, that was of continuing interest. Such works as 'The morphology of landscape' (1925), 'A geographic sketch of early man in America' (1944), *Man and Nature: Early America Before the Days of the White Men* (1939), 'Foreword to historical geography' (1941a). 'The personality of Mexico' (1941b), 'A geographic sketch of early man in America' (1944) and *The Early Spanish Main* (1966) are good examples of the method and materials used by Sauer in the reconstruction of early primitive environments. One of the best examples of the reconstruction of early environments, which had attracted the attention of Sauer as a model for his own work, was Fox's *Personality of Britain* (1932). This particular work, which was to have a profound influence on the thinking of a whole generation of pioneer human and historical geographers and archaeologists, owed more than a little to the input and ideas of a young Welsh geographer Bowen and to the work of Crawford of the Ordnance Survey (Thomas, 1985, 21; Crawford, 1922). It was part of an era of extensive study, through distribution maps, of the relations between environmental conditions and the evolution of human settlement (Goudie, 1976). The main thesis of Fox's book relates to the importance of natural environment, especially the division between highland and lowland Britain, in the analysis of the distribution of prehistoric sites. Mapping was very much of the essence of this work, especially the patterns of vegetation and other areas of environmental difficulty such as marsh and fen (see Fig. 5.1) that faced the iron and bronze traders at the dawn of the Iron Age (500–400 BC in Fox's reckoning).

A parallel development in the attempted mapping of aspects of prehistoric environment in Britain was that of Wilcox (1933), with her production of a map of the prehistoric woodlands and marshlands of England. In his preface to the work, Roxby, professor of geography at the University of Liverpool and a pioneer worker in the field of historical geography, states that 'The reconstruction of primitive conditions of vegetation is a need which constantly confronts workers in the field of historical and regional geography and indeed of archaeology, and it is hoped that the two maps and accompanying text may be of real value to many students and teachers' (Roxby, 1933, 5). The two maps

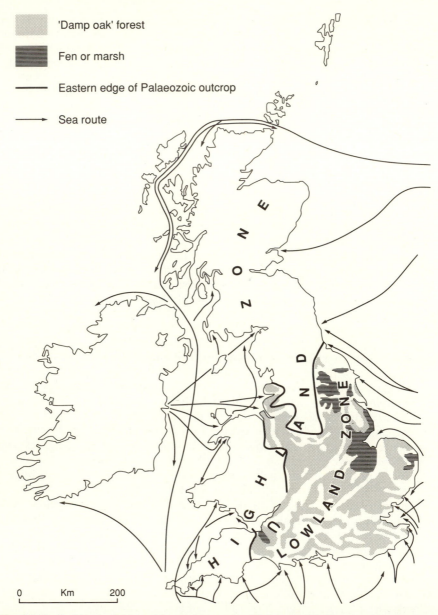

Fig. 5.1 *Sir Cyril Fox's division of the environments of Britain into Highland and Lowland zones in relation to prehistoric colonization. Source: Fox,* The Personality of Britain *(1932, opposite 28)*

were of the woodlands and marshlands of prehistoric England (map A) and of 'early' England (map B), and were intended to yield correlations with other facets of prehistoric and early geography, particularly sites of human activity. While Fox drew heavily on the pioneering work of such palaeobotanists as Tansley and Godwin, Wilcox, while noting the broad principles which underpinned Tansley's work, attempted to map vegetation *de novo* using climatic, topographic, and geological evidence. The influence of this type of work on the thinking of early historical geographers in Britain was quite profound and evident, seen, for example, in the extensive referencing and use of Fox's *Personality of Britain* in the chapter on 'The peopling of the land' in Mitchell's seminal and still attractive short work *Historical Geography* (1954), and the chapters by Bowen ('Introductory background: prehistoric south Britain') and by Wooldridge, a physical geographer, on 'The Anglo-Saxon settlement' in Darby's edited volume, *An Historical Geography of England Before AD 1800* (Darby, 1936). Langton (1986; 1988) has drawn attention to the significance of this human ecology approach, characterized by the Aberystwyth school of geography and anthropology and its links with archaeology.

The problems of reconstruction of physical background may also be seen in those major historical works which set the scene for the play of the major events of history by describing the geographical background in detail, what Prince (1971, 6) describes as studies in 'géohistoire', one of the most notable of which, perhaps, is Braudel's magisterial narrative study of the Mediterranean world in the age of Philip II. Braudel states in his introduction to Part One ('The role of the environment') of the first volume:

> Even if there had been more properly dated information available, it would have been unsatisfactory to restrict our enquiries entirely to a study of human geography between the years 1550–1600—even one undertaken in the doubtful pursuit of determinist explanation. Since in fact we have only incomplete accounts of the period, and these have not been systematically classified by historians—material plentiful enough it is true, but insufficient for our purpose—the only possible course, in order to bring this brief moment of the Mediterranean to life, between 1550 and 1600, out of the shadows, was to make full use of evidence, images and landscapes dating from other periods, earlier and later and even from the present day. The resulting picture is one in which all the evidence combines across time and space, to give us a history in slow motion from which permanent values can be detected. Geography in this context is no longer an end in itself but a means to an end (Braudel, 1972 edition, 23).

This is not to say that Braudel's reconstruction of the geohistorical environment of the Mediterranean is without its flaws. One recent critic has drawn attention to Braudel's neglect in *The Mediterranean* of a number of key works by French and German geographers on the Mediterranean environment that were available at the time of writing, and the absence of reference to the work of Spanish and Italian geographers. These geographical lacunae, contends Péguy, are not entirely accidental (Péguy, 1986, 78). One tendency of this geohistorical approach is to assume relatively few, if any, major changes in the physical environs of the region studied throughout the period concerned, and an apparent view that a general statement about the broad features of the physical geography of the region is a sufficient introduction to its historical geography. The chapter by Diarra, on the physical aspects of the historical geography of Africa in the methodological and prehistory volume of the UNESCO *General History of Africa* (Diarra, 1981), is an example of the problem, for it contains primarily an account of the physical geography of modern Africa, with virtually no attempt, even in summary, to describe past climatic and biotic changes and variations.

Most of the recent attempts, at least on a large scale, to reconstruct environmental conditions at times of 'early' settlement tend to be for times of pioneer European settlement in various parts of the New Worlds from the sixteenth century onwards, mainly because of the relative wealth of documentary evidence in the form of early travellers' and explorers' accounts and official surveys and maps. Watts, in his extensive study of patterns of development, culture, and environmental change in the West Indies since 1492, reconstructs in great detail in the first two chapters of his book, the 'complicated, multi-facetted and yet very vulnerable environmental milieu of the West Indies' (Watts, 1987, 41) as experienced by aboriginal and European settlers, as evidenced by the early accounts of Spanish settlers and the archaeological record, the latter in particular affording a basis for retrospective views of the environmental and cultural milieux of what are termed palaeo- and meso-indians, whose cultures date back to 5000 BC. It is interesting, and worthy of note, that this fine example of the reconstruction of early or primitive environs is a continuation, as also is Harris's research, both of the early environs of the Leeward Islands and Venezuela and of the general problems of plant domestication (Harris, 1965; 1967; 1971; 1984) of the approach and influence of the Sauer 'school' of cultural geography at Berkeley (Watts, 1987, xx) which, as with the British work on prehistoric geography and environment discussed above, very much operated at an interface with archaeology and anthropology.

Another example of the reconstruction of early environments is found in the maps (Plate 17) and text on ecological regions *c.* 1500 in the *Historical Atlas of Canada* (Harris, 1988), the basic classification being into large-scale ecological provinces and smaller-scale ecological regions (see Fig. 5.2).

Of similar but chronologically later ilk is Heathcote's (1975) mapping and analysis of the ecosystems of Australia in 1770, comprising the coastal reefs and marshes, the rainforests, the schlerophyll forests, the woodlands, and shrublands, the grasslands, the deserts, and the alpine ecosystem.

A most useful synthesis of the early environs and inhabitants of North America is contained in Butzer's study of the Indian legacy in the American landscape, which includes a series of informative maps of the ice, lake, steppe parkland and forest environments of palaeoindian America (12,000–9000 BP), of Indian settlement in late prehistoric and European contact times, and of patterns of Indian subsistence in Euro-American contact times (from the sixteenth to the nineteenth century) (Butzer, 1990). A major role is afforded, especially in the period 8000–3000 BP, to environmental change, which effected increased regional differentiation through, for example, reductions in the complexity of vegetation on the Great Plains during the change from glacial to non-glacial environments, the disappearance of the large pluvial lakes from the south-west, and increased aridity in the Mississippi Basin. The importance of environmental change to early societies, and therefore the vital necessity for development of sophisticated methods for environmental reconstruction, is properly and appropriately emphasized by Butzer in relation to North America, but is equally applicable elsewhere (1990, 31):

The potential role of environmental change at the end of the Ice Age and

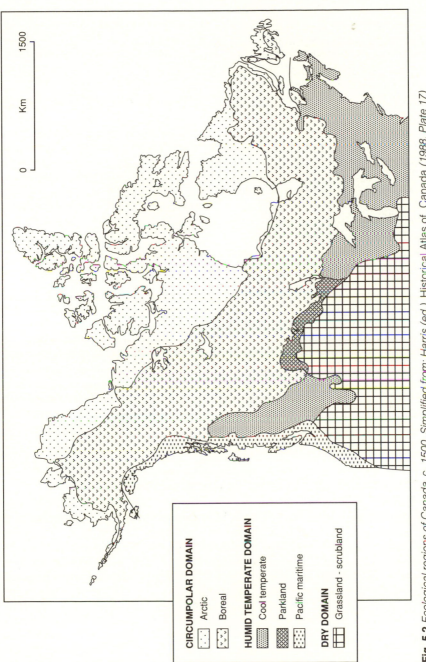

Fig. 5.2 *Ecological regions of Canada, c. 1500. Simplified from: Harris (ed.), Historical Atlas of Canada (1988, Plate 17)*

CIRCUMPOLAR DOMAIN
Arctic
Boreal

HUMID TEMPERATE DOMAIN
Cool temperate
Parkland
Pacific maritime

DRY DOMAIN
Grassland - scrubland

0   Km   1500

during post-glacial times has not been widely appreciated. The shift from a glacial to a non-glacial environment on the Great Plains greatly reduced the complexity of the open vegetation, in favour of a more monotonous grassland with fewer plant species and specialized environments, while the faunas indicate that post-glacial climate was, contrary to expectations, more continental, despite higher temperatures. Accelerated aeolian sedimentation has been verified on the High Plains about 8000 to 4500 BP, contributing perhaps to the demise of the palaeoindian way of life and probably explaining the limited archaeological record for the Early and Middle Archaic in this area.

Butzer has developed this theme extensively within the conceptual framework of cultural ecology, as applied to prehistoric and historic cultural environmental relationships and to contemporary situations (Butzer, 1982; 1989), identifying the roots of cultural ecology in late nineteenth- and early twentieth-century German attempts to integrate research in physical and human geography and in Marsh's work on human influences on the environment, and stressing the complexity of the relationships and the necessity for interdisciplinary work towards the solution of the key problems. The range of scientific techniques for the reconstruction of a variety of aspects of prehistoric or primitive environments is very wide, and it is unnecessary to attempt to describe them in substantial detail, but it is important for historical geographers to have a working notion of the range of techniques available and of their potential application to historical research. Their significance derives from the fact that they make possible surprisingly accurate reconstructions of past environs and climatic conditions and provide indices for evaluation of human impact over time. In many cases there is overlap with documentary and artefact evidence, and interdisciplinary studies employing this multiplicity of perspectives are becoming more frequent. Curiously, in some respects, there is closer linkage at present between archaeology and environmental history—as practised by physical geographer and geologists—than there is between historical geography and these specialists, though there are some signs of improvement (Wagstaff, 1987; Dodgshon, 1988, Petts *et al.*, 1989).

Techniques of Environmental Reconstruction

Summaries of the basic techniques of environmental reconstruction are contained in methodological treatises by historical geographers, by Jäger (1969), for example, in his book *Historische Geographie*, at greater length in his volume on European cultural landscapes (Jäger, 1987), and by Hooke and Kain (1982) in their guide to sources and techniques for studying historical change in the physical environment. Techniques for the reconstruction of physical environments involve palaeoecological methods which permit reconstruction through the use of fossil organisms including animal bones, beetles, palynology or pollen analysis, palaeolimnological indicators such as diatoms, and a range of geological, palaeoclimatic and geo-archaeological methods, dendrochronology, varved sediment analysis, and lichenometry (Roberts, 1989).

Micro- and macro-flora and fauna

Palynology, or the analysis of pollen grains preserved at particular sites, is an important and dominant feature of palaeoecological reconstruction. The basis of this method is the assumption, subject to certain important major qualifications about the differing propensities of plants to release different quantities of pollen, of different media and sites to preserve it, and processes of sorting and transportation, that the nature and relative proportion of pollen grains and spores found in site samples partly reflects the vegetation complex at and in the vicinity of the site, and that changes in the proportions of particular plants and species through time are indicative of climatic change and also of change induced by human impact. While the examination of fossil plant remains, including seeds, in peat bogs goes back to at least the early nineteenth century, the first calculations of relative percentages of pollen types date from the early twentieth century, when the Swedish state geologist Von Post lectured to Scandinavian scientists on the subject in 1916, and since that time pollen analysis has been the primary method for examination of vegetation sequences and climatic changes in the late Quaternary period (Faegri and Iversen, 1975). This early work was taken up by major scientists such as Iversen and Godwin, with the emphasis in Europe from the 1940s to the 1960s having been on areas of north, west and central Europe which were intensively occupied in prehistoric and early historic times and therefore on the subject of human-induced changes in vegetation, but more recently European scientists have shown more interest in marginal areas of less intensive occupation. Additional technical innovations in the 1960s and 1970s included the adoption of absolute pollen frequency techniques, the use of modern pollen samples as comparators for fossil pollen, and the use of multivariate analytical techniques (Birks and Birks, 1980).

Pollen is obtained, as is much field evidence of environmental change, by sampling cores from field sites, often from peat bogs or lake sites that have preserved the pollen in good condition and have continuous records of accumulation, and after laboratory processing the individual grains can be classified and counted, and pollen diagrams constructed showing change through time of the various groups selected. The diagrams show the relative percentages of pollen from the various species relative to the total amounts in the sample, and a distinction is made between tree and non-tree pollen. The whole process is very complex, and is greatly simplified in this brief account. The pollen record provides relative scales of change through time, but specific dates can only be obtained by recourse to carbon-14 or other dating methods, including reference to documentary evidence. In addition to these plant microfossils, visible plant macrofossils, including seeds, are important evidences of change. An example of the plotting of pollen data into a diagram is given in Fig. 5.3, which shows a human-agency clearance phase in south-west Turkey from 3500 BP to about 1500 BP, which in the vegetation sequence was succeeded by a dominance of pine forest (Roberts, 1989, 140).

Fossil fauna can also be used for environmental reconstruction, including coleoptera (beetles), gastropods and molluscs (land snails), whose physiological sensitivity to changes in environment, including temperature, enables them to be classified and used as indicators of local changes in environment. The analytical use of micro-fauna such as diatoms, tiny algae with silica shells,

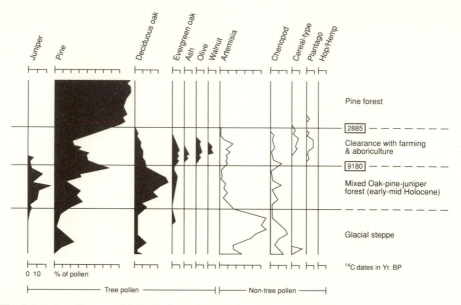

Fig. 5.3 *Pollen diagram, Sögüt, Turkey, showing the clearance phase. Source: Roberts (1989, 140)*

occupies an important role in the study of environmental change, for diatoms, which are found in a very wide range of environmental habitats are very sensitive indicators of ecological contexts, including climate (Roberts, 1989, 173). As with the case of pollen, the mode of retrieval and analysis is generally via the taking of sediment cores, sampling, and the use of high-powered microscopes for identification. Ecological indicators of natural and human-induced change in major rivers and lakes includes diatom frustules, algal pigments cladoceran (microscopic crustacean) and chironomid (insect group, for example mayfly) remains (Amoros and Van Urk, 1989).

Morphological methods, including erosion studies and palaeohydrology

Changes in the rates of activity of processes of, for example, erosion and deposition of rocks and sediments and in consequence the complex and often partly fossil landforms which they produce have been extensively studied by physical geographers, and a substantial body of theory and case studies is available which can be of considerable value to the historical geographer seeking to correlate and associate human activity with features and processes of environmental change.

Regional associations of geomorphic processes and associated changes in landforms and sediments can be identified and used as bases for the study of human-related environmental change, such as the different processes of erosion and sedimentation associated with lacustrine, fluvial, coastal marine, aeolian, glacial and mass movement geomorphic regimes. Some regimes, such as those associated with lacustrine and aeolian processes, can be very sensitive indicators of climatic change: in the case of lakes, the complex evidence of shoreline changes, together with lithological evidence from lake sediments, can provide not only direct evidence of the effects of climatic change on the lakes themselves but also evidence of major regional or even global changes in climate (Roberts, 1989, 30–7; Gregory, 1977).

A study by Thornes of the palaeoecology of hillslope erosion, particularly of the role of vegetative cover (Thornes, 1987), stresses the crucial links between this set of processes and anthropogenic and climatic change, especially the possibility offered of dating sites and sediments and of assessing the constraints within which prehistoric agriculture operated. Vegetation acted as a control or brake on soil erosion, was effected by climatic change and also by human and animal action, especially clearing.

Major contributions to environmental reconstruction have been made in the field of palaeohydrological river investigation. In an important study of valley alluviation in south-western Wisconsin, Knox (1972) has linked the three distinct river valley sedimentary sequences in the region to three phases of change. The lowest sequence, a base unit of coarse-textured debris is ascribed to a bedload sediment of a channel active near the end of a mid-Holocene drought *c.* 6000 BP. The second sequence is a silty clay series covering the first, and is ascribed to vertical accretion on a floodplain during more humid conditions of the late Holocene. The top sequence comprises laminated loam sediments, explained by reference to destruction of natural vegetation for cultivation of uplands and valley sides since about 1830, a process which has increased the size and frequency of peak discharges with consequent losses of sediment from the surface of cultivated fields. Additional factors have been the erosion of waste from mining activities and the denudation of construction site surfaces. A study of the effects of removal of forest cover on erosion rates in southern Michigan was carried out by Davis (1976), based on Frains Lake near Ann Arbor. Using what she describes as an 'historical approach', that is 'comparing the rate of sediment accumulation in a small lake during primeval time, when the landscape was forested, with the accumulation rate during the last 146 years, when the land has been used as farmland' (Davis, 1976, 139), the effect of human settlement is shown by a ten-fold increase (over the lake as a whole, but thirty-fold increase in the centre) in mineral materials in the sediment, indicating increased erosion from the watershed. The main technique used was the plotting of the ash-weight of sediment, but other techniques used in this type of study also include estimates from coring, analysis of chemical constituents of sediments, and analysis of the remains of phytoplankton.

Perhaps the most significant aspect of palaeohydrological studies for historical geographers are those which are concerned with the ways in which channel form, flow rates and sedimentation rates reflect human activity in catchment areas. In addition to the above studies, there are many collections of palaeohydrological research publications which offer a wealth of examples from different parts of the world (Gregory, 1977; Gregory, 1983; Petts *et al.*, 1989; Starkel *et al.*, 1991). In a short history of the forms of river regulation in western Europe Petts (1989, 5) illustrates the changes in forms of human interference, starting with weirs for water power and river improvements for navigation in the thirteenth and fourteenth centuries, continuing with flood-control systems and the development of the science of hydraulics and river regulation in the sixteenth century, major channelling and floodplain reclamation in the eighteenth century, extensive floodplain reclamation in the nineteenth century and major impacts via hydroelectric and river regulation dams in the twentieth century. Midel and Raukas (1991, 377) have reviewed the evidence for changes in river systems in the East Baltic region, and concluded, in relation to the Subatlantic period (2500 BP to the present) that 'The time when the human impact first influenced the hydrological river regime has not yet been precisely dated, although it is known that the first dams were built on rivers by as early as the thirteenth century. The greatest changes were due to a wide-scale land reclamation in the nineteenth century, which increased in the post-war years'.

The distinct possibility exists for major interdisciplinary research on human interaction with river catchments and regimes, using documentary and environmental evidence, and it would be encouraging to see historical geographers and palaeohydrologists taking a lead in such projects, which could focus on a range of different scales.

Archaeological evidence

The archaeological evidence for prehistoric and early historical change in environment is a vast and complex topic, for which space here allows only a brief synthesis and series of indications of possible use. Human occupation of settlement sites and the use of near and distant areas for hunting, gathering, fishing, pastoralism and cultivation, has over long periods of time left a complex array of types of direct and indirect evidence of former occupation. These include: human and animal remains, the former frequently though not always in ritual burial sites; a range of tools and artifacts, earthworks and stone structures related to ritual and to economic activity; the remains of cultivated plants and weeds preserved in their original form or indicated by pollen grains; and a range of geo-archaeological indicators of environmental modification. The extent, contents and contexts of sites of human occupation in the distant past, both individually and collectively, can be studied both by direct methods such as field investigation through excavation and by indirect methods such as remote sensing of various kinds. Sophisticated laboratory analysis of the artifacts and remains from archaeological sites allows for dating, classification by type and origin, the possibility of studies of the diffusion of economic practices and cultures, and the formulation and testing of models and hypotheses.

Dating techniques

Once an ancient environment is reconstructed in outline, using the techniques outlined above, attempts are made to establish relative and absolute chronologies of change. A wide array of dating or chronometric techniques is available, by use of radiocarbon or carbon-14, potassium-argon (with a date range from hundreds of thousands to several million years) and uranium series (used for time-periods over 125,000 years), palaeomagnetism, thermoluminescence, amino acid racemization, and the use of varves and dendrochronology.

The method of radiometric dating most commonly used in environmental reconstruction studies involves the use of the radioactive isotope carbon-14, which decays at a fixed rate, like most unstable isotopes, and which has a half-life (the time taken for half the original level of radioactivity to be reached by decay) of 5730+/−40 years. Carbon-14 is absorbed by most living organisms, and the decay of radioactivity sets in with the death of the organism, allowing dating to be made through measurement of radioactivity levels. Because of atmospheric contamination in industrialized countries, the method is only applicable for objects dating from before the middle of the nineteenth century AD, and complications can arise from other forms of contamination of the sample. Many dates have been obtained since the inauguration of this technique by Libby in Chicago in the 1940s, using a variety of media including wood, bone, shell, soil, charcoal, peat, and seeds, going back to 40,000 years before present.

Carbon-14 dating can be used in combination with a range of documentary and geochronological sources. It can be used, for example, in connection with dendrochronology and with palaeomagnetic dating—a technique employing the secular variations of magnetic alignments in samples such as fired clays or sedimentary deposits to construct regional geomagnetic curves. The basis of palaeomagnetic studies is the fact that iron oxides are present in significant quantities in the earth's crust and are 'among the most sensitive and ubiquitous indicators of environmental conditions and processes' (Oldfield, 1983, 141), and their measurement by various forms of magnetometer enables sophisticated reconstructions of, for example, the synchroneity of sediments in different catchment and lake systems.

Thermoluminescence involves the measurement of radiation created in, for example, the firing of pottery, and can also be used for dating sediments. Amino acid racemization involves the measurement of the ratios of different types of amino acid present in fossil organisms, especially the aspartic acid from bone, which has a half-life of 15,000 years, and can be used to date and measure temperature changes through time.

Dendrochronology is one of a number of relative dating techniques that relies on the evidence, in this case in the trunks of trees, of rates of growth. The study of the growth rings of trees dates back to prehistoric classical times, but the main scientific understanding of their implications has occurred in the twentieth century, initiated in 1901 by the study by an American, Douglass, of the correlation between tree-ring data and sunspot cycles, leading later to his correlation of tree-ring data with the archaeological evidence of early Indian settlements in Arizona. The width of the annual tree-growth rings reflects environmental fluctuations and a count of the number of rings enables the age of the tree to be determined. Broad rings reflect favourable, and narrow rings unfavourable climatic growth conditions, and the patterning of these can be used as indicators of climatic change. The technique is not only applicable to living trees, but to dead wood in various conditions, and this allows for linkages or cross-dating between various types of wood, including the wood from ancient structures, and uncrushed charcoal. The pioneer work in Arizona was mainly on the record of the bristlecone pine, which can live to nearly 5000 years and has allowed chronologies of up to 5400 years to be established, but other tree species, notably oak, have been used elsewhere. These chronologies can be related to carbon-14 dates, and of course, to written accounts for historic time, and are extensively employed by archaeologists in studies of regions and particular sites.

Lichenometry involves the measurement of the size of lichens growing on various media, there being a relationship between their size and age because they are assumed to grow at a constant rate. This technique allows for the dating of natural features such as glaciers and river channels and also of features of human construction such as walls and houses.

Climatic change

Of the fact that there have been major changes in the climate of the world in the past, with major local variations, and with major impact on human habitation and environment, there is no doubt. It is important, therefore, for the historical geographer, whether researching on events in the remote and distant past or in more recent times, to have sufficient knowledge of the major and minor changes in climate which affected the area of research. Broadly speaking, the major changes that have affected the earth since the time of the earliest human habitation (that is from the time of the late Pliocene and the Pleistocene Ice Age, the Pleistocene era lasting about 2,500,000 years until the Holocene period, which began about 10,000 years ago) have included five colder periods of ice advance and glaciation during the Pleistocene when ice sheets and glaciers advanced in many parts of the world and indirectly affected the climate of many other areas, each of these separated by periods of interglacial warming and ice retreat, followed by a period of warming from the beginning of the Holocene up to about AD 1500 when there occurred what is generally known as the 'Little Ice Age' lasting to about 1850, when climatic warming occurred again. The specific contexts of human habitation history relate to the fact that although there were ape-like hominids in Africa before the Pleistocene, progress even to the level of Palaeololithic cultures was slow, with modern *homo sapiens* appearing in the last glacial period about 40,000 years ago. By about 20,000 years ago, ice covered much of Canada and Europe, and Palaeolithic cultures existed in Europe, Australia, Asia, but much of the southern part of North America, and large areas of South America, were largely uninhabited, even though Palaeolithic people had reached the southern tip of South America. The earliest phase of habitation by hominids had involved East and southern Africa, followed by southern Asia and Europe, thence with later expansion in Australia and New Guinea, and the use of the Bering Strait land bridge in the case of North America, both facilitated by low sea levels. The final major phase of colonization stems from the warmer period of the Holocene, when settlement took place around the Greenland and north Canadian ice sheets, on the Mediterranean islands, the islands of the eastern Pacific, Madagascar, and New Zealand (Roberts, 1989, 55–6). The advancement through the complex and regionally varied cultural stages of the Megalithic, Neolithic, Bronze Age and Iron Age, sometimes through diffusion, sometimes through parallel developments in different sites, is a very complicated story which is still being researched, and requires a detailed scrutiny of the archaeological literature, which cannot be provided here.

During the late prehistoric and historic periods the fluctuations of climate on larger and particularly smaller scales remain of importance in the understanding of the history of human settlement and environmental change. The major fluctuation in climate is thought to have been that of what has been called the 'Little Ice Age'. Some have dated its onset from about 1500, others earlier, from about 1200–1400, and its termination in the nineteenth or twentieth centuries. This climatic worsening of the late Middle Ages seems to have been accompanied, according to Lamb (1977, 449), 'by shifts of the zones of most cyclonic activity as the polar cap and circumpolar vortex expanded, and . . . in the seventeenth century seems to have produced a world-wide cold stage . . . this particular climatic change was probably a change for the worst for most people in most places. The only exceptions are the change towards more moisture for crops and pasture detected in the drier parts of the southern United States and, apparently, in the thirteenth century in central Asia'. Lamb's view of this era is that the Little Ice Age lasted from about 1550–1850, with an intense period from 1550–1700. Recent critiques and re-evaluations of the concept, originally developed from documentary records and the obvious experiences of advance of European Alpine glaciers, conspicuously in the eighteenth and nineteenth centuries, have suggested greater complexity of experience on a global scale. The review by Bradley and Jones (1992), for example, suggests that the last 500 years have not, on a global scale, experienced a consistently cold Little Ice Age, for certain intervals were colder than others, the coldest periods varied chronologically between regions, and there were also seasonal anomalies between regions. The experience was, inevitably, varied and complex. The fact seem to be emerging that in Europe the seventeenth and the nineteenth centuries were cold, but that the sixteenth and eighteenth centuries were relatively warm. Also: 'In eastern Asia, the 17th century was the coldest period; the late 18th and early 19th century was also cold, but there is little evidence for persistent low temperatures throughout the 19th century, as in Europe . . . Southern Hemisphere records are consistent in showing the main period of negative anomalies occurred earlier than in the Northern Hemisphere, with widespread cool conditions in the 16th and 17th centuries' (Bradley and Jones, 1992, 659). Seasonal fluctuations in rainfall, amount of sunshine, intensity of storms and other phenomena, over short periods of time are of considerable importance in the study of, say, agricultural change, success and failure, conspicuously in regions of marginal agriculture and settlement. The occurrence of famine through time is of major significance (Le Roy Ladurie, 1972), not only in relation to the immediate effect at specific times on the people in the regions affected, but also in respect of longer-term trends of global warming and environmental dessication. Parry (1981) has examined the effects of climatic change in Britain and Ireland in the period AD 1300–1600 on the abandonment of marginal land in the upland regions, demonstrating the significant consequences for agriculture and livelihood of the climatic cooling of that period (see Fig. 5.4).

The efficacy of reconstructions of climatic change and its relationship with human settlement is partly, of course, dependent on the data and method-ologies involved. Some of the environmental indicators have already been mentioned above. To them may be added the evidence from ice cores for polar and high mountain regions, varved sediments for continents and some coastal basins, and the evidence of corals in tropical oceans. Documentary records are very important, but by definition are much more restricted in the period of time for which they are available. Bradley and Jones (1992) divide doc-umentary records of climatic change into three types: observational weather phenomena, records of weather-dependent natural phenomena, and pheno-logical records. The first type include weather observations, initially by amateurs and increasingly by scientific measurement. Early diaries giving

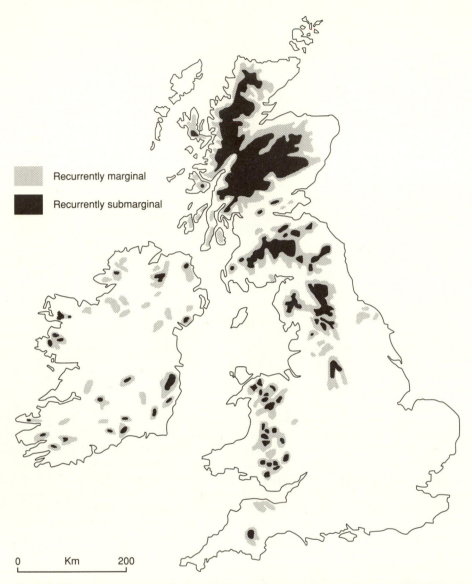

Recurrently marginal

Recurrently submarginal

0   Km   200

Fig. 5.4 *Changes in cultivation limits indicative of climatic change in Britain and Ireland, AD 1300–1600. Source: Parry (1981, 15)*

details of occurrence and amounts of rainfall or snowfall, or the onset of frost, for example, have been used in the reconstruction of weather patterns. Instrumental measurement of windspeed and rainfall by vane and gauge are of great antiquity, but newer instruments from the sixteenth and seventeenth centuries herald the beginning of scientific observation of climatic phenomena. Regular daily observations were made in Florence from 1654 to 1670, and were encouraged by the Royal Society in England from the late seventeenth century. Continuous records of weather observations exist for places in central, northern and western Europe from the eighteenth century (Lamb, 1977, 22–6). The second type of meteorological data source relates to what are sometimes known as parameteorological phenomena, that is to phenomena related to particular types of weather, for example floods, droughts, the dates and occurrences of the freezing-over of seas, lakes, and rivers. The third type, the phenological record, derives information from biological data and phenomena which reflect aspects of weather and weather change, including the dates of harvests, ripening of grain, flowering of trees, and the arrival of birds. The analysis of this type of data, much of which is highly subjective, including diaries, letters, estate records, government surveys, company records, and travellers' accounts, is difficult but rewarding. Content analysis may reveal items of importance. The information has to be subject to tests of reliability and accuracy, and needs, for wider pictures to be drawn, to be calibrated with other and more recent data sets. The problem of reconstruction of weather and climate is less difficult for the last 200 years, the main task being the verification of large meteorological observation data sets, but prior to this the problem is greater. Much advantage can be derived from the combined use of varied methods in reconstruction, combining, for example, the evidence of documentary texts dealing with settlement and farming with the evidence of glacial moraines, the pollen evidence from bogs and marshes, and carbon-14 dating.

Grove and Battagel (1981) have used an interesting combination of Norwegian tax and land rent records, moraine and glacier evidence and indications of other environmental hazards including landslides, rockfalls, avalanches, river erosion, and floods, as a basis for the study of Little Ice Age environmental and economic deterioration in the Sunnfjord Fogderi (a 'fogderi' was an administrative division) in western Norway for the period 1667–1815. They demonstrate, *inter alia*, that in the years 1740–60 the glaciers of the region reached their most advanced extents, and thereafter there was a slow retreat, but the effects of the glacier advance were evidenced most particularly in flooding, landslides and rockfalls (see Fig. 5.5), ruining the arable and pasture lands and initiating claims for tax relief from the farmers.

An interesting study of an unusual data source is Catchpole's (1992) use of the ships' log-books of the Hudson's Bay Company to derive indices of summer ice severity in Hudson Bay, Hudson Strait, and the western margin of the Labrador Sea. The log-book record extended from 1751 to 1870, and the records are relatively homogenous in form, providing a basis for ordinal data and thus for a ranking of the years covered according to the severity of summer ice.

Changes in sea levels, and the flooding of land

Changes in sea level, and the storminess of and extent of flooding of land by seas, are important factors in the consideration of the historical geography of coastal regions in particular. Changes in sea level in the past have either been of an 'isostatic' (related to movements of the earth's crust) or 'eustatic' kind (unrelated to crustal change). Sea levels have varied greatly through time in relation to variations in the quantities of water stored as ice and snow, the variation in ocean water volume according to temperature, tectonic changes,

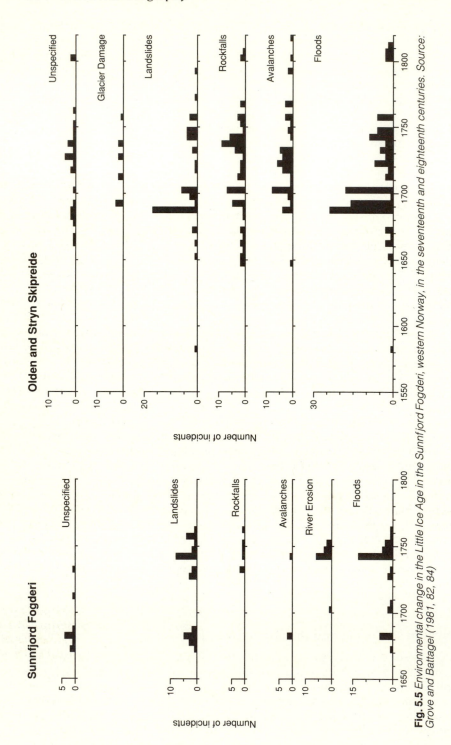

Fig. 5.5 *Environmental change in the Little Ice Age in the Sunnfjord Fogderi, western Norway, in the seventeenth and eighteenth centuries. Source: Grove and Battagel (1981, 82, 84)*

and in relation to variations in atmospheric pressure and wind speeds (Lamb, 1977, 112–13).

Within historical times the occurrence of floods caused by the sea has attracted the interests of historical geographers and historians of environmental change. Two principal causes are storm surges (the combination of high tides and strong onshore winds) and 'tsunami', tidal waves initiated by tectonic action under an ocean and which travel long distances, causing great damage in coastal regions. The records of such events are, prior to modern seismic and oceanographic recordings, subjective—in the form of personal accounts, descriptions of the damage done and loss of life effected, official studies of the extent of the damage, and statements of possible means of prevention of such effects by various means, including coastal defences.

Extensive studies have been undertaken of storm surges in the North Sea (Fig. 5.6), which indicate, for example, increases in intensity of storminess in

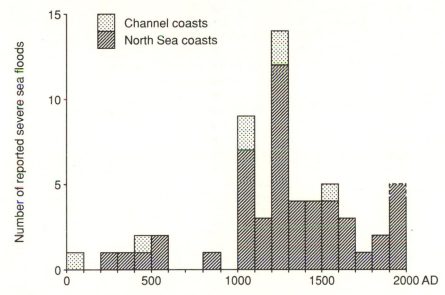

Fig. 5.6 *Number of reported severe sea floods, causing loss of life or land, in the English Channel and North Sea per century. Source: Lamb (1980, 264)*

the thirteenth century and in the late sixteenth and seventeenth centuries, with at least 54 sea floods recorded for the thirteenth century, 116 for the sixteenth and 128 for the seventeenth century, compared with 68 for the eighteenth century and five for the nineteenth, this last figure reflecting the increased efficacy of sea-coast defence engineering (Lamb, 1977, 119–28).

Documentary records for sea- and river-flooding in the Netherlands up to 1700 were extensively studied by Gottshalk (1971; 1975; 1977), and this work has been extensively co-ordinated with the work of other historical geographers, historians and coastal geomorphologists (Fig. 5.7), working with historical cartographic and morphological evidence (Verhulst and Gottshalk, 1980).

One of the most interesting and potentially rewarding aspects of multi-

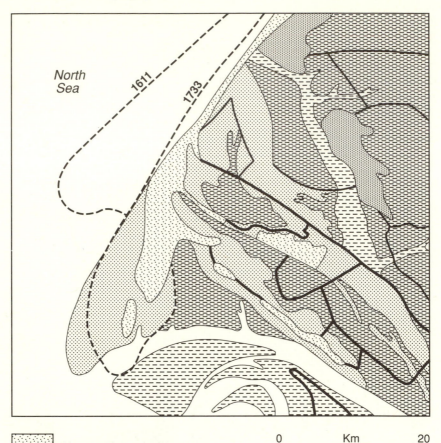

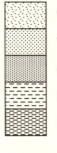

Younger dune sands

Younger beach sands & spits

Older dune & beach sands

Dunkirk III deposits, gully deposits

Dunkirk III deposits, mud flat deposits

——— Dikes constructed before 1300

——— Younger dikes

- - - - The 1611 & 1733 coastlines

Fig. 5.7 *Reconstruction, based on historical cartographic and geomorphological evidence, of the changing coastlines and landforms, natural and artificial, of the region to the north of the Maas delta in the Netherlands. Source: Hallewas and van Regteren Altina (1980, 200)*

disciplinary studies of environmental change is the opportunity offered to historical geographers for the combination of their insights into the historic documentation of, for example, sea and rivers floods and the many attempts made in the past to control such major events, with the morphological and palaeoecological evidence analysed by geomorphologists and palaeoecologists. A major volume on the subject of historical change of large alluvial rivers in western Europe (Petts, Möller and Roux, 1989) contains a number of interesting illustrations of this possibility, including the study of Bravard and Bethemont (1989) of the combination of maps and other records housed in the French national and local archives of rivers and river changes with field evidence of river pattern changes, including floods. Braga and Gervasoni (1989) also exemplify the application of the analysis of historic maps to the understanding of river changes in their study of the evolution of the River Po from the seventeenth century to the late twentieth century.

Environmental Perception and Historical Geography

There is evidence of the revival of an environmentalist perspective in historical geography, free from the deterministic connotation with which it was once associated. It is hardly surprising that the bulk of the work has come from studies of pioneer or frontier societies, where the perception of and responses to new and unknown environments (and their inhabitants) led to a wide range of patterns of occupance.

Powell has outlined, in a fascinating and important work, and within a humanistic framework, the role of images and image-makers in the settlement process in the New World (Powell, 1977), and in a review of work in Australia has also drawn attention to what he describes as 'the painful and engrossing theme of race relationships' (Powell, 1981) as a major related theme. The frontier and new environmental experiences are a constant theme in work on the United States, Canada and Australia, and well symbolized in the readings edited by Ward in *Geographic Perspectives on America's Past* (1979a), Harris and Warkentin's *Canada before Confederation* (1974) and the essays in the *festschrift* for Clark (Gibson, 1978). An important study of the strategy and ecology of the American fur trade of the Trans-Missouri West has been undertaken by Wishart (1979), and studies by Christopher (1984) and Harris and Guelke (1977) have charted people—environment relations in Africa. Overlap with work on landscape idea and myth has been interesting, as in Kay and Brown's study (1985) of Mormon beliefs about land and natural resources, and Olwig's (1984) study of the Danish heathland, which provide a link with the applied historical geography of Newcomb's *Planning the Past* (1979). An ecological approach in historical geography is evidenced also in recent work on the historical geography of attitudes to and perceptions of potential remedies for various kinds of sickness and disease, including Dobson's study of malaria in England (Dobson, 1980) and Kearns' study of cholera in London (Kearns, 1985b), which point also to a rapidly growing interest in research into the social history of medicine.

Human Modification of the Environment

The extent of human modification of natural environments has occupied much of the research time of historical and human geographers, and provided some of the most important insights into and stimuli to the understanding of human relationships with environment. The range of topics studied is vast, and illustrations of only a selection of themes will be provided in the following section.

Marsh and fenland drainage

The history and reclamation for cultivation and human habitation of large areas of former marshland, fenland and swamp has been a major interest of historical geographers over a long period of time, and detailed research has shed much light on the complex relations between humans and their natural environments. Among the major factors to be considered are: the dynamics of the physiography of the region concerned, the history of the technology available through time to those who sought to effect superior drainage schemes, the fluctuating financial incentives to do so, legal aspects of landownership and, very important, the powers of local and regional drainage authorities, the institutions involved (including the state and private entrepreneurs), and the nature of opposition to drainage schemes. The best way of illustrating the fascination and complexity of this issue is to use some specific examples from different countries. Three will be given: the swamplands of Russia; the East Anglian Fenlands, in England; and the wet prairies of the United States.

Swamp reclamation in Russia
French (1964), in his account of swamp reclamation in pre-revolutionary Russia, calculated that approximately one-tenth of the total area of the former Soviet Union comprises swamp or waterlogged soil, most of it in the mixed forest zone of European Russia, whose two largest areas are the Poles'ye in the basin of the River Pripyat and middle Dnepr (modern Byelorussia and northern Ukraine), and the Meschera depression in the Oka valley south-east of Moscow.

In spite of the fact that Byelorussia and north-west European Russia were the areas of longest settlement of the country, effective attempts at reclaiming this land were not made until the late nineteenth century, because better quality and largely uncolonized soils existed to the south and east. A few pioneer attempts at drainage of the peat bogs and grass marshes had been made, through the initiative of Peter the Great, around St Petersburg in 1775, 1802, and 1807–40, by German, French, and English engineers (French, 1983a, 17), but the main efforts came from the 1870s, when a combination of factors led to major attempts at drainage. These included: increased population and related demand for increased natural fodder supplies; health and sanitation problems, including anthrax, malarial fever and amoebic dysentery, which confronted people and animals in these unhealthy environments. Human interference with drainage, by means of dams built on the smaller rivers by millers and fishermen, actually caused an increase in these wetland areas, as did the effects of forest burning and the blocking of channels by waste from felled and cut timber.

In the early nineteenth century state engineers were sent by successive tsars to drain a number of areas around St Petersburg, and it is estimated that by 1850 11,500 acres has been drained. An edict was issued in 1857 by the Ministry of State Property to drain and cultivate swamps (French, 1964, 178). In 1872 a government commission reported on the need for wetland drainage, and this was followed by the initiation in 1873 of a Western Expedition for the Drainage of Swamps, led by an army engineer, with a goal of reclaiming land around Moscow, in the Meschera depression, and in the Poles'ye swamp and later a Northern Expedition, with the initial, though soon expanded brief of draining swamps in the Novgorod region. There was much preliminary work to be done before the drainage technology could be applied, and the preliminaries for the draining of the Poles'ye included extensive topographic, geological, and hydrographic surveys, together with the establishment of meteorological stations.

As with all drainage schemes attempted in populated areas, there was opposition from local interests, including those of the fishermen and millers, and from scientists who feared the effects of changes in climate, soils, and vegetation. Nonetheless the improvements encouraged the peasants of the region to participate in the schemes, paying for drainage by their labour, though in the initial stages two-thirds of the cost was paid by the state, with the balance shifting after five years to majority payment of costs by private landowners and local authorities (French, 1964, 182). Further funding was provided by industrial concerns. By the end of the century the Western Expedition had cut nearly 3000 miles of drainage canals (effecting relatively shallow drainage depth and not providing protection against major floods), 30 sluice gates, 87 miles of roads and 549 bridges (French, 1964, 184). These drainage schemes effected improvements in road and water communication, in tree growth, in meadow quality and the quantities of hay produced, and they also increased the value of the drained land. The effects on health conditions were also dramatic:

> In Poles'ye, elflock [a malady indicated by the matting of the animals' coats] was completely obliterated; in the north, the incidence of anthrax was drastically reduced. The Nilovetskoye swamps on the river Sheksna had been one of the worst areas for anthrax and indeed had provoked a special survey by the director of the Novgorod Medical Department in 1867; in the 1881 outbreak of anthrax, not one case was reported in these swamps. A number of drainage works were carried out in towns to improve sanitation, including Vologda, Mologa, Vyetgra, Yamburg and outlying parts of St Petersburg itself (French, 1964, 185).

The work of the expeditions continued to almost the end of the nineteenth century, though the disruptions of the early decades of the twentieth century caused some deterioration of the systems created.

The Fenlands of East Anglia

The Fens of eastern England form a large 1300 square mile (3367 km^2) basin, floored by different types of clays, the surface comprising peat and silt. Island uplands (such as the Isle of Ely) provide variations from, and important settlement sites in, the otherwise flat surface. The main drainage channels of the Fens are the Great Ouse and its tributaries, which originally flowed by means of a very tortuous course, to the North Sea at King's Lynn. The other main drainage channels of the Fens are the rivers Nene, Glen, Welland and Witham. Large volumes of water are discharged from the uplands, especially in winter, into the Fenland basin. The peats themselves are generally no more than about 5 feet (1.6 m) maximum above sea level, and in some are actually below sea level, so that comparatively slight differences in height have in the past frequently had profound effects on human survival in the region.

Although attempts had been made to drain the Fens since Roman times, as late as the early seventeenth century the state of the major rivers and watercourses was far from compatible with good drainage and advanced agricultural practice, with major impediments to effective drainage and navigation, including the collapse of banks, trees falling into the watercourses, the growth of aquatic plants and weeds, and the development of gravel and sand bars at the confluence of rivers and streams. There were also large areas of water—lakes and meres—especially in the southern part of the Fenland, which were a hindrance to those who sought to promote more extensive cultivation, though they did provide fish. Human negligence affected the efficiency of water flow, both through failure to clear and maintain channels and ditches and through the erection of a variety of structures such as mills, weirs, and staunches. Much of the history of the changing landscape of the Fens is therefore the history of success and failure to modify the watercourses of the region. Additional problems were those posed by difficulties of water outfall to the North Sea, and of North Sea storm surges (Darby, 1983; Gottshalk, 1971; 1975; 1977).

Before the seventeenth century the Fens were in a largely untamed state, valued for their natural products including fish, eels, birds, timber, turf, reeds, sedge, and salt, and the pastures, some seasonal, provided for the grazing of cattle, sheep, and horses. The economy of the parishes on the edge of the Fens not only comprised large areas of low-lying Fenland, but involved a dual upland/lowland system of agricultural production. The villages themselves were on elevated dry sites and were until the early nineteenth century surrounded by open arable and pasture fields, moor and meadow.

During the seventeenth century a combination of circumstances led to intensive efforts to render the Fens more productive. The first major drainage scheme was approved in 1630, whereby the fourth Earl of Bedford, who owned a very large area of land in the Isle of Ely, contracted to drain the very large area of the southern Fenland, later called the Bedford Level, within a period of six years receiving a substantial grant of an additional large area of the drained land in return, a benefit also accruing to the other investors in the proposed scheme. These speculators or 'adventurers' employed the Dutch engineer Vermuyden, whose main strategy for the agreed purpose of transforming the wetlands into arable, meadow, and pasture was the cutting of new, straight, artificial channels. Drainage work ceased during the Civil War, but resumed thereafter. Vermuyden's system for the drainage of the Fens was based on gravitational principles, assuming, partly incorrectly, that the relative relief of the region would enable gravitational discharge of the water to the Wash. Fenland drainage in the seventeenth century met with strong opposition, especially from the Fen-dwellers on account of their fear of loss of rights of common (including grazing, peat-cutting, fishing, and fowling) through enclosure of the drained land.

In both short- and long-term the drainage schemes helped to increase agricultural productivity in the Fens, though clearly the commoners lost much. The new agriculture introduced in the fully drained areas included the cultivation of cole-seed, rape-seed, hemp (for ropes), onions, peas, flax, oats and woad, and improved grasses, introduced to intensify the productivity of animal husbandry.

The state of the Fens at the end of the seventeenth century has been characterized by Darby:

> The immediate consequences of the draining promised more than was fulfilled for many years. Some of the complaints of the time were summarized in the General Drainage Act of 1663: that some lands still remained drowned; that the draining of some localities had only made other areas worse; that there were many discrepancies in the allotments of lands between owners, commoners and townships; and that the maintenance of the Level involved a clash with the interests responsible for navigation (Darby, 1983, 96).

An additional problem for the south peat Fenlands, consequent upon the drainage schemes, was peat shrinkage, which lowered the surface and thus increased the problem of lifting water from the fields to higher drainage channels and outfalls. The problem of raising water to the main rivers and channels was not a new one in the Fens, and windmills (often called 'engines' in descriptions of the region from the sixteenth to the eighteenth centuries) were used for this purpose from at least the sixteenth century.

At the beginning of the eighteenth century the major problems were those of maintaining the existing system of drainage, the difficulty of coordinating a growing number of independent drainage administration units, and of course, the continuing natural hazards such as major floods.

The principal uses of the peat fens in the eighteenth century included the digging of turf for fuel and housing material (turbary), the cutting of sedge, fishing, the grazing of animals, notably cattle and sheep, and, when drained, for high-quality arable land. Animals were still grazed on the Fens in the drier summers, and also on the uplands. The traditional conversion method of the black peat fen soils into land suitable for cultivation involved the paring and burning of the peat and its fertilization with the ashes produced, and also the mixture of lower clay with the peat, to give greater body to the soil, and make it more fit for wheat cultivation. The open-field system, continued in the eighteenth century without being subject to parliamentary enclosure, but with some modification to the crops and rotations. The use of fallows continued into the nineteenth century, and a four-year rotation frequently employed on the open fields, the main crops being wheat, barley, peas and oats (Butlin, 1990).

During the course of the nineteenth century major changes were effected in the region, including the use of steam-power for pumping off the excess water, new schemes for controlling the flow of river and floodwater out to the sea, and the conversion of much of the common land, including the majority of the open arable fields, to private ownership. The advent of the railway extended the potential of existing markets such as London and opened up new ones. In a relatively short space of time, by the early twentieth century, the Fenland had become one of the most productive farming regions in Britain, specializing in a range of cereal and horticultural crops.

The wet prairies of the United States

The Midwestern prairies of the United States may briefly be considered as an interesting historical example of relatively recent land drainage. Mainly found in Illinois, southern Wisconsin and Iowa, these areas of humid grassland with sparse woodland were colonized from the mid-ninteenth century onwards (though significant areas remained on the eve of the First World War) and transformed for the production of wheat and corn. Hewes and Frandson's definition of this ecological type is that 'Wet prairie was the designation in common use for poorly drained prairie and other non-forest vegetation of poorly drained land by early farmers, at least from Indiana to Iowa. It included the lower-lying areas of big bluestem [*Calmagrostis candensis*], other more hydrophytic prairie grasses, and slough grass [*Spartina Michauxiana*], sedges, rushes, and similar plants. It was distinguished from other unwooded areas as being too wet to cultivate' (Hewes and Frandson, 1952, 25).

Real problems attach to attempts to establish the former extent of the wet prairie, partly because of exaggerated accounts of its extent and degrees of wetness by early settlers, though the problems of winning a living from the poor, malarial-ridden environments were real enough. Winsor has studied the effect of such images on the late settlement of the wet prairies of Illinois, and concluded that 'The pervasive wetness, coupled with the spectre of malaria and the inherent isolation prior to the coming of the railroad stigmatized the region in the minds of many. The region suffered from adverse spatial stereotyping with particular areas dominating the shared spatial memories, the images of which remained long after the particular wet features were drained. It was prophetic that east-central Illinois, initially a region which repelled travellers and settlers, with reclamation has become some of the nation's most valuable farmland' (Winsor, 1987, 394).

The wet prairies were one of the last settlement frontiers of the American Midwest. Among the pioneer settlers of these lands were groups of Scandinavians, notably Danes and Norwegians, with experience of wetland management and drainage. Before effective artificial drainage systems were introduced, partial drainage was by means of ditches, and the normal land-use practice was for the harvesting of the natural or 'wild' hay (bluestem with some slough grass) and open grazing of cattle. From the 1880s significant improvements were made by the laying of tile drains. In Storey County, Iowa, about one-eighth of the total area was tile-drained (by smaller and shallower-depth tiles than at present) by 1894, the main areas of tile drainage being adjacent to the major streams and watercourses. By 1920, about 60 per cent of the county had artificial drainage, this major increase having been assisted by the increase in the number of formal drainage districts (from two in 1904 to 75 in 1919) allowed by changes in the Iowa constitution (Hewes and Frandson, 1952).

Irrigation

Land drainage by definition is an activity most common in areas which for climatic, lithological and topographic reasons have a surplus of water on or below the surface. This phenomenon features strongly in the historical geography of temperate regions. In semi-arid and arid regions, however, a major feature of the history of human habitation has been the complex variety of attempts, some successful, some not, to channel water to support life generally, and various forms of agricultural activity.

The history of hydraulic civilizations and communities is a dominant theme in the history of the habitation of the earth's surface, with immensely strong cultural associations. As with land drainage history, its understanding involves knowledge of changes in technology, cultures and belief-systems, and hydrology. The term 'hydraulic civilization' has been used to describe major, culturally and technologically sophisticated, states or concentrations of settlement, whose power and authority may be ascribed to their mastery of the waters of great rivers in such regions as the valleys of the Nile, Tigris and Euphrates, the Indo-Gangetic lowland of north India, the riverine regions of China, south-east Asia, and meso-America. The main proponent of this thesis has been Wittfogel, who argued that large-scale irrigation schemes (as opposed to small-scale irrigation, or 'hydroagriculture', and, of course, 'rainfall' agriculture), required a scale of management and control which gave rise to an intensely centralized, bureaucratic, and despotic state apparatus, a hydraulic bureaucracy and theocracy which totally dominated the lives of the majority of the servile labouring population which was used to create these large irrigation works and to maintain them (Wittfogel, 1956; 1957). Such civilizations were thought to be subject to cyclical decay and subsequent regeneration, rather than internally generated evolutionary development.

A number of major criticisms have been made of these thesis, including that of Wheatley, who in his major study of the origins of Chinese urbanism contests a number of its basic tenets, and suggests that, for example, flood control and irrigation were not constant unitary common factors in all instances, but in reality were much more diverse, reflecting variations in physiographic, technological and socio-cultural circumstances; that these societies did not remain static over long periods of time; that the concept of total despotism is a sociological concept which is untenable; and that the historical facts of the thesis are incorrect (Wheatley, 1971, 289–91).

Many of the world's larger river systems did not experience extensive control for irrigation until much later in time than those discussed above, largely though not entirely because of the lateness of settlement of the regions through which they flow.

The Modification of Vegetation by People and Animals

Forest and woodland clearance

One of the major themes of the history of human habitation of the earth's surface is the modification and clearance of natural vegetation, especially trees, for the creation of space for human habitation and agriculture. As Darby has suggested,

Perhaps the greatest single factor in the evolution of the European land-scapes has been the clearing of the wood that once clothed almost the entire continent. The presence of woodland, and the effort to use it or subdue it, has been a constant motif throughout the history of successive centuries; and the struggle has left a mark, often upon the form and intensity of human settlement, and always upon the general character of the landscape (Darby, 1956, 183).

From initial temporary clearings, usually under a migratory system of agriculture, clearance took place at increasingly larger scales and with permanent effect at times of significant population increase. Attempts to redress the imbalance so caused, through extensive replantation schemes, come much later in time, largely in the twentieth century. The general scale of forest and woodland modification has been assessed by Williams (1989), on the basis of calculations by Matthews (1983) of the areas covered by pre-agricultural and present-day major ecosystems. In essence, Williams suggests that 'the total area of forest in the world has possibly decreased by 15.15 per cent and the woodlands by 13.8 per cent, a massive amount of one calculation, but not, perhaps, the world-wide devastation that is commonly supposed' (Williams, 1989, 178). The estimated change in total area of forest from pre-agricultural times to the present is from 46.28 to 39.27 million km^2 and of woodland from 15.23 to 13.10 million km^2, involving primarily the clearing of the temperate deciduous and coniferous forests, mainly of Europe and eastern America, initially by small-scale peasant farming and subsequently for the needs of commercial farming. Extensive forest and woodland clearance has also taken place in the temperate evergreen forests, subtropical drought-resistant forests, in the dry African miombo, the Mediterranean, and the dry eucalyptus and mallee lands of Australia (Williams, 1989, 177–8). The chronology of this clearance is complex. We know that major phases of deforestation occurred in Europe in the Neolithic and in the early Bronze ages, especially through the use of 'slash-and-burn' techniques, particularly in the deciduous forests. In addition, there was extensive cutting for the timber trade in the eastern Mediterranean lands from the fifth century BC, and evidence that this and other processes of tree clearance, including fire and the grazing of animals, especially goats, had effectively removed the tree cover from the Attica region of Greece by this time. The temperate woodland of North America has been affected by clearing since about 12,000 BP (8000 BC), and the equatorial rainforests of Africa, South and Central America, and India and New Guinea, since approximately 3000 BP (1050 BC), 7000 BP (5050 BC), and 9000 BP (7050 BC) respectively (Flenley, 1979; Goudie, 1990).

Major phases of clearance also occurred in Europe in the late Middle Ages, from the eleventh to the thirteenth centuries, notably through the German colonial drive eastwards into the Slav lands of eastern Europe, and also in the period from the sixteenth to the early twentieth century, when the population of Europe increased dramatically, and vast areas were cleared for cultivation and for timber for a variety of uses, including house construction and shipbuilding. The lack of timber, notably oak, for building ships was a major complaint in England by the late seventeenth century, and the Baltic countries became major suppliers of naval store materials such as ships' masts, pitch, and tar. Figure 5.8 shows a reconstruction of the extent of woodland and

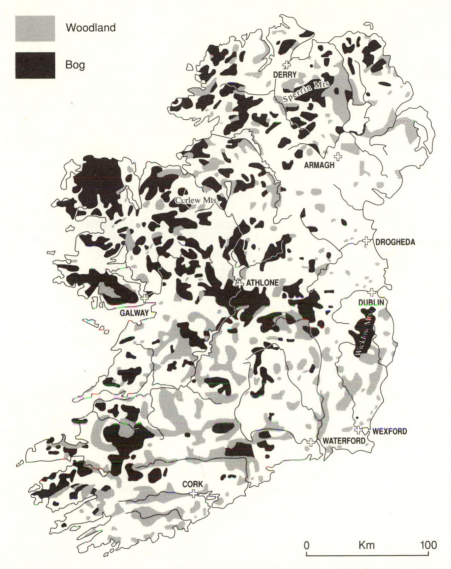

Fig. 5.8 *Reconstruction of the woodland and bogland of Ireland, c. 1600. Based on map by Davies in Butlin (1976, 144)*

bogland in Ireland *c*. 1600, already modified by human action in prehistoric and medieval times, but to be further changed by clearance and drainage in early modern and modern times (Davies in Butlin, 1976, 144).

In the period of European colonization overseas from the sixteenth century, extensive forest clearance took place in North America, South Africa, Australia and New Zealand, and in large areas of the tropics and subtropics. The search for new raw materials to feed the mouths, the domestic and public tastes, and the industries of the inhabitants of the industrializing countries of Europe incorporated initially a pragmatically experimental and ultimately a scientific imperialism, using indigenous plants and crops for more intensive production systems geared to export. The dramatic examples mainly come from the tropical and subtropical regions, where forests were managed for the extraction of rubber and timber (especially hardwoods), and cleared for the cultivation of sugar, coffee, tobacco, and cotton.

Plants and animals

The reconstruction of the varied outcomes of human agency on changing environments via the introduction and diffusion of new species of plants for cultivation and landscape planning and the domestication and diffusion of a variety of animals is a major topic in human and historical geography, but space only permits here a brief summary of some of the more important facets and reference to a small group of examples of published research in this field. Some of the early theories for the domestication and diffusion of plants and animals were of a simplistic kind, such as that postulated by the American geographer Sauer (1952), suggesting origins in a single major area of the world (in Sauer's thesis the major agricultural hearth area for plant domestication having been south-east Asia) with gradual diffusion elsewhere, but current opinion is that the processes were complex, and that the chronology of domestication and diffusion differed and evolved at different rates in different parts of the world (Goudie, 1990, 17). An important feature of the analysis of hearths of domestication is that there appears to have been very little regional and species overlap between the different domesticated plants and animals, so that, for example, the main cultivated crops (wheat, maize and rice) originated in the Near East (*c.* 7000 BC), meso-America (*c.* 6000 BC), and eastern and south Asia (3500–2500 BC) respectively. The origins of domesticated cattle, sheep, goats, pigs, donkeys, dogs, and the dromedary are in the Near East (covering a period from 12,000 BC—dogs—to 2000 BC—dromedary, with sheep, cattle and goats (*c.* 6500–5000 BC), the horse and the Bactrian camel in central Asia (*c.* 3000 BC and 1500 BC), and the llama and alpaca in South America (*c.* 1500 BC). (Roberts, 1989; Goudie, 1990). There is, however, some overlap and regional similarity for the domestication of species of pig and duck for south and south-east Asia, West and Central Africa, and the lowland tropics of the Americas (Donkin, 1985, 100).

While these major innovations and their diffusion are of considerable importance, viewed inevitably at global and large regional scales, it is more likely that the interest of the historical geography will focus on smaller scales and more local effects on landscape and livelihood. A number of species and regional examples will be considered.

In meticulously documented studies of the domestication of animals in the New World, especially the humid tropics of Central and South America, Donkin (1977; 1985) has indicated that the processes of cultural change among the unspecialized, horticultural (hand-implement) cultivators of the humid tropics of the New World were very slow. The partial taming of the peccary, a species of pig, came about as a consequence of the pig being a scavenging animal, its frequent proximity to human settlements having led to juveniles being reared for economic and ceremonial purposes, and being kept as pets, in the period prior to European colonization. Donkin suggests, however, that the peccary was never fully domesticated, the evolutionary processes that would have led to this having been interrupted by European colonization and the introduction of the domesticated pig from Spain from the late fifteenth century. The prime role of the peccary was as a hunted source of food. The two dominant species of peccary were the collared and the white-lipped species, the former found in a region from the southern United States to northern Argentina, the latter in the hot and humid tropics from southern Mexico to Paraguay (Donkin, 1985, 9). Hunting methods included cage and ditch traps, nooses, drives into nets, and in some cases the use of dogs in the hunts. Meat was the primary product, but others included hides for local use and for trade, and teeth and bones for implements and for decoration. Certain taboos attended the eating of peccary meat, and may have acted as factors in conservation. Donkin concludes his study with the view that 'the peoples of lower Central America and northern South America engaged in activities that could have led to domestication. Here Muscovy ducks were bred, many animals were kept as curiosities, and the peccary was sacrificed, traded, and indeed carried by man to some of the nearer islands. Future research may show, however, that this was only a peripheral manifestation of the developments closer to the Amazonian heartland of South America' (Donkin, 1985, 102).

Historical geographers writing on the New World have focused particularly on the ecological and environmental changes effected by the introduction of exotic species of plant and animal, both in the early phases of European colonization in the Americas from the fifteenth and sixteenth centuries, and on the later colonial activities in the eighteenth and nineteenth centuries in Asia and in Australia and New Zealand. A major study is Clark's *The Invasion of New Zealand by People, Plants and Animals: the South Island* (1949), in which the sequence of colonizations by people, plants (potatoes, wheat, fodder crops, trees and shrubs) and animals (sheep, cattle, smaller animals and animal pests), primarily from Europe, radically transformed the landscape and ecology of the South Island of New Zealand. Meinig described this, for its time, as 'a fresh kind of historical geography. It was the first detailed application of the Berkeley genetic approach to the study of European overseas colonization of such middle-latitude new lands during the nineteenth and twentieth centuries' (Meinig, 1978a, 8).

A major feature of the historical geography of North America is the invasion of the Great Plains grasslands by horses, then sheep and cattle, from the seventeenth century onwards. The horse spread slowly northwards and eastwards from Santa Fe and other places as a result of escape, trading, or capture from Europeans by Indians, some going wild into a feral state, others becoming part of the Plains Indians (Clark, 1956, 742–3). Initially the horse seems to have little effect, through competition for grazing, on the numbers of bison on the plains, but the intense period of destruction of the bison in the period 1840–70 so that it was almost completely gone by 1890, changed the balance. Cattle-grazing spread to the whole of the plains by 1880, having spread from the south, notably Texas, from about 1830. From 1880 onwards, there was serious risk of overgrazing and thus environmental damage, exemplified by dust storms and soil erosion. The shorter grass areas were affected by the rearing and grazing of sheep and goats.

While proper and appropriate emphasis on the major and larger species of animal has been given by historical geographers and others in historical studies of the diffusion of domesticated animals and their effects on the natural environments, smaller animals have had in some cases devastating effect, notoriously the rabbit in the mid-temperate grasslands. In addition, both larger and smaller fur-bearing animals have been targets of human attention for the production and trading of cured skins for clothing. Two examples of work by historical geographers in each of these contexts will be outlined. In his study of the historical ecology of the rabbit in post-medieval England, Sheail (1978) indicates that this animal was introduced, probably in the twelfth century, from the Mediterranean for fur and meat, and was both protected in warrens and coursed (hunted for sport). There is distinct evidence of an increase in the significance of the rabbit in the rural economy of post-medieval England, partly as a response to declining grain prices and partly as a conscious attempt at agricultural improvement, parallel to and in some respects an integral part of the better known introduction and spread of the 'new' crops and grasses such as the turnip and clover. The significance of the breeding of the rabbit in warrens varied regionally, one of the most important areas being the sandy Breckland of East Anglia, where, as a result of the late medieval increase in sheep numbers and consequent erosion of grassland-heaths, the rabbit, grazing closer to the ground, could adapt more readily to the reduced sheep-carrying capacity of the land, so that by the eighteenth century rabbit warrens covered about 15,000 acres of this region (Sheail, 1978, 350). There was, however, a decline in interest in profiting from rabbit rearing during the eighteenth century, sometimes for conversion of the light-soil lands for the production of grain. Rabbits, however, were impossible to clear from the land, and their feral state led increasingly to environmental damage, notably the eating of cultivated crops. The improvements in agriculture, including the new roots and grasses and the development of more open environments through land drainage, heathland reclamation, and landscaping, facilitated the spread of what was increasingly being regarded as a pest. While this role was never catastrophically devastating in England, the transfer of this animal to Australia and New Zealand had quite dramatic effects on the environment, to which expensive and ugly solutions were ultimately applied. The hunting and trapping of animals for fur is a major theme in economic history and in historical geography, and another indicator of the negative interaction between humans and animals, effecting severe environmental and ecological change. Wishart's major study of the fur trade of the American West in the period 1807–40 (Wishart, 1979) shows how small but diverse groups of generally young men, some escapists, some romantics, but mainly people trying to earn a living, set about the intensive and insensitive withdrawal of an easily exploitable resource from the wilderness environment, specifically the skins and furs of principally the beaver and the bison, but also of a wide range of other animals, including the muskrat, otter, deer, mink, marten, sable, weasel, racoon, bear, wolf and fox. Differing environments and ecological systems led to different trapping and hunting systems in, for example, the Rocky Mountains and the upper Missouri regions. While the fur trade was never in national terms an important part of the American economy, its significance at regional level was much greater. In a geopolitical context it may be contended that the fur trade played a major role, that is as a prelude to the settlement of the West via exploration and the opening of major routes such as the Missouri River and the Oregon trail, the influence of the pioneer fur trappers and traders in the new communities of the western frontier, and the influence of the fur trade on the missionary and military frontiers. It had, however, a destructive effect on both flora and fauna of the environment in which it operated. In contrast with native American 'ecosystem people', Wishart describes the fur trappers and traders as 'biosphere people'.

One important and fascinating aspect of the diffusion and modification of environment by plants and animals subject to human agency is that effected by imperialism and colonialism from the sixteenth to the twentieth century. In an important study of the impact of imperialism on the natural world, MacKenzie and others have reassessed the relations between European science and the theory and practice of empire (MacKenzie, 1990). In his introduction MacKenzie contests the conventional periodization of science and empire, that is the view that sees eighteenth-century science as 'pure', and that of the nineteenth century as more 'applied': in practice there was always a mixture of the two. Hence:

> The science of economic botany had emerged from the search for colonial staples in the British colonies in North America and the West Indies, and had been promoted by the foundation of botanical gardens in the eighteenth century. Botanical and geological surveys were developed at an early stage of East India Company rule in India. Here commercial enterprise and imperial rule were intertwined and the efforts to move beyond the old mercantile trading patterns have their origins in the last decades of the eighteenth century (MacKenzie, 1990, 5–6).

Conspicuous diffusions and transfers in the British empire were those of plants for commercial growth. Tea was taken from China to India for commercial growth in plantations, the cinchona plant (the source of the anti-malarial drug, quinine) illegally smuggled from the Peruvian Andes to Kew Gardens in London and thence for commercial growth to India, and conspicuously the rubber tree, again transferred via Kew Gardens from the Amazon Basin of South America to south and south-east Asia, where by the end of the nineteenth century the rubber produced from adapted species had become a major commercial commodity (Christopher, 1988, 181). Botanical gardens, and their predecessors the 'physic' gardens (for the cultivation of medicinal plants, such as the one established at Oxford in 1621) were crucial points in the preservation, propagation and diffusion of tropical and equatorial species for scientific, commercial, and decorative purposes, and this role was not confined to an imperial context. Denecke's study of the diffusion of the potato in Europe from its importation from America in the late sixteenth century emphasizes the significance of royal and university botanical gardens in the spread of knowledge of its characteristics and commercial potential (Denecke, 1976).

In a study of the history and geography of plant introductions to England in the period 1500–1900, Jarvis (1979) has linked the British exploration and colonial expansion with the spread of exotic species into England at various times of domestic demand through changes in landscape fashion and taste. Thus, there was a major rise in the importation of woody species from the Atlantic seaboard of North America from 1625 to 1820, from the Pacific seaboard from 1825 to 1900, from Latin America from 1820 to 1870, and from the Far East and China from about 1750 onwards. Importations from

Europe and Asia Minor showed a steady increase through the period. In 1600 103 alien hardy woody species were known, and this number had increased to 239 by 1700, 733 by 1800, and 1911 by 1900 (Jarvis, 1979, 153), facilitated by the agency of such sites as orchards, herb gardens, kitchens, nurseries and timber plantations and accelerated with the transition from horticulture to commercial field culture. A damaging effect of imperial environmental policy was the adoption by colonial officials and scientists, especially British and French, of policies of appropriation and conservation, especially of forests, which were totally alien to the symbiotic and ecologically more balanced practices of the indigenous inhabitants, resulting often in environmental deterioration and destruction of the economic basis of the indigenous cultures (Grove, 1990; Elliott, 1990).

6

Historical Geographies of Landscape

Introduction

Landscape is everywhere: it is a present and potent concept for the novelist with a strong sense of place, as also for the landscape painter, photographer, landscape historian, and the geographer. The concept of landscape, particularly in a material sense, is well rooted in the history of geography, and remains an important part of historical geography. One difficulty involving its use and conceptualization derives from an ambiguity of meaning in the German term 'landschaft' from which it derives. As Hartshorne (1939, 150) has pointed out in a long disquisition on the subject 'The major, though by no means the only difficulty, results from the fact that the German word "landschaft" has long been used in common speech to indicate either the appearance of a land as we perceive it, or simply a restricted piece of land. Both these concepts were introduced into German geography not later than the beginning of the last [nineteenth] century'. Hartshorne also suggests, however, that while the term 'landscape' in English has a variety of uses and potential meanings, it does not usually have the somewhat additionally confusing connotation of 'region' which it does in some German readings.

The term 'landscape', like historical geography, has therefore changed its meaning and connotations through time, and its use by German geographers has shown a remarkable series of shifts and variations, with Schlüter, for example, including human beings within its scholarly remit and Passarge excluding them. Some of the ambiguity has been in part imported into the geographical interpretations of landscape employed in the English-speaking world. The major influence of German ideas in North America, especially the United States, has been Sauer's essay 'The morphology of landscape' published in 1925. The key to the paper lies in his definition of landscape: 'Landscape is the English equivalent of the term German geographers are using largely, and strictly has the same meanings: a land shape, in which the shaping is by no means thought of as simply physical. It may be defined, therefore, as an area made up of a distinct association of forms, both physical and cultural' (Sauer, 1925; 1963, 321). Sauer stressed the generic or dynamic basis of studies of the component parts or morphology of landscape, involving strong elements of personal judgement and historical sensitivity in the selection of particular landscape components for study. Williams suggests that this is perhaps one of the most important elements of his essay, 'Though what might be termed the mysticism of observation and contemplation in the field (almost a cult with Sauer) the problems of objects and behaviour were revealed and some of the answers given. This demanded "Verstehen", the empathetic understanding and intuitive insight of object or behaviour from within, as opposed to knowledge from without' (Williams, 1983, 5). While this approach may now seem clear in meaning, especially through Sauer's major regional analyses of landscape, it was not clear to his contemporaries, including Hartshorne, and Williams has claimed that the most important parts of his essay are those which have been least well recognized and understood, partly because of Sauer's attempts to incorporate some of the complex German thinking on the subject. It may also be that Sauer's emphasis on the need for geography to be a form of positive science may have confused his critics' thinking about his more subjective views of landscape.

Hartshorne suggests that the use of the term 'landscape' by English geographers in the 1930s, a concept which he thinks many of them received from the United States (Hartshorne, 1939, 157), showed a similar ambivalence and uncertainty to that which he contended prevailed in the United States at the time. Dickinson, however, in an essay 'Landscape and society', published in 1939, suggested that for the early generation of academic geographers in Britain working in the 1930s 'it is the scene within the range of the observer's vision. As many German geographers express it, "It is subjectively experienced by the artist. The geographer tries to describe it objectively and to understand it in its entirety"' (Dickinson, 1939, 1–2).

The incorporation of the landscape element into studies in historical geography has been a strong and favoured activity since the inception of classical historical geography in the 1920s and 1930s, though more perhaps in those pioneer societies which had recently undergone or were still undergoing rapid changes of settlement and resource use. The element of 'scientific' classification of the morphological elements of landscape remained important in such countries as Germany and France and those which were strongly influenced by their geographical methodologies. One aspect of this type of approach was and is the emphasis placed on material remains from the past as historical evidence, to be sought directly by field mapping, air photography, and other techniques of recovery or inventory. The type of evidence used varies enormously, from primitive relict features of past agricultural communities to those of advanced urban and industrial societies. For studies of societies from the remoter past, for which there is precious little if any literary or documentary evidence, the skills and ingenuity employed in the recovery of the past from material cultural remains are vital, and involve overlap with the techniques of cognate disciplines such as archaeology.

Landscape Traditions in Britain and Ireland

In Britain and Ireland the amalgam of field and documentary evidence and expert analysis, coupled frequently with a highly polished literary style by such leading practitioners as Hoskins, Beresford, Darby and Evans encouraged the development of both professional and amateur interest in landscape history and historical geography from the late 1940s onwards. Links with historical geographers are evident from the work of the historian pioneers, and their profound interest in the historical changes in landscape epitomized in Darby's classic paper 'The changing English landscape', delivered to the Royal Geographical Society and published in its *Geographical Journal* (Darby, 1951). This paper centred around a series of themes such as 'clearing the wood', 'the changing arable', 'the landscape garden', and 'towns and seats of industry', and such themes are central to many of Darby's other publications, notably those on Fen drainage in England and woodland clearance in England and in Europe (Darby, 1940a, 1940b; 1956; 1983). The 1950s seem, in fact, to have been a singularly productive time for the genesis of research and publications on the theme of landscape change, often tied in to a resurgence of interest in local history, and the effective marriage of investigations in local archives and of fieldwork. The essence of the work by geographers and historians in Britain was a study of the landscape both as evidence of broader socio-economic changes in prehistoric and historic times, but also as illustrator of changing landscape *per se*. Relict features of landscape, as seen directly on the ground or as more 'remotely' sensed via air photographs and historic maps and documents, were crucial and critical elements of this type of approach and analysis, used in the solution of a very wide range of problems such as settlement desertion, changes in the fields and field systems of the rural landscape, and changes in urban economy, society and topography. Hoskins' *Making of the English Landscape* (1955), and Beresford's *History on the Ground* (1957) were among the seminal and influential works of this period. These reflect a new-found enthusiasm for the history of landscape through scholarly search of documents and fieldwork.

A strong school of the use of landscape evidence and landscape as a prime focus was that developed at the University of Birmingham by Thorpe, whose studies of green villages in Co. Durham, rural and urban settlement evolution in the West Midlands, notably Warwickshire, and on the Danish heathland settlement, together with those of his students, provide good evidence of the linked use of documentary evidence and fieldwork, examples of which are to be found in the *festschrift Field and Forest* (Slater and Jarvis, 1982).

There were in some cases other, broader, themes, notably what may be described as an implicit and explicit lament for a past, pre-industrial Utopian landscape which was steadily being eroded by the rapid spread of industry, communications and towns and cities. This type of critical regret has its roots earlier in the century, conspicuously in the 1930s, and is notably evident in the last chapter of Hoskins' *Making of the English Landscape*, in which he says that

> especially since the year 1914, every single change in the English landscape has either uglified it or destroyed its meaning, or both . . . England of the arterial by-pass, treeless and stinking of diesel-oil, murderous with lorries; England of the bombing-range wherever there once was silence, as on Otmoor or the marshlands of Lincolnshire; England of battle-training areas on the Breckland heaths . . . . Barbaric England of the scientists, the military men, and the politicians: let us turn away and contemplate the past before all is lost to the Vandals (Hoskins, 1955, 231–2).

It would probably be true to say, however, that Hoskins' statement is not typical of the academic work on landscape history and historical geography of this period, though it did voice a wider concern of a group of intellectuals and policy-makers from a wide range of disciplines and backgrounds for the erosion of the countryside, especially in the 1930s, often focused on such bodies as the Council for the Preservation of Rural England.

Landscape Analysis in Europe

The general thematic treatment of landscape elements as scientific evidence of landscape change has been a central feature of modern 'classical' historical geography in many parts of the world. It is a strong tradition in Europe where such themes as the evolution of fields and field patterns, rural settlements of all kinds, house types, deserted villages, green villages, woodland clearance, and cultivation systems have been extensively researched and published. A large number of major and influential works exemplifies this type of approach to the cultural landscape and its evolution, many of which are reviewed and incorporated in Jäger's overview of European cultural landscape— *Entwicklungsprobleme Europäischer Kulturlandschaften* (Jäger, 1987), and in the 'national' reviews of progress in historical geography in Baker's edited volume, *Progress in Historical Geography* (Baker, 1972). A map of the Netherlands showing the various components of physical and cultural landscape, strongly indicating processes of change such as land and coast reclamation and defence, is shown as Fig. 6.1.

The intense interest in the question of historic landscape evolution in Europe is reflected in the establishment of the Permanent European Conference for the Study of the Rural Landscape, whose regular conferences since 1957 have stressed the evolutionary cultural landscape approach, especially since the influential Vadstena conference of 1960 and the resulting publication, *Morphogenesis of Agrarian Cultural Landscapes* (Helmfrid, 1961a; Baker, 1988).

There is plentiful evidence of landscape-orientated historical geography, notably in the territories colonized from Europe from the sixteenth century onwards. Australia and New Zealand have been well studied from the perspectives of their changing landscape, for example Clark's *The Invasion of New Zealand by People, Plants and Animals: the South Island* (1949) is a study of the cultural modification of landscape from what might be termed a Sauer-influenced Berkeley perspective, using a thematic approach. Heathcote's (1975) *Australia* volume in the Longman *World's Landscapes* series focuses on the regional and ecological aspects of landscape change in Australia between 1770 and 1970, a somewhat similar approach is taken in the equivalent volume for New Zealand by Cumberland and Whitelaw (1970). Heathcote and McCaskill (1972) have listed the main contributions in this aspect of historical geography in their review, and more recent publications are listed in Wynn's review of historical geography in Australia and New Zealand (Wynn, 1977).

Landscape Analysis in the United States and Canada

As far as the United States and Canada are concerned, the morphological aspects of landscape change have been less favoured than broader aspects of

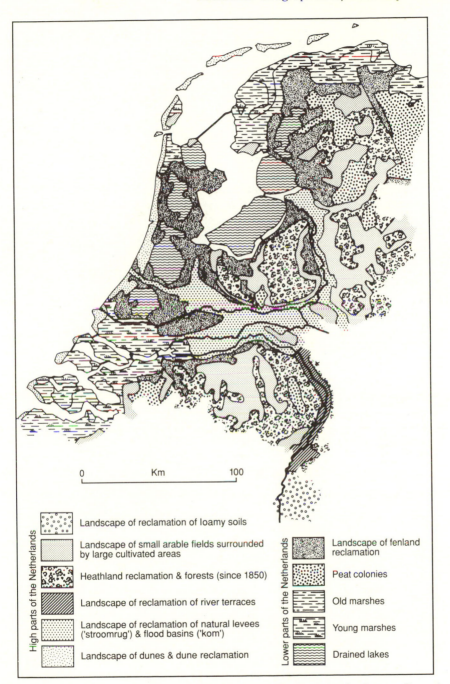

Fig. 6.1 *Historical and cultural landscape regions of The Netherlands. Source: Barends, Haartsen, Renes and Stol (1988; 1991)*

cultural impacts on landscape changes. Clark's analysis of North American historical geography suggests that apart from the contribution of Kniffen to 'what we might call morphological aspects of the cultural landscape, beginning with covered bridges and county fairgrounds and ending with an immensely detailed and comprehensive description and interpretation of the diffusion and location of American house types' and a small number of other scholars, 'what has been referred to elsewhere as the "chimney-pot" type of morphological interest has had little following in the United States and Canada' (Clark, 1972, 140–1). Lewis, in an essay 'Axioms for reading the landscape' has confirmed this view: 'it remains a sad fact that most academics in those fields where we might expect to find expert landscape-reading are egregiously inept. To be sure, there are glorious exceptions . . .' (Lewis, 1979, 14), among the exceptions he cites the work of Sauer, Kniffen, Zelinsky, Hart, Mather, Swain, Lowenthal and Jackson.

Historical geography as a study of landscape change is a prominent feature of the subject in Japan. Senda, for example, has indicated (Senda, 1982) how the influence of Sauer in the United States was paralleled by the work of Fujioka in Japan, initiating traditions of landscape study which continue to the present.

The tradition of historical landscape analysis is therefore universal in the older tradition of historical geography, and its appeal easily understood. It is not a subject confined to geography, and broadens progressively to include a wide range of disciplines and sub-disciplines, including archaeology, industrial archaeology, and urban and planning history. It does, however, pose some difficulties to those who seek a broader, more consciously theoretical engagement with the past, for it does seem to reflect or epitomize a seemingly neutral, objective approach, generally free from explicit theoretical statements and formulations and free from value judgements: the evidence of the landscape is allowed to speak to its skilled interpreters as hard or factual evidence. Attractive though the end-product of his type of viewpoint may be, it still leaves a number of important questions unanswered, and a range of potentially valuable evidence largely untapped. It also tends to deceive, in the sense that its implicit value systems, especially those which involve a linear, progressive, Whiggish approach to the past, overplay the technological and heroic perspectives of the material and cultural worlds, and underplay the role of the underprivileged and the deprived. What is being suggested, therefore, is that there are alternative ways of looking at, or seeing, past and present landscapes, ways which require a more explicit theory base and a wider range of contextual evidence.

The Ideologies and Symbolisms of Landscape

There has of late been a stimulating growth of work on landscapes, rooted in the Sauerian tradition of historical cultural geography but more closely related to theory of change in the idea of landscape and the representation of landscape in literature and art. The landscape as ideology, as symbol and as a moral statement are elements of this new cultural/historical geography of landscape. In effect, they represent in part attempts to answer questions about the kind of past or pasts that we seek to recover or reconstruct. Landscape thus becomes not just a book with statements that can be read only one way, but a text to be read in a variety of different ways, subject to a wide range of interpretations. The historical study of landscape as evidence, as we have already seen, has a long tradition in human and historical geography in Europe, and the work of economic historians like Hoskins has been of the utmost importance, as has that of Jackson in reading the meanings of past and present landscapes. It is with the meaning and messages of landscape, however, that much recent work has been concerned.

One of the reasons for the development of a new set of perspectives on landscape and on representations of landscape—in paintings and literature in particular—is that there has clearly been in the social sciences a decline of interest in positivist scientistic approaches to the study of society, and a preference for the adoption of more humanistic perspectives. A different kind of problematic has emerged, more focused on such notions as social justice, symbolism, and the relationship of landscape to a very wide range of cultural issues and perspectives. This new set of approaches renders all landscapes and landscape elements symbolic, that it turns landscape into a subject rather than an object. As Duncan has put it: 'The landscape serves as a vast repository out of which symbols of order and social relationships, that is ideology, can be fashioned. . . . The landscape should thus be viewed as a text that can be interpreted by those who know the language of built form' (Duncan, 1985, 182–3). Hence, the landscape, in past and present form, may be seen as a symbol of changing social orders, including feudalism and capitalism in their various temporally and spatially located and experienced forms.

Cosgrove has developed this theme in a major work *Social Formation and Symbolic Landscape* (1984), in which he analyses the history of the meaning of landscape in a materialist/humanist perspective, and proposes a theory of symbolic landscape, which is illustrated by studies from Italy, England, and North America. The essence of his argument is

> that landscape is a social and cultural product, a way of seeing projected on to land and having its own techniques and compositional forms; a restrictive way of seeing that diminishes alternative modes of experiencing our relations with nature. This way of seeing has a specific history in the West . . . in the context of the long processes of transition in western social formations from feudal use values in land to capitalist production of land as a commodity for the increase of exchange value. Within that broad history there have been, in different social formations, specific social and moral issues addressed through landscape images (Cosgrove, 1984, 1).

The origins of the landscape idea as a way of seeing has its origin in Renaissance humanism (Cosgrove, 1985), but has changed and been modified since. Cosgrove's (1988; 1990) research on Italy from the fourteenth to the sixteenth centuries has clearly demonstrated the complex links between beliefs, power, science and technology, perspective and the construction and management both of Utopian and more functionalist landscapes and landscape elements. In a study of the Venetian land territories of the sixteenth centuries, the processes of land acquisition and drainage are linked with perspectives and belief systems which are equally reflected in the artistic portrayal of landscape (Cosgrove, 1990).

The landscape within this mode of understanding and interpretation thus becomes not a source of hard historical facts and elements, but a text to be read, deconstructed and reread, sometimes with emphasis placed on the perceived intentions of the designers, in the case of clearly designed landscapes such as urban and rural landscape gardens and estates, in other cases to be experienced and sensed in a subjective way in a liberal and personal mode of interpretation. Landscapes which contain elements of the past can be experienced directly, or indirectly through paintings, air photographs, written descriptions in prose and poetry, maps and plans. Landscapes themselves, and the experience of seeing and sensing them, constitute therefore complex ways of seeing. The terms 'iconography' and 'iconographical analysis', derived from the methodology of art history and interpretation, are now used by landscape historians and geographers to signify the process of experience and analysis of landscape, that is of landscape as image and as symbol. Hence, 'To understand a built landscape, say an eighteenth-century English park, it is usually necessary to understand written and verbal representations of it, not as "illustration", images standing outside it, but as constituent images of its meaning or meanings. And of course, every study of a landscape further transforms its meaning, depositing yet another layer of cultural representation' (Daniels and Cosgrove, 1988, 1). The array of meanings available to an observer and interpreter of landscape at any given point of time will be conditioned by personal feelings, informed experience, and scholarly fashion, and these change through time, sometimes reflecting senses of stability and confidence, at other times instability and uncertainty, of complex processes of social and environmental change experienced. Thus, the analysis of landscape through painting and through direct experience of the powerful architectural environment of Venice of the Victorian scholar Ruskin is seen to symbolize an attempt to find stability from landscape such as that of historic Venice at a time of rapid industrial and social change in England, and offers an interesting contrast with current post-modern perspectives whose premises involve an 'inherent instability of meaning, our ability to invert signs and symbols, to recycle them in a different context and thus transform their reference' (Daniels and Cosgrove, 1988, 4–7). Such approaches offer some exciting prospects for historical and cultural geographers, but they do also have attendant problems, including the difficulty of finding appropriate criteria by means of which the freer 'textual' interpretations of text and landscape themselves may be judged and evaluated, sceptics seeing the subjective interpretations of texts (and presumably also landscapes as texts) as 'a hall of mirrors reflecting nothing but each other, and throwing no light upon the "truth", which does not exist' (Stone, 1991, 217). This is, of course, one of the significant dilemmas of post-modernism as a whole, a question that has been dealt with in Chapter 3.

Present insights into the meanings of landscape owe much to the pioneering work of such geographers as Appleton, Lowenthal, Prince, Yi-Fu Tuan and Relph, and the work of scholars of landscape literature such as Barrell and Williams. In his book *The Country and the City* (1973), which portrays the representation of town and country in literature, Williams indicates not only the ambiguity of town/country distinctions, but also firmly attaches concepts of town and country to rigid social and political contexts, generally read from a Marxist perspective. One of many interesting sections of this book is that which discusses the political and moral contexts of 'improvement' in the eighteenth century where Williams indicates the importance of seeing enclosure as only part of a set of complex processes which drive the advance of agrarian capitalism, in which the idea of development, 'an ideology of improvement—of a transformed and regulated land—became significant and directive. Social relations which stood in the way of modernization were then steadily and at times ruthlessly broken down' (Williams, 1973, 61), a process of vital change reflected in changes in the way in which agricultural tenants were portrayed in eighteenth-century poetry.

Interesting developments in the study of the symbolism of designed landscapes include Daniels' studies (Daniels, 1982a,b; Daniels and Seymour, 1990) of the form and of the 'morality' of landscapes, notably those designed by the English landscape gardener Repton, which show that the political context of Repton's early career was that of Whig party politics, for land was the basis of political power and the advance of a landscape gardener such as Repton required appropriate political patronage, and the ideological basis of his designing maintained this conservative flavour, so that

> From the early years of the nineteenth century Repton was as concerned with the organization of English society as he was with the appearance of the English landscape. His writing became more ideological, his designs more emblematic. He connected the aesthetics of landscape gardening more to a benevolent morality of estate management. Repton's ideal of landscape improvement had its basis in a conservative respect for landed property and its attendant duties. This ideal was threatened by the forces of industry and commerce represented by some of Repton's later clients (Daniels, 1982a, 118).

The designed landscapes of early modern and modern rural England included large-scale landscaped parks, with formally and informally planted trees, lakes, classical temples and statues, and with herds of deer. Some were of completely new design, others bore the traces of landscape design through successive phases, such as Hampton Court (Fig. 6.2) on the River Thames, west of London, which dates from the reign of Henry VIII but was redesigned in the reigns of Charles II and William and Mary.

They are strongly symbolic of the power associated with ownership of land, both by long-established landowning families, such as the Dukes of Northumberland (see Fig. 6.3) and those who were beginning in the eighteenth and nineteenth centuries to make money from industry and commerce which was invested in land.

Formal planning of gardens and rural landscapes is not, of course, a phenomenon confined to Britain. Many of the ideas for landscape design in Britain, America, and other countries in the seventeenth, eighteenth and nineteenth centuries were directly influenced by the designs of the sixteenth-century Italian architect and landscape designer Palladio (1508–80), developed in his *I Quattro Libri dell'Architectura* (1570). Palladio's designs were for churches and other buildings in Venice, where he was official architect, and other cities of the Veneto, including Vicenza, and conspicuously for villas on the landed estates around Venice, including the Godi Villa at Lugo, the Villa Capra (La Rotonda), and the Villa Barbaro, designed in the 1560s for the brothers Barbaro. The villa designs are for house and for formal garden, with elements of the former frequently continuing into the latter. Palladio's designs translated to both town and country England in the eighteenth century

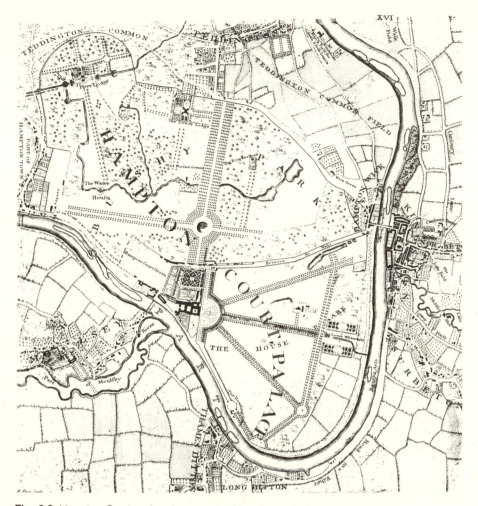

Fig. 6.2 *Hampton Court and environs, west of London: a designed landscape. Source: Rocque. An exact survey of the citys of London, Westminster and borough of Southwark and the county near ten miles round begun in 1741 and ended in 1748.*

(Cosgrove, 1984; Hunt, 1986) and to the design of Washington, DC. The designed landscapes and gardens of Italy extend from well before and after the sixteenth century, of course, and an inventory of types would include the Sicilian gardens of southern and central Italy in the twelfth century, Tuscan villas and gardens of the late fourteenth and early fifteenth centuries, the architecture, designed urban spaces and Roman baroque gardens of early seventeenth-century Rome, and the baroque gardens of Como. The formal layout of estates and gardens in France owes much to Italian influence, especially the French Renaissance garden of the fifteenth and sixteenth centuries, though by the early seventeenth century a distinctively French classical style of landscape design had developed, with formal gardens surrounding the magnificent chateaux, such as those at Richelieu (where the

Fig. 6.3 *Alnwick Castle and demesne, Northumberland. Engraving from C. and J. Greenwood's Map of the County of Northumberland, 1831. Alnwick Castle is the seat of the Percy family, the Dukes of Northumberland, and is part of a symbolic landscape of power and patriarchy, which included landscape planning and agricultural improvement from the early seventeenth century onwards*

town, chateau and gardens were designed by Lemercier for Cardinal Richelieu in the early seventeenth century), Versailles, and Vaux-le-Vicomte. In the eighteenth century the English garden was favoured, mirroring such gardens as Stowe and Kew, and there were further changes to an Empire style in the nineteenth century.

Outside Europe major processes of landscape design were experienced in many countries, regions and places. In China, which has a very old tradition of urban and rural landscape design, the combination of Daoist and Confucian philosophies formed much of the planning, so that

> ... the classic Chinese house, with its symmetrical progression of rectangular courtyards, may be seen as a reflection of the Confucian desire to regulate human relationships, while the Chinese garden, with its apparent disorder, its irregular winding waterways, its rocky hills and pavilions tucked into trees, mirrors the Daoist principle of harmony with nature. This is true equally of both main types of Chinese garden—the great parks of the Emperors, and the private gardens, made sometimes by merchants but traditionally by scholar-officials who were the old élite of China (Keswick, 1986, 111).

The Ming palace and gardens built at Beijing in 1408 are good examples of formal planning on a large scale. In the world of Islam from the seventh century the garden, especially the 'paradise garden', symbolized peace and tranquility and provided an environment which contrasted markedly with the dry barren wastelands of desert and steppe, and the formal garden, whose elements were a rectangular shape, enclosure by a wall, symmetrical design, incorporating pools and water channels, pavilions or similar buildings at the centre, fountains, and terraces and waterfalls where the site sloped. Islamic gardens were developed in Spain from the early eighth century, in North Africa (Tunis) from the ninth century, in Turkey from the tenth century, and had reached advanced stages of design in central Asia by the fourteenth and fifteenth centuries, and in Mogul India, especially in Delhi and Agra, Lahore and the Vale of Kashmir, frequently attached to Buddhist monasteries, by the sixteenth century (Lehrman, 1986, 280–1). Formal rural design in North America dates from the eighteenth century and is seen in the designs by Jefferson for his estate at Monticello in Virginia, where he built a hilltop small classical house surrounded by an oval area of lawn, shrubs and flowerbeds, and lower terraces for fruits and vegetables, and by George Washington at Mount Vernon. Formal plans were developed for the planters' mansions along the coast and on the tidal rivers from Maryland to South Carolina. In the nineteenth century, there were major developments in the form of the layout of public parks, with Downing using the principles of the English garden designer Louden for such gardens as Central Park, New York, and the grounds of the Capitol, the White House, and the Smithsonian Institution in Washington (Lambin, 1986, 572–5).

In all parts of the world the new designs for landscapes and gardens from the Middle Ages onwards were facilitated by the diffusion of many species of plant and tree, often over very long distances, a process accelerated by the discovery, exchange and propagation of exotic species by imperial scientists in the nineteenth and early twentieth centuries. Jarvis (1979) has documented some of the more formative influences of plant importations into Britain on landscape innovations from the medieval period to the late nineteenth century (Fig. 6.4).

The Nature of Landscape Myths

While actual and imagined landscapes are frequently encountered through the prose of novelists, playwrights and poets, some images of landscape, based on partial or inaccurate geographical information, have been influential on the settlement policies and intentions of governments and would-be settlers seeking to extend their frontiers of settlement into *terrae incognitae*. One classic case is that of the Great American Desert, the notion that parts of the High Plains of the Great Plains region of the United States was a desert or series of deserts. The context is that of the exploration of the region in the early nineteenth century: in 1806 Pike led a government expedition into the area of the Louisiana Purchase (1803) to explore the Arkansas and Red rivers, going west from St Louis, north to the Republican River, and west along the Arkansas River to the region of Peake's Pike. In his diary he spoke of the existence of internal deserts, a view repeated by the Long expedition of 1819–20. Not surprisingly, 'a popular idea so firmly grounded was bound to survive beyond the time of their original pronouncement. Geography text-books took up the refrain, adding apparent authenticity with their maps,

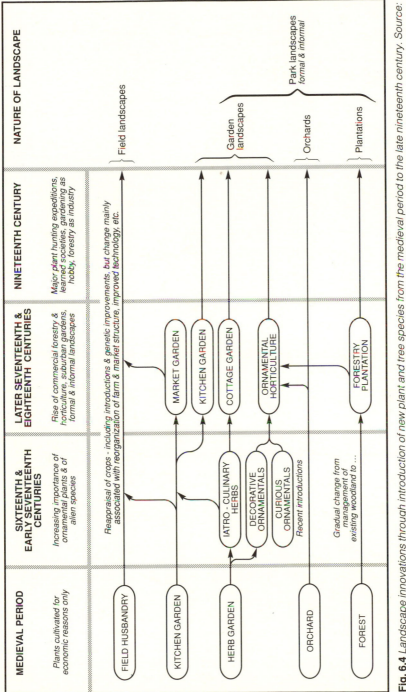

Fig. 6.4 *Landscape innovations through introduction of new plant and tree species from the medieval period to the late nineteenth century. Source: Jarvis (1979, 146)*

which carried the words "Unexplored Deserts" or "Great American Desert" over the western portions of present-day Nebraska and Kansas' (Brown, 1948, 370), and the idea prevailed until the early railroad surveys of 1855. The complex origins and variations of this myth have been examined by Lewis (1966). Powell (1977, 114–18), and Bowden (1969). Powell suggests that a clarification of the changing views of the existence of a desert involves the following sequence of perceptions:

> the desert notion was born of disinterest, neglect and misperception in the earliest days of European contact; it was then fostered by the imperfect transmission of information to the Anglo-American inheritors, who in turn exaggerated the supposed characteristics of aridity, leaving it to their more enlightened successors to demonstrate by careful promotion and scientific research, as well as by technological innovation, that the region was predominantly a massive and complex subhumid grassland ecosystem, and a perception whose erasure was effected in part by a Republican need to perceive a homogeneous America, and by the understanding of climatic fluctuations (Powell, 1977, 114–16).

The misunderstanding of the nature of deserts can be particularly potent when driven by a combination of political purpose and geographical and technological ignorance. Heffernan (1988) has provided an interesting example in his analytical narrative of the attempts of Roudaire, a surveyor in the French Armée Afrique, to create between 1872–83 an immense inland sea in the Algerian and Tunisian Sahara, by flooding saline depressions or 'chotts' with water by a complex system of canals. This venture, inspired by Saint-Simonian ideals of progress through the application of science and technology—conspicuously by railway and canal—to effect transcultural commercial exchange in order to link different peoples, was a tragic failure.

The desert through time is one of the most powerful images or sets of images fixed in the minds of students of geography, history, and culture, and of the educated populace at large. One reason is the fascination afforded for those, usually Europeans, who have no familiarity with this type of alien or 'other' environment, and with the exotic life-styles and senses that it stimulates. Images of deserts given in paintings are very powerful, and offer interesting sources of information and analysis for historical geographers and others. The orientalist movement in painting is an interesting aspect of British and French painting in the nineteenth century, and is associated with a number of developments, including the increasing accessibility of the Orient to travellers via steamships, the overland route fully established in the late 1840s for travellers from Europe to India, the intense interest created by archaeological excavations such as Petra in 1812, the Assyrian cities in the 1840s, and the temples and tombs of the Pharaohs of Egypt during the course of the nineteenth century (Lewellyn, 1989), and the political and scientific interest generated by intense imperialism in the critically important regions of the Middle East and the Mediterranean. The images presented vary greatly, but frequently emphasize sensual, erotic, violent and dramatic perceptions of life. In a study of French paintings of deserts, Heffernan (1991) stresses the ambiguity of the desert images presented, contrasting the landscapes of ruins and death (the desert as a place abandoned by civilization) with the landscapes of movement and spirituality (the desert as a place of peace and inspiration).

Similar contrasts and ambiguities are to be found in the accounts of travellers in the Middle East in the eighteenth and nineteenth centuries.

The evidence for the nature and experiencing of deserts is, however, mainly that of men, and alternative perspectives are offered in the book edited by Norwood and Monk, *The Desert is No Lady: Southwestern Landscapes in Women's Writing and Art* (1987), in which women scholars explore women's reactions to the deserts of the south-western United States. Common threads include the value by women of all cultures of ordinary, as well as exotic, erotic and romantic aspects and images, respect for and a sense of continuity and tradition, and the equation of female with the landscape, what Rodrigue (1990, 23) describes as 'a highly creative and original exploration of the distinctively female engagement with landscape', which also contrasts women's with men's experiences of deserts, the latter including a sense of opposition between nature and culture (stressing isolation), the depiction of the land as a source of wealth, the use of psychosexual metaphors, and romantic images of the West which exclude the female (Rodrigue, 1990, 22).

The use of paintings as sources of evidence and texts for understanding the genesis and perceptions of landscape is becoming an important part of historical and cultural geography. In an important study of art and agrarian change in England in the period from 1710 to 1815, Prince (1988) examines the fascinating question of the apparent neglect by landscape painters of the major changes—enclosure, new farming systems, new social relations of production—and asks whether this points to an overestimation of the importance of these processes of change influenced by the strongly supportive writings of agricultural writers of the time. He concludes that the six paintings which he analyses in the study, together with other landscape paintings, 'play down the impact of agrarian changes, dwell on aspects of continuity, emphasis ties with the past, highlight signs of ageing and allude to old traditions. None of the pictures I have seen provokes any firm evidence that an agricultural revolution was taking place. I think that this neglect may be attributed partly to artistic fashions, partly to patrons' preferences and partly to widespread feelings of nostalgia' (Prince, 1988, 114). In the same volume Osborne (1988) looks at the way in which a search for Canadian national identity is reflected in artistic images of Canadian lands and peoples, picking up the theme of symbolic landscapes as part of the iconography of nationhood examined earlier by Meinig (1979b).

Landscape as Heritage

A conspicuous feature, at least of western society, in the late twentieth century, has been the rise of the heritage industry, reflected in a proliferation of museums of rural and urban life, the increasing promotion of visits to country houses, historical theme parks, and the incorporation into the tourist industry of historic landscapes and relict features of agriculture, industry and commerce. The academic study of the powerful influence of relict features of past landscape on popular consciousness has a long history, and in the more recent past has attracted important and sensitive analysis by, for example, Lowenthal (1985). A number of views can be taken by the historical geographer of this interesting phenomenon. Hardy (1988) has suggested two general and relevant perspectives: the use of heritage in a conservative sense and as a radical perspective. The conservative sense of the term includes the concept of heritage as nostalgia, used to support and promote a looking back into the past in sentimental terms, and a particularly powerful appeal in times of economic depression, a sense which can be criticized as uninformed and contextually as a means of controlling the cultural consumption of a supposedly undiscriminating public. Wright's (1985) counter to this is the assertion that heritage as nostalgia is understandably found attractive for the plausible reason that it contains some elements of truth and is a valid item of cultural production, and Hardy suggests that 'it is all too easy to be disparaging, and it would certainly be over-simplistic to dismiss all aspects of modern heritage as, at best, superficial, at worst, exploitative' (1988, 335). The critical and radical aspect of heritage is one which advocates an informed, open and radical dialogue between past and present, not simply a passive presentation of exhibits, in whatever form, as though they are unquestionable in their symbolism and degree of representation. Hardy (1988) suggests two ways in which historical geographers can be more actively involved in heritage studies, one involving the application of the strong empiricist skills and tradition within historical geography to the identification and interpretation of past landscapes, and the other is to situate such work on a sound basis of theory, which enables meanings of the sites and artifacts and their contexts to be suggested and debated. Such an involvement is to be commended, but caution has to be sounded about the ethical issues which may arise through conflict of the more crass commercial interests with the canons of sound scholarship. The work of Newcomb (1979) on the role of historical geography in the preservation of the past offers a sound starting point from which this potential new role may be examined and developed.

7

Historical Geographies of Power and Control

Introduction

While it would perhaps be somewhat of an exaggeration to say that until recently historical geographers have tended to take primarily a linear, progressive and 'Whiggish' approach to the past, nonetheless many writings in historical geography do tend to overlook the negative experiences and catastrophes. The briefest reflection on personal experience, however, confirms that setbacks, disappointments, traumas and even catastrophes are part of the direct and indirect experiences of life. Add to this knowledge of deprivation of various kinds, and the obligation and necessity is immediately obvious for historical geographers to take cognizance of many aspects of conflict, power, advantage and disadvantage, and the consequences for short- and long-term trends, and individual, community, and spatial system changes. While the interesting possible range of interpretations of the past offered by such an approach is perhaps now more obvious than it was, its proponents have sometimes gone too far, and have striven too hard at times to impose a conspiracy or class-struggle perspective on what often seems to be an unsuspecting, unhelpful and intractable past.

War, famines, earthquakes, fires, floods, plagues and other extreme events have also been given remarkably little attention by historical geographers, the field having largely been left to the physical geographers, earth scientists, and more ecologically minded historians. This may be partly explained by the highest densities of historical geographers being in regions where extreme events are comparatively rare.

The basic premise of this chapter is that the changing control of people and space or territory through time by the exercise of different kinds of power is a legitimate and important part of historical geography. Power is, of course, a term with broad and complex meanings, ranging from direct conscious desire for and practice of control and subjugation to a deeper and less overt structural context of application of ideological norms and rules produced by conjunctures of cultural and economic beliefs and practices. The understanding of notions and practices of power has its own historical geographies, which are still a long way from being written. Mann (1986) identifies four sources of social power: ideological, economic, military, and political.

Ideological power offers to society firstly a transcendent means of power, which for most of early history is a divine form, and an immanence means, which is some form of strengthening the cohesion and self-confidence of social groups, the two means being different and sometimes in opposition. The means of economic power are termed 'circuits of praxis' by Mann, and include 'the intervention of human beings in nature through labour' and the circulation and exchange of goods from nature for modification and consumption (Mann, 1986, 520). Concentrated coercion is the main means of military power, and the first means of political power is territorial concentration, ultimately seen in the formation of states, though the varying and conglomerate nature of human societies makes for shifts and changes, enabling the second means—geopolitical diplomacy—to come into play. Most of the examples cited below might be allocated to one or several of these headings, but Mann's theoretical framework deals in terms only of the time before AD 1760, and has to be supplemented for later time-periods by reference to the work of Foucault.

A broad history of power would have to take into account the familiar notion that it is assymetrical, that is for the greater part of historical time it was in the hands of a privileged and powerful few. In medieval Europe power was assymetrical under the widespread feudal system of control of land and feudal services by monarchs and lords, while at the same time characterized by a spatial geographical fragmentation between complexes of states (some very small) and empires. In the early modern period there was in Europe a change to more absolutist monarchies with strong control over subjects and interests in strengthening the relative economic position of their kingdoms by aggressive commercial trading, or mercantilism and by overseas colonization. With increasing capitalist relations of production, the centralizing tendencies of control and administration, including those of the emergent nation-states, gradually and eventually produced tensions between various orders: the old aristocracies, the landless and rural poor, the middle-class bourgeoisie, and the varied elements of the growing industrial labour forces and the urban underprivileged. In extreme form these tensions expressed themselves in revolution, as in the case of the French Revolution of 1789, but in other cases the tensions were less overt, though no less real, in the case of land appropriation for example. The outcome in Europe was the establishment of various democratic systems of government in the late nineteenth and early twentieth centuries, but with a very strong and dynamic totalitarian element, seen in the fascist states of the 1920s, 1930s, and beyond, and the extreme socialist/command economies which developed after the Second World War. This broad outline is based on mainly political and religious factors, but there are many other ways and other scales in and at which the changing historical geography of the understanding and exercise of power can be comprehended, including those based on language, culture, and imperialist territoriality. One important concept which has been extensively used by historical geographers is that of hegemony, in the more recently derived sense, based on Marxist writings, especially that of the Italian Marxist Gramsci, of the dominance of one class or group over another. Thus, 'The feature which this usage stresses is not only the political and economic control exercised by a dominant class but its success in projecting its own particular way of seeing the world, human and social relationships, so that this is accepted as "common sense" and part of the natural order by those who are in fact subordinated to it' (Bullock, 1977, 279). An interesting demonstration of the utility of the concept is that of Billinge

(1984) in his study of the changing hegemonic positions of the landed aristocracy and the commercial middle-class bourgeoisie of late Georgian and early Victorian England, viewed specifically through a study of involvement in and patronage of science and culture in the city of Manchester, where bourgeois counter-hegemony was evidenced, for example, in support for the Manchester Literary and Philosophical Society. Ultimately what is described as the eighteenth-century 'schism' between rural and urban patrician classes was renegotiated and their hegemonic interests, although somewhat changed and reordered, accommodated.

The following examples may offer some insights into this complex notion of power and control and the way in which it may in part be incorporated into a set of ways of seeing the historical geography of the past.

Social Control in the Nineteenth Century

In the mid- to late nineteenth century, the rapid industrialization and urbanization of Britain in particular led to major problems of overcrowding, dreadful living conditions, poverty, deprivation and disease on a large scale, notably in the growing urban and industrial areas. Concerned administrators, philanthropists, social scientists and politicians attempted to understand, map and solve these problems for a variety of reasons and from differing perspectives. The broader ideological context was that of:

> a particular moment in the history of social policy when the environmental and educational concerns of the Enlightenment were being fused with new strategies of reform and government. The social scientists of the 1830s and 1840s were concerned with the relationships between antisocial conduct and the spaces in which it thrived. They mapped the moral geography of the city, explored the distribution of social ills (crime, delinquency, pauperism, disease, drunkenness, insanity, prostitution) across the urban landscape. They paid special attention to standards of discipline; to the *morale* of the population. . . . The new social science was, after all a science of improvement; it sought social regeneration through the design of moral landscapes and the manipulation of space (Driver, 1990, 273).

The historical context was that of advancing capitalism manifest in industrialization and urbanization and the dissolution of the older rural-based patriarchal systems of control and poverty relief, which produced a series of pragmatic experiments with social control and order which attempted to cope with the stresses and difficulties of urban and industrial existence. One consequence, noted and studied by the French philosopher and social scientist Michel Foucault, particularly in his books *Madness and Civilization* (1961), *The Birth of the Clinic* (1964), *The Archaeology of Knowledge* (1969), and *Discipline and Punish: the Birth of the Prison* (1975), was that of the geographical isolation and correction through work and punishment of those deemed to be deviant from the norms of social and moral behaviour. Foucault posits that such phenomena can be understood by documentary investigation through and of the discourses which attended such phenomena, the field of this discourse being, according to Philo (1989, 217) 'a hypothetical space occupied by speeches and sayings, academic papers and books, imaginative novels and poems, government publications, and all manner of other productions, the "oral or written utterances" of which fall into distinctive though interwoven medical, legal, political, literary, and related "bodies of discourse"—or individual discourses—homing in on important social matters such as "madness" and its treatment'. The more specific context was that of Victorian Britain and a time of material prosperity, political stability, and massive economic expansion, in which sets of belief-systems grew and flourished, including those of religion and a general sense of a proper public morality, primarily promoted by the upper and middle classes, within a period of substantial increase in the power of the state. The relationship between state formation, state intervention and major changes in administration in nineteenth-century Britain is interesting but complex, offering links between, for example, Benthamite philosophy and reform on the one hand and more pragmatic explanations of reform on the other. It is too easily possible to see the major events of social control, reform and 'improvement' in a simplistic way as the outcome of a zealous, reactionary, improving central state authority bent on the prevention of social and environmental problems, their means, philosophies and data sources assisted and in some cases provided by the more talented and dedicated social reformers and experimenters. The situation was, of course, far more complex, and it is perhaps useful to bear in mind Harvey's contention that space-relations and geographical structure cannot be reduced to a theory of the state, and that the more important end is the construction of 'a theory of space-relations and geographical development under capitalism that can, among other things, explain the significance and evolution of state functions (local, regional, national, and supranational), uneven geographical development, interregional inequalities, imperialism, the progress and forms of urbanism, and the like' (Harvey, 1985d, 144). The local and regional aspects are particularly important, for the state as a central agency of capitalism often had to negotiate the obstacles and particular requirements of particular localities. Many examples could be cited, though a few will have to suffice for present purposes, of attempts at reform and control of a society deemed to be in need of control and improvement.

A major preoccupation of Victorian society was with rules of behaviour and the institutionalization of corrective measures for those judged to have broken them or who were deemed morally or psychologically incapable of observing them. Deviance, as Sack (1986) has indicated, was seen in Victorian Britain and other areas undergoing rapid industrializing capitalism, as an inability to cope satisfactorily with the transition to a commercial economy related to an impersonal resource-allocating market economy.

> It therefore seemed natural that the typology of deviance should be guided by the extent to which people were unable or unwilling to work and the reasons for their disabilities should be explained in terms of the characteristics of work. Thus, the able-bodied poor could be separated from the poor who were too ill too work, or from the poor who were mentally defective and could not attend to the drudgery of work, or from those who would not do an honest day's work (Sack, 1986, 180).

Separation and supervision were two of the key facets of this type of social and moral philosophy and practice. Thus, in the case of those classified as the pauper insane, boroughs and counties in England and Wales, after an Act of

Parliament passed in 1845, were legally obliged to construct asylums within their own territory or to make arrangements for the institutionalization of the insane in neighbouring asylums, and within a period of eight years 27 county and four borough asylums had been constructed (Philo, 1987, 399). The spatial implications of physical separation of those judged insane are important, as much from the perspective of changing attitudes towards the diagnosis and treatment of mental health as from a basic geographical perspective. Some contemporary reasoning suggested that removal from home to special rather than general hospitals was the means for curing those deemed to be curable, though there were some views that this was too much of a policing type of action and excessively restrictive on those involved, preferring a more open type of caring in rural communities, as was the case in Gheel in Belgium. The location of the asylums elicited much debate, with some preference for their siting outside the squalid environs of industrial cities, that is in the countryside, where exercise and rural work could form part of the treatment (Philo, 1987, 403–8). In a short study of the discourse on the possible location for the Cumberland and Westmorland public county lunatic asylum in the 1850s, Philo emphasizes the importance of the broader context, showing that the example illustrates 'a chain of influence leading from an over-arching "medico-moral" discourse—which can be said to have possessed its own "special *is*ness"—through the specific intervention and associated discursive fragment of the Cumberland memorialists, to the siting of an actual asylum on a particular patch of land blessed with particular locational attributes' (Philo, 1989, 227).

Interesting parallels are afforded by efforts at the establishment of corrective institutions, including prisons and reformatories. In a study of the agricultural reformatory colony founded at Mettray, just north of Tours, France, in 1839, Driver (1990) has shown that the basic principles involved were widely diffused to other parts of Europe. The agricultural colony was founded on the assumption that young delinquents from such large cities as Paris could be reformed by exposure to a disciplinary regime and outdoor labour in a rural setting. Similar reformatories already existed in Holland, Belgium and Germany, and the basic features of discipline—wholesome work, the arrangement in dormitory houses, in 'families' of about forty boys, with provision of chapel and of punishment cells—were replicated in other parts of Europe up to the 1870s. There was strong British interest in the principle, especially by reformatory scientists, and gentler variations on this theme were to be seen in the 'cottage homes' provided in parts of England and Scotland for orphan children. As Driver has indicated, British reforming zeal in this respect was epitomized in the 1854 Reformatory Act which allowed the establishment of reformatories for delinquent children, and which effected the creation of 60 such reformatories, mainly located in rural areas, in the period 1854–74 (Driver, 1990, 281–2). The amelioration of human conditions was also a common theme among the reformers in Britain who sought improvement in conditions in hospitals and in prisons, mainly through new designs and layouts of the buildings involved. The fact remained, however, that the organization and architecture of schools, prisons, hospitals and asylums and indeed of factories reflected a strong element of control and discipline. An early concept had been that of Bentham's idea (proposed between 1787 and 1791) of a 'panopticon', a building conceived and designed in a circular layout to facilitate observation and supervision of those under institutional control, an idea translated into designs in Britain of prisons in Edinburgh, Lancaster, and at Pentonville, and in the United States in Philadelphia. The design, with geometric variations, was also used in schools (Sack, 1986, 187–8). A further example of the integration of political and social ideologies, means and ends in Victorian Britain was that of the new Poor Law, that is the Poor Law Amendment Act of 1834. This act was the outcome of an extensive review of the inadequacies of provision for the poor and of the rising cost of rural relief to the landowners, based as it was on legislation dating from the late sixteenth century, and geared to a predominantly rural population and related to the provision of outdoor work for the unemployed, punishment for the indolent, and almshouses for the infirm poor. The responsibility for the poor was that of the parish (there were about 15,000 parishes in England and Wales). As a result of the General Workhouse Act of 1723, the construction of workhouses for provision of work for relief of the able-bodied poor was made possible, again by parishes, and by 1776 there were almost 2000, holding 20–50 inmates (Digby, 1982, 6). The 1834 Act radically changed the territorial basis and the underpinning assumptions of poor relief, by focusing on the provision of work under difficult conditions in workhouses administered by Poor Law Unions, and on the abolition of payments for outdoor relief. The basic assumptions were that those who were able-bodied and able to work, even though in some cases not inclined to work, would prefer to find work out of doors (one of the main concerns being rural poverty, especially in the east and south of England) rather than be confined to the workhouse, and that this institution would provide relief of poverty for those genuinely unable to find work. The fear of the moral and political effects of pauperism was a major driving force behind this new legislation, not least on account of the agrarian riots in south-east England in 1830. There was, however, much variation in the interpretation and practice of the new law, and much opposition to it and to the new unions, notably in the industrial districts of the north of England. The new Poor Law is therefore an interesting example of the way in which a major piece of legislation enacted and effected by the power of a central state was in practice modified by local interests and opposition. Its weaknesses derived from an excessive emphasis on the solution of the problem of rural poverty and a lack of consideration to the relief of poverty for those who were very young, old, infirm, or mentally and physically handicapped, but in spite of its low level of effectiveness, it was not fully replaced until the twentieth century.

Imperialism and Colonialism

One of the most important historical manifestations the exercise of power and control is the experience of imperialism and colonialism, by means of which more developed countries, generally though not exclusively of western Europe, have deliberately chosen to exercise various degrees of political, economic and cultural control over other territories of temperate and tropical zones. The term 'imperialism' is applied to the process of subjugation, usually by force, of territories by a dominant, imperial state. The acquisition of empires in a broad sense is a very old habit, going back to prehistoric and early historic times. Much later in history, specifically the nineteenth and early twentieth centuries, the term 'imperialism' acquired a more specific connotation, namely the rapid economic and political dominance of territories in Africa and the Far East by a group of rival European powers, the period 1870–1914 being known as the 'age of imperialism'. Imperialism as a major dominant economic form of capitalism was not without its radical critics, including Lenin and the English economist Hobson, Lenin seeing imperialism as a necessary search for profits in overseas territories by advanced capitalist states exposed to falls in capital accumulation at home. The term 'colonialism' is generally applied to that particular type of imperialism which is manifest in the maintenance of clear distinctions between colonizers and colonized, in terms, for example, of settlement systems, land allocations, laws and rights, and the maintenance of a major economic trading difference between colonies and metropolis.

The colonization and exercise of sovereignty over other lands comprised, from the sixteenth century to the late eighteenth century in the case of European overseas colonies, a mixture of mercantilism (the name given in writings and theories of the seventeenth century to the strategy and philosophy which viewed trade and the influence of merchant capitalism as important means for the development of one country's wealth advantage, and therefore power, over another) and cultural and religious fervour, whose combined effects on the native populations, resources and environments of the territories colonized were devastating. Imperialism and colonialism took various forms, but had certain common elements, including transfers of sovereignty, the administrative reorganization of the territories affected, the creation of various forms of urban and rural settlement, and the general assumption of superiority by European powers, settlers and colonists over the indigenous inhabitants. The initiators of the first phase were the Spanish and the Portuguese, driven mainly by searches for gold and other forms of wealth which would help solve the economic crisis experienced in the Iberian Peninsula in the late Middle Ages, though there is evidence that some regions, such as Castille declined, after the benefit of inputs of colonial bullion (Dodgshon, 1992). The most dramatic effects were in Central and South America. Kriedte captures this tragedy in the following terms:

> Looting, plunder and naked exploitation were the main features of the colonial system of the 16th century. The feverish search for precious metals overruled all moral scruples. Faced with the *conquistadores* and the excessive demands which they made on native labour, the demographic and economic equilibrium of the old American culture collapsed. The population of the Antilles was exterminated within a few decades. The population of Mexico which had numbered 25.3 million in 1519 slumped to 1 million by 1600. The inhabitants of Peru were in all probability similarly decimated (Kriedte, 1983, 43).

The Spanish were initially the most active in the Americas, conquering and colonizing vast tracts of territory in the Caribbean, western and central South America (notably Mexico and Peru), and exporting large quantities of silver to Spain by the last third of the sixteenth century. The Portuguese interest had initially been in gold from West Africa and the spice trade of south and east Asia, but expanded to include the cultivation of sugar-cane on plantations established in Brazil from the mid-sixteeth century, worked by slaves mainly imported from Guinea and then Angola. In the seventeenth century, other European nations began to establish colonies in the Americas and in Asia. The

St Lawrence valley (New France) was settled by the French from 1608, as was Nova Scotia (Arcadia) from 1604, and the whole of the Mississippi valley claimed from the early 1680s. Many English settlements were established along the eastern seaboard of North America, the earliest being Virginia, settled by the Virginia Company from 1604. A parallel phase of activity by the north-western European states came in the Caribbean region in the period 1620–70, with the establishment of 25 new colonies by France, England and the Netherlands, and the capture of six colonies by England and the Netherlands from Spain and Portugal, the main economic outcome of which was the development of sugar plantations using first indentured then slave labour (Taylor, 1985, 85). The demand for sugar and later tobacco indicated clearly the growth of a world economy or world-system, focused on north-west Europe. A third area of colonial activity was Asia, where the Dutch were the main traders, having established a main operating base at Batavia on the island of Java for the Dutch East India Company, founded in 1602. A provisioning settlement for the Dutch routes to the Indies was established at the Cape of Good Hope in South Africa from 1652. The British trading presence in the East was largely that of the East India Company, founded in 1600, trading cotton and pepper from India and later in the century tea and porcelain from China.

Taylor, using the Wallerstein model of the elements of a world economic system (core, semi-periphery and periphery) outlines the possibility of viewing these first two periods of European colonization (sixteenth century and seventeenth century) as the opening stages in a cyclical process of formal imperialism, the essence of which was the search by European states for low-cost labour forces, facilitated by the development of particular systems of slavery in the Americas, so that 'formal imperialism has been the prime means of ensuring the transformation of external arenas into the world-economy's division of labour' (Taylor, 1985, 85). The legacy of the first phase of European colonization and control of the periphery has had a permanent legacy, notwithstanding the cessation of imperial control in the nineteenth and twentieth centuries.

The second major phase of colonialism and imperialism began with the growth of British power in India in the mid-eighteenth century. The British East India Company had been involved with trade with India since the early seventeenth century, but the major change in the eighteenth century came with the conquest of Bengal in 1757, and by the early nineteenth century much of north-east, east and south India was under direct British control, and locked into an imbalanced system of trading with the financial advantage massively in Britain's favour. In the late eighteenth century the scientific voyages of Cook awakened British interest in the settlement possibilities of Australia and New Zealand, and the first British settlement was established at Botany Bay in New South Wales in 1778, leading to the establishment of coastal settlements of various kinds, the establishment of Pacific and Indian Ocean trade ports, and ultimately settlement expansion inland (Fig. 7.1).

The major part of this later phase of imperialism came in the nineteenth century, partly, as with Australasia, through the increased interest in scientific exploration, facilitated in Europe by the interests of the newly founded geographical societies (the Paris Geographical Society 1821, the Berlin Geographical Society 1828, and the Royal Geographical Society 1831 but with a

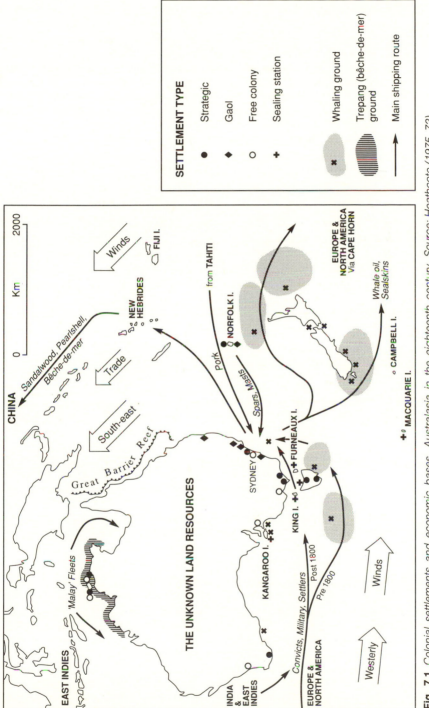

Fig. 7.1 *Colonial settlements and economic bases, Australasia in the eighteenth century. Source: Heathcote (1975, 72)*

precursor The African Association, founded in 1788) and the expeditions which they promoted, notably in Africa. Although there had been extensive settlement of the coastal areas since the sixteenth century by traders and the military in the related forts, the only substantial area of settlement by Europeans was in South Africa at the Cape, and the major imperial division of Africa came in the nineteenth century and was effected in a very short time, mainly in the last 15 years of the century. What is generally known as 'the scramble for Africa' was initiated by the French occupation of Tunisia in 1881 and the British occupation of Egypt in 1882, territories contested by Italy and France respectively. The concern of the major European powers for profitable acquisition of territory in Africa resulted in the Berlin conference of 1884–85, which attempted to establish agreement for the division of the continent. Although it has been viewed as the event which agreed and effected the partition of Africa, recent research places it in a somewhat different light. As Wesseling suggests,

> what was true, was that the partition was taking place at high speed and under the supervision of the European heads of state and government. The misunderstanding was that people thought the partition took place in Berlin. Politically speaking, the role of the Berlin Conference was not to do the partitioning itself, but to draw the attention of the world to this process and to legitimize it. Historically speaking, the meaning of the Berlin Conference is that it represents the partition in a symbolic form (Wesseling, 1988, 33).

The partition did take place rapidly, with the major powers with colonies in Africa being France and Britain, followed by Germany, Belgium, Portugal and Spain. French involvement in North Africa began in June 1830 and continued to 1962 when the terrible war of independence in Algeria ended. As Mackinder stated in his chapter on 'Imperial Britain' in *Britain and the British Seas*:

> The career of annexation once commenced is for reasons of strategy difficult to check. Britain undertook the conquest of India in the course of trade-competition with France; she extended her Indian domain to prevent interference with her rule from without; she became mistress of Egypt and of the Cape because they command the roads to the Indies; she conquered the Sudan for the purpose of ensuring the water supply of Egypt; she annexed Rhodesia and the Transvaal in order to protect her position at the Cape. Thus, and by similar processes, has Britain incurred vast Imperial responsibilities both in Asia and Africa. Internal and external peace and just administration are the returns made to India for freedom of trade and security of capital (Mackinder, 1915, 344).

Elsewhere in the world the main colonial activities and acquisitions were those of continuing British control in India, the domination of Indochina by France, achieved in the period 1858–87, British acquisition of Singapore and the Malay states, together with North Borneo and southern New Guinea, German acquisition of part of New Guinea and part of the Samoa Islands, and a large area of Indonesia by the Dutch. American imperialism was manifest in the acquisition of part of the Samoa Islands, Hawaii, Puerto Rico, Guam, the Philippines, and Cuba. Thus, by the beginning of the First World War the United States occupied and controlled Samoa, Midway Island, Hawaii, Puerto Rico, Guam, the Philippines, Tutuila, Cuba, Santo Domingo, Haiti, Nicar-

agua, and the Panama Canal Zone (Hunt and Sherman, 1972, 131). Colonization and control was effected by extensive and expensive military campaigns,
such as those of the French in Western Sudan, Dahomey, Madagascar,
Morocco and Indochina, the British against the Ashanti, the Transvaal and the
Orange Free State, and the Belgians in the Congo, and the Germans in south-
west Africa (Fieldhouse, 1982, 222).

The consequences of this massive exercise of power and control, from
complex and changing motives including military, strategic, political, economic, cultural, humanitarian and religious, and via a complexity of direct and
indirect administrative systems, were far-reaching. They affected trade and
capital flows of an imbalanced nature, movements of population to and from
and within the colonized territories, a culture of imperialism based on
assumptions of the superiority of western cultures, segregation of colonial
élites, the transmission of killer diseases to devastating effect, and large-scale
interference with natural environmental habitats (though this to some extent in
later years redressed by protection and restoration policies, especially through
afforestation) (Pawson, 1990). Figure 7.2 portrays one aspect of the 'civilizing
mission' of the Europeans overseas: the sites of the religious missions in Africa
in the late nineteenth century, which represent a varying amalgam of piety,
altruism, and assumed superiority, and whose perception by those whom they
sought to convert is only just beginning to be researched and understood.

While the majority of accounts of European imperialism have been written
from the perspective of the European colonizing and imperial powers, more
recently attempts have been made to document the experiences of those whose
lands were taken and whose ways of life were so radically altered by the
process. These alternative visions of the process should form one of the most
important aspects of historical geography in the future (Mabin, 1986). Crush,
writing of this theme in relation to the historical geography of South Africa,
points to such themes as 'class struggle and social control in the diamond
mining industry, the historical roots of South Africa's notorious migrant
labour system, the contradictions between segregation and capitalist production in the South African city and the modes of survival of marginal social
groups on the Witwatersrand' as being part of a 'joint endeavour to fashion a
contextual people's historical geography. . . . The first step must be to narrow
the gap between those who write about racial capitalism in the present and
those who have borne the brunt of it in the past' (Crush, 1986a, 3).

New perspectives on the nature of European imperialism in the period
c. 1870–1945 and the way in which geography as a science and a focus of a
heterogeneous discourse engaged with the complex territorial, cultural, and
economic ambitions of imperial powers are currently being explored. The role
of individuals, and groups (men and women), governments, geographical and
commercial societies and, increasingly, the attitudes and responses of those in
the colonized regions whose lands and ways of life were deeply affected, are
being investigated, and will produce a much more complex and kaleidoscopic
picture.

Questions of Minority Groups and Territorial and Other Rights

One of the most interesting and harrowing aspects of the application of power

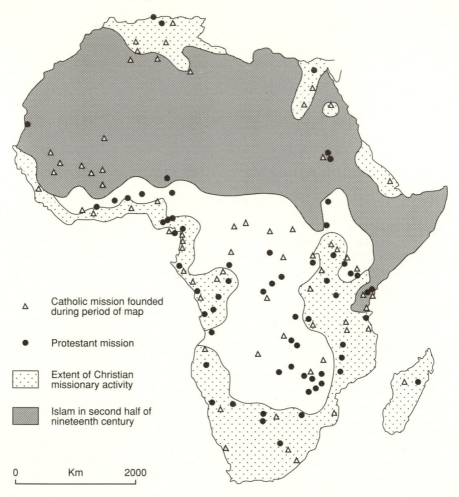

Fig. 7.2 *Mission stations in Africa in the late nineteenth century. Source: Ade Ajayi and Crowder (1985, Section 53)*

in a particular ideological context has been that involving the appropriation of indigenous land rights by the process of colonialism and imperialism, a highly fractious and contentious issue which continues to the present day. The basis of that appropriation has, of course, changed through time, from the late feudal/early mercantilist appropriations by the European powers in Central and South America, North America and the Caribbean, and Australasia and Africa in the sixteenth, seventeenth and eighteenth centuries, to the advancing capitalist land-grabbing of the nineteenth and twentieth centuries. The effects, however, have been much the same, and what has been termed the 'native lands question' continues to burn.

The context of the early attempts to settle parts of the New World is that of the advance, through exploration and settlement, of European interests of commerce and culture, especially religion, into territories deemed to be rich in minerals, precious metals and exportable agricultural products. Prevalent theories and models of colonization and settlement involved the transfer to these new lands of many basic assumptions about property and territory from the homeland countries, and an increasingly ethnocentric view of the native inhabitants of the colonized countries, developing eventually in the nineteenth and early twentieth centuries to a quasi-scientific form of racism. Powell (1977, 85) asserts that 'The Europeans clearly entered the New World with a vital sense of mission. Part of that mission entailed a conversion of the native peoples to "civilized" ways, and it incorporated a strongly ethnocentric application of the increasing emphasis in post-Reformation Europe on the "perfectibility of man". So, for example, the Indians [of North America] could only be "improved" if they were settled upon their own cultivated farms'. European belief was that patterns of land occupation should be fixed rather than seasonally migrant, as in fact was the case with many hunters, gatherers and shifting cultivators, with the consequence that land which visually seemed to be unoccupied, but which frequently was part of complex land-use systems, was appropriated into a European system of ownership and property rights. Similar assumptions were made in Africa in the nineteenth century. The designation of the indigenous inhabitants of colonized territories as primitive or subhuman overcame both the legal and moral difficulties of territorial appropriation. This having been said, it is very important, particularly for the geographer, to recognize and acknowledge the diversity of colonial and imperial experience, especially at point of contact with native inhabitants. Meinig (1986, 71–2), for example, suggests for North America three basic types of experience: the first involving the elimination or expulsion of native peoples from an area to be settled by colonists, as in Virginia; the second, the 'benign articulation of the two peoples at a point of exchange, each group operating largely within a separate territory but bound together in an encompassing economic system, as in Canada'; and thirdly, a system of greater fusion, as in Mexico. The precise nature of land acquisition and control was also affected by the political situation in the home territories, competition between colonial groups in the new territories, and the character and environs of the indigens involved. Thus, Meinig shows that the initially benign negotiations between English Puritan settlers and Indians for land rights in New England changed dramatically with competition between colonialists for land, resulting in the wars of the 1670s in which 3000 Indians were killed (Meinig, 1986, 94–5). An approximation to assimilation was achieved by the end of the eighteenth century, but changed substantially when in the early nineteenth century the movement of the settlement frontier westwards brought in a policy of clearing Indians from east of the Mississippi, initiated by the Indian Removal Act of 1830, and continued by a series of treaties, leading by 1869 to the establishment of Indian reservations and to widespread individual property rights on reservations from 1887. The nineteenth century witnessed the brutal appropriation of land from Indians by means which until recently western culture has dramatized and glorified in literature and cinema, very much in keeping with 'the whites' ceaseless projection of their own self-image in their dealings with the new environment and its inhabitants' (Powell, 1977, 87). The extent of dispossession and decimation, symbolized by the massacre of the Sioux at Wounded Knee in 1890, was massive: by 1890 the total Indian population in the United States amounted to only about 10 per cent of the original number in the year 1500. The geographical extent of the decimation of Indian territory is an equally depressing story, starting in modern times with the reservations policy of the US government from the late eighteenth century onwards. The maximum extent of the reservations was reached in 1875, with an area of 166 million acres, reduced after the Dawes Act of 1887, to 78 million acres in 1900, and 39 million acres in 1930 (Fig. 7.3).

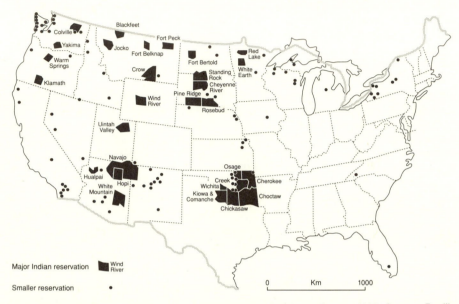

Fig. 7.3 *Major native American Indian reservations in the United States, 1900. Source: Paullin,* Atlas of the Historical Geography of the United States *(1932, Plate 36)*

There were similar experiences in Australasia, Latin America, and Africa. Christopher has described the varied experience of land appropriation in the British Empire in the following terms:

> British colonial policy regarding the indigenous population in the rural areas lacked any consistent direction. Attitudes ranged from impulses to convert and save souls on the one hand to exploitation and extermination on the other. Recognition of the land rights of the indigenous population similarly varied from the complete recognition of the pre-colonial land system to the assumption that all land on annexation became the property of the Crown. It was the latter that tended to predominate in the temperate lands and the former in the tropical areas of late incorporation into the Imperial system (Christopher, 1988, 162).

In the majority of cases, appropriation in various forms was the norm, especially in the earlier settlements. In the case of New Zealand, the Waitingi Treaty of 1840 guaranteed Maori chiefs possession of their lands and their land-use rights in exchange for accepting sovereignty to the British Crown, together with virtually unlimited purchase rights, in spite of Maori traditions against the sale of land. A series of Land Acts in the later nineteenth century, however, regardless of strong Maori resistance in the North Island in particular, succeeded by assimilation and confiscation in effecting a major reduction in the amount of Maori-held land, on the familiar grounds that white settlers had a higher economic and moral purpose and more efficient means of using the land resources of New Zealand (Fig. 7.4).

In the longer term, as Powell has suggested, the Maoris strong political base gave them a better chance for protection of their traditional ways of using land than the North American Indians (Powell, 1977, 93–4). The Australian Aborigines experienced progressive appropriation of lands and land rights from the time of the earliest British settlements from the late eighteenth century, reflected in a movement away from the coastal areas of early European settlement inland, and from the 1830s for a variety of motives, some out of concern for their decimation through contact with Europeans (through disease and deliberate extermination), were subject to a native reserves policy, the majority now being in remote, arid, inland areas. The essence of the problem was again the contrasts in attitudes to and traditions of land rights and the concept of ownership and property, a formidable and vicious expression of the contrasts between pre-capitalist and capitalist societies. Reynolds (1982, 66) explains that 'Aborigines reacted less to the original trespass than to the ruthless assertion by Europeans of exclusive proprietorial rights often from the very first day of occupation. It was behaviour probably unheard of in traditional society'. The outcome has been a very familiar one, the marginalization from every perspective of the original inhabitants of a continent, though fortunately recent interests in mineral exploitation and more general concerns for justice have at least given an airing to this outstanding problem.

The system of colonial land appropriation and use in Latin America varied through time and according to the policy of the colonizing power. The essence was, however, that of land and labour appropriation, including the use of local and imported slave labour, for the purpose of the production of wealth through farming of large estates and plantations, especially for the production of sugar, and the extraction of mineral wealth through mining. The extraction of tribute from the native populace through the medieval Spanish 'encomienda' system and the later development of the system of large rural estates, the 'haciendas', 'estancias', or 'hatos', operated by settlers and by the larger religious orders, obtained by royal grant and subsequently by purchase. The development of sugar plantations along the coast of Brazil by the Portuguese in the sixteenth century involved the use of African, Indian, and local slave labour, a practice repeated in the West Indies by other European powers in the seventeenth and eighteenth centuries.

The effects of colonial power and control go much further than land-rights abuse, but this topic offers an important example of the historical geography of power which continues to have meaning for the present day. Powell's comment on the fate of the Australian Aborigines has general bearing on the whole question: 'For many years the best treatment they received was that odd brand of patronizing care, tinged with a kind of high-minded fatalism, which characterized the experience of each indigenous group in the New World in varying degrees: it was born of a white belief that either the natives themselves, or their culture, or both, were irrevocably doomed' (Powell, 1977, 96). The power of such beliefs still awaits further detailed examination, but of their

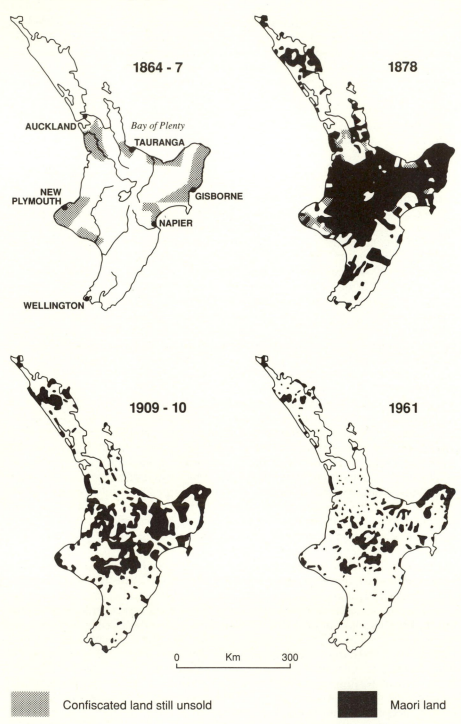

Fig. 7.4 *The reduction of Maori lands in New Zealand, 1864–1961. Source: Powell (1977, 93)*

existence their can be no doubt, as evidenced in the statement in 1894 by an international lawyer:

> The inflow of the white race cannot be stopped where there is land to cultivate, or to be minded, commerce to be developed, sport to enjoy, curiosity to be satisfied. If any fanatical admirer of savage life argued that whites ought to be kept out, he would only be driven to the same conclusion by another route, for a government on the spot would be necessary to keep them out. Accordingly international law has to treat natives as uncivilized. It regulates, for the mutual benefit of civilized states, the claims which they make to sovereignty over the region and leaves the treatment of the natives to the conscience of the state to which the sovereignty is awarded (Westlake, 1894, cited by Uzoigwe, 1988).

Internal Colonialism

Political, economic and cultural hegemony does not only occur in the context of overseas colonization and imperialism by European powers, for example. There are many instances of what has been termed 'internal colonialism'. The concept of internal colonialism derives in part from modern studies of underdevelopment in the Third World, especially dependency and modernization theories. Williams (1983) identifies the major conception of internal colonialism as that involving the intranational exploitation of cultural groups, deriving from studies of power relations in Latin America, but employed influentially in Hechter's sociological model of internal colonialism in western Europe, especially the islands of Britain and Ireland (Hechter, 1975), which emphasizes the dominance within a state by the core (London) of the economic, political and cultural life of the peripheral regions (Scotland, especially the Highlands, Wales, and Ireland) and the extensive means adopted to secure and maintain control, through military, language, religious and economic strategies, emulating in many respects the relationship between a colonial power and overseas subject territories. The assumptions made by the dominant strategists working from the core seem to be similar to those of the imperial strategists of the nineteenth century in particular, including assumptions about the innate inferiority of the inhabitants of the periphery, whose habits and practices, especially those of the Irish in the sixteenth and seventeenth centuries, were regarded as those of 'primitive savages'. Withers (1988) has studied this phenomenon in Scotland, with particular reference to the removal of the Gaelic language, 'improvement' through military subjugation, the creation of new urban and rural settlements, together with the establishment of industries and changes in the nature of agriculture and education. Of particular importance in Withers' study is the analysis of the reaction of the Highlanders to such attempted subjugation and control, especially his point that the geography of counter-hegemony or resistance has varied through time: 'In the century from 1782, protest was concentrated particularly in the more fertile areas of the north-east Highlands. . . . By the later nineteenth century, however, protest was concentrated in the north and west, in the crofting Highlands' (Withers, 1988, 390). The Irish experience of attempted colonization and control had common elements with the Scottish experience and with the early British colonies in North America, military activity being followed by attempts in the sixteenth and seventeenth centuries at the 'plantation' of agricultural and urban settlements for the purposes of stabilization, security, and favourable terms of trade. Only in Ulster did these plantations have any success, and they have obviously had long-lasting effect, reflected in the community tensions which last to the present day. The Hechter version of the model of internal colonialism has been criticized on various grounds, including assumptions about the homogeneity and identity of cultural groups, the underweighting of class distinctions within Celtic cultures, its structuralist affiliation, and its failure to analyse structures of Celtic colonial relations with the metropolitan core in a broader imperialist and expanding capitalism theoretical framework. Many attempts have been made at the application of several versions of the concept of internal colonialism, one of the earliest being Gramsci's study of the Italian south (Williams, 1983, 5). More recent applications include Drakakis-Smith's (1983) analysis of Aboriginal underdevelopment in Australia, Goodman's (1983) study of the province of Guizhou in China, and Corbridge's (1987) study of industrialization, internal colonialism and ethnoregionalism in the Jharkhand, eastern India, in the period 1880–1980. Many possibilities exist for further study, including nineteenth-century Russia, twentieth-century Germany, South Africa, and Israel.

8

Rural Transformations

Introduction

For the greater part of the history of human occupation of the earth the majority of the inhabitants have lived in non-urban, non-industrial milieux. The term 'rural' as applied to such environments does give some semantic and practical problems, having perhaps too much of a connotation of separateness from urban life, ignoring the essentially symbiotic relationship between all elements of production and cultural systems, and the extent of non-primary production which has been carried out, in the form of the production of clothes, farm and other implements, and, at a later date, cottage industry, in non-urban areas. The term here is therefore used in a qualified sense that recognizes the distinctive physical, social, economic and cultural patterns of the countryside without implying a totally separate and independent existence from other productional systems and locations. The basic entity or common denominator in all types of rural economy and society is the use of land and the natural resources of the habitat. Land is for much of historic time a repository of highly complex use-rights and privileges, but relatively late in the human time-scale becomes in advanced economies a commodity to be bought and sold, a status symbol, or property, these concepts and practices involving a concomitant loss or appropriation of communal use-rights by a variety of means but generally through the agency of the market system, privileging a minority of the population, often at the expense of a majority of land users, living at the margins of existence. This concept of property is an important one, with the direct meaning of exclusivity of use-rights to one individual and, therefore, the exclusion of the use-rights of others.

The historical geography of rural land use and settlement is inevitably and predictably a complex question, with major regional and chronological variations that can only be fully understood by intensive regional study. An attempt is made here to present a digest of some important concepts, and is followed by a brief and selective account of significant aspects of the historical geographies of rural change in different places through different times in the past.

Peasantry and Peasant Cultures

The word 'peasant' conjures up a variety of images, most of which pertain to a basic and largely subsistent existence based on cultural appraisals of natural resources and resourcefulness, primitive technologies, the use of family labour, and production at a small scale from land which for the most part is exploited by use-right rather than ownership. It tends to have connotations of a noble primitiveness and dignity of labour, communal endeavour, common resources, and intense knowledge of local productive environments, often at precarious margins of existence, conditions which in time are eroded and changed by the exploiting and selective process of market-orientated capitalism, with which peasant society and culture is generally incompatible, and by which it is drastically modified, enfeebled or destroyed. Peasant families provide for themselves food, drink, tools, utensils, and shelter, are units of production and consumption, are normally of necessity involved in complex subdivisions of specialist agricultural activities with other groups with whom they are bound into a wide array of assemblages, whose main aims are long-term survival and whose character is essentially conservative (Clarke and Langton, 1990; Shanin, 1971; Redfield, 1956).

The precise history of peasant farming and culture is regionally specific, and within the European context, for example, major differences occurred between those regions which were subject to a feudal regime until quite late in historical time, and those which were not. Particular difficulties attach to unqualified uses of the terms 'peasant' and 'peasantry'. As Williams (1973, 194) has indicated, the roots of the word 'peasant' derive from Old French via the Latin *pagus* or country district, with the connotation of working on the land and living in the country, and suggests that the collective noun 'peasantry' in English derives from the sixteenth century, but that 'The social and economic transformation of English agriculture, from the sixteenth to the nineteenth century, created a special difficulty in uses of the word. The classes of small working landholders in feudal or semi-feudal relationships to a landowning aristocracy, as found in pre-revolutionary France or Russia, and often described by this primary French word, had virtually ceased to exist in England by the eighteenth century, and had been replaced by the new capitalist relationships of landlord, tenant, and labourer'.

Approaches to Farming Systems of the Past

The consideration of the productive aspects of rural economies in the past has been a major object of research by historical geographers and others, and has resulted in an enormous quantity of literature, organized on regional and chronological lines. It would be quite impossible to present even a digest of this work here, so what is offered is a limited range of examples of the ways in which different types of farming systems have evolved through time.

Shifting cultivation

One of the main types of agriculture from the earliest points of the development of tillage of the soil has been shifting cultivation. The essence of this mode of cultivation is the clearance of trees and vegetation from a patch of land by cutting ('slashing') and burning, and the cultivation and harvesting of a variety of planted crops in a very basic and non-labour-intensive way, a use of land by the shifting or changing of the location of the fields cultivated rather than a rotation of crops within a given arable field area.

Variations also occur in relation to the nature of the settlements of the cultivators, some working a bush-fallowing system from a permanent village, others changing the site of their temporary settlement to move to new areas for cultivation. The density of population maintained under such a system of swidden cultivation is low. The plough is generally absent, and livestock normally associated with this system are usually pigs and poultry, though cattle (outside the tropical regions), sheep and goats have been and are kept in Africa. The main implements are the digging-stick, hoe, and axe, and the main crops are roots, cereals and shrubs (Grigg, 1974, 57–8). The present location of this system of agriculture is largely the tropical regions of Central and South America, Africa and Asia, but formerly it was characteristic of parts of China, south-west Asia, Europe and the Americas, in a very large and complex range of forms and with varying chronologies of development, from prehistoric times onwards, and involving not only indigenous inhabitants but also, in the case of regions colonized in the early modern period, European settlers. Chaudhuri has described the system in Asia:

> The usual method of shifting cultivation in the forested areas of Asia was to clear a plot of land by cutting down trees and burning the wood. The ash acted as a fertilizer to the ground which was dug with either a sharpened stick or a hoe. Dry rice, millet, and maize (after its introduction in the sixteenth century) were the most common crops grown in the clearings, and these were left fallow after two or three seasons. It has been estimated that the period of rest required by the soil in the tropical regions of Indonesia was about nine years and after the average yield is taken into account, a family of five would have needed about 25 acres of suitable land to support itself (Chaudhuri, 1990, 220).

Nomadism

The movement of groups of pastoralists with their animals has long been a feature of semi-arid and arid regions of the earth, characteristic of particular phases of economic and social development and having very close links with environmental conditions, notably climate, water supply, and vegetation. The major type is pastoral nomadism, which has generally been characterized by the movement of large herds of animals, sometimes over long distances, in order to feed on pastures which are seasonally available. A more restricted semi-nomadic type is that related to sedentary farming systems in areas where there is a distinctive wet season. At the far end of this spectrum of nomadic types is that in which the movement is predominantly altitudinal, as in the case of the transhumance practiced to the present day in parts of the Alps of western and central Europe and in Scandinavia. It is important to recognize the variety of types of nomadism: 'Nomadism is a convenient theoretical term. It is also a continuum. A wide variety of people with different types of social organisation, degrees of mobility, and livelihoods can be classified by the term'

(Chaudhuri, 1990, 263). The ecological logic of pastoral nomadism is that it permits the existence of larger numbers of livestock under the migratory system than a given piece of land would normally accommodate, that it facilitates an easy way of capital accumulation, and also has the advantage of movability of livestock as potentially taxable items, a greater measure of security and a greater freedom of choice of political regime. Its dynamics in history indicate that communities of pastoral nomads have moved towards a sedentary way of life, but also that there are many instances of settled agricultural communities taking up a more nomadic existence (Wagstaff, 1985, 63–4).

In his long account of nomadism in Asia before the advent of the European colonialists, Chaudhuri (1990) makes a distinction between free and encapsulated nomads, the former, characteristically associated with the deserts and mountains of central Asia, the steppe lands of Eurasia, the arid deserts of Arabia and of the Sahara, existing in lands relatively devoid of population and with weak state formations, the latter in more densely populated regions with stronger state formations such as Anatolia, upland Syria, Iraq, Iran, Afghanistan, the Himalayas, and the plains of northern and western India. The free nomads were very much more difficult for the administrators of the states across which they migrated to control, and the effect of their invasions of settled territories, both in Europe in the Dark Ages and of the settled lands of China, India, and the Middle East through to the sixteenth and seventeenth centuries, was profound and disruptive.

The animals chiefly involved in nomadic pastoralism were horses, camels, cattle, sheep, and goats. There was a tendency to have more than one kind of animal, for example sheep and goats, in the system, to have supplementary economic activities, such as spinning and weaving, and distinctive social systems. By their very nature they leave very little landscape evidence of their existence, and the written record, apart from travellers' descriptions, is sparse. Yet their ways of life and militaristic capacities have captured the imaginations of scholars and novelists, and they perhaps deserve even more subjective and objective research than hitherto they seem to have attracted.

The Bedouin of the Middle East may serve as a useful illustrative example of a number of the points made earlier about the nature and development of systems of nomadic pastoralism. The steppe and desert lands of the Arabian peninsula and of parts of North Africa, punctuated irregularly with oases, have been since late prehistoric time the territories of nomadic pastoralists to whom the name Bedouin (the French transcription of the Arabic term 'Badawin', meaning occupant of the desert) has been given. The basis of their existence has been the pasturing of camels, sheep and goats, the use of tents for dwellings, and their social and political basis a tribal structure, comprising groups of families led by chiefs or sheiks. Associated with these groups was a strong 'ethos of courage, hospitality, loyalty to family and pride of ancestry' (Hourani, 1991, 10), together with a sense of cultural identity reflected in the development of a common poetic language. The appearance of the Muslim religion in the sixth and seventh centuries gave a greater sense of culture and purpose to the nomadic (as well as the settled) Arabs. During the period of expansion of the Muslim Empire in the Middle East and the Mediterranean, the dynamics of nomadic life were complex: in some areas change to sedentary agriculture took place, in others the land over which they ranged increased and took in some of the land of settled cultivators. Initial movements of pastoral nomads from Arabia were to Syria, Mesopotamia, Egypt and Persia. The experience was repeated in the early tenth century, and various processes, including politics, religious fundamentalism, and local shortages of grazing in the aftermath of droughts caused further expansions and movements of Bedouins away from their bases. Reports by early European travellers in the Middle East in the eighteenth century contain tales of ferocious attacks by some of the Bedouin on pilgrims and travellers, as well as intertribal warfare, but these accounts are often balanced by an undisguised admiration for the Bedouin way of life and hospitality (Wagstaff, 1985, 228–9). The administrators of the Palestinian provinces of the Ottoman Empire were concerned in the course of the eighteenth century with harnessing and controlling the militaristic energies and inclinations of the Bedouin, though their raids, for example on Jerusalem and other inland cities from the Judaean desert, were thought by the Ottoman rulers—quite mistakenly—to be a less serious problem than attacks on coastal cities such as Haifa and Jaffa by Christian pirates (Cohen, 1973, 270). During the course of the nineteenth century there were widespread attempts to effect sedentarization of the pastoral nomads in the countries of the Middle East, in order to lessen their threat to political order and to settled agricultural communities. These attempts were not very successful, owing to the nomads' superior knowledge of the terrain of the desert, but these attempts became more successful with the advent of the aeroplane in the twentieth century and with other sophisticated weapons of war. The process continues to the present day.

One interesting feature of the desert nomad is the image created in the minds of western Europeans, through the media of travellers' accounts, poetry, novels, paintings, operas, and more recently through films, of the desert and its inhabitants as a place and as peoples of exotic, romantic, mystery, part of a broad and long-lasting engagement of the minds of westerners with the 'other' and with the cultural phenomenon of orientalism (see Chapter 6).

Wetland cultivation

The main form of early wetland cultivation was the cultivation of rice, an obvious prerequisite for which is an annual rainfall of between 1780 and 2200 mm and high temperatures during the growing season, together with the necessary technology for the control and management of water. This is a labour-intensive method of cultivation, which by damming or ponding water in rivers and streams, to create flooded fields or terraces partly overcomes the disadvantages of uneven and unpredictable rainfall. Its main regional concentration historically has been in the river basins and deltas of the monsoon lands of south and east Asia, where elaborate systems of water control, including protection of farms from flooding by embankment of rivers and streams, and the irrigation of the rice-fields, has been an important part, though not necessarily always the most important part, of the rural economy. Wet-rice cultivation was always characterized by intensive labour input, and therefore generally with high densities of population and sophisticated systems of social organization. Rice cultivation started as a dry land system, with the use of the wild rice plant having occurred in the forested regions of south-east Asia during the early Holocene, but wet-rice cultivation may be traced to the lower

Yangtse River in the early Neolithic (Roberts, 1989, 103), though its larger-scale development comes later. The migration of the Han Chinese—who had large-scale irrigation schemes for rice cultivation in the Hwang-Ho valley from the first century BC—from the Yangtse valley along the middle Han, the Hsiang Chan, and the Chiang Kan, after the fourth century AD, led to further extension of rice cultivation, and Grigg (1974, 86) shows that the main rice-growing areas as identifiable in the twentieth century were already established by the fourteenth century in such regions as the Yangtse delta, the Hsiang valley, Szechwan, and the lowlands of Kwantung. Major increases in intensity of rice cultivation were achieved from the eighteenth century, through double-cropping systems and application of newer intermediate technology methods, but a crisis point was reached in the nineteenth century because of substantial population pressure.

The production of rice for export from south and south-east Asia was an important feature of the nineteenth century, with profound implications for the economies and societies of the rice-producing regions. British control of the delta region of the Irrawady River in Lower Burma from 1855 resulted in a massive increase in production over the next 30 years, using immigrant labourers from Upper Burma and capital and rural credit provided by the owners of the rice mills of Rangoon and Bassein, with the exported rice going primarily to India. Other rice-exporting regions were Thailand and Cochin China (Wolf, 1982, 321).

The evolution of mixed farming areas: medieval Europe

One of the major determinants of the nature of European medieval rural landscapes was the complex dynamic of colonization of thinly peopled areas from more densely settled areas, notably from the eleventh century to the early fourteenth century when, for example, Germans from west of the River Elbe moved eastwards in very large numbers to appropriate and settle the lands of the West Slavs, of the Baltic tribes, and the Magyars in the northern part of the kingdom of Hungary. A parallel movement of smaller proportion involved the expansion of the Anglo-Normans westwards into Wales and Ireland. Included in this complex territorial and political dynamic was the reconquest of Spain from the Arab colonists.

The outcome in many instances was a transformed landscape. In the Slav territories east of the Elbe, professional planners were employed to survey and supervise the layout of new planned villages: green-villages or street-villages with regular forms and planned three-field arable systems. In western Europe, notably Ireland and Wales, however, the impact of the Anglo-Norman colonizers on the rural settlements and rural landscapes of the conquered regions resulted in less formal and regular layouts. One term frequently used to describe the complex arrangements of land tenure and labour service in medieval Europe is 'feudalism' or the 'feudal system', essentially a system of devolved political and economic control from a lord or king to a vassal, indicative of the gradual fragmentation of responsibilities of administration, law, and military defence from larger scales, such as those of early medieval states and empires, to smaller scales such as those of fiefs (Latin *feudum*), land held by subordinates of kings and lords in exchange for military service and payments of various kinds, right down to the level of the individual manor or seigneury and village. The basic division of agricultural land in the feudal manors was that of the lord's own land or demesne and the rest which was managed by free and unfree peasants under a complex variety of tenurial systems. The exact nature of feudalism varied chronologically and regionally within Europe.

In the Mediterranean a particular feature of agriculture was the provision of water for cultivation purposes in the many regions where it was in short supply. The extent of irrigation was limited by the availability of surface water supply and relatively shallow wells, the means of damming very large areas of water and of tapping deep aquifers being a very late and modern development. Irrigation ditches and water-meadows were in existence in the northern Italian lowlands by the twelfth century, and large irrigation canals were built by cities such as Milan in the twelfth and thirteenth centuries. The success of irrigation was partially dependent on the regularity of river flow, hence the increasing difficulty as one went farther south in Italy, though it was used in the south for the production of fruit and of rice.

Irrigation systems had been developed in Mediterranean Europe by the Romans, with some continuity after the collapse of the Roman Empire, but the major diffusers of irrigation in many parts of the Mediterranean were the Moors, who by the twelfth and thirteenth centuries had developed extensive systems around Saragossa, in Andalusia, Murcia, and Catalonia, based on the rivers Genil, Segura, and Segre. A major and famous system was the 'huerta' of Valencia, partly based on an intricate network of wells, dams and reservoirs developed in Moorish times.

In southern France revival of irrigation systems after the decline of earlier Roman systems occurred in the lower Rhône valley in the eleventh and twelfth centuries, providing a means of facilitating the supply of market-garden crops to the towns around which the irrigation systems were located, such as Avignon, but on a very much smaller scale than that of Spain. One of the key factors in the extent of irrigation was the tradition of water-use rights, the traditions of the Arab parts of the Mediterranean treating water as a communal resource, with many non-Arab areas treating it as a private resource.

Open- and communal-field systems and agricultural systems in Europe

The landscapes of medieval Europe comprised a mixture of arable land, pasture, meadow, wasteland or poor-quality common grazing land, and woodland and forest. A key feature was the arrangement and organization of arable land, much of it in very large, generally unfenced or unenclosed fields, subdivided into ownership and cultivation strips and parcels and managed under a variety of systems. The basic product was grain for domestic consumption, notably wheat to be eaten as bread, with a gradual increase through time of the area of wheat grown. The system in its variations maintained a balance between grain and livestock, through complex systems of land use and use-rights (Fig. 8.1).

Three major types of field system may be identified. The first, the so-called open-field system, was long characteristic of much of north-west, central and south-central Europe north of the Mediterranean, and consisted of very large

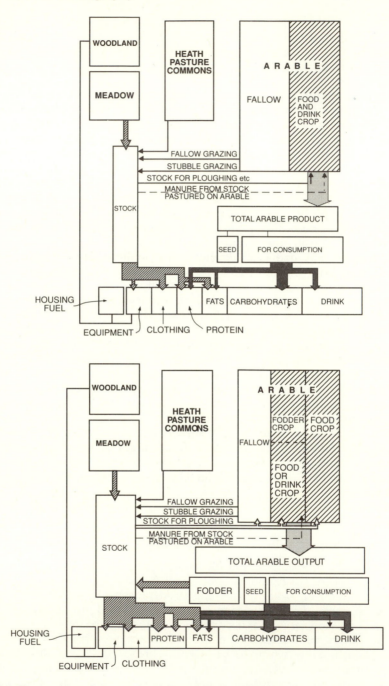

Fig. 8.1 *The ecology of the medieval European open-field system. Top: two-course fallow rotations. Bottom: three-course winter corn, spring corn, fallow rotation. Source: Smith (1967, 206)*

open arable fields, in combinations of three, four or more, managed under a communal control system which regulated every aspect of use, including the distribution of cultivation strips, the rotation of crops, the grazing of animals on the fields after crops were harvested and when they were left uncultivated during periods of rest or fallow. These large areas of arable land were most frequently found in lowland and plateau areas with fertile soil, for example loess or limon, and in association with village settlements managed under a feudal manorial system. A feature of such a system was the often long and always narrow strips which were units of cultivation and of tenure, the direction and form of the longer axis of the strip frequently being determined by ploughing technique, a reversed 'S' shape often indicative of the use of a heavy plough and a large team of oxen. This 'ridge-and-furrow', as it is known in England, can be seen in many parts of England which subsequently changed to grassland in the modern period, and where the undulations are well preserved on the ground.

By the beginning of the seventeenth century major forces of change had begun the further transformation of the local and regional patterns of open fields developed during the Middle Ages, and which according to some commentators, had reached their maximum extent in the thirteenth and fourteenth centuries. The geographical pattern of open-field systems in England in the early modern period related to three basic types: regular systems, irregular systems, and enclosed systems. Variants on the classic 'Midland' three-field system were to be found in a strip of territory running from the south coast of England between Devon and Dorset, running northwards and narrowing to the north-east in the coastal plain of Northumberland. The elements of the system in 'idealized' form included three large open arable fields, subdivided into tenurial and cultivational strips, allocated to various members of the farming community according to status, tenure and entitlement, the pattern of use reflected in an intermingling of strips. The ideal rotation was three-course. In practice there were major variations within the Midland zone. More irregular systems were to be found in the north of England and in East Anglia. Figure 8.2 shows the field systems of two open-field settlements in Cambridgeshire in the mid-seventeenth century, reconstructed from a survey of 1656, the main fields at Soham to the north being North Field, No Ditch Field, Down Field and Clipsall Field, the latter intercommoned and cultivated with Fordham, whose additional main open fields were Fordham Hales, Biggen Field and Chippenham Field (again intercommoned) to the south (not marked on the survey map).

Open fields were not, of course ubiquitous. Systems of agricultural practice based on enclosed fields were quite extensive, and were frequently found in areas of woodland clearance, including parts of Essex, Hertfordshire, the West and East Midlands, and the Kent and Sussex Weald (Baker and Butlin, 1973; Dodgshon, 1980).

A second type of field system was that of the northern and western maritime fringes of Europe, sometimes known as a 'Celtic' system because of its apparent association with areas of Celtic speech and settlement in prehistoric times, though it is not at all possible to attribute the variety of cultivation systems given this general name to a Celtic or even a common origin. In such areas, where there is in fact much more emphasis on the pastoral aspect of the rural economy and landscape than on the arable, the proportion of grassland

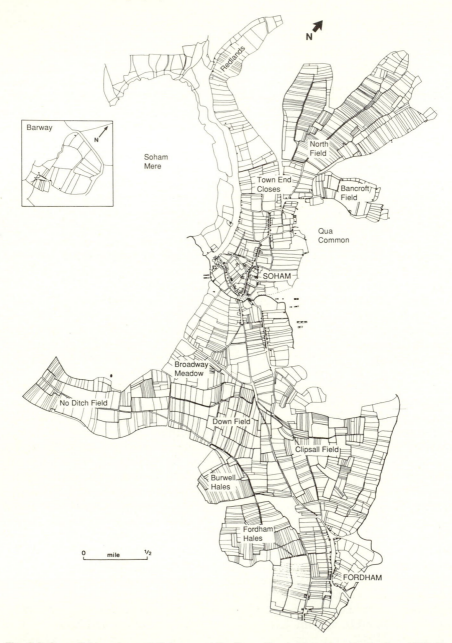

Fig. 8.2 *Open-field systems at Soham and Fordham, Cambridgeshire, England, c. 1656. The main elements of these systems are the four open fields, in which the holdings of the farmers were scattered, together with the meadow, pasture and commons. Based on the survey by William Palmer. Cambridgeshire County Record Office, 107P.*

being far greater, the form of arable fields and cultivation was essentially that of a small area of open arable field, cultivated intensively and often without fallow or rest, intensively manured, and used for the growing of cereal crops, notably barley, rye and oats. The fields were subdivided into strips, which in some regions were reallocated from one year to another, often by drawing lots. This small area of arable was, especially at times of population pressure, supplemented by the ploughing-out of temporary patches of arable from the surrounding waste areas, which were intensively manured and cultivated and then allowed to revert to their former condition. The main arable field is sometimes referred to as the 'infield' and the surrounding area as the 'outfield'. In some parts of western Europe, for example western Brittany, the cultivated fields were not open, that is unfenced, but enclosed. A variety of types of such a rural economy were found in medieval Europe (Fig. 8.3), one example being the 'drubbel' and 'langstreifenflur' systems of north-west Germany, where in the 'Geest' or heath regions were to be found many small hamlet-type settlements whose economy was based on the cultivation in open fields with 'langstreifenflur' or long strip fields of raised islands of better sandy soils, on which islands the farmsteads themselves were located.

The medieval field system of northern Europe varied regionally, reflecting the nature of the physical environment and the social and economic structures, including the size and distribution of population. There were large areas of Scandinavia which were sparsely populated or totally devoid of population. The most densely populated area was Denmark. Figure 8.4 shows the main variations in field systems in Denmark in the seventeenth century, illustrating the great variation in types of land-use management.

The actual settlement forms in northern Europe were predominantly dispersed individual farmsteads, notably in Norway, Iceland and the Faeroe Islands. Two types of field system were the 'bolskifte' and the 'solskifte' systems, found in Denmark and parts of Sweden, especially the south. The 'bol' of the 'bolskifte' system was an arable area of about 25 hectares, subdivided into tenurial and cultivation units, the 'solskifte' system involved the layout of the strips of the open arable field or fields according to the direction of the passage of the sun. Laws providing for this 'sun-regulation' were codified at an early date in Jutland and south-central Sweden. The main crops cultivated were rye, barley, and oats, with a fallow (rest) period incorporated. Additional products were peas and beans, flax and hemp, some fruit and, of course, hay from the meadows.

The third major variant of European field-system type was that of the Mediterranean, where in a different environment a wider range of crops was involved, reflecting topographic and climatic variation. The three topographic elements were and are plains, mountains, and hills, matched in the system of agrarian production by a respective emphasis on arable, grazing (particularly for sheep and goats), and woodland. The relationship between these three types of land use was never fixed, the tendency being for increases in arable and pasture to be at the expense of woodland. The field systems of the Mediterranean were of a greater variety than those of northern and north-western Europe.

An additional important characteristic of this region was the growth of tree- and shrub-crops, including the olive, the vine, the fig, and citrus fruits, together with vegetables and fruits such as almonds, chestnuts, sugar, and melon. Rice

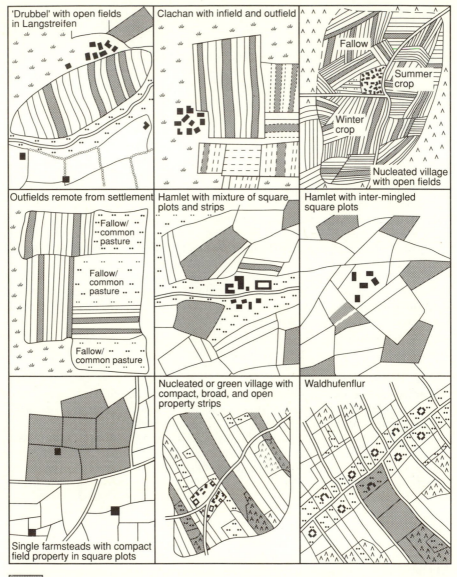

Fig. 8.3 *Different possible types of open fields in western and central Europe. Source: Uhlig (1961, 306)*

was an important irrigated crop, grown in the delta and alluvial river lands of the Mediterranean.

An important feature of the rural landscapes of Mediterrean Europe was the practice of transhumance, the movement of animals to summer pastures in the uplands and mountains. In Spain there were many routes by means of which vast numbers of sheep from the regions of the central Meseta and the

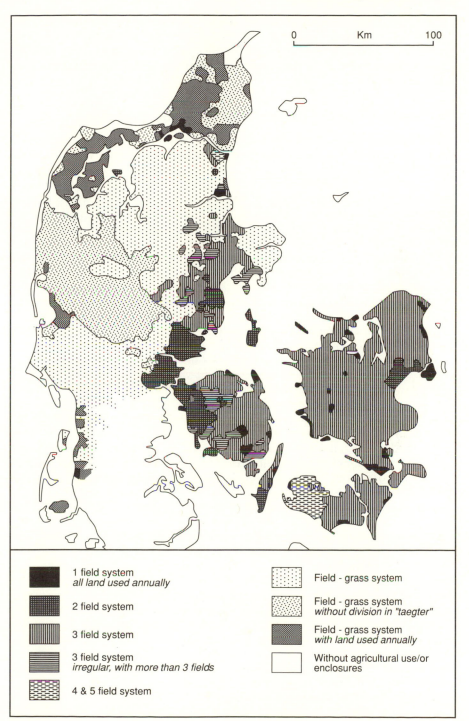

0   Km   100

1 field system
all land used annually

2 field system

3 field system

3 field system
irregular, with more than 3 fields

4 & 5 field system

Field - grass system

Field - grass system
without division in "taegter"

Field - grass system
with land used annually

Without agricultural use/or
enclosures

Fig. 8.4 *Field systems of Denmark, 1682–83. Source: Frandsen (1985, 305)*

Guadalquivir valley were taken to the summer pastures in the Pyrenees and the Cantabrian mountains. Similar movements occurred in southern France from the lowlands to the summer pastures for sheep and goats in the Alps and the Massif Central, and in Italy from the coastal plains and marshes to the pastures of the Apennines.

The farming systems of Europe in the early modern period

An accelerating characteristic of rural Europe in the early modern period was that of differences of regional experience. The most rapid pace of agricultural change through improvement of techniques of cultivation and the diffusion of new crops was in the Low Countries and England, and parts of northern Italy, southern France and small areas of eastern Europe. A region which experienced major increases in agricultural output through a combination of innovation in crops, cropping systems and in the extension of the amount of land cultivated was the Low Countries, where, since the fifteenth century, a combination of factors, including population growth, increased urbanization, the challenge of what were generally difficult soil and drainage conditions, and the northward movement of the economic centre of gravity of Europe from the Mediterranean, led to major agricultural innovations. In the greatest period of prosperity, that is 1590–1670, these included: the intensification of arable cultivation by, for example, the progressive elimination of the fallow year in the three-course crop rotation through its replacement by a fodder crop like lucerne or turnip or by a sown grass; the introduction of commercial crops like flax, hops, madder, woad, and tobacco; light-wheeled ploughs on light soils; cultivation of seeds on raised beds; and use of a wider range of fertilizers, many of them artifical; and the intensification of animal husbandry. The new crop rotations varied widely, from three and four to six or more courses of crops. There was a major extension of farmland around the coasts of north-west Europe by land reclamation, both from the sea by poldering and from large inland lakes by pumping. The major regions affected were the coastal polders of the Low Countries (about 45,000 hectares reclaimed between 1565 and 1615), Schleswig Holstein (25,000 hectares by 1650), western France, and the Fens of East Anglia in England (about 160,000 hectares in the seventeenth century). The reclamation of the inland lakes or meres required a new technology of pumping out water, provided by the spread of the windmill, and accelerated by the major investment of capital in this type of reclamation by the burgesses of the larger cities, notably Amsterdam. Land reclamation from river and coastal marsh also was rapidly underway in Italy, with 100,000 hectares drained in Venezia and smaller areas of the Maremma in Tuscany, Campania, and the Pontine marshes during the seventeenth century. This phase of reclamation was part of a wider movement of land improvement in Europe, reflecting the rise in grain prices and also reflected in the cultivation of waste land and the recovery of land which had often remained uncultivated since the settlement desertions of the fourteenth century. Other areas of conspicuous agricultural improvement at this time were England, and parts of northern and western France.

The rural economies of southern Europe varied regionally and topographically. The mountain areas of the Apennines, Pyrenees, Sierra Nevada, Sierra Morena, and the southern Alps were characterized by a pastoral economy using the extensive upland pastures for sheep and cattle, related to the seasonal transhumance movement of animals and their keepers to and from the upland and lowland pastures, and also the forest resources of these regions. The rural economy was marginal, however, and such regions frequently were subject to loss of population by emigration. On the foothill and lower hill slopes of the Mediterranean, an active and generally mixed agriculture was practised, within a zone of Mediterranean scrub (*maquis, macchia*). The generally terraced slopes of the coastlands contained olives, vines, almond trees, mulberry trees, and fruit trees. In the hotter, more southerly areas citrus fruits were produced, and there were attempts to increase the extent of the production of rice, sugar and cotton. Maize had spread eastwards into south-west France from Spain by the mid-sixteenth century, and Italy by the late sixteenth century, and became commonplace in the moister regions of the Mediterranean by the late seventeenth century. Cereal production was also an important part of the Mediterranean economy, including the cultivation of such crops as wheat, rye, barley, and millet.

In Scandinavia the early modern period is one of both stability and change in rural societies, economies and landscapes, the fundamental basis of the agrarian economy being a mixed cropping/pastoral economy with fishing, forestry-related activity and some hunting. The older open-field system persisted in the areas of better soil and climate, but with some indications of the beginnings of enclosure, notably in Sweden. Varied forms existed in Scandinavia, ranging from the large multiple fields of eastern Denmark and Skåne in southern Sweden to the more irregular systems in the more marginal areas.

Some parallels have been drawn between the rural experiences of northern Europe and eastern and central Europe at this time, notably in respect of the creation of areas of cultivation from the extensive areas of woodland and forest, with the rise in cereal prices from the mid-sixteenth century effecting an increase in the production of wheat and rye and a relative reduction in the extent of use of natural pastures for animal husbandry. The social and tenurial features of this period are the increase in serfdom and feudal relations of production on the larger estates.

Changes in Rural Europe from the Eighteenth to the Twentieth Century

Although major changes in agricultural production had been making their mark on the rural landscapes of Europe from the late Middle Ages, it was the period from the eighteenth century onwards that witnessed the most dramatic changes. These included the consolidation and enclosure of the open fields and their replacement in many regions by systems of enclosed fields and the removal of communal land-use rights; the development of new implements, crop rotations, and animal breeding systems; the development of new methods of fertilization of crops and genetic improvements in plants; the opening up of new markets; the intensified investment of capital in the countryside for production and for pleasure, the latter reflected in the magnificent designed and planned landscapes; and the extension of cultivated and managed land by reclamation from marsh and heath. The term 'agricultural revolution' has been applied to the major changes that occurred in the rural regions of Europe in the eighteenth and nineteenth centuries. While there can be no doubt of the significance of the complex changes that did occur in many regions, notably England and Germany, the term is not particularly helpful as it simplifies the technical, chronological and regional complexity of agricultural change, and also perhaps disguises the negative effects for the rural poor.

One of the conspicuous features of this period was the consolidation of scattered holdings, especially in regions of open fields, and the appropriation of communal rights of land use to a smaller group of landowners. The rationale behind such movements had a lot to do with the notion that the older system of widely scattered holdings, especially the arable strips, was uneconomic and travel was time consuming, though the question is by no means as simple as this. In England and Wales, the process was known as 'enclosure', that is the land which was consolidated was enclosed, in a physical sense, by hedges, stone walls and ditches. The mechanism was the use of Acts of Parliament, called Enclosure Acts (introduced by pressure from the landowners and agreed by a strongly landed interest in Parliament) and the redistribution of land via awards by specially appointed enclosure commissioners. The outcome was not only, in the areas affected, a new regular geometrical pattern of field shapes, but also a landscape with new roads and farmsteads. While enclosure had been a continuous process, accelerating in the seventeenth century, the movement of the eighteenth and nineteenth centuries virtually completed the elimination of the open fields (especially in Midland and eastern England) and commons, with the exception of some of the remoter upland pastures.

A similar consolidation and enclosure process also occurred in Scandinavia. Land reorganization known as 'storskifte' began with legislation in Sweden in 1749 (Fig. 8.5), which effected some measure of consolidation in a number of small hamlets, and was followed by further legislation in 1757, though the overall effect seems to have been more important for the introduction of progressive ideas than for major landscape and tenurial change. Consolidation ('udskiftning') started early in Denmark, and peaked between 1780 and 1800, effecting the dissolution of the nucleated village communities related to open-field farming and the spread of newer patterns of dispersed individual farmsteads. A newer form of consolidation (Fig. 8.6) occurred in Sweden and in Finland, the 'enskifte' (consolidation at the request of one owner, legalized in Sweden from 1803) and 'lagaskifte' (from 1827, which allowed more than one piece of land for each farm, including allocations of former common arable, meadow, pasture and forest land), also produced the dissolution of villages and the spread of isolated farmsteads, particularly in forested regions: an estimated total for dispersed farmsteads in the period 1828–1922 in Sweden is 83,000. Consolidation and redistribution of open-field strips is later in Norway, where the open fields were smaller; the process dates from 1821.

It would be wrong to assume that this major process of appropriation of use-rights of common land was achieved without protest and resistance by the peasants deprived of such rights. There were many instances throughout the eighteenth and nineteenth centuries of rural protest in various forms, some dramatic and causing physical damage, others more modest, attempting to stop the process by legal means.

Land consolidation was encouraged by the Prussian government in northern

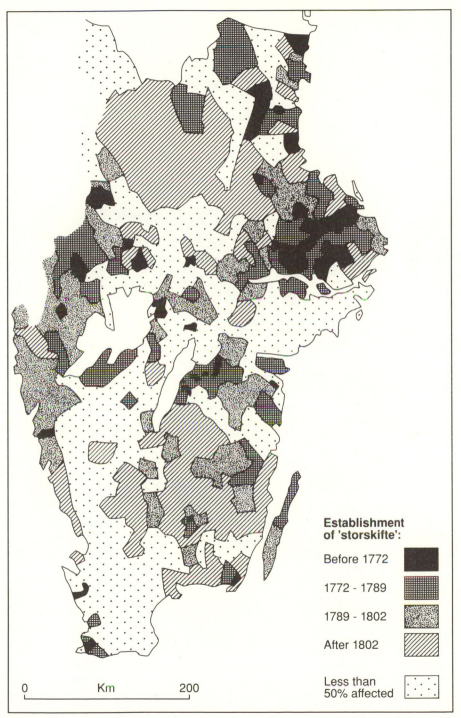

Fig. 8.5 *'Storskifte' in Sweden in the eighteenth and nineteenth centuries. Source: Helmfrid (1961b, 120)*

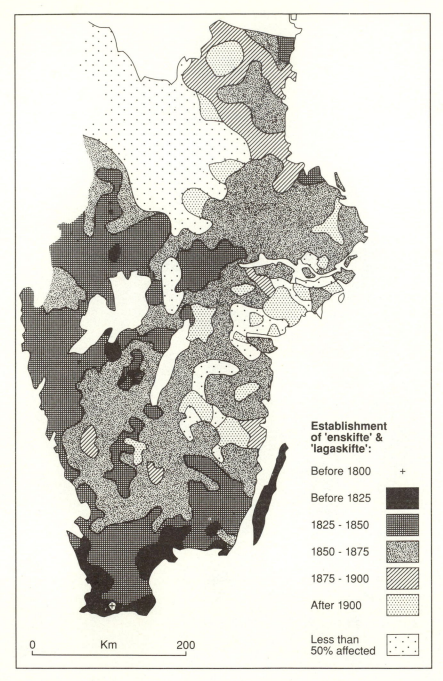

Fig. 8.6 *'Enskifte' and 'lagaskifte' in Sweden in the eighteenth, nineteenth and twentieth centuries. Source: Helmfrid (1961b, 123)*

Germany in the first half of the nineteenth century. In most of the rest of Europe such rationalizations of farm holdings came gradually, and the major reforms much later. In the case of such countries as Switzerland, France, and Belgium, the major reforms came after the Second World War. Progress in this direction was also slow in eastern Europe and the Balkans, major change only being produced in the Soviet Union and other socialist countries through the creation of collective and state farms. Although attempts at consolidation have been made in the Mediterranean countries, large areas of Spain, Italy and Greece remain under highly fragmented patterns of landholding.

The accommodation of the rapidly growing population of Europe in the modern period and the consequent demands for increased food supplies was partially achieved by the extension of cultivable and managed land, through land reclamation and improvement through draining and underdraining and the reclamation of extensive areas of sandy heathland. The major area of land reclamation from the sea is the Netherlands, with the revival of drainage of small polders and inland lakes, through the means of windmills and then by steam pumping, in north Holland throughout the nineteenth century (the Anna Paulowna polder and the Haarlemmermeer, for example), and the beginning of the reclamation of land from the sea through the creation of larger polders. The most dramatic changes were those of the Zuiderzee, sealed to become the IJsselmeer in 1932, enabling the creation of the Wieringermeer, Nordoost, Oost-Flevoland, Zuid-Flevoland and Markerwaard polders, in one of the most spectacular engineering feats in Europe of the twentieth century. In the Netherlands there was also major reclamation of sandy heath and waste land, notably after the Enclosure Act of 1886, the foundation of the Nederlandsche Heide Mij in 1888, and the application of artificial fertilizers. Estimates for land reclamation from the sea and from the waste in the period 1833–1911 are 93,000 and 370,000 hectares respectively. Parallel development in heathland reclamation occurred in Denmark, with the establishment of the Danish Heathland Society in 1866 and the reclamation of the extensive heaths of Jutland.

Major changes in rural landscapes of Europe were influenced by additional technological innovations, too extensive and complex to mention except in outline. They included: the accelerated adoption of new crops and trees, such as the potato, turnip and swede, beetroot, maize, and tobacco, and (more recently) rape-seed, aloes, cacti and eucalyptus; rotations including clover and lucerne; the development and adoption of tile underdrainage of wet farmland, especially clay; improved ploughs; machine-driven implements such as combine harvesters, threshing-machines, seed drills; the ubiquitous tractor; the coming of electricity to rural communities; the application of artificial fertilizers to the soil; the improvement of pesticides (though not without negative consequences for the environment); and the genetic improvement of plants and farm animals. Cooperation in agriculture has several faces, including the successful cooperative dairying movements of Scandinavia and Ireland from the nineteenth century, and the state-enforced agrarian cooperatives of eastern Europe and the Soviet Union from the twentieth century, both with marked effects on the rural landscape.

Dairy farming and the introduction of agricultural cooperatives

One interesting institutional development in Europe in the nineteenth century was the agricultural cooperative movement which effected economies of scale for marketing agricultural products and for purchasing in bulk seed, fertilizers, feeding stuffs and machinery, and for processing of farm products, notably milk. Reflecting a long tradition of communal cooperation in a wide variety of agrarian tasks, the formal cooperative movement emerged in the nineteenth century mainly as a peasant response to the power of the market and of large-scale commercial agricultural production, but also as a political statement about the autonomy of peasant farmers relative to the owners of large estates. The exact nature of cooperatives and the history of their development varies from place to place. One of the earliest cooperative movements was in Denmark, where agrarian reforms at the end of the eighteenth century had given security to a large number of emancipated peasant landowners, where rural education advanced, and for which large world markets in dairy produce were opening up. The first cooperative dairy was established in Denmark in 1882, mainly to make butter by use of the centrifugal separator, invented in 1878. The number of cooperatives had increased to 1503 by 1914 (Milward and Saul, 1979, 506–7).

The Danish system was influential on the pattern of cooperatives developed in Ireland, initially under the influence of Sir Horace Plunkett who settled permanently in Ireland in 1889 and addressed the problem of the poor packing and grading of butter and eggs for export. He started a cooperative society at Doneraile in Co. Wexford in 1889, which accelerated the movement towards cooperative dairies or 'creameries', and the increase in cooperatives was swift, there being 33 by 1894, mainly in the counties of Cork, Tipperary and Kilkenny. This work was further promoted by the Irish Agricultural Organisation Society, founded in 1894 (Lyons, 1973, 209–10).

The cooperative movement in agriculture was also experienced in other parts of Europe, including the Netherlands, France, and Germany. The Netherlands had an extensive agricultural cooperative movement, with the first purchasing cooperative set up to buy fertilizers in 1877, and from 1987 a large number of auction societies was established, in which the descending-price Dutch auction method was used for the sale of market-garden produce. The first credit bank was opened in 1896 (Huggett, 1975, 136).

In France the earliest establishment of cooperative dairies followed the ravages of the vineyards by phylloxera, and cereal and wine-producing cooperatives were established mainly after the depression of the 1930s.

Baker (1980; 1984a) has outlined the context of the emergence of agricultural 'syndicats' in France in the second half of the nineteenth century: groupings of peasants formed to make efficient use of labour and resources, to preserve their existence and their freedom in the face of strong market pressures, and to implement a range of ideologies of moral, social and political goals, including those of Republicanism and Social Catholicism.

Baker's studies of the 'syndicats' and some of the fraternities of the Département of Loir-et-Cher, the former mainly comprising livestock insurance, threshing and general-purpose agricultural syndicates, have added considerable theory and detail to the analysis of agrarian cooperation and community organization (Baker, 1980; 1984b; 1986; 1990). The Syndicat des

Agriculteurs de Loir-et-Cher, based at Blois, was the first agricultural 'syndicat' to be established in France, and its main economic purpose was the bulk purchase of fertilizers to be supplied to its members at advantageous cost, but it also provided them with technical information, through its monthly *Bulletin* and subsequently its weekly journal, and with credit facilities, through the establishment of a 'Caisse Régionale' (Baker, 1986).

In Germany an early model for cooperative structures was set up by Friedrich Raiffeisen, first through the establishment of a loan society for peasants in the Rhineland in 1862, and then through the creation of a coopeative bank in 1862, which was extensively adopted elsewhere in Europe (Huggett, 1975, 136).

Cooperatives for agriculture and the processing and marketing of its products was not simply a European phenomenon. Cooperative cheese and butter making began in the mid-nineteenth century in the eastern United States, especially New York State (Gates, 1960, 245–6), and cooperative creameries were established in New Zealand, notably in the North Island, from 1882 (Cumberland and Whitelaw, 1970, 40). The cooperative ideal and the movements associated with it spread beyond agriculture, to include cooperative wholesale purchase for urban dwellers, a common form found in Britain in the 1830s and 1840s and later through the medium of the Co-operative Wholesale Society, a consumer's society which became a global organization and 'developed manufacturing, retailing and farming interests in scores of countries, supported by millions of predominantly working-class subscribers' (Powell, 1977, 147–8). In the twentieth centuries, different forms of cooperative, with different ideologies, also developed in Israel and in the Soviet Union.

A colonial farming system: the plantation

The plantation had developed in many tropical and subtropical areas as part of the commercial strategy of European colonizing powers in the sixteenth, seventeenth and eighteenth centuries. Their main products in the seventeenth century—sugar, tobacco and indigo—met the demand of the changing tastes of European populations and the changing needs of European industry in the case of crops such as cotton. Cheap land, cheap labour, and overseas markets in the parent colonial countries were the three elements of plantation agriculture. Some of the earliest were the Portuguese sugar plantations along the northeastern coast of Brazil, established in the sixteenth century in response to rapidly rising sugar prices in Europe by wealthy colonists, each plantation comprising the cultivated or fallow cane fields, the pasture for oxen, the land cultivated for food, and the woodland areas used as reserves for future cultivation (West, 1982, 71–2). Brazilian sugar dominated the European market until the early eighteenth century. The labour used, as in all early plantation systems, was slave labour, initially of local Indian populations and subsequently of black slaves from Africa. The low cost of slave labour and the cheapness of transport—in appalling conditions—meant that normal labour costs, including those of family farms, were always undercut by this system.

The plantation system diffused from Brazil and Barbados to other islands in the Gulf of Mexico and the Caribbean to the southern mainland of North America, and by the late eighteenth century the large plantation was a common feature of the landscape and culture of the South, with regional mosaics of specialization in sugar, cotton, tobacco, rice and hemp, though the question of whether such crops were grown on plantations or smaller farms was influenced by such factors as transport facilities and the availability of large tracts of land (Hilliard, 1990, 104–7).

Grantham has suggested the analogy of the plantation with industrial factory organization: 'it was entrepreneurial, centralized production decisions afforded considerable scope for the division of labour, and depended on a smoothly functioning commercial system to attain its extremely high level of specialization. It was eminently suited to respond massively to market opportunity' (Grantham, 1989, 4).

During the course of the nineteenth century the nature and distribution of plantation agriculture changed. Although the demand from industrial Europe for cotton intensified production in the plantations of the American South, the abolition of the slave trade and of slave labour in British colonies, the abolition of the slave trade by the United States, France and the Netherlands, the effects of the Napoleonic Wars, and the broadening of British hegemony outside the Caribbean led to a move away from sugar production on plantations based on slave labour towards other labour systems of production, in the Caribbean in particular. Slave labour intensified, however, in Brazil and Cuba in the nineteenth century. The British control of other tropical areas of the world was accompanied by the demise of the old planter class and its replacement by major metropolitan corporations which controlled the commercial plantations of the tropics in the nineteenth and twentieth centuries, moving control from the local planter classes to more distant locations from the areas of production (Wolf, 1982, 315–17). Indentured labour, especially from India, was a new form of labour provision introduced in the 1830s to the British Caribbean and British Guiana, and later in the century to new plantation colonies of Natal, Fiji and Malaya. New plantation crops developed in the British colonies in the nineteenth and early twentieth centuries included tea, notably in Assam in India, and rubber, particularly in Ceylon and Malaysia (Christopher, 1988, 176–85).

Modern Commercial Farming Systems

Large-scale wheat farming in the nineteenth and twentieth centuries

The development of large-scale grain farming in countries such as Canada, the United States, Australia, Argentina, South Africa, and subsequently the Soviet Union is a feature of a world market for foodstuffs consequent on the industrialization and population expansion of the developed and developing economies in the nineteenth and twentieth centuries. The incapacity of the industrializing nations of Europe to provide sufficient food from their own agricultural systems for their expanding populations, together with the development of more efficient transoceanic shipping, and legislative changes such as the repeal of the British Corn Laws in 1846 (removing laws which hitherto had protected Britain from competition from cheaper important grain from Europe and North America), pointed to the dramatic opening of markets for countries where large-scale production of the crops required, notably wheat, was possible.

In the instance of Australia there were major changes in the production of wheat—indeed in the nature of Australian agriculture in general—from the mid-nineteenth century, partly occasioned by increased domestic demand, notably the gold rushes which started in 1850, and by international market demand facilitated by the repeal of the British Corn Laws, and the later post-First World War Imperial preference system, together with improvements in the flow of price and availability information via the international telegraph system, fast sailing clippers and subsequently steamships. The expansion of the agricultural area in Australia was initially, from *c.* 1850 to 1880, on grassland or savannah woodland, but thereafter the move was to shrubland, where new clearing methods, including the use of the stump-jump plough, were required when farmers were faced with mallee and acacia scrub. An additional factor was the necessity of moving the grain from inland regions to the ports, made possible by the development of railways from the 1860s to the 1890s. (Heathcote, 1975, 106–7). The major expansion of wheat farming in the late nineteenth century was on the red-brown earth soils of the south-east in South Australia, Victoria, and New South Wales. The movement of this wheat farming frontier did not take place, of course, in a proprietorial vacuum, and part of the story of wheat farming involves an understanding of methods of land allocation, survey, settlement and management. The allocation system in South Australia, for example, produced an administrative hierarchy of counties, hundreds and farm blocks, mainly on a gridiron system, with the 1869 Land Act setting 640 acres as a maximum allocation, though many were much smaller. Technological improvements in South Australia included the Ridley stripper and the small stationary winnower, and the advent of locally adapted combine harvesters in the 1880s (Meinig, 1963, 106–10). Problems associated with this type of commercial farming in a pioneer environment incuded criticisms of shallow ploughing, inadequate fallowing, the lack of livestock in the system, and the almost exclusive production for export.

In the United States the development of commercial grain farming involved an initial period of a moving wheat frontier, between 1840 and 1870 on the prairie fringe of Illinois, Wisconsin and Minnesota, the frontier having reached western Minnesota by the 1870s, but with the appearance of rust and other crop diseases, this region moved to dairying and the advent of newer disease-resistant strains of wheat enabled spring wheat production to focus on North Dakota and Montana. The drained wet prairies south from Chicago to Omaha developed into a maize-growing region, and from the advance of the agricultural frontier westwards across the Mississippi in the mid-nineteenth century there emerged the wheat belt of Kansas. After 1900 grain farming reached the grasslands of western Oklahoma and Texas. The use of dry farming techniques enabled moisture conservation to take place in the semi-arid regions of the west and north (Hudson, 1990, 176–81). International trade in grain was stimulated by the expanded demand and high prices for wheat at the time of the Crimean War in Europe and the record crops in Wisconsin and Illinois in 1854, together with the extension of the railroads (bringing modern transport to most of the upper Mississippi valley) and the development of a boom in demand for land for wheat growing. Gates reports that: 'The 72 per cent increase in wheat production in the fifties, which took place entirely in the

Mississippi valley, made possible large sales of wheat abroad during the Crimean War and again during the Civil War. The wheat exports contributed to the prosperity of the United States in the fifties and were a major item on the credit side of her balance of payments and an important factor in her international relations' (Gates, 1960, 167). In 1851 1,026,725 bushels of wheat were exported from the United States, and the figure had risen to 31,238,057 bushels in 1861. The advent of more efficient means of sowing and harvesting wheat, particularly through combine harvesters, in the period 1860–90, intensified production but also in many instances increased the cost to the environment, resulting in crop failures and lowering of yields. The dramatic outcome of grain farming in marginal environments is evident in the experience of the Dust Bowl conditions of the Great Plains of the 1930s.

Cheap land, allocated under both market conditions and specific government and state settlement policies, together with increasing world demand for grain, were the main stimuli for the development of commercial grain-growing in the nineteenth and twentieth centuries. The positive consequences were the ability to provide the rapidly increasing urban and industrial populations with cheap food, but the consequences in terms of vulnerability of the specialist producing regions to slumps in demand and in price and to environmental exhaustion and degradation were profound.

Commercial grazing enterprises of the nineteenth and twentieth centuries

One of the major impacts of the areas of European settlement in the nineteenth century in Australasia, Latin America and Africa, and of the changing economy of the United States, was the development of the specialist rearing of animals, notably cattle and sheep, on a very large scale, in order to cater for and profit by the demand for meat from the increasing populations of the rapidly industrializing countries of Europe, and subsequently of increasing domestic populations. The patterns of demand were thus similar to those for grain, especially wheat, but the environments and regions affected and involved were different.

The emergence of commercial cattle production or ranching as it became known is a feature of the second half of the nineteenth century, when the demand from industrializing nations for meat and meat products could be met from the pastoral areas of New Zealand, Australia, South America and parts of southern Africa, thanks to the speeding up and cheapening of cost of transoceanic transport, but also the invention and incorporation of refrigeration into ships and railways, and the advent of meat canning (Grigg, 1974, 241). The term 'ranching' is normally applied to the grazing of large areas of natural grassland vegetation by herds of cattle and flocks of sheep, but many of the natural grassland areas have been transformed by the sowing of artificial grasses such as lucerne and alfalfa.

In South America the commercial possibilities of the temperate grasslands or pampas of Argentina, Chile, and Uruguay were recognized in the early nineteenth century, and Britain negotiated a treaty of friendship and commerce with Argentina in 1824, leading initially to the export of wool from the poor-quality sheep of the pampas, with the quality improving from the 1830s as better sheep were introduced. The export potential of cattle was limited by the lack of means of refrigeration and preservation of meat, factors that changed with Liebig's development of a method of producing a meat extract in 1847, and the initiation of transport of refrigerated meat from 1877 onwards. New breeds of cattle were introduced in the 1870s, notably the Aberdeen Angus, to cater for British markets, and though at first exported live, this practice ceased after 1900 in consequence of the foot and mouth disease outbreaks, and meat thenceforth was mainly exported in frozen form (Lobb, 1982, 171). Major attempts were made by the Argentinian government to open up the pampas for agricultural settlement, including rather unsuccessful equivalents of the United States' land grant programmes, but the development of railways from the 1860s and the modification of traditional patterns of stock-grazing by the introduction of sown alfalfa grass to the Buenos Aires province intensified productivity.

The transformation of the economy of New Zealand through the commercial development of sheep-raising is a well-known story. Planned settlement of New Zealand dates from 1840 with the formal annexation of New Zealand as a British colony and the beginning of implementation of the Wakefield plan for colonization. From the 1850s new land laws gave greater liberty to settlers to move into the eastern plains, downlands and basins of the South Island, occupied on the basis of sale, free grant, and lease systems, and Australian and English pastoralists introduced and built up huge flocks of merino sheep, managing the tussock grassland by burning it to eliminate the tussock leaves. By 1881 there were more than 13 million sheep in the colony (Cumberland and Whitelaw, 1970, 34). Shipment of frozen meat to Britain began in 1882, initiating a long period of high dependence on the British market and a transfer of emphasis in sheep farming from the production of wool to the production of meat and the consequent introduction of a wide range of cross-breeds more appropriate to the market than the merino.

In Australia pastoral systems of land use had been in place from the late eighteenth century around the coastal settlements, but only after the discovery of high-quality natural grasslands across the Blue Mountains was sheep and cattle farming intensified and specialized. Ultimately expansion took place into the semi-arid shrublands and poorer grasslands of the interior. Early expansion to the grazing lands was in the south-east prior to the 1830s, thence in the south and south-west, involving sheep, cattle, and horses, and by the 1890s the northern gazing lands had been occupied. The system of land acquisition and allocation varied through time, initially involving a mixture of private enterprise, grants leases, and illegal squatting, but after 1847 a leasing system for pastoral land was introduced, a measure by means of which revenue could be derived from the rent of crown lands and control maintained over the system of land use, facilitating, where appropriate, a transition to cultivation (Heathcote, 1975, 87–93.) Problems in the interior were posed by the nature of the vegetation, the lack of water, and towards the end of the nineteenth century with the removal of vegetation by the rabbit which had been introduced in the 1860s. The water problem was partially solved by the drilling of deep boreholes to tap the artesian water supplies between about 1880 and 1900, though major losses of livestock were still occasioned by drought. The precarious nature of livestock farming was a reflection of cycles of drought, overstocking, environmental degradation and fluctuations in demand, and there were dramatic reductions in sheep and cattle populations in the last decade of the nineteenth century, but further expansion was made possible through refrigeration of meat for transport over long distances, with some very large-scale investment by international companies in Australia early in the twentieth century (Christopher, 1988, 208–9).

Common denominators in the historical geography of commercial grazing enterprises of the new lands of the nineteenth century included their mono-cultural aspect, their existence at frontiers of settlement and land use, their overexploitation of resources, resulting in degradation and catastrophe on many occasions, the large scale of the unit of enterprise, their very close links with European markets, and their frequent promotion or facilitation through a complex series of national and local land allocation policies. Each region differed in its particular experience, and a full appreciation of the geography of this type of activity can only be made by focus on detailed studies, for example Powell's (1970) study of land allocation and settlement policy in Victoria.

The Concept of the Frontier: the Turner Hypothesis

The concept of a frontier of settlement or a farming frontier is a familiar one to the geographer, having the connotation of a dividing line between, for example, the territory of two separate states or polities. A more dynamic version has the notion of a frontier as a temporary notional line, marking the point reached by a moving set of processes of settlement, occupation, and use of land and territory deemed to be either empty or underpopulated. This version is quite important to the study of the historical geography of changing economic and settlement systems, so some short discussion and exemplification of it is appropriate at this point.

The best known use of the frontier concept or hypothesis is that of the American historian Turner (1861–1932), conspicuously in his publication 'The significance of the frontier in American history' (1894). The basic tenets of Turner's hypothesis were that the westward-moving frontier of settlement and land-use modification that was characteristic of the United States, beginning in the east in the seventeenth century and moving rapidly for much of the nineteenth century, facilitated by the supply of a large area of what he deemed to be free land accompanied by a rich and varied resource base, was fundamental and instrumental in shaping the nature of America's historical development, moving progressively away from its European origins and towards a very different national character, democratic in nature and based on the individualism and opportunism derived from confrontation with a wilderness environment. The frontier ended in effect in the 1880s.

In a re-evaluation of Turner's hypothesis Walsh (1981, 15) suggests that within the context of the economic history of America, and

> From the perspective of the modern interest in growth and welfare, Turner's West can be viewed as a vast arena of free land and abundant resources waiting to be used by successive generations of native-born and foreign settlers. Defining the frontier in three distinct ways, firstly as a *condition* or as unused resources awaiting exploitation, secondly as a *process* of recurring stages of settlement, and finally as a specific *location* or geographic region, then the historian is discussing growth in a newly settled area or the economics of underdevelopment.

This categorization is a useful starting point for critical examination of the hypothesis. In the context of the frontier as a process, there are problems with the assumed evenness of change at all stages of the westward movement of the frontier, for the heterogeneity of the geography of the Plains and West of the United States, for example, necessitated an unevenness of movement and a heterogeneity of cultural and economic regional developments, each of which constituted a frontier in their own right rather than a convergent common experience, and some areas of which were in any case re-evaluated from an economic perspective. An additional problem, in the context of the frontier as a condition and as location, and particularly pertinent to current thoughts about European colonization of supposedly 'new' worlds (which had long been occupied by indigenous populations) is the bypassing and overlooking of the land rights of the American Indian, both as they existed and as they were appropriated to create an apparent free and vacant space into which the new settlers could move. The demographic and gender characteristics of frontier society also need redefinition and re-examination. A particularly helpful and constructive statement in this respect but with much wider and very important consequences for the future study of historical geography and cultural history as a whole, has been made by Kay (1991) in her re-evaluation of the regional historical geography of the United States and Canada. Questioning and challenging the gender bias of many accounts of the historical geography of regions of the United States and Canada, and the gender-specific writing of the national epic type of account of American development (which includes the Turnerian approach and emphasizes regional economic development, agricultural systems and export staples), Kay points to an alternative approach which involves the examination of the experiences and perspectives of women at a different geographical scale from that used in the dramatic, larger-scale landscape planning and modification processes associated with a minority of male community leaders.

While there has been much critical evaluation of the Turner hypothesis and attempts made at revision in order to correct some of the obvious weaknesses, there have also been attempts to emulate and apply the idea to historical situations in other countries. Treadgold (1952), for example, identifies some conceptual parallels between the American experience and the eastward movement of the Russian frontier into Asia, from the seventeenth century onwards, intensifying from the middle of the nineteenth century. He identifies a character-modifying and reshaping experience for the peasant colonists of Siberia, and the temporary use of the frontier as a safety-valve for the tsarist regime, but draws no particular and specific conclusions other than the general usefulness of the Turner hypothesis as a comparative conceptual tool.

An equally interesting aspect of the Turner hypothesis is the intellectual and socio-political context in which it was raised, including the integration of new concepts from biology, notably those on evolutionary biology from Darwin, and from geography (including environmental influence) into a closed-space hypothesis (Kearns, 1984), whose components were appropriate to the political debates in America at the time, concerned as they were with the nature of American nationalism in the late nineteenth century and the future directions of the public domain given the closure of the frontier.

Rural Settlement Patterns

The term 'rural settlement' is generally applied to the farmsteads and farm buildings which form an essential and integral part of rural economy and habitat, the relationship in functional and spatial terms with the component units of agricultural or pastoral production such as fields, and the pattern, layout, or morphology, formed by the arrangements of these units of habitation, shelter, and storage. One of the strongest traditions in European historical and human geography has been the detailed study of the forms and functions of such settlements, of the dynamics of both gradual and cataclysmic change which they have experienced through time, and of their complex relationships with their physiographical sites and situations. The form and style of the buildings themselves has also been a major focus of attention.

The classification of rural settlement types has long held the attention of historical and human geographers. The German geographer Meitzen in 1895 produced a classification of settlement and associated agricultural and field-system types in France and Germany, based on the assumption of close correlation of these phenomena with ethnic or racial origins (Meitzen, 1895), so that areas of Celtic settlement were characterized by dispersed individual farmsteads, Germanic or Teutonic expansion after the fall of the Roman Empire expressed in settlement by irregular-shaped nuclear settlements or villages, such as in western Germany, Alsace, Lorraine, and north-east France, and Slavic settlement by regular-shaped round and elongated street-villages. The detailed geography of settlement types in Europe, including the existence of areas of dispersed settlement in older areas of German settlement such as north-west Germany, pointed to the inaccuracy of this ethnic explanation. A later attempt at rural settlement classification was made by the French geographer Demangeon (1928), who divided settlements into two types, 'agglomerated' or 'dispersed', the agglomerated types subdivided into three: the village with open-field systems; the village with contiguous fields such as the marsh and forest villages of the Low Countries and central Europe; and the villages with dissociated fields, as in the Mediterranean. The four types of dispersed settlement were: areas of primary dispersion, such as western France or highland Britain; intercalated or interspersed settlements between areas of earlier village settlement, as in parts of western France and Midland England; areas of secondary dispersion from former nucleated villages, as in Mediterranean France, the Swiss plateau, or Sweden after enclosure; and areas of primary dispersed settlement of comparatively recent origin as in the United States in the nineteenth century. In 1939 Demangeon produced another classification, this time the agglomerated settlements of France were sub-categorized as: long or linear, as in eastern and northern France; massed, as in the Midi, and star villages throughout France whose form was much influenced by their trade functions and expansion along main roads. The new division of dispersed settlement was into linear, nebular, hamlet, and totally scattered types (Demangeon, 1939; Smith, 1967, 263–4). There has been a fairly steady flow of case-studies and typologies of settlement based on morphology from the earlier part of the twentieth century down to the present day. German scholars have been particularly active in this field, and their example has been widely followed in, for example, Sweden and Poland. The major study of settlement geography by Schwarz (1959) made the familiar distinction of dispersed and grouped rural settlement, but since then there have been many syntheses and regional studies of settlement types and associated field systems in Germany, extensively reviewed in the major two-volume study of the genesis of settlement forms in Mitteleuropa and its neighbouring regions, published in 1988 by the Arbeitskreis für genetische Siedlungs-forschung in Mitteleuropa based in Bonn (Fehn, Brandt, Denecke and Irsigler, 1988). The chronology of settlement development in central Europe is divided into old and young settled lands, the areas of 'older' settlement being those to the late Merovingian period of the eighth century, 'younger' settlements thereafter. The descriptive terminology is complex, but key terms include those of 'Drubbel' (an early hamlet form of settlement, characteristic of north-west Germany, comprising a small number of farms with long strip holdings in an open field) and 'Gewanndorf' (an open-field village, usually with a large number of farms and extensive areas of open fields) (Uhlig and Lienau, 1972). Much of the terminology of German settlement classification has come from the forms of settlement resulting from the colonization of regions east of the River Elbe in the twelfth, thirteenth and fourteenth centuries. The street-village ('Strassendorf'), with the peasant farmsteads equally spaced along a road or track and the cropped land, often cleared from forest, stretching beyond to the territorial limits of the settlement, was a common form found in the colonized regions. The linear forest village ('Waldhufendorf'), associated with the extension of German law of land layout and organization, usually had a field pattern of long relatively wide strips of land, under various kinds of land use, and a double row of farmsteads, but had various forms, including the short or concentrated 'Kurzwalhufendorf'. The 'Waldhufendorf' were found in the eastern uplands from the Saxon Erzegebirge to the Carpathian mountains. Villages based around a circular or oval-shaped ('Angerdorf') green, some-times derived from pre-existing Slav settlements, were morphological variants, frequently having the crop-land laid out in units radiating from the farmsteads. Examples of some of these types are given in Fig. 8.7 from the work of Nitz (1976).

One of the distinctive features of early medieval settlement in Europe in the early Middle Ages, whose presence is still clear in upland Mediterranean Europe, is that of the hilltop settlement, the chronology of whose development varies regionally and altitudinally.

The form and content of medieval rural settlements was one of bewildering variety, which archaeologists and others are only just beginning to unfold from the sparse field and documentary evidence available. The main material for construction of houses and farm buildings was wood, with reed and straw thatch used in some regions as a form of roof covering. The use of stone on the whole, at least as a common means of construction, came later. The main components of the built parts of the landscape were peasant houses, the manorial houses of the feudal landholders, and the more substantial houses and castles of those at the top of the socio-political hierarchy, including kings and chiefs.

An important feature of the major changes in the early historic, medieval, and modern European countryside was the desertion or abandoning of settlements through plague, warfare and economic decline either separately or in combination. Much detailed research has been carried out on these settlements, known as 'Wüstungen' in Germany, especially in Germany itself,

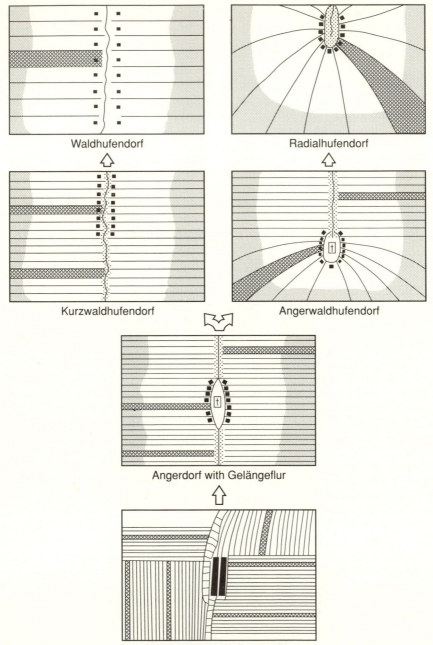

Fig. 8.7 *Settlement types and associated field systems, central Europe. Source: Nitz (1976, 223)*

where three basic phases of desertion occurred, the first in the eighth and ninth centuries, the second during the eleventh to the thirteenth centuries, during a very dynamic phase of settlement change which included expansion, the third in the fourteenth century, which was a general phase of settlement abandonment over much of Europe because of plague, especially the Black Death or bubonic plague. In the later period the regions of high desertion included northern Thuringia and the eastern Hartz mountains (Simms, 1976; Jäger, 1979). This major theme in the historical geography of European settlement evolution has also been extensively studied in England, exemplified by the studies of Beresford and Hurst of the village of Wharram Percy in Yorkshire within the context of deserted villages in England as a whole (Beresford and Hurst, 1971). Such changes were not confined to the medieval period: successive cyclical agricultural depressions in the capitalist phase of farming in the modern era have left their mark on the landscape through settlement desertion by emigration and by political changes in land organization, seen most dramatically in the Highland clearances in Scotland in the eighteenth and nineteenth centuries, the effects of the Great Irish Famine on settlement desertion in the mid-nineteenth century, and the totalitarian destruction of peasant life and livelihood in the Stalinist era in the former Soviet Union in the twentieth century.

The tradition of morphological analysis and the tracing of the evolution of settlement types through changes in plan and in social and economic bases has been well developed in Britain and in Ireland, following a variety of traditions. Roberts (1987) has synthesized from his extensive studies a history of the evolution of the English village, based on a range of morphological types and the identification of various processes of change, including planning. Jones (1961; 1971; 1973; 1976; 1989) has extensively studied the settlement patterns of Wales and England in the Dark Ages, paying particular attention to the longer-term influence on the settlement pattern of the multiple-estate structure, wherein groups of hamlets and villages were bound to a chief central place of authority or lord's court. The study of rural settlement in Ireland has ranged extensively from studies of prehistoric and Dark Ages settlement to the era of modern settlement planning from the sixteenth through to the nineteenth and twentieth centuries. Thus, Evans' studies of the whole span of peasant settlement in Ireland have been particularly influential (Evans, 1951; 1957; 1959; 1973; Stephens and Glasscock 1970; Buchanan, Jones and McCourt, 1971), as also has been that of Jones Hughes on landlord settlements of the nineteenth century (Jones Hughes, 1965; 1981; Smyth and Nolan, 1988).

Studies in Poland by Szulc and others have extended the morphogenetic type of rural settlement pattern analysis, thus in her study of morphogenetic types of rural settlements in Pomerania, Szulc (1978; 1988a, b) has shown that irregular green-villages (centred on a green) are the nuclei of the oldest network of Slavonic settlements in Pomerania, and that the more regular oval or circular-shaped green-villages represent later developments and modifications, dating from periods of medieval and later colonization. Planned settlements also date from the Frederician colonizations from 1740–1806, and from the nineteenth and twentieth centuries.

The mapping of settlement patterns and their evolution in Europe has formed an important component of their analysis and interpretation. Figure

8.8 shows a classification of rural settlement types in Italy, based on morphology and function, and indicating a wide range of influences, including that of physiography, climate, defence, the 'latifundia' (sizeable estate system with very large villages of landless agricultural labourers) system of the south, and the influence of land reclamation from early modern to modern times.

The morphological approach, however, when used alone, has proved insufficient for the purpose of credible explanation. Austin (1985) has expressed doubts about morphogenesis specifically in relation to the difficulty of reconstructing complex and changing patterns of settlement, even on a single site, the general neglect through this methodology of the processes of change, and the difficulty of dating from the typology of settlement alone. Different types of rural settlement are clearly the result of different types and

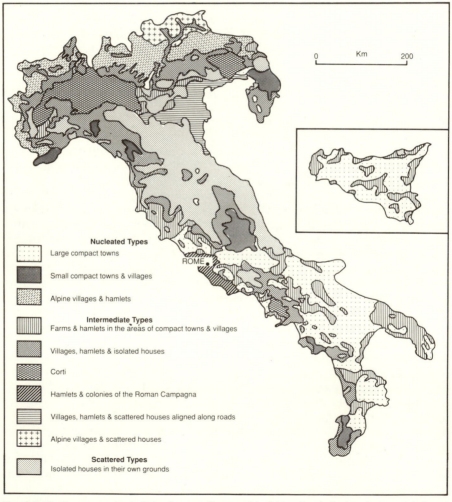

Fig. 8.8 *Settlement types in Italy. Source:* Geographical Handbook Series, Italy, *vol. II (1944, 506)*

stages of cultural and economic development. One significant area in this respect is the planned settlement, and although there are many examples from areas of ancient settlement, the remainder of this section will concentrate on planned settlements in areas of comparatively recent settlement and development.

The export of settlement patterns and field systems from an old country to a new region of colonial settlement is well exemplified by the case of French-influenced landscapes in North America. In the wake of the successful development of the fur trade by the French, in the early seventeenth century permanent agricultural settlement began in Acadia and along the valley of the lower St Lawrence River near Quebec. Early trade monopoly concessions in the period 1609–20 to associations of merchants were unsuccessful, and responsibility for colonization and development was transferred to the Company of New France, which was established in 1627, and comprised of the Hundred Associates, but it also signally failed in its task and voluntarily surrendered its charter in February of 1663, with control reverting directly to the French monarchy. The allocation of land along the St Lawrence to the new colonists who came chiefly from the west of France in increasing numbers in the late seventeenth century. The basis of land allocation was the seigneurial system, a system which combined feudalism with the need to devolve the initiative for colonization to individuals. Thus, as Harris (1990, 70) has indicated, 'Land in Canada, as in France, was held by seigneurs from the crown. The seigneur subgranted land to farmers (habitants) who acquired security of title in return for annual rents and charges for seigneurial services. In theory the seigneur was to behave towards his tenants as "un bon père de famille" '. But the system was already in decay in France, and produced little seigneurial revenue and little protection for the farmers in Canada. The method of land allocation, according to the cadastral system of the colony, involved the laying out of long thin parallel strips of land ('rotures' in French, 'long-lots' as they became known), 50–100 arpents in size, with one end at the river, where the farmstead was also located. The shape of the lots, cleared from the forest, was a familiar one from the source-region of many of the immigrants (Normandy), was not unlike the 'Waldhufendorf' system mentioned earlier in this chapter, and gave advantages of access to the river, ease of survey, variety of soil and vegetation types, and proximity to other farmers. From 1666, attempts were made by the French government to concentrate farmsteads into village settlements, for reasons of security, but these were largely unsuccessful. Later allocations of land took similar form, laid out in rows behind the first 'rangs' near the river. The system of inheritance was partible, and the subdivision of holdings and the later increases of population in the eighteenth and nineteenth centuries led in many regions of the lower St Lawrence to the existence of six or seven double rangs parallel to the river, and to an increased density of settlement within them. The pattern was also established in parts of Louisiana and Wisconsin (Harris and Warkentin, 1974, 37–40).

A formal system of land survey and allocation was adopted for much of the land in the Great Plains and West of the United States, following the establishment of the township and range method of land subdivision used from 1795 onwards, giving to large areas the gridiron layout of square or rectangular farms and a regular dispersed settlement pattern. Planned settlement in more recent times has been associated with voluntary or enforced concentration for purposes of protection or defence. Many new villages were, for example, created in Algeria by the French after the uprisings of the mid-1950s, involving the displacement of over 1 million people (de Planhol, 1961). The colonization of Palestine in the nineteenth and early twentieth centuries by Jews from Europe was effected in rural areas initially by agricultural settlements, the 'moshava', with populations of about 200 by the beginning of the twentieth century, and their successors the cooperative moshav and the kibbutz, whose primary function was agricultural but which diversified in the later twentieth century, many of which had distinctive geometrical forms of layout, with defence a contributory factor. Ideologies of many kinds have been key factors involved in the planning of rural settlements, notably in North America from the seventeenth to the late nineteenth centuries, and many of them had Utopian, cooperative and millenaristic ideals (Powell, 1977, 144–72).

In addition to the study of settlement patterns on a typological and morphological basis, attempts have also been made to model the processes of change in settlement type and in the spread of settlement. An early model was Whittlesey's 'sequent occupance' model, which sees each successive stage of occupation and settlement of a region as a reflection of the previous stage of occupation and a contributor to the next stage, analagous in some respects to models of ecological change (Whittlesey, 1929).

Deterministic simulations of the processes of settlement colonization have also been attempted, for example by Bylund (1960), using a gravity model to assess and simulate the main foci of attraction for new settlers in a district in northern Sweden. Current trends in settlement studies reflect a combination of both detailed morphological, documentary, ecological and theoretical modelling bases for research, related to intensive and very detailed field investigation, including archaeological excavation and dating in many cases, and this is likely to be the most widely used approach in areas of both old and recent settlement for some time to come. An interesting constituent part of such work, though in the past tending to be a separate study, is the investigation of the materials and architectural and functional forms of rural house and building types. This type of work is of importance not only in relation to the scholarly investigation of material and cultural aspects of rural life in the past, but has long been associated with the increasingly favoured question and possibility of the preservation and reconstruction in museums of rural life of buildings whose origins lie deep in the past (Newcomb, 1979). The changing form of rural house types is, for example, a consistent theme throughout Pitte's study of the history of the French countryside (Pitte, 1983) and has been extensively studied elsewhere in Europe and in North America (Rapoport, 1969; Kniffen, 1965; Zelinsky, 1973a).

9

Historical Geographies of Urbanization

Introduction

Towns and cities are so central to modern life that the idea of large-scale urbanization being a recent phenomenon may appear initially to be a strange one. Nevertheless it is a fact, for urban growth on a large scale, and particularly the growth of great cities with populations of over 1 million inhabitants, is largely tied in with advancing industrial capitalism in the nineteenth and twentieth centuries. Stretching well back into prehistoric time, however, is a long history—and therefore geography—of urban development, part of a complex dynamic which incorporates to varying degrees political, economic, military and strategic, cultural, religious and belief-system elements, bound up into changing systems of production, their outward material manifestation including construction of buildings for habitation, industry, ceremonial and cultural purposes. Historical geographies of urban change are numerous, especially for the nineteenth and twentieth centuries, and although only a brief outline of some of the principal features and a small number of examples can be given here they should suffice to indicate the challenges and excitements of this important sector of the subject.

The question of the origins of urban settlements is complex, and partly vexed by definition. 'Urban' is a term which connotes a concentration of population (many of whom are not primary producers), a built environment, systems of administration and exchange, and links with proximate and more distant rural hinterlands and related regional hierarchical urban systems. The urban/rural distinction is in some respects an arbitrary one, in the sense that the notion of towns being a separate driving force in economic development in a given region is, to say the least contestable, especially in the pre-factory age, a symbiotic relationship being a more realistic perspective (Langton and Hoppe, 1983). The question of urban origins is also difficult, obviously dependent on regional experience and to a degree on definition of urban. Carter (1983) and Gregory (1986a) have suggested four types of explanation of urban origin: the ecological or environmental model, seeing urban development as related to production of a surplus, sometimes associated with such technological advancements as irrigation and hydrology; economic models, focusing on economic integration, exchange, reciprocity and differential allocations of surpluses of production, and within the Marxist views the socially preferential alienation of surpluses; cultural models, which emphasize the importance of ritual, including religion; and politico-military models, which ascribe early urban origins to the need for fortification and defence. This is a helpful taxonomy, but none of the categories can be accepted uncritically. The environmental model poses problems of the definition and role of 'surplus' production, which may well owe as much to the efficacy of social organization as to the richness of the natural environment, a view shared by Marx in his acknowledgement of the cultural determination of surplus. The mercantile and market models (economic models) of urban origins encounter difficulties when faced with the controls of trading in pre-modern times, the effects of non-settlement related markets and fairs, some itinerant, and the lack of clear association with markets and strong political and administrative organization. The problem of circular argument arises in the case of the military stronghold hypothesis, for war and defensive structures may be the outcome of the concentration of surplus rather than an initiator of it, and the religious theory, though strong in historical supporting evidence, faces problems of areas where strong religion did not produce strong urban development (Carter, 1983, 3–8). The question is complex, and may conveniently be investigated by brief analysis of some regional examples, followed in a chronological sequence.

Ancient Towns and Cities. Mesopotamia and Central America

One of the hearthlands of early urbanization was the region called Mesopotamia, the valleys of the rivers Tigris and Euphrates, largely within the territory of the present state of Iraq. The beginnings of a major wave of urban development in the region are dated to the period 4000–3000 BC, in the Uruk and Jemdet Nasr periods, characterized by the concentration of populations in larger groups, the political organization of society, the development of an élite which imposed taxes, and scientific and technical innovations including the invention of writing.

The best known city from this region is Ur in southern Mesopotamia on the lower Euphrates, founded in the early Ubaid period (sixth century BC) and buried beneath alluvial deposits from flooding, thought initially to have been the biblical Great Flood, but extensively rebuilt when it became the capital of the Third Dynasty in the period 2112–2004 BC. The importance of Ur was partially revealed by its excavation by Sir Leonard Woolley (1880–1960), and his discovery of the royal cemetery which proved to be astonishingly rich in grave goods. Its major functions included that of port city for the Mesopotamian trade with other regions of the Arabian Gulf and as a major religious and defensive site. Major elements were the ziggurat and temple of the moon god Nanna, contained within a large walled sacred precinct, or tenemos, a large number of other temples, two-storey mud-brick houses arranged around paved courts, and a large defensive wall (Roaf, 1990). Carter (1983) suggests that this was largely an unplanned city, with the exception of the sacred precinct (massively replanned by the king Nebuchadnezzar), in contrast to the geometrically planned ancient city of Mohenjo-Daro in the Indus valley in India. It is likely that the abandonment of the site of Ur in the fourth century BC was caused by a change in the course of the Euphrates and its tributaries.

Another region of early urbanization was meso-America, with, early complexes of ceremonial centres in Guatemala, Oaxaca and the valley of Mexico developing from 1000 BC, but with major urban ceremonial complexes from about 300 BC, particularly in the Mayan territories. The largest was that at Teotihuacán in the valley of Mexico, a major and monumental ceremonial complex covering an area of 30 km^2, and including the massive Pyramid of the Sun (Wheatley, 1971, 235). The early Chinese experience of urbanism under the Shang dynasty (1630–1520 BC) has been exemplified by the sites of Cheng-chou and An-yang on the edge of the north China plain, both with traditions of bronze metallurgy, writing, and distinctive class and political structures. Cheng-chou was rectangular in shape with an earthen wall, focused on a major ceremonial and administrative core, with residential quarters and workshops outside the walls (Tuan, 1970; Wheatley, 1971).

Greek and Roman Towns and Cities

The beginnings of urban settlements in Greece and her territories go back to the eighth century BC and the emergence of the Greek 'polis' or city-state, a region of varied size comprising groups of rural settlements whose administrative and defensive focus was a fortified hilltop citadel, the 'acropolis', which frequently developed into a full urban settlement. Greek colonization of the Mediterranean in the period 750–550 BC resulted in the establishment of Greek town and city colonies in southern Italy and Sicily, southern France, North Africa, the shores of the Dardanelles and the western end of the Black Sea, fed and sustained by trade. Similar settlements derived from the Phoenician traders of the eastern Mediterranean with their bases on the Levant coast and their colonies in the central and western Mediterranean focused on the premier colony of Carthage in North Africa. An additional region of urban development was that of the Etruscan culture in Italy. Characteristics of the Greek cities were: near-coastal locations, with outports; elevated and fortified locations (acropolis); defensive walls and, in the case of the older towns, irregular plans; and large, distinctive public buildings, including temples (Pounds, 1990, 35–6). Grid-plan geometric layouts, probably a pattern diffused from the Middle East, were incorporated into the plans of later cities, including those of the Greek colonies, for example at Miletus in what is now south-west Turkey. The next major wave of urban development in southern and in western Europe was the creation of the spread of the Roman Empire in the fifth and fourth centuries BC from modest beginnings in Italy to a major empire covering much of Europe, North Africa, and the Middle East before its collapse under the impact of barbarian invasions in the fifth century AD. The city was one of the essential elements of the Roman Empire, whose origins and characteristics reflected the region and stage in the history of the development of the empire. Their greatest density was in central Italy, Crete, the Balkan Peninsula, and southern Spain. Many were major forts, others adjustments to pre-existing native fortresses or 'oppida', some were administrative centres, some newly founded 'coloniae'. These were settlements with distinctive plans and form, incorporating geometric grid-plan designs and many public buildings spaces and buildings, including the forum, basilicas, temples, heated baths, amphitheatres, shops, residences, water supply and waste-disposal systems. They were generally but not inevitably fortified with walls. The Roman inheritance has been long-lasting, and is still to be found in place-names and many relic features, including amphitheatres. The question of the continuation of the Roman influence through occupation of Roman urban sites after the barbarian invasions is a complex and regionally specific one, with a high degree of continuity of occupation of the sites, even where much modified, through the Dark Ages.

Medieval Towns and Cities

There is a wide array of theses which attempt to account for the origins and character of the towns of medieval Europe. Carter (1983, 34–5) categorizes them as: mercantile settlement theories; market theories; artisanal theories; association or guild theories; military or garrison theories; ecclesiastical theories; free-village theories, and Romanist theories. One of the most influential mercantile settlement theses concerned with the growth of towns in early medieval Europe, especially the Low Countries, is that of the Belgian historian Pirenne, who in a series of publications in the inter-war period, and notably in his *Medieval Cities* published in English in 1925, promoted the idea that the origin of towns (places of industry and trade with a distinctive form of municipal administration) was in international trade, and that the towns of medieval Europe both grew and shrank with changes in trade, especially in the Mediterranean. Thus, the decline in trade which he contends resulted from the Arab invasions of the western Mediterranean in the eighth century AD and Viking invasions in the North Sea resulted, in his view, in the almost total disappearance of towns, urban life being revived from the tenth century by the restoration of links between western Europe and the eastern Mediterranean. There are quite a number of factual and theoretical flaws in the theory. Verhulst (1989), for example, has reviewed a range of evidence that, *inter alia*, indicates that: long-distance trade in the North Sea and in Scandinavia continued from the seventh century onwards; the decline in trade within the Mediterranean was not caused by Arab invasion in the eighth century, for it had been in slow decline since the end of the third century, effected by Byzantium military operations and the Lombard occupation of north Italy in the sixth century. Verhulst contends that trade was only temporarily affected by the Arab invasions, and that there were signs of the revival of trade, especially in north-west Europe, from the end of the seventh century. The notion that urban life and development continued and even flourished during the ninth and tenth centuries has also been promoted by Hodges (1982), who takes the view that the trading stimuli were at regional levels.

The significant elements of urbanization in medieval Europe, from the ninth to the late fourteenth century, include: increase in numbers, especially through the foundation of new planned towns; increase in size and functions of established towns; the increasing interrelationship of town and country at a time of increased rural productivity and urban demand; and the legal separation of towns within the feudal system (this a much debated topic). A major feature was the establishment of large numbers of new planned towns in the twelfth, thirteenth and early fourteenth centuries, including the fortified frontier bastide towns, notably in Gascony in France but found elsewhere. Friedman (1988) has, for example, studied in detail the foundation of five new towns (San Giovanni, Castelfranco di Sopra, Terranuova, Scarperia, and

Firenzuola) in Tuscany in the period 1299–1350, towns founded as fortresses and market centres, with a conspicuously symmetrical and geometrical layout around a central square, designed by architects with artistic vision and setting a basis for the further imaginative urban development of the Renaissance.

In England and Wales a complex of urban bases had emerged by the eleventh century, reflecting origins from royal residences, trading settlements and ninth-century defensive structures. They were distinct not only by concentration of population but also by their having been granted privileges of burgage tenure, customs and guilds, the latter often including rights of freedom of payment of tolls and linked to the granting of charters for markets and fairs, giving boroughs greater freedom to trade and accumulate merchant capital and thus, as some would argue, sowing the seed of the transition from feudalism to capitalism (Unwin, 1990, 124–6). The largest towns at this time were London, Bristol, York, Lincoln, and Norwich, in which, as in other places, new castles had been constructed in the eleventh century. New town construction was a major feature of England and Wales from the late eleventh to the early fourteenth centuries, numbering 166 in England and 83 in Wales. Within Wales there was a spate of urban foundation consequent on the Norman conquest of the south, including Cardiff and Swansea, and later of the north-west in the thirteenth century where fortified 'bastide' towns such as Caernarvon and Harlech were constructed. The social geography of the early medieval town was one of generally unsegregated residential and commercial activity, though some places had distinctive quarters in which people of the same trade lived and worked, and also market-places, some of them specialist in the larger towns and cities (Dodgshon, 1978, 106, 110). The main occupations of town-dwellers, in addition to administrative, military and ecclesiastical functions were manufacturing and trade. The major items traded internally were grain, fish, salt, wool, cloth, and metals, and externally lead, tin, hides, dairy products and cloth. (Donkin, 1973, 116, 120). After the mid-fourteenth-century demographic crisis, dominated by the Black Death, urban populations generally declined, but this was not necessarily matched by commercial decline, for the changes in trading patterns within western Europe facilitated the export, initially of wool and later, in the late fourteenth and fifteenth centuries, of cloth, from England.

Ireland and Scotland had somewhat different experiences, certainly from England, though there were some similarities. Graham (1988) has reviewed the position for medieval Ireland in terms of an initial feudal relationship with England which then turned into a colonial relationship after the loss of French territory and the attendant need for supplies of primary goods. The question of urban settlement continuity from earlier origins through the Dark Ages does not seem to have the same significance as in England, for Ireland experienced no Roman settlement or occupation and the Roman forts in Scotland did not develop into towns, but urban origins do nonetheless pose some important questions. In Ireland there is fairly clear consensus that early urban origins were essentially Norse, in the case of the major port cities such as Dublin, Cork, Waterford, Wexford and Limerick, which sites were developed by the Anglo-Normans in the twelfth century. The idea of monastic sites as bases for urban development is generally not accepted, for there seems to have been no regionally specialist space-economy to support towns and the political structure of the Irish was also against it. The number of boroughs in medieval

Ireland up to 1500 has been estimated at about 300 (many of which, however, were not towns in the physical sense) and about 400 in Scotland. Graham (1988, 47–50) notes that the location of boroughs in Wales, Scotland and Ireland reflects the pattern of Norman colonization, with the majority of them in Scotland being either in the Forth–Clyde lowlands or along the east coast, while in Ireland they are mainly in the south and east. Later urban development through newer foundations and through expansion of existing sites is evident in both countries, though there were also desertions and decline. One of the dominant fortified towns of medieval Scotland was Edinburgh (see Fig. 9.1).

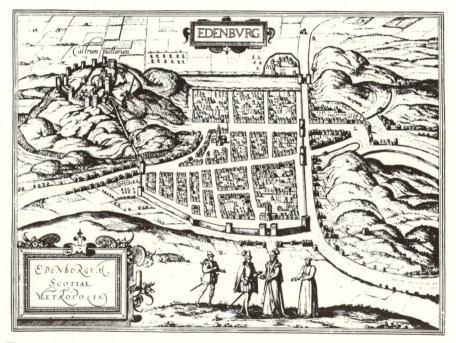

Fig. 9.1 *Edinburgh, Scotland, 1581. Plan by G. Braun and F. Hogenberg,* Civitates Orbis Terrarum, *vol. 3. The map shows the medieval town, contained within the town walls, with Edinburgh castle as the dominant feature*

Eastern Europe and Russia offer different histories of medieval urbanization. In eastern Europe, one significant facet of urbanism was that the eastward colonizing movements of the Germans in the twelfth and thirteenth centuries produced waves of new town settlements, some on entirely new sites, others from older villages, many to a planned, standard design with walls, castles, and central market-places. For Russia, French (1983b) has outlined two major areas of urban origin, one in central Asia, where towns developed among the hydraulic societies of the rivers Amu-Dar'ya, Zeravshan, and Murgab, including Afrosiab (Samarkhand) from about AD 500, and where continuity was maintained through many invasions and conquests, there being about 35 towns in this region from the sixth to eighth centuries. The second region was that of foundation of Greek colonies on the Black Sea coast from the mid-seventh century. Additional evidence for possible urban origins elsewhere in Russia comes in the form of settlements within fortified enclosures, or 'gorodischa', dating from the sixth to the ninth centuries AD, and by the ninth century trade was becoming an important urban function. Growth of new towns was rapid in the period 1000–1240 (the time of the Tartar invasions)— about 250 in this period—and Moscow's foundation is officially dated from this time (1147). After the disruptions of the Tartar invasions, new urban growth slowed to almost a standstill in the Russian lands though there was some continuation in the lands lost to the Lithuanians. In the fourteenth century, some modest urban recovery is evidenced in the foundation of frontier strongholds and the colonization of the north for the purposes of obtaining fur, with monasteries often being the nuclei for urban growth. Renewed major urban growth did not occur until the sixteenth century, though for part of that period urban decline was effected in the reign of Ivan the Terrible, but with the advance of the Russian frontier in his reign southwards and eastwards into Asia, many frontier forts were established which ultimately took on broader urban functions (French, 1983b, 264). French has characterized the morphology of the medieval Russian town as 'a combination of features, a single nucleus of lay and church authority (unlike so many medieval German towns for example), the growth of defended cells, the extensiveness rather than the intensiveness of buildings, all of which added to the cultural distinctiveness of architectural style [which] would seem to produce a recognizable "Russian" medieval town' (French, 1983b, 274–5).

In the Islamic territories of the Mediterranean and Middle East, urbanism developed on the basis of Islamic conquest of existing towns and their modification to include mosques, though there were some new military and palace towns. Islamic values influenced the style of urban development, with the 'model' Islamic town (Fig. 9.2), focusing on the Friday mosque, near which was

> the principal commercial area of the town, with its shops, workshops and warehouses, *khans* (combining residences with commercial premises) and *qaysāriyyas* (lock-up markets). Localization was never complete, however. Bakers and grocers tend to be found in residential areas and noxious trades (like tanning) are forced to the periphery of the built-up area. Public baths may be centrally located because of the importance of ritual ablution. The citadel is the centre of political and administrative power, its walls serving to accentuate the division between the mass of the population and the often alien governors and soldiers. Streets through the town are described as narrow and meandering; culs-de-sac are common. Residential quarters are distinguished on the basis of community affiliation, particularly religious allegiance (Wagstaff, 1985, 173).

Full flowering of an Islamic influence on urban morphology occurred from the eleventh and twelfth centuries, with the addition of more mosques and religious schools and colleges. Regular layout is found in those towns actually founded, rather than taken over by, the Muslims, such as Basrah and the Round City of Baghdad. Hourani (1991, 110–11) contends that the great cities of the Islamic territories were by the tenth and eleventh centuries the largest in the western world, citing population estimates for Cairo of a quarter of a million inhabitants by the early fourteenth century, as many if not more for

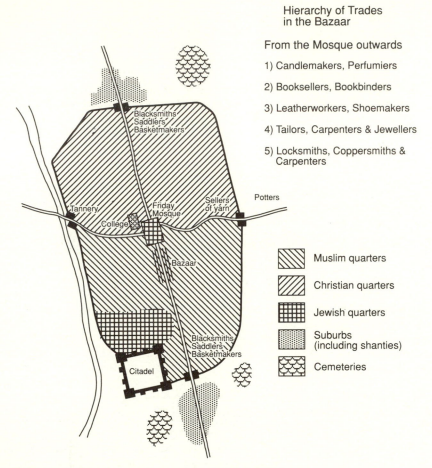

Hierarchy of Trades
in the Bazaar

From the Mosque outwards

1) Candlemakers, Perfumiers

2) Booksellers, Bookbinders

3) Leatherworkers, Shoemakers

4) Tailors, Carpenters & Jewellers

5) Locksmiths, Coppersmiths &
   Carpenters

Fig. 9.2 *A 'model' Islamic town. Source: Wagstaff (1985, 174)*

Baghdad, with population estimates of 50–100,000 for Aleppo, Damascus and Tunis by the fifteenth century. The fate of the Islamic towns varied in the Middle Ages, many suffering extensively from warfare, including invasions by Turks, Crusaders, and Mongols, epidemics, problems with water supply, and economic decline. A city which shows influences of not only Islamic but also Jewish and Christian belief systems in its morphology and style is Jerusalem, the centre of these three major faiths and of strategic concern over a long period of time (Fig. 9.3).

Early Colonial Towns and Cities

With the major voyages of discovery in the fifteenth and sixteenth centuries and the beginnings of European settlement in the Americas, Africa and Asia, it was inevitable that urban life, initially in a European form, would be exported, and there came into being a large number of early colonial towns which

Fig. 9.3 *Panorama of Jerusalem. Copperplate by Matthias Merian, 1647*

reflected both European ideas on town layout and function but also elements of the societies and environments in which they were located.

The bases of Spanish and Portuguese urbanization in Central and South America were laid in the late fifteenth and sixteenth centuries (Fig. 9.4), with initial settlement activity in Caribbean areas and the north coast of Brazil in the period 1496–1550, and a later phase of penetration of Spanish America up to about 1700.

In the Spanish Americas early urban foundations included Santo Domingo (1496), Trinidad (1512), Havana (1514), and Santiago (1515). In Mexico the Spaniards found well-established large cities within the Aztec Empire, such as Texcoco with a population of about 100,000. Mexico City was founded by Cortez on the site of Tenochtitlán in 1521, and many other new towns were established in Central America in the mid-sixteenth century. Colonization of

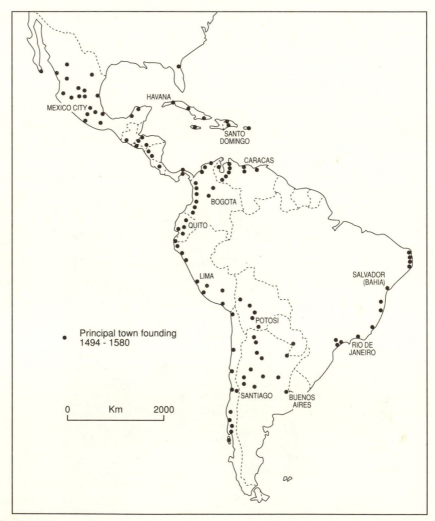

Fig. 9.4 *Main town foundations in Latin America, 1494–1580. Source: Sargent (1982, 206)*

Andean America in search of gold and silver resulted also in urban foundations. Portuguese foundations in Brazil included São Vicente (1532), Recife (Pernambuco, 1536), São Paulo (1554), Salvador (1534) and Rio de Janeiro (1567) (Sargent, 1982). Further urban development in interior areas was more significant in the next 200 years in the case of Portuguese activity in Brazil than in the Spanish colonies.

The morphology of the towns of this major phase of Iberian colonization in Central and South America reflects, in the case of Spanish settlements, for the most part the regulations for town planning issued in and after 1514, which required grid-plan layouts with central plaza and church or cathedral, long narrow blocks with narrow streets, and major administrative functional building at the centre. Portuguese towns were less formal in layout (as were Spanish mining towns, on account of topography). In some instances, especially in California, the mission and 'praesidio' (fort) was an important focus of settlement. Six basic characteristics of Spanish urbanization in the New World in the sixteenth century indentified by Houston are: the instability of urban sites (ill-chosen, affected by storms, earthquakes floods, plagues and diseases); the weak development of urban networks in this early phase; a tendency towards decentralization rather than concentration of urban life; the primacy of a small number of metropolitan centres, notably Lima and Mexico City; a sustained distinction between Spanish and Indian urbanism in the form of racial separation; and a distinctive regional pattern to the experience of urbanization (Houston, 1968).

Elsewhere in North America new towns were established by other European colonial powers in the seventeenth and eighteenth centuries, including the towns of the tidewater colonies in Virginia and Maryland (including Jamestown and Baltimore), New England (with Boston as the main town), the Middle colonies (notably New York and Philadelphia), and those of Carolina and Georgia, notably Charleston and Savannah (Carter, 1983). Urban settlement in the French colonial areas of North America, principally Acadia on the Bay of Fundy and the colony of Canada in the lower St Lawrence valley, which were settled from the early seventeenth century, included the foundation of Port Royal, Montreal, Trois Rivières and Quebec, initially as fortified villages.

Baroque and Renaissance Towns and Cities

The period from the early sixteenth to the end of the seventeenth century witnessed in Europe a growth in the number of towns and large cities. Of particular note were the changes in formal systems of town planning and style, effected by the influence of architects, urban theorists and military engineers. The source of much early urban theory was Vitruvius, a Roman architect and military engineer of the first century BC, whose work on architecture—*De Architectura*—was translated and published in Rome in the period 1484–92. This was emulated by the publication of a series of treatises on urban plan, architecture and design, started and much influenced by Leon Battiste Alberti (1485). The new notion of linear or single-point perspective was very important (Cosgrove, 1984; 1985), the principle of which came in the fifteenth century 'as a complete revolution, involving an extreme and violent break with the medieval conception of space, and with the flat, floating arrangements which were its artistic expression' (Giedion, 1954, 31, cited by Carter, 1983, 115). The actual designs of cities varied with topography, taste and the extent to which they were new or rebuilt towns, and the significance of military considerations. This latter consideration reflected the new technology of warfare, especially the use of the cannon and the propulsion of various types of missile through the explosive force of gunpowder. Cities were thus designed in part to advance the cannon's position as near to the enemy from the city walls as possible, resulting in the design of star-shaped forts and cities from the late fifteenth century onwards. Their concept was wider than that of mere military convenience, and Carter has indicated an amalgam of Vitruvian ideas, holistic design incorporating science—geometry—and art, autocratic control of the town by the prince or ruler, and ancient cosmographic symbolism (Carter, 1983, 116). There were many such towns, some named after the rulers, some in frontier positions. Famous examples include Palma Nuova in Italy, founded in 1593 (Fig. 9.5), and Naarden in the Netherlands, fortified in the early fifteenth century with major earth banks in bastions. A large number of fortified frontier towns were constructed in eastern France, following designs by the architect and military engineer Vauban, including Marienbourg and Philippeville.

The tradition of tasteful and fashionable aristocratic and regal influence on urban design continued through into the seventeenth and eighteenth century in what is called the Baroque period, a name given to a style of architecture and design that emphasizes the ornate and the elegant, and that is exemplified in Europe in a large number of newly designed or redesigned houses, palaces, gardens, estates, and urban plans which gave priority to wide streets for display and for facilitating troop movement. Major replanning was under-taken of old cities and also the establishment of new towns in the seventeenth and eighteenth centuries, with the trend in somewhat different styles of expression continuing into the nineteenth century, occurred, for example, in Copenhagen, Oslo, Karlsruhe, Dresden, Munich, Hanover, Paris, Vienna, Berlin and London, and in the port towns of Nantes, Bordeaux, Le Havre, Rouen, Lorient, Brest and Rochefort (Smith, 1967, 337–8). A particular feature of the eighteenth century in many parts of Europe was the spa town, whose functions related to the presence of hot mineral springs thought to be conducive to health improvement and cure, but which also developed a wide range of fashionable social functions and particular types of layout. One of the best examples is Bath in south-west England, whose earlier spa functions, dating from Roman times, were revived in the eighteenth century, and whose elegant crescents and 'Circus'—curving and circular terraces of Georgian buildings—made up a very attractive townscape (Fig. 9.6). New planning was often associated with royal and aristocratic estates, such as the 'residenzstädte' in Germany (Dresden, Weimar, Würzburg and Weimar). Not all towns and cities in the eighteenth century were newly planned: the vast majority developed informally, their townscapes reflecting their functions as places of residence, religious, market and commercial centres, foci of transport net-works, centres of industry, and as places of leisure and entertainment of many different kinds. Figure 9.7 is a map of one such place: a small cathedral and market town in Midland England—Lichfield in Staffordshire—reconstructed by Thorpe (1954) from a survey of 1781.

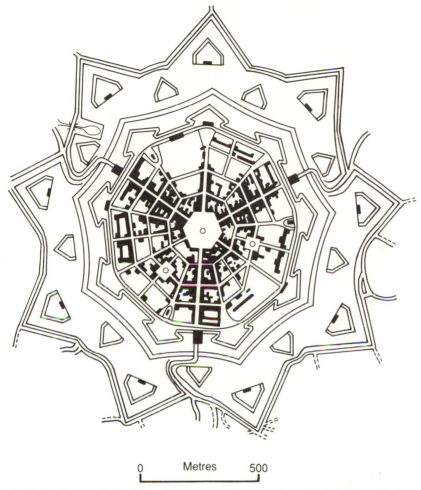

0   Metres   500

Fig. 9.5 *Palma Nuova, Italy. A Renaissance Venetian star-shaped fortified town, fortified by walls, towers and moats, and founded in 1593. Source:* Geographical Handbook Series, Italy, vol. II (1944, 540)

The urban experience outside western Europe and its distinctive cultural contexts was different. The rise of the Ottoman Empire, to become a major cultural and political force in the period from the sixteenth to the nineteenth century, and with it the increase of the percentage of its population living in towns and cities. The growth of urban population in the sixteenth century was in part effected by immigration, some forced, for the repopulating of Istanbul, some a drift from the land. Old towns grew, and new ones were established, conspicuously in Anatolia, both through the economic forces provided by stable political conditions and also the specific administrative organizations of the empire. An increasing urban hierarchy developed, dominated by Istanbul, whose population may have reached 1 million by 1600 (Wagstaff, 1985, 193–5). A specific Turkish Islamic character was stamped on the cities of the empire, including particular designs for palaces and mosques. In the sev-

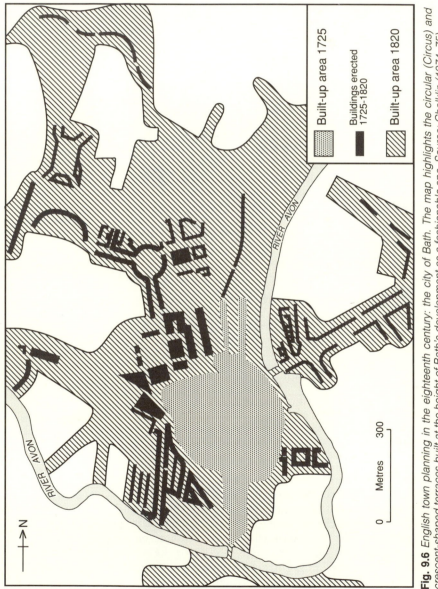
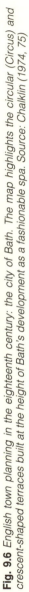

Fig. 9.6 *English town planning in the eighteenth century: the city of Bath. The map highlights the circular (Circus) and crescent-shaped terraces built at the height of Bath's development as a fashionable spa. Source: Chalklin (1974, 75)*

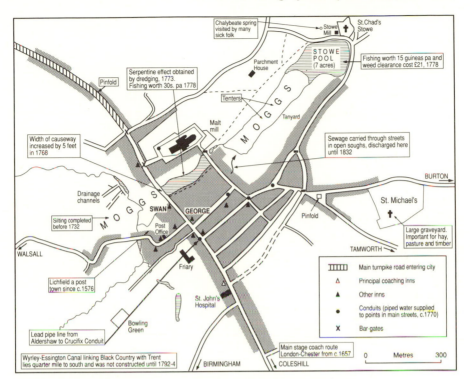

Chalybeate spring visited by many sick folk

St.Chad's Stowe

o Stowe Mill

STOWE POOL (7 acres)

Fishing worth 15 guineas pa and weed clearance cost £21, 1778

Parchment House

Serpentine effect obtained by dredging, 1773. Fishing worth 30s. pa 1778

Pinfold

Tenters

M O G G S

Malt mill

Tanyard

Width of causeway increased by 5 feet in 1768

Sewage carried through streets in open soughs, discharged here until 1832

BURTON

St. Michael's

Drainage channels

M O G G S

SWAN GEORGE

Silting completed before 1732

Post Office

Pinfold

WALSALL

Large graveyard. Important for hay, pasture and timber

TAMWORTH

Friary

Lichfield a post town since c.1576

St. John's Hospital

	Main turnpike road entering city
Δ	Principal coaching inns
▲	Other inns
●	Conduits (piped water supplied to points in main streets, c.1770)
X	Bar-gates

Bowling Green

Lead pipe line from Aldershaw to Crucifix Conduit

Wyrley-Essington Canal linking Black Country with Trent lies quarter mile to south and was not constructed until 1792-4

BIRMINGHAM

Main stage coach route London-Chester from c.1657

COLESHILL

0   Metres   300

Fig. 9.7 *Lichfield, Staffordshire, England. A reconstruction of Lichfield's urban morphology in 1781 from a survey by John Snape. Source: Thorpe (1954, 193)*

enteenth and eighteenth centuries there was decline of the empire in economic terms, at least relative to the rise of western Europe, but urban development continued, with increase in size of Aleppo, Damascus, and Cairo, for example, and the establishment of new centres including Smyrna and Acre. In the Persian East, in the Safavid Empire, Tehran and Esfahān grew in size in the seventeenth centuries, and a major development was that of the royal suburb south of Esfahān in the early seventeenth century, with its ceremonial avenue, square for use for polo and archery, and garden palaces (Wagstaff, 1985, 207–8).

While the roots of the Japanese urban system go back to the eighth century AD, when towns such as Nara and Kyoto were founded and their design based on Chinese designs of the T'ang period, including rectangular outline, the major basis for modern Japanese urbanization was laid in the Edo or Tokugawa period from 1603–1868. From the late twelfth to the early sixteenth centuries the main settlement nodes were Kyoto and the many small and isolated castle towns, together with a small number of port towns, including Sakai, whose basis was foreign trade and piracy. The Edo period from the early sixteenth century saw the growth of castle towns in a trading and administrative system, focused on the castle city of Edo. In addition, other types of town at this time, when Japan was a highly urbanized country, were internal ports, post or stage towns, religious centres, market towns and spas, the latter based on the thermal hot springs which are widespread in Japan (Kornhauser, 1976, 69–71).

Chaudhuri in his interesting study of the Indian Ocean and its coastland territories in the period before AD 1750, ascribes the development of perennial (as opposed to 'firefly') towns such as Constantinople, Damascus, Baghdad, and Fustat, as the outcome of 'favourable geographical location, transport facilities, concentration of population and the symbolic value of an exalted reputation' (Chaudhuri, 1990, 362). He stresses the significance of major towns for the acquisition and retention of political power, citing the importance for the historical geography of Mughal India of eight primate cities— Lahore, Delhi, Agra, Patna, Burhanpur, Ahmedabad, Kabul and Quandahar. The actual physical nature and morphology of the towns of Asia reflected a range of cultural, social, and economic factors. Chaudhuri (1985) identifies three urban traditions in Asia: the Indo-Islamic, south-east Asian, and Chinese. Thus

> The morphology of the planned city in China presented a complete contrast to that of the congested, circular Indo-Islamic towns with their multi-storied buildings. . . . In a Chinese town, the buildings were mostly single-storey, and the prosperous houses were surrounded by landscaped gardens. . . . Canals running at right-angles to one another supplemented a similar network of streets and public squares. . . . An Islamic town was typically identified in our period by the presence of the Friday mosque and the square surrounding it. . . . The buildings were mainly rectangular with flat roofs and constructed in stone or brick, though the poorer housing was made of clay mixed with straw. In south-east Asia stone was only used in areas where it was easily available, and the remains of vast palaces in Java and Cambodia reflecting Hindu architectural and artistic traditions demonstrate that the technique of construction in stone was neither new nor a challenge to the people of the area. But the most common form of house building was wood or bamboo (Chaudhuri 1985, 180).

Urban Explosion and the Development of Great Cities

At the beginning of the nineteenth century the major urbanized regions of the world were Europe and the Mediterranean, south and south-east Asia, and China and Japan. The number of very large cities in the world, that is with estimated populations over 500,000, was very small (probably no more than four or five), with the majority of major cities having populations of between 200–500,000. Major changes were experienced in the course of the nineteenth century, through a variety of complex processes including the expansion of European empires, the broad advance of capitalism and its massive implication in urbanization, changes in patterns of consumption and demand, industrialization and, of course, dramatic changes in population and demographic regimes. The phase of urban expansion in the first half of the nineteenth century has been described by Lawton (1989, 3) in the following terms: 'By 1800 there were relatively few great world cities, arbitrarily defined as those with a population of over 100,000, a figure which was exceptional prior to the fifteenth century. The total rose rapidly from 65 to 106 between 1800 and

1850, and nearly trebled again by 1900. Moreover, whereas Peking was the only 'million city' (narrowly defined), by 1850 it had been joined by London and Paris and by 1900 there were 16 such cities—mainly in Europe and North America, a tribute to the triumph of the Atlantic economy—and another 27 of over half a million'. The regional balance of urbanization gradually changed throughout the nineteenth century, with Europe equalling Asia in the number of cities with populations of over 100,000 by 1850, and overtaking Asia by 1900, with growth also marked in the north-eastern United States. By the mid-twentieth century the pattern had changed again, notably in respect of urban growth in North and South America and in Asia.

This rapidly changing pattern with its tendency towards the creation of a distinctive urban hierarchical structure, dominated by major metropolitan areas, reflected major changes in the nature of national and global economies. Harvey has analysed the relationship between capital and urbanization with particular reference to crises of over-accumulation, over-production, under-investment and class struggle, using an overt Marxist theoretical basis (Harvey, 1985a). The solutions, he argues, to the crises of capitalism operating in the processes of urban change included the adoption of such strategies as the export of surplus capital, the exploitation of new markets of areas of cheap labour, together with major investment in the redesigning of the central areas of cities such as Paris and in suburban development, all operated from the perspective of short-term returns, resulting in crises and struggles with those who suffered in consequence, the working-class labour force. His studies of Paris in the nineteenth century (Harvey, 1985b) attempt to situate this theory in the experience of an individual city, but at a level of abstraction and generalization which requires much more empirical support before the case made can be properly evaluated (Dennis, 1987; Harvey, 1987).

Studies of the historical geography of urbanization in the nineteenth and twentieth centuries have been conducted at a variety of scales and with different objectives, ranging from studies of the global experiences of urbaniza-tion to detailed studies of the social and morphological structures of individual towns and cities. Two aspects in particular will be examined here: first, the meso-scale experience of urbanization, at national and regional levels; second-ly, aspects of the internal geography of towns and cities of the modern period.

Urbanization in Britain in the nineteenth century

The British urban experience was closely tied to population increase and to industrial development. By the mid-nineteenth century almost 50 per cent of the population of Britain was urban-based, and by the end of the century the overall figure was above 70 per cent. A major feature was the increase in the number of cities with populations of over 100,000, and cities like Liverpool, Manchester, Glasgow and Birmingham had reached over 1 million by the end of the century, London having reached that size earlier in the century. The changes of the nineteenth century partly reflect the increase of larger-scale industrial and retailing functions in and near towns, some of which were already growing rapidly in the seventeenth and eighteenth centuries as a result of their incorporation into a world-trading mercantile system, but in other cases, especially where new inorganic bases for industry were located, such as coalfields, the link with heavy industry and technical innovations was close and more recent. The towns and cities of Britain on the one hand became part of an integrated system, with diffusion of certain utilities occurring down a conspicuous hierarchical system, from larger to smaller, yet also maintained a distinctive regional identity and association, the nature of many towns reflecting the specific but complex nature of regional economies and societies (Lawton and Pooley, 1992). Increasing specialization of function was also a distinct characteristic of this period. The essence of the dynamics of urban location, size and function was a change from the early modern system comprising London, the expanding port towns such as Liverpool, Glasgow and Bristol, the historic regional centres including the old county towns, and the newly developing industrial towns such as Birmingham, Manchester, Leeds and Sheffield (Borsay, 1990, 49), to a pattern dominated by industrial towns and the rising service centres of the south and east. The process is very complex. Shaw (1989) has outlined for England the differential rates of growth of towns in relation to specific industrial changes, mapped against Kondratieff cycles, and suggested an early phase of growth to the mid-1820s of textile and manufacturing towns in northern and Midland England, a second phase of growth from about 1840 to 1870 involving expansion of urban areas with specialist industrial functions, including factory-based power-loom weaving, and a third phase from *c.* 1870–86 associated with a broadening economic base of urbanization. Carter and Lewis (1990, 65) have characterized urban developments in England and Wales in the nineteenth century as a system developing initially through industrialization as 'a series of independently organized regional systems which, during the century, were very gradually synthesized by the development of the capitalist system, in all its aspects, into a single interacting system under the metropolitan dominance of London. But that state was only reached towards the end of the century'.

The internal social, cultural, functional and morphological features of the towns and cities of Britain in the nineteenth century have been extensively studied, and these complex fields of investigation for the historical geographer can only be presented here in a brief digest. The major morphological characteristics were the development of distinctive central commercial and business districts in the larger towns and cities, outside of which was a zone of mixed functions including poor-quality slum property inhabited by immigrants and ethnic minorities, together with various commercial activities, a third sector or zone of middle-class housing which linked outwards to the growing suburbs, and a fourth element of working-class terrace houses (Carter and Lewis, 1990, 148–9). The actual layout of individual towns and cities reflected a host of variables, including competition for space for such functions as transport, industry, commerce, administration, public utilities and institutions for residential purposes, each of which demands represented and symbolized different positions in the hierarchy of capital formation and investment and the power structures of urban politics and cultures.

An important factor was the nature and geography of landownership. In some of the towns that grew in the eighteenth century the major landowners were private landowners, including the aristocracy and the rising merchant, professional and business classes, municipal corporations, charities and schools, some of whom, notably the municipal corporations, regulated the nature of design and densities of housing development, and which also made preliminary attempts to control the spread of infectious diseases through the creation of Improvement Commissions.

By the mid-nineteenth century, within a changed context of much wider municipal powers and much changed administrative urban systems and geographies, and particularly of much larger and more mobile populations, the internal social geography of the major towns and cities was generally characterized by the predominance of rented accommodation for the working classes in particular, taking the form of cheaply constructed low-rent terrace housing, constructed earlier in the century, or slum housing, including insanitary cellar dwellings. The pattern of work in the inner city also changed, and was reflected in standards of living and of accommodation. Thus, in London there was a change in the early nineteenth century in the pattern of manufacturing from small workshops in the West End catering for the wealthy residents of that location to the mass production of lower-quality goods for the increasing working-class and lower middle-class markets, with a greater division of labour, de-skilling, piece-work and extensive use of female labour, with a change in location to the East End to make use of a large potential labour force of women and children (Dennis, 1990, 430). Locked into a system of casual labour and a cycle of poverty, the working-class poor of the larger cities such as London, Manchester, Liverpool and Glasgow experienced dire living conditions and high death rates. An intensified pattern of residential segregation between rich, middle class and poor led not only to new patterns of residential geography but also to ignorance by the better-off of the conditions of the poor, so that

> out of sight, if not out of mind, the poor could be blamed for their poverty and urged to greater efforts of self-help. Even among philanthropic agencies, a distinction was drawn between deserving and undeserving, and the Charity Organisation Society—an umbrella agency for large numbers of different charities and trusts—was as concerned to restrict aid as to dispense it, in order to ensure that the poor were not demoralized by too generous or too easily available forms of assistance' (Dennis, 1990, 430).

The residential separation of people by class in urban areas varied from one place to another: although there was a general or model pattern of working class in the inner city, lower middle class in the residential suburbs constructed for the most part by speculative builders in the middle and late nineteenth century, and the upper classes in the outer suburbs, cities such as Manchester and Leeds demonstrated variations therefrom. Ward's study of residential patterns in Leeds in the mid-nineteenth century (Ward, 1980) indicates that apart from the segregation in exclusive sectors of a small percentage of the middle-class population, the residences of the rest of the population in the middle-class, lower middle-class and working-class categories were inter-mingled, this weak level of residential differentiation by class being a phenom-enon that increased during the later nineteenth century. Manchester had a social geography which was more complex than the model suggested by Engels in 1844 which incorporated a series of concentric zones, the innermost comprising a generally non-residential commercial district, beyond which lay a zone of 'unmixed working people's quarters', then the planned streets of the middle bourgeoisie and finally the superior residences of the upper bourgeoisie, a model system complicated, *inter alia*, by the ethnic and intra-working class differences within the inner city (Dennis, 1990, 435–7).

The built environment of the Victorian city in Britain reflected the pace of change and range of demands for housing, the changing fashions of style and design of public buildings and of urban plan, legislative controls on development, provision for improvement in water supply, sewerage, public health, and for recreation. Building was subject to slumps and booms, and the cyclical nature of suburban and fringe-belt development and its effects on urban morphology has become an important focus of study for historical geographers (Whitehand, 1987; 1988). London was an indicator of the changes in the economy and society of early Victorian England, where the 'remodelling of parts of central London from its foundations symbolized the vitality of the mid-century scene; new, grander buildings for government, finance, religion, clubs, city guilds, museums and art galleries were daily altering the skyline' (Harley, 1973b, 594). There were major contrasts between the open spaces of the extensive royal parks on the one hand and the appalling conditions of the East End on the other.

The public and private architecture of the rapidly expanding towns and cities of Victorian Britain reflected both social and economic change and also the rise of architecture as a profession and the increase in the scale of competitions for public and commercial buildings, together with a major increase in the scale of private commissions. Most of the major monuments of Victorian Britain were the outcome of competitions, including the Houses of Parliament, the Royal Exchange, the Oxford Museum of Natural History, the Foreign Office, the Albert Memorial, the Law Courts, Manchester Town Hall, and the Glasgow School of Art (Dixon and Muthesius, 1978, 10–11). The styles changed through the century: Greek and Roman classical, neo-classical (often incorporating French and Italian Renaissance designs), Gothic, neo-Gothic, free and eclectic and late Victorian baroque styles. An example of the neo-classical Greek revival style is the British Museum in London by Sir Robert Smirke. Victorian national and civic pride is well exemplified in the major public buildings of London and the other major cities of Britain, and their architects also were influential in their designs for the country houses of the industrial and commercial magnates of the period. Housing for the working class was very different, generally taking the form of a variety of terrace-house forms in England and Wales, and higher-rising tenements in Scotland, paralleling Belgian and German patterns respectively (Daunton, 1983).

Urbanization in the United States in the nineteenth and early twentieth centuries

The percentage of the population of the United States living in urban areas was 5.1 in 1790, 8.8 in 1830, 15.3 in 1850, 25.7 in 1870, 39.7 in 1900 and 51.2 in 1920 (Ward, 1971, 6). The regional balance of urban population increase varied: in the early nineteenth century the percentage of the total urban population of the United States in the north-east was 10.9, with 0.9 in the north-central region, and 4.6 in the south. By mid-century the respective percentage figures were: north-east 26.5, north-central 9.2, south 8.3, and west 6.4. By 1900 the figures were: north-east 61.1, north-central 38.6, south 18 and west 39.9 (Ward, 1971, 7). The phasing of the varied regional experiences of urbanization in the United States has been characterized by Ward (1971) into three periods. The first involved the establishment prior to 1830 of the commercial and administrative centres necessary to link the colonial peripheries with their European centres, and the development of Boston, New York, Philadelphia and Baltimore on the north-eastern seaboard, and Charleston in the South, as the largest towns, with a small number of smaller towns on the coast of New England. The most rapid growth by the mid-nineteenth century had been that of New York. The second phase, between 1830 and 1870, witnessed the 'emergence of the core in the old periphery and the differentiation of the new periphery' (Ward, 1971, 32), a period of increasing intensity of industrialization, especially associated with New York, Boston, Philadelphia, Baltimore, southern New England, upstate New York and southern Pennsylvania. At the periphery of this core, and influenced by the development of the railroad and river and lake transport systems, cities such as Chicago, Detroit, Cleveland, St Louis, and Cincinnati grew rapidly, the latter having been the largest inland city in 1850. Urban expansion was facilitated by the construction of canal networks in mid-century and the beginnings of interregional railroad construction in the 1850s. The third phase, that involving the enlargement of the core and the greater integration of the new periphery, occurred between 1870 and 1910, in which 'the small economic core incorporated adjacent industrialized sections, and a newly completed continental transportation system stimulated the enlargement and metropolitan organization of the new periphery' (Ward, 1971, 39), including the extensive urban growth within the American Manufacturing Belt of the north-eastern and Great Lakes states. An important facet of all phases of urban growth in the United States was that of immigration, 33 million immigrants entering the country in the period 1820–1920, the great majority of them becoming urban residents.

The social geography of the nineteenth-century city in the United States evidences the emergence of specialist functional zones, conspicuously the Central Business District and varied residential areas and groupings. The extent of distinctive social segregation within the growing cities of the United States is as contentious a question among researchers as it is for posited parallel developments in Britain. The image or model projected by contemporary observers and twentieth-century scholars is one of the existence of an area of residence of unskilled labour near to the Central Business District of the city, with cheap housing (including older houses abandoned by high- and middle-income residents) and poor living conditions, and which increasingly attracted immigrants, the areas in which they were concentrated in largest numbers becoming ghettos. Ward has suggested that this general model must be qualified by the understanding that before 1875 the labour requirements and housing provision meant a much greater spread of the working class over wide areas of the city and in peripheral shanty towns in some cases, with greater inner-city concentration only occurring after that time. Thus, before the Civil War many Irish and German immigrants in Boston and New York had to locate outside the central immigrant area on account of the insufficiency of abandoned housing for their large numbers, also there was a movement of middle-class residents to outer suburbs, awaiting in some measure the later development of streetcar transport. In addition, he adds the qualification that even within the inner city in the later nineteenth century the conditions varied, with the worst forms of ghetto environment (overcrowding, high death rates and very poor social conditions) experienced only by a part of the immigrant population (Ward, 1979b).

Reference to Ward's comparative essay on images of residential segregation in the cities of Britain and the United States in the early nineteenth century is pertinent here, especially his idea that the models and descriptions of Booth and Burgess for late nineteenth-century London and early twentieth-century Chicago offer and demonstrate scales of residential differentiation quite different from those of the early Victorian cities, and that 'Descriptions of the social geography of early Victorian cities might then be viewed as geopolitical images designed to justify reform and derived from new concepts of poverty' (Ward, 1978, 189).

The location of the black population in the cities of the United States is an important question. Data sources have been reviewed by Wacker (1975) and Clarke (1975) and Radford's analysis of race, residence and ideology in Charleston in South Carolina in the mid-nineteenth century indicates a tight control of black residential location, free blacks being confined to the northern part or 'Neck' of the city, some by choice, others by obligation of the city's élite. According to Radford (1979, 354), 'Planter ideology, including powerful notions of social control, permeated the whole of Charleston's existence. In particular, a curious amalgam of aesthetic taste, medical ignorance, and racial myth affected the evaluation and allocation of residential space within the city. In comparison, those market forces assumed to be dominant in nineteenth-century US cities were insignificant. The main process was residential control'.

The emergence of areas of black alley-dwellers in late nineteenth-century Washington has been studied by Groves (1974) and the broader question of black residential areas in late nineteenth-century cities by Groves and Muller (1975), the latter study indicating a difference of chronology in the emergence of major black ghettos between the cities of the South, the border and the North.

The built form of the cities of the United States in the nineteenth and early twentieth centuries is a massive topic, and only one or two important trends can be mentioned here. A central feature is the development of skyscraper buildings in the city centres. Domosh has shown that 'New York's first generation of skyscrapers reflected the city's unprecedented economic growth in the late nineteenth century. Between 1875 and the first decade of the twentieth century, New York was transformed from a predominantly hor-izontal to a vertical landscape' (Domosh, 1987, 233). The combination of rapid economic growth, change in transportation systems, and new systems of building construction, (especially the steel building frame) plus the elevator, intensified and dramatized the concentration of retail and financial districts of the American city from the last decade of the nineteenth century. 'By stacking offices a dozen or more stories high, the skyscraper solved the constraints of earlier walk-up buildings, but it also unleashed the businessman's burgeoning sense of power and importance. Originally a profitable solution to spatial demands, the skyscraper in its awe-inspiring verticality and behemoth scale became the symbol of corporate prestige and a means of competition for status among the captains of industry' (Muller, 1990, 274). In addition to the spectacular high-rise temples to the new capitalism of finance, retailing, and administration, the late nineteenth-century city in the United States was characterized by the building of luxurious townhouses for the affluent in such prestigious locations as Fifth Avenue in New York, Commonwealth Avenue in Boston, Prairie Avenue in Chicago, and Euclid Avenue in Cleveland. The railroad from the nineteenth century and the automobile from the twentieth extended the spread of élitist residences into and beyond the suburbs of the expanding cities, and was further accompanied by the growth of both inland and coastal resorts (Wyckoff, 1990). The particular form of suburban expansion was conditioned by a whole range of factors. In the case of Boston Conzen (1990b, 156) has suggested that there were three influential factors: the irregular framework of colonial and early-age routeways dividing the unbuilt zones between Boston and other nearby towns; early suburban railway lines; and current fashions for the layout of suburban lots. The architectural styles of the new élitist residences and the major public buildings of the central city moved through the nineteenth and early twentieth century through a variety of designs and trends: Georgian, Grecian (after 1825), Gothic Revival, and increasingly from 1865 to 1925 a greater eclecticism, driven by the varied tastes and the massive wealth of the rich. According to Wyckoff (1990, 349), this was 'a grand and gawdy era of ostentatious townhouses, mammoth resort "cottages", and plush metropolitan theaters. Architects such as R.M. Hunt, H.H. Richardson, and McKim, Mead, and White gave the wealthy whatever they wanted, whether it was a French Second Empire mansard roof, a Moorish minaret, a Victorian tennis court, or an Egyptian dining room'.

The major monumental urban construction was Washington DC, conceived in the late eighteenth century but whose construction and modification occupied much of the nineteenth and early twentieth centuries. By the 1870s, in spite of the completion of many of the major public buildings and monuments in the classical style, there was still a great deal of unfinished work. A substantial burst of activity in the early 1870s effected major improvements, including construction of sewers, the paving and lighting of streets, though the large blocks envisaged by L'Enfant in his original design had been subdivided into smaller blocks, in whose alleyways lived the urban poor in conditions of great squalor (Green, 1957, 229–30).

Many of the urban characteristics described above were also experienced, with different chronologies and styles of building, in other countries and regions, notably in western Europe, undergoing rapid industrialization and intense capital investment.

The well-known reconstruction of much of central Paris under the prefecture of Baron Haussmann (prefect of the Département of the Seine from 1853) and the emperor Napoleon III may be read one way as a piece of inspired modern urban reconstruction, involving the clearing out of many slums and the creation of a modern, functioning and visually attractive townscape, including the grands boulevards and such new buildings as the Paris Opera House. It was more, however, than a novel piece of modern town planning and renovation. Clout (1977, 509–10) shows that, 'The need to maintain law and order loomed large in Haussmann's plans for the "new Paris". Broad, straight avenues were to be laid out to facilitate the movement of cavalry'.

Harvey (1985c, 67), however, sees the period of the reconstruction of Paris during the Second Empire as 'a deadly serious experiment with a form of national socialism—an authoritarian state with police powers and a populist base. It collapsed, like most other experiments of its ilk, in the midst of dissention and war, but its tenure was marked by the imposition of intense labour discipline and the liberation of capital circulation from its preceding constraints'. He maps out its history of change in terms of broader space relations, distribution (credit, rent, taxes), production and labour markets, reproduction and consciousness formation.

Colonial Towns and Cities

To a degree the western urban experience was translated to less developed regions of the world by the mechanism of colonialism, though its exact nature depended much on the strength or otherwise of indigenous urban tradition. In the British Empire, in such places as India, Malaya, and some parts of Africa, which had strong urban traditions, the nature of colonial urban development was, as Christopher (1988, 130–1) suggests, dualist and segregationist, that is to secure the separation of colonists and colonized in separate quarters, for military and ethnic reasons. Places like Delhi and Agra in India, which had been major pre-colonial walled cities, had new colonial towns laid out adjacent to them in contrast to Bombay, designed *ab initio* as a colonial town, where the European population inhabited the core and the indigenous population the periphery. The precise form of plan could either be of a regular, grid-plan type, or irregular, related to the form of existing indigenous cities, but in both cases having all the necessary social and commercial functions to enable almost total self-sufficiency. The crowning achievement of British imperial formal urban design was New Delhi, in India, designated in 1911 as the capital instead of Calcutta, and constructed according to plans prepared by the architects Sir Edward Lutyens and Sir Herbert Baker.

The form of physical and social segregation of the indigenous and European populations varied from one colonial territory to another. The Chinese in particular suffered from residential exclusion from colonial towns. In Africa the experience of segregation was complex. In Southern Rhodesia the pattern of residence of black African servants in such towns as Salisbury and Bulawayo—in their own quarters at the back of each house—was similar to that of the black slave populations of the cities of the ante-bellum American South (Pawson, 1990, 529). In South Africa, although there had been quarters for freed slaves within Cape Town and Port Elizabeth after 1834, by the beginning of the twentieth century the European perception of the links between the indigenous population and disease led to deliberate policies of separate permanent locations for such people at a distance from the European town, exemplified by Ndabeni in Cape Town, New Bright in Port Elizabeth and Pimville in Johannesburg, established in the period 1900–04 (Christopher, 1988, 117–18). The apartheid city has been viewed by some commentators as a later and more extreme variant of the colonial city, the accentuation of the ideology of apartheid being achieved by the South African Group Areas Act of 1950 (Christopher, 1983), though Mabin (1986a) has pointed in his study of residential segregation in Kimberley in the period

1880–1920 to the significance of the African labour force compound and its later variant, the hostel, in the history of labour control.

An interesting variant on the theme of the colonial, or at least the colonizing, city is to be found in the urban history of Palestine in the nineteenth and early twentieth centuries, evidenced in the development of new cities by Jewish colonists, mainly from Europe, and continuity and change of the much older cities such as Jerusalem. Ben-Arieh (1989) has outlined the 'new beginnings' experienced by Palestine in the nineteenth century, including changes within the Ottoman Empire (especially modernization, constitutional reform, and increased Jewish immigration), greater involvement by the Christian churches, and 'the third factor portending momentous change was the enormous growth during the nineteeth century of what had for hundreds of years been a very small Jewish community in Palestine. This development was accompanied by ferment in the Jewish world as a whole, heralding Zionist ideology' (Ben-Arieh, 1989, 52). Within the older cities dramatic increases in population enhanced the distinctiveness of residential quarters. In Jaffa, for example, whose population increased from about 2750 in 1800 to 45,000 in 1921, the Muslim community, which had increased in size from *c.* 3000 in 1805 to 30,350 in 1915, largely inhabited the old city, but upper-class Muslims also had elegant houses on the outskirts. There were residential variations between different groups within the Muslim community: Egyptian farmers, working in groves as gardeners, lived outside old Jaffa; North Africans lived near the mosques; gypsies, working as blacksmiths, lived in tents within the city; and there were also Asian Muslims (Kark, 1990, 160). The Christian communities in Jaffa, initially within the town wall on the south side of the town, subsequently expanded outside the wall on the south side. The Jewish population began to increase rapidly from the 1830s, with the majority being North Africans and Sephardic, but in the 1880s these groups were overtaken in size by the Ashkenazi Jews who migrated both from within Palestine and from outside. This late nineteenth-century increase effected spatial changes from the groups within the walls, residentially separated by country of origin, to new locations outside the walls (Kark, 1990, 163 *seq.*). In Jerusalem there is also clear evidence of the historical tendency for religious and national groups to separate into particular residential quarters, so that within the walls there are Muslim, Jewish, Christian and Armenian quarters, whose precise locations have changed with time. Thus the Jewish quarter was originally in the vicinity of the south-west section of the Western Wall, then in the southern part near the Temple, then in the north-eastern part of the city, removing after the Crusader invasion to the southern part, south-west of the Temple Mount (Har-El, 1977; Ben-Arieh, 1984).

The westernization and European physical penetration of towns in the Middle East during the nineteenth century, according to Katz (1986), took three different forms. In the first a modern European town or quarter, planned by European planners, was built near the old town, and from this new quarter ultimately grew a new town. Examples are the Italian development of Misurata in Libya and French foundations at Fez and Marrakesh in Morocco. In the second type, a whole new town was built by Europeans adjacent to the old town: examples include the English construction of Abadan, now in Iran, and the French construction of Rabat in Morocco. Thirdly, as in the case of Beirut and Tripoli in Lebanon and Casablanca in Morocco suburban development by locals and Europeans occurred around the old town. Tel Aviv was an example of the first type, a garden suburb near the old port of Jaffa being constructed by Zionists from 1906, which became an independent town in 1921 and a city in 1934. It was distinctive, however, in that the ideological and political motives behind its creation were very closely allied to the Zionist plans for the colonization of Palestine, the site near Jaffa being chosen for its trade and production potential and for its perceived healthiness, which it was hoped would encourage increased Zionist immigration and capital investment (Katz, 1986, 402–6).

10

Historical Geographies of Industrialization

Introduction

One of the dominant features of the evolution and development of the landscapes of the world from prehistoric times onwards has been the sites associated with and the distribution of the products of a very wide variety of types of industry. Over a long period of time industrial change was partly conditioned by technological advance and the opportunities for sale of industrial goods both near the areas of production and, in the case of products which commanded high demand, further afield, especially where effective transport and trade links existed. The most intensive periods of industrialization, however, came in the eighteenth, nineteenth and twentieth centuries, with the development of new technologies, the use of large quantities of inorganic raw materials, the investment of capital in very large quantities and the employment, often in very poor working conditions, of very large industrial labour forces. Three phases of industrial development will be used here to discuss and illustrate the historical geography of this important and complex set of processes: medieval industry, 'proto-industry', and modern industry.

Medieval Industry

Industry was carried out both in the towns and the countryside of medieval Europe. According to Parker (1979) there were five types of industry to be found in late medieval Europe (in the late fifteenth century): village industry; the industry of peasant households; the workshops of urban artisans; 'montanindustrie' (mining, smelting, charcoal-burning and quarrying), in the mountains and forests of central Europe in particular; and the industry associated with merchant-organized networks combining rural and urban labour. At the level of the village industry took the form of produce for local markets by shoemakers, smiths, carpenters, thatchers, masons, millers, weavers and the like, and was supplemented both by the work of itinerant craftsmen and, largely for their own use, by the production of utensils and clothes by the individual peasant households. The workshops of the urban artisans were a long way removed in style, output and organization from those of the peasant households, particularly those which were producing luxury goods, including works of art, for a sophisticated aristocratic and merchant market. The organization of the units of production was in the hands of the master workman who controlled the journeymen and apprentices, and who himself was subject to the control of the craft guild. There was a wide range of guilds or confraternities in medieval towns, serving social and religious as well as economic purposes, but the craft guilds were the dominant form, expanding in the twelfth and thirteenth centuries into specialized guilds from the more general Guild Merchant. This distinction between merchant and artisan guilds is highlighted in Langton and Hoppe's analysis of the relative roles of town and countryside in the economic development of early modern Europe, the artisan guilds being seen as a form of pre-capitalist natural economy (Langton and Hoppe, 1983). Cologne, the largest city in the Rhineland, had 36 guilds at the end of the fourteenth century; the smaller city of Frankfurt-am-Main had 14 in 1355 and 28 in the fifteenth century (Pounds, 1974, 296–7). Paris had 101 guilds in 1260 (Braudel, 1982, 317). The extent of control of the urban guilds on the extent of industrial production and the expansion of the craft trades through recruitment of apprentices has perhaps been exaggerated, partly because of the stagnant population and therefore demand during their time of greatest influence together with the slow pace of technological change. A key question for the historical geographer, however, in the particular context of theories of the nature of the pre-industrial town, is the effect of guild affiliation on the social geography of particular cities. Sjoberg (1960) has argued the centrality of importance of the guild or craft districts to the character of the medieval town, though the phasing of the emergence of socially distinctive regions of such 'pre-industrial' cities varied enormously, hence 'The early and sharply-accentuated divisions between "fat" men and "small" men in Florence did not dissuade the rich from building their palazzi evenly across the town rather than defensively clustered in one rich sector, whilst rich and poor jostled each other for the same living space in the Old Town of Edinburgh until the late eighteenth century' (Dodgshon, 1987, 133).

The dominant industry in medieval Europe, apart from food production, was textiles, of which the woollen industry was the most important. Clothes were made from a range of fabrics, including wool, flax, hemp, and to a lesser extent cotton and silk. The regional historical geography of the textile industries was essentially that of the dominance in the production of better-quality cloth of the Low Countries, with advantages of good-quality local wool, effective waterway communications and port systems, and northern Italy, which finished cloth produced in the Low Countries for markets in the eastern Mediterranean. Its largest centre of production was Florence, where production, reaching its zenith in the late thirteenth century and well declined by the mid-fifteenth, was controlled by the guild Arte di Calimala (Pounds, 1974; 1990). North Italy also developed cotton and fustian weaving, and the weaving of cloth from silk was a regional speciality initially of central Italy, in Lucca. In England, a pattern of export of wool to the Low Countries changed to the export of cloth in the late fourteenth and the fifteenth centuries, the wool cloth being produced in East Anglia and the south-west, and in central Europe there was a specialist region of linen and barchent (a mixture of flax and cotton) production in southern Germany and northern Switzerland. As indicated above, a major sector of medieval European industry was ore mining and smelting, charcoal-burning and quarrying, the 'montanindustrie'. Alluvial gold was found in central Europe and supplemented by gold imported from

Africa, and silver, often found in close conjunction with lead, was mined and smelted in the Hercynian uplands, including the Hartz Mountains, the eastern Alps, the Pyrenees, Carpathians, and in the Balkans. Copper, iron and tin were also mined in these regions, and in south-west England. The most extensively worked metal was iron, which required large areas of timber for charcoal for smelting, especially given the low level of smelting technology.

In China, in contrast, there was in the early medieval period, especially in the Northern Sung period (960–1126) major progress in industrial development, especially in ironworking and coal mining, and Tuan has suggested that 'The extent of China's industrial development in the eleventh century was comparable to that which took place during the earlier phases of England's Industrial Revolution. It was stimulated by the demand for iron currency, iron and steel weapons, agricultural implements, salt pans, nails, anchors and armour' (Tuan, 1970, 131). Extensive industrial development occurred both in the cities and the countryside, especially in the north of the country. Although the cities had traditionally been the main centres of industrial activity, the new heavy industrial centres, especially ironworks, were in the countryside near to the sources of supply of the raw materials, in the case of those producing the pans for salt production, near the salt-producing areas themselves, close to shipbuilding areas and the iron mines.

Towards the end of the medieval period there was, notably in parts of Europe, a conspicuous growth in the extent of rural industry which, it is argued, represents the historically specific (late feudal) increase in freedom from the controls of urban guilds to adapt to changing market opportunities and to undercut the prices of urban-based industries and crafts, together with the realization of marginal ecological environments which supplied such industrial raw materials as timber, leather, wool, dyes and metal ores. The communities involved were on the whole free, frequently practising partible inheritance, having small holdings which only partly provided for subsistence and had predominantly pastoral economies whose seasonality allowed time for non-agricultural economic activity (Dodgshon, 1987, 268). Although such activities had been opposed and limited by urban guilds in the thirteenth, fourteenth and fifteenth centuries, there was a change of balance towards the rural artisan from the late sixteenth century.

Proto-industrialization: Concept and Reality

Of the existence in Europe and elsewhere of regionally specific, rurally located, industries in the period prior to that of intense, large-scale, capitally intensive and generally urban-based industry there is no doubt. The common characteristics of these industries appear to include: the production of a wide variety of goods for markets beyond the immediate locale, sometimes for other regions of the same country or territory, sometimes for more distant, foreign, markets; the general tendency for proto-industries to be part of a marked dual-economy, in which farming and industrial production were combined, with a marked but not inevitable tendency for location in pastoral or woodland, that is marginal, environments; the creation of demand for foodstuffs by the development of this only partially producing sector of the rural economy; the special relationship in the marketing process with towns in the region; the effect of such proto-industries on the processes of demographic change, notably by facilitating a lower age at marriage and therefore higher birth rates and higher population densities; and the expansion in due course to full industrialization. The idea of the expansion of rural industry in areas of agricultural seasonality and marginality has been part of the literature on economic and social change, especially in Europe, for some time, early contributions coming from Thirsk (1961) and Jones (1968). A major early seminal contribution was Mendels' paper 'Proto-industrialization: the first phase of the industrialization process' (1972), in which distinction was made between areas of Europe characterized by pastoral regimes and subsistence-level economies, where early and growing domestic industries developed, and areas of commercial farming where generally they did not develop. The system of proto-industrial work organization was markedly different from that of the earlier medieval merchant guild system and from the later system of industrial capitalism. A distinction was also made by Mendels and others, using German terminology, between two ideal-type systems of proto-industrial production: the 'Kaufsystem' and 'Verlagsystem'. The 'Kaufsystem' was one in which independent peasants or artisans sold their own goods, produced from their own raw materials and using their own machines, for cash in the market: a system where the producers largely owned and controlled the means of production. The 'Verlagsystem', which sometimes evolved from the 'Kaufsystem', was one in which merchant capitalists took over control as middlemen in the provision of raw materials and machines and marketed the end-products, paid wages or piece-rates and furnished credit, thus to a marked extent separating the workers from the means of production.

Medick (1976) argued that demographic characteristics and tendencies of proto-industrial communities and families included a lowering of age at marriage and therefore higher birth rates and higher population densities. The conceptual basis of this rather loose bundle of theory of proto-industrialization ranges from models based on neo-classical economic theory, described by Gregory (1990) as 'ecological', to a more Marxist-related view of proto-industrialization as a second phase in the transition from feudalism to capitalism, which Gregory (1990) describes as 'economic'. Critiques of the theory of proto-industrialization abound. Coleman (1983) objects on the grounds that: the timing or chronology of proto-industrial change is wrong, especially for Britain; that there is a wider range of causes; that there is little evidence of the process leading to earlier marriage and population growth; and that the theory rests excessively on the experience of cottage-based and textile industries, whereas little is said about more centralized forms of manufacturing such as mines, mills, furnaces, forges, or urban industry. Other critiques have stressed the inadequacy of a linear theory, particularly in view of the complexity of processes and conditions leading to rural industrial development in a very wide variety of economic and social environments. Houston and Snell (1984, 492) advocate the abandonment of the term, notwithstanding the usefulness of the debate which it has launched, for with particular reference to the publication by Kriedte, Medick and Schlumbohm (1981) they conclude that 'we are still little closer to a general or theoretical understanding of the transition from an agrarian to an industrial world. For this reason, proto-industrial theory will have to be abandoned, and replaced by a less schematic and limiting approach which takes more account of the diversity of European social and economic development in the passage to industrialization'. The need for more detailed analyses of the phenomenon has been supported in critiques and reviews by Berg, Hudson and Sonnenscher (1983), Clarkson (1985), Butlin (1986), and Hudson (1989). The theory has been empirically tested for an astonishingly wide array of places.

The English experience of rural industries

The existence of rural regions of industrial production in England, producing for distant markets, is well documented, though not all such industries and regions have been exposed to equally intensive levels of investigation.

In essence the balance of the theoretical and specific empirical work undertaken suggests a period of active rural industrial activity between the seventeenth and the early nineteenth centuries. The predominant rural industries were textiles, but there were in addition significant areas of metalworking and other craft industries. The relationship between the sources of capital and the organization of the labour force is thought to be of particular importance, especially in cases where the capital came from outside the region. Dodgshon in this context has stressed the distinction between circulating and fixed capital, the latter more important in the proto-industrial period before the intense period of heavy investment in fixed capital (buildings and machines) of the periods of the so-called Industrial Revolution and involving mainly 'raw material, semi-finished and finished products moving through the various stages of production via scattered craftsmen and artisans and whose gross value far exceeded the plant and equipment involved' (Dodgshon, 1987, 320). One effect of this was the relative mobility and freedom of circulating capital to support changes from one area of comparative advantage to another, witnessed in the shift in the location of major domestic industries within England in the sixteenth, seventeenth and early eighteenth centuries away from the iron-producing region of the Weald of southern England and from the cloth districts of East Anglia towards a growth of industrial activity in the Midlands and the north, especially the north-west, with parallel changes in active industrial regions in, for example, the Low Countries and in France. The dynamics of this kind of industry reflected far more, however, than the predominance of circulating capital and its perceived consequential effect on spatial mobility of location. As Hudson has indicated, explanations of the comparative advantages experienced by regions of growth and the disadvantages of regions of decline have to go well beyond considerations of lists of basic environmental and crude economic pre-conditions, they have to examine 'how systems of landholding, inheritance and wealth distribution conditioned the nature, organization and finance of industrial activities in an area, how urban production functioned in relation to rural manufacturing, how the family, household and personal life adapted to changes in work regimes and market opportunities, how these were reflected in demographic behaviour and how all these variables related to one another' (Hudson, 1989, 25).

In early modern and modern Britain, as elsewhere, industry was almost without exception not a separate and distinctive economic activity but part of a complex set of economic and social relations or 'ecologies' bound up together at both small and larger scales, that is at the household and regional level, with other activities such as agriculture and urban change. If one includes in the term 'industry' various trades and crafts, in addition to manufacturing, then the complexity deepens, and the experience was geographically extensive.

At the outset of the early modern period, however, it is clear that what might be seen as the integration of the space-economy in relation to capital, goods, and even information was very imperfect and uneven, partly due to the poorly developed inland transport systems. By the mid- to late eighteenth century a more sophisticated system had developed, with price-fixing markets, national and international, determining the tighter integration of the space-economy and the expansion or demise of proto-industrial regions.

An important and obviously relevant feature of proto-industry is its connection with non-local markets, sometimes far removed from the place of production. By the mid-eighteenth century, the national economy was led by export industries, with a very high percentage by value of exports being of cloth. Of particular importance were the markets in the British colonies, but there was intensive interaction with European countries also.

Most accounts of proto-industrialization in England stress the importance of the textile industries, and not without justification, for the output of the textile industries increased substantially between the early sixteenth and mid-eighteenth centuries. There was a striking increase in the early modern period in the numbers of people employed in England in crafts and trades, that is from about 25 per cent in the early sixteenth century to 40 per cent by the late seventeenth century. What is especially important is the way in which competition, changes in supply of raw materials, and changes in technology, effected dynamic changes in the nature of success, and thus in the rise in importance of some producing regions at the expense of others. In late medieval times the major producers were Wiltshire and Gloucestershire, which produced broad cloth for export, West Yorkshire, producing lower-grade cloth for the home market, the worsted-producing region in East Anglia, centred on Norwich, and the traditional cloth-producing regions of Essex, Suffolk, Devon and Somerset. Subsequently there was a northward shift in emphasis, with the decline of the south-western and eastern regions and the rise of the textile areas of Lancashire and Yorkshire. The complexity of early production systems in the rural areas of the north has been well illustrated in studies, for example, by Gregory (1982b), Hudson (1986) and Walton (1989), which stress, among other aspects, the interactions between basic environmental and labour endowments and the detailed and dynamic nature of production systems and capital circuits.

Rural Industries in Europe

Studies of the regional experiences of early rural industry in Europe and elsewhere abound, many of them addressing the question of 'proto-industry' and therefore of continuity into fully fledged factory-based industry, others indicating regions of industrial decline. The experience of early rural industry in Scandinavia is well documented. Schön (1982) in a study of textile industries in Sweden in the mid-nineteenth century offers three contrasting locational experiences. In Sjuharädslygden there was increasing dependence on domestic industry from the end of the eighteenth century, especially among smallholders and the landless. Linen and then cotton weaving were the initial activities, mainly carried out by women. A putting-out system operated, with merchants and wealthier peasants providing the yarn and taking responsibility for marketing. In the Ångermanland a different system of peasant production of linen was based on locally grown flax, involving both men and women in production and some peasant control over marketing. In a third region, the wool-production industry of Norrköping was an urban factory form of production, including state-provided woollen factories. In the eighteenth century the central organization of spinning and weaving combined with the putting-out of carding and spinning to women outworkers, but mainly in the towns. Magnusson and Isacson's (1982) study of smithcraft in Eskilstuna and southern Dalecarlia in Sweden show two characteristics of this type of proto-industry: much of it comprised small-scale peasant iron-making, having tenuous links with agriculture; and that there was only partial intervention of merchant capital.

In France rural industry was widespread in the seventeenth, eighteenth and nineteenth centuries (see Fig. 10.1), with some indication of decline beyond the 1830s (Clout, 1980, 26).

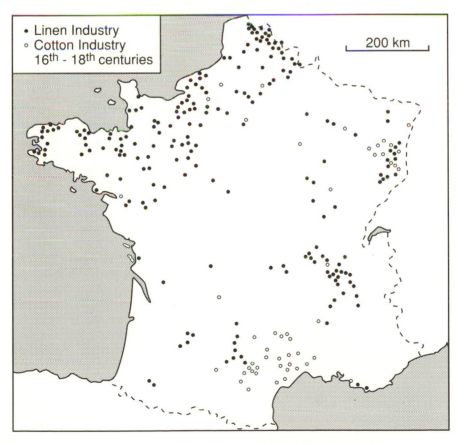

Fig. 10.1 *The French cotton and linen industries from the sixteenth to the late eighteenth centuries. Source:* Geographical Handbook Series, France, *vol. II (1942, 98)*

Regions with high population densities supported by rural industries included rural Normandy and Maine, Picardy, Touraine, Poitou, Languedoc, with the Lyonnais district the principal areas of the silk industry. Few villages in France did not have workshop trades (Clout, 1977b), and those industries which were based on imported raw materials such as silk and cotton tended to be organized by merchants or other industrial capitalists. Departures from the standard model of proto-industrialization have been found in France. Gullickson (1983) in a study of rural industries in the Pays de Caux in Normandy has illustrated the compatibility of commercial agriculture and proto-industry, for this region was a very large textile (putting-out) region in the eighteenth and nineteenth centuries while also characterized by commercial grain-growing. Important aspects of this system were the seasonality of labour use in the production of grain, a significant gender division of labour (employment for women in the textile industry) and the connections with the merchants and labour market of Rouen and the urban markets of Paris and centres in England and Spain.

Rural industries in Asia

Perlin (1983) has, in challenging the basic assumptions of the proto-industrial theory with specific reference to the experiences of pre-colonial south Asia, offered a broader framework for the analysis of such systems, which in fact draws both Europe and Asia into an analytical context. He replaces the term 'proto-industrialization' with 'commercial manufacture', this including all forms of pre-factory industry, and argues that its essential contextual characteristics, demographically including high fertility, large families and rapid population growth, generally living in conditions of poverty, although associated with manufacturing of goods for regional, national or international markets, have much in common with predominantly agrarian regions. Also the strategy of increasing the size of the family labour unit is a demographic response to 'a contextual development of exploitation relationships which demand ever more labour for less rewards from particular household units', implying that 'different kinds of relationship—between landlord and serf directly for labour, between colonial state and peasantry for taxes in kind or cash, between market and industrial producers mediated through "hostile" competitive market forces—produced similar results' (Perlin, 1983, 49). This phenomenon he claims is characteristic of European and Asiatic systems of both agricultural and industrial production in the seventeenth and eighteenth centuries, and is the product of 'the secular increase in the use and exploitation of large collections of dispersed labour based on the use of simple technologies, and the increasing sophistication and extension of these commercial methods of exploitation over ever larger distances (thus of commercial practice and banking institutions, for example)' (Perlin, 1983, 50). The mixed occupations (agricultural and industrial) of this period should better be viewed as indicators of structural change at a time of increased freedom from guild restrictions and expanding domestic and international demand for lower-cost goods rather than as indicators of either backwardness or transition to either more efficient use of resources or a complete reversal away from industrial activity. The additional question in the case of India is the extent to which intensification of colonial influence and control in the eighteenth century led to decline in industrial activity.

The major craft goods produced in Asia as a whole in the pre-factory period were textiles (cotton, silk and wool, for clothes and carpets), metal goods including jewellery, ceramics, glassware, and subsidiary products such as the manufacture of paper, gunpowder, bricks, musical instruments, furniture, cosmetics and perfumes (Chaudhuri, 1990, 302). Regional specialization in the production of textiles was evident in all areas of Asia, conspicuously in the carpet-producing areas of Iran and Ottoman Turkey from the sixteenth century, the cotton fabric-manufacturing regions of India (the Punjab, Gujarat, the Cormandel coast and Bengal), and the silk-weaving regions of China, notably Szechwan, the lower Yangtze regions, Chekiang and Kiangsu (Chaudhuri, 1990, 309). The contexts of regional industrial production in the sixteenth, seventeenth and eighteenth centuries differed, though there were common denominators including the links with overseas markets and merchant capital. Analysis of the textile industries of Asia suggests that different factors affected the types of regional specialization, some more strongly influenced by the supply of raw material and hereditary local skills, others by transport, technology, and mode of organization of production and distribution. The chains of production and sale were frequently very complex. The similarity of this system to the European putting-out system is a debatable question, a difference, especially in the case of India, being the advance of capital rather than raw materials by the owners of the commercial capital. The complexity of production of textiles in India reflected social (including considerations of caste), economic, technical and environmental conditions, the complex division of labour involved in the production of a given type of textile good often being a major influence to the point of requiring movement of raw materials over considerable distances for different stages of treatment.

Modern Industry and Theories of Modernization of the Economy

The transformation of the economies and societies of the West by the complex processes associated with the intensive development of capital- and labour-intensive industry commenced in the eighteenth century, accelerated in the nineteenth century and changed course in the twentieth century, but the precise form and chronology of industrialization varied substantially from one region to the next.

Central to the understanding of processes of advancing industrialization and modernization of societies and economies or transitions to new modes of production is at least a minimal understanding of theories of the role of capital and capitalism. Capital is a resource created through the release of profit (surplus value, that is the market value which is normally in excess of the actual labour cost or exchange value of production of a good or service) by means of the use of money for purchase of critical commodities (materials, machines and labour power) and by their use the production of new commodities for profit, which can be further invested in extended or new production processes for further profit. Different theories accommodate the various processes of production of profit in different ways. Classical and neo-classical economics, deriving from work by the political economists of the eighteenth century and the marginal utility theories of mid- and late nineteenth-century economists, views the principal mechanism of economic change as being the way in which the market perfectly and disinterestedly balances the inputs of factors of production such as land, labour and capital, with technology seen as a key factor influencing the rate at which the marginal returns to each of these factors diminishes relative to others, and is also the impersonal factor which in effect determines the ultimate distribution of income in conditions of market competition. Value and profit, therefore, are viewed as the outcome of a mechanistic market process. In contrast, Marxian economics sees value or profit as the outcome of the unequal and class-specific appropriation of the surplus value of labour to a particular bourgeois or capitalist class, the consequence of the exploitation of the labour of the working class who are in this process impoverished, and whose control over the means of production, including their own labour, is weakened or severed. The emphasis is not on the impersonal effects of market mechanisms, but on the social and political contexts and consequences of the unequal exchanges and allocations from the control of resources and labour by a small fraction of the population. Key additional concepts are those of the 'mode of production' (a specific and historically identifiable system of relations of production) such as feudalism or capitalism and the relations of production, that is the relationship engaged in, independently of individual choice, in the process and organization of production. In the historic context, the Marxist interpretation of change from a pre-industrial political economy to an advanced industrial political economy is that of a transition from a feudal to a capitalist mode of production, from a predominance of circulating—including merchant—capital to a predominance of fixed capital. An important feature of capitalism, according to Marxist theory, is that it does produce spatial as well as social inequality, the product of an international scale of resource allocation and the search for capital accumulation, capital circulating along varied paths and associated in this circulation with crises or disequilibria of production.

The initiation of an advanced form of industrialization from the late eighteenth century onwards, notably in Britain then in other resource-rich parts of Europe, was in part occasioned by the adoption of new technologies of production and transport, involving a change in the balance between circulating and fixed capital (money invested in machines, buildings, canals and railways, for example). Although traditional forms of technology were dominant in the early part of the Industrial Revolution, and modest fixed capital ratios prevailed until the 1830s, from that time there emerged large production units with increasing outputs, together with increased investment in mining, canals and railways (Dodgshon, 1987, 321–2). Fixed capital and social capital (networks of place-specific skills and social relations) had their spatial ties, but with a profit equilibrium and equalization being reached new strategies had to be found to create more profit, including new technologies and new locations, so that 'the history of capitalism should be read as a series of locally or regionally specific investments, each moving through a cycle of innovation, adaptation, then crisis as capital moves on to areas of unused freedom' (Dodgshon, 1987, 324). What we should look for, therefore, in a broad analysis of the spatially specific experiences of industrial capitalism is not a geographically ubiquitous experience of technological innovation and increase in scale of production (the conventional linear progress to and through an epic industrial revolution), but complex and uneven developments within particular sectors of industry, embedded in locally and regionally specific physical and social environments within which dynamic changes, including decline, may take place as comparative advantage is maintained (often by frequent and complex adjustments to the production system), yielded, or gained. The nature of the markets for which industrial goods were provided and the role of the entrepreneur capitalists were, of course, extremely important.

With these basic theoretical notions in mind, it is now appropriate to examine some national and regional experiences of advanced industrialization in the period from the eighteenth to the twentieth centuries, on both an individual and comparative basis. The first example is that of England.

Industrialization in England

The study of what is generally regarded as the first country in the world to undergo rapid and advanced industrialization has an interesting historiography, of which brief mention might help to highlight changing contexts of analysis and of theory. Cannadine (1984), for example, has traced the changing ideological bases of interpretation of the English Industrial Revolution in writings on the subject in the period 1880–1980. He identifies a number of phases. First, in the period from the 1880s to the 1920s, a period of concern at the general declining economic health of the country and with questions of health, housing and poverty and a consequent fear that the Industrial Revolution had not brought great improvements for all sectors of the population, reasons for this failure (capitalism) were at the centre of radical writings of such authors as Toynbee, the Hammonds and the Webbs, and therefore, 'because most economic historians were defining themselves against the *laissez-faire* theoreticians, the majority of them—regardless of their general ideological and political standpoint—wrote of the Industrial Revolution as nasty, mean, brutish and fast' (Cannadine, 1984, 138). The second phase of writing was that from the 1920s to the 1950s, in which prime concern of economists was with cyclical fluctuations in the economy, with booms and slumps, in the aftermath of the collapse of the international economic system after the First World War. Economic historians therefore were interested in tracing back such cyclical fluctuations to the Industrial Revolution and examining the internal dynamism of that period of change in similar terms, that is of trade cycles, price fluctuations, the main exemplar from the perspective of explanation of fluctuations rather than growth being Rostow's *Growth and Fluctuations of the British Economy, 1790–1850* (1953). From the mid-1950s to the early 1970s the successful advance of western capitalism led to a third phase of writing about the Industrial Revolution, one which emphasized growth and development models as a means of explanation and seen, interestingly, in Rostow's *The Stages of Economic Growth. A Non-Communist Manifesto* (1960).

From the mid-1970s and the energy crisis, together with an increasing view that the theories of development economics had not worked in practice, a more pessimistic view returned. From the neo-classical economic perspective came a series of revisions of the scale, timing, and extent of dramatic change, the new view being that change was slower and more restricted, that steam-power, traditionally and properly allocated a major role in the explanation of the pace of industrialization in Britain (Fig. 10.2) was late in its impact, that manual labour and basic technology remained important well into the nineteenth century and that major changes by the middle of the nineteenth century were local and limited, all contributing to what has been described as a 'limits to growth' view of the Industrial Revolution. A second and not unrelated perspective was provided by neo-Marxist commentaries which stressed the class-struggle element of industrialization, the most influential work undoubtedly being Thompson's *Making of the English Working Class* (1963).

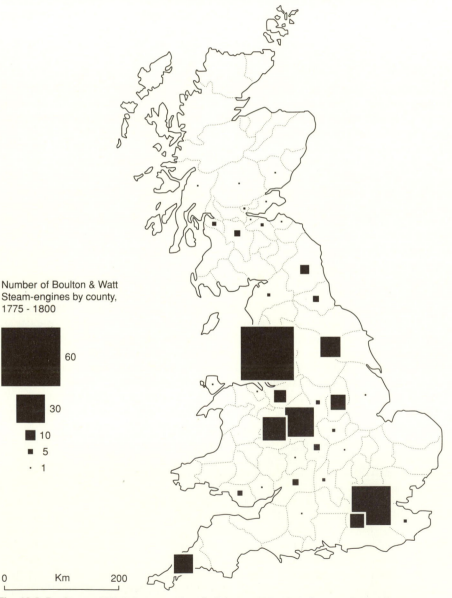

Number of Boulton & Watt
Steam-engines by county,
1775 - 1800

60

30

10

5

1

0   Km   200

Fig. 10.2 *Boulton and Watt steam engines in Britain, 1775–1800. Source: Smith (1949, 96)*

Current views of industrial change in England in the eighteenth and nineteenth centuries tend to favour the notion that although the period *c.* 1750–1850 was a time of major transformation of the economy, notably from an emphasis on agriculture to a predominance of industry (and services) the full period of transition was very much longer, stretching from the late sixteenth to the early twentieth century. In addition to a longer-term view of change, which includes such aspects as economic and social developments and changes in markets, including overseas markets, there is a recognition that the whole experience was also made up of a bundle of shorter-term changes, like parliamentary enclosure, transport improvements, mechanization of industrial production, with different general and regional chronologies. The classic model of the Industrial Revolution—a relatively short period of rapid growth, steam power and factory production—is now thought to be characteristic of one or two unrepresentative sectors such as cotton and iron (Hoppit, 1987; Verley, 1991). Crafts' (1985) analysis of British economic growth during the Industrial Revolution suggests a period of quite slow gradual growth in most sectors of the economy, including agriculture, traditional industries and transport, from 1760 to the 1830s, a view interestingly reflecting the much earlier perspective offered by Clapham (1926–38), and an overall character-ization of the experience of the eighteenth and nineteenth centuries as one primarily involving a shift of emphasis in the balance of the economy.

An important perspective offered by historical geographers in the extensive debate on the nature of industrial and economic change in modern England concerns the extent to which, for the greater part of the eighteenth and nineteenth centuries, it was a regional experience. Langton (1984) has argued for the recognition of the accentuation of regional specialization of production until the late nineteenth century, an expression of regional separation through transport discontinuities, social characteristics and regional cultures, and of the realization of new opportunities in specific places (and therefore locational shifts) via the new technologies and commercial prospects. The financing of industrial development is an important aspect, and Hudson (1989) has argued that the markets for industrial capital and commercial credit and the banking systems were essentially regional before the 1830s and 1840s, with most industrial and commercial finance up to then raised and remaining within its generating region. There was also a strongly regional dimension to commercial crises and bankruptcies. That is not to say that there was only a regional dimension to the economy: the metropolitan influence of London was always present, and growing stronger towards the end of the nineteenth century.

Resource endowments played a major part in the new geography of industry in this period. Langton and Morris (1986, xxvii) comment on the historical and process-specific pattern of industrial development in regions endowed with water power and minerals, and Wrigley (1988) has made the distinction between the organic basis of the pre-industrial economy—the advanced organic economy of the eighteenth century—from the mineral-based energy economy of the peak period of industrialization, the latter offering sub-stantially greater quantities of raw material than the more limited stocks of organic material such as wood.

Some regional and sectoral examples may serve to illustrate some of the topics just considered. One of the leading sectors of industrial advance was the cotton industry, primarily associated with Lancashire. The use of cotton in the manufacture of cloth was localized in south-east Lancashire from at least the late seventeenth century, with intensification throughout the eighteenth century. The major changes in the Lancashire textile industries in the late seventeenth and eighteenth centuries involved the expansion of the area producing fustians, and the development from it of the beginnings of the cotton industry. The geography of textiles in the early eighteenth century involved three distinctive production regions: the wool area of the eastern uplands and valleys, with packhorse transport and a dual economy being characteristic features; the linen area of the west of the county, whose products were marketed at Warrington, Preston and Ormskirk; and the third region was the fustian region of the centre and south-east, with an extension into the Manchester lowland, on account of the large amounts of imported cotton available from Manchester via the Mersey–Irwell Navigation Canal. Although handlooms were still employed into the nineteenth century, the eighteenth century witnessed an increase in water-driven machinery. A greater specialization of occupation was a consequence of the increase in production in the eighteenth century, and new machinery included the flying shuttle. More and more families were devoting all their time to domestic manufacture. The spectacular changes which were to transform the area to a major manufacturing region in the period of full industrial revolution only date from the late eighteenth century.

The spinning and weaving of cotton and cotton cloths was initially on a domestic basis, with high densities of production units near to and in Manchester, associated in the rural areas with rapid growth of population in the eighteenth century and with the subdivision of holdings: a classic proto-industrial arrangement. The putting-out system was increasing in the late seventeenth century, and was the most common system by the mid-eighteenth century. The pace of technical change accelerated after about 1750, with the introduction on a wider scale of the Dutch loom for smallware (tapes) production, Kay's flying shuttle in weaving, and new techniques for printing, dyeing and bleaching (Walton, 1989, 62–3). The effect of external and national demand on the growth of the Lancashire textile industries was an important factor. The early British colonies such as North America and India became markets for textile exports, including coarse cloth, but the inappropriateness of such cloth for hot climates led to the exploitation, through regulated trade, of the Indian market by imitation of Indian production of cotton and calico, and to the development of colour printing on cloth. Local as well as London capital and finance was employed in the seventeenth and eighteenth centuries.

Lancashire and its cotton industry achieved what many early industrial regions did not: a breakthrough to a very large scale of factory-based manufacture. The reasons are complex, and the introduction of new technologies and methods uneven, but the main reasons include the versatility of cotton, the elasticity of its supply, the massive scale of growth in demand, Lancashire's production and marketing expertise, and regional transport improvements (Walton, 1989). A particular feature is the continuation well into the factory era of large areas of rural domestic cotton manufacture, in the vicinity of Blackburn, Oldham, Rochdale and Bolton, for example. The Lancashire cotton industry is a good example of a feature of the textiles industry in general which, viewed from a national perspective, showed a very marked tendency to regional specialization. The concentration of cotton textiles in Lancashire, measured by statistics of employment in factories, accelerated between 1838 and 1900, at the expense of Scotland, Ireland, and Cheshire, and within Lancashire there was increasing polarization between spinning and weaving districts. The degree of dependence on the cotton industry is most marked in smaller weaving settlements, where almost 90 per cent of women, for example, worked in the cotton mills (Laxton, 1986, 108, 112).

The geographical implications of the changes in production systems and markets and the use of new raw materials have been usefully demonstrated by Dodgshon in the case of the iron and steel industry (Dodgshon, 1987, 327–9), the early hearths, using coke-based (as opposed to charcoal-based) smelting of iron, being in Shropshire and Staffordshire. Subsequent introduction of the Cort puddling process effected growth in south Wales, and the Neilson hot blast technique in the Clyde valley in Scotland. Later in the nineteenth century with more effective coal-using techniques location shifted for cost advantage nearer to the ore-fields of Cleveland and the East Midlands, and the use of the Bessemer converter, open-hearth furnace and other innovations particularly facilitated growth in the Sheffield, south Lancashire and south Wales regions. Specific regions also saw and benefitted from particular demands for different industrial products, some domestic, some overseas.

In marked regional contrast to the classic industries of the Industrial Revolution in Britain were the service industries, whose share of the employed population increased from about 25 per cent in 1851 to 40 per cent in 1911, an increase which was most marked in London and the south of England, though there were degrees of variation of patterns of employment between, for example, the professional classes and domestic servants (Lee, 1986). Within this broad category there were also major changes in the distributive systems, including retailing. The increasing differentiation by the mid-nineteenth century of wholesaling and retailing, with large-scale retail organizations and department stores developing rapidly towards the end of the century. Shops were already important in the urban distributive system by the 1830s, their numbers having grown rapidly from the late eighteenth century, and they continued to increase in number in many places until the late nineteenth century, undergoing spatial changes within the cities during this period, notably following the trends of suburbanization of the population. There were also changes in the wholesale and retail markets of the major towns and cities, a conspicuous feature being the creation of new markets in the industrial regions of Lancashire and Yorkshire (Shaw, 1986).

The process of industrialization in Britain, as elsewhere, involved far more than new patterns of industrial technology, resource use, and location. The class, political, economic and cultural dimensions, for example, were of lasting importance. The move to greater industrial employment and the poor conditions associated with it led to increasing attempts by the workforces to improve their conditions and rights. Early in the nineteenth century, in 1811–17 handloom cotton weavers in south-east Lancashire attacked power-looms, croppers in the West Riding of Yorkshire attacked gig-mills, and framework knitters in Nottinghamshire and Derbyshire also physically and symbolically attacked the machines which they saw as threatening their livelihood and customary working practices, these separate events being known as Luddite Riots and the movements associated with them as Luddism. These were particular protests with particular objectives, but the wider context, as Thompson has indicated, was that of a period between the passing of the Combination Acts of 1799 and 1800 and their repeal in 1824–25 had 'forced the trade unions into an illegal world in which secrecy and hostility to the authorities were intrinsic to their very existence', the Acts codifying existing laws against trade unions and allowing two magistrates to effect summary jurisdiction over those deemed to be in breach of these acts, though earlier statutes, including the common law of conspiracy and Elizabethan Statute of Artificers were also used (Thompson, 1968, 550–3). In part, as Thompson states, 'Luddism can be seen as a violent eruption of feeling against unrestrained industrial capitalism, harking back to an obsolescent paternalist code, and sanctioned by the traditions of the working community' (Thompson, 1968, 601), that is as a protest at the change from a moral and paternalistic set of relations of production to that of a more impersonal and abstract political economy. Out of Luddism, the 1832 Reform Bill and increasing Whig anti-labour sentiment, came Chartism, a major industrial labour rights, social and electoral reform movement in the period 1837–48, based on a manifesto—*The People's Charter*. The main centres of Chartist support were the industrial regions of England, Wales, and Scotland, the centre of organization being Leeds, this being well reflected in the geography of support for the general strike of 1842 (Charlesworth, 1986). The pattern of formal trade union organizations can be seen through the grouping of occupation- and trade-related friendly societies in the early nineteenth century, the main centres being in London, the Lancashire cotton region, and the north-eastern coal-trading region. Amalgamation of various regional and trade-specific unions at national level came much later in the nineteenth and in the twentieth centuries (Southall, 1986). A whole range of popular institutions, including an array of friendly societies, cooperative societies, public houses, women's cooperative guilds, working men's clubs, and sport and recreational societies and facilities developed during the nineteenth century to accommodate the needs of the urban and industrial working classes for saving, insurance, low-cost food and drink, comradeship, sport and recreation (Purvis, 1986; Vamplew, 1986).

Industrial change in France and Germany

The pace, scale, and emphases of industrial development in France and Germany in the nineteenth and early twentieth centuries were different from that of Britain and from each other. The French pattern was nearer to that of Britain, while the German experience was of later achievement of full industrial development. The rate of French economic growth in the first half of the nineteenth century, after the end of the Napoleonic Wars, increasingly fell behind that of Britain, and her rate of population growth was slower. There was some acceleration in the 1830s and 1840s, a pause during the revolutionary year 1848, then a resumption of growth to a point where France was catching up on Britain. To the east, however, the rate of growth in the German lands accelerated from the 1850s and by 1871, the year of German unification, had caught up with France and was to move on rapidly to a superior position. One major difference between the two countries was that of resources, with

France's coalfields, including the Nord, Pas-de-Calais, and eastern Massif Central fields, of small size in comparison. The northern coalfields were producing only about one-quarter of France's total output at mid-century, but thereafter increased to about two-thirds under the stimuli of new transport networks, the demands of Paris and of the textile and metallurgical complexes that grew rapidly in the Lille–Roubaix–Tourcoing–Armentières and Sambre and Schelde valley regions (Clout, 1977a, 474). The leading sector of French industry up to the last quarter of the nineteenth century was textiles. Cotton had replaced linen and wool in the rural industrial areas of Picardy, Flanders and Brittany, and major changes had occurred in Alsace before mid-century, involving the use of spinning jennies and flying shuttles from the beginning of the century, the use of weaving sheds as opposed to cottages, and the use of steam-power on a small scale from 1812. Between 1815 and 1850 there was major technological change and acceleration in the cotton industry around Mulhouse, with power-looms increasing between 1830 and 1846, matching, it is thought, Lancashire for new technological adoption rates (Clapham, 1928, 65–6). Shifts in metallurgical industry regions occurred with the use of the Bessemer converter from 1856, and a move to develop steel-manufacturing at such coastal sites as Boulogne, Calais, Marseilles, and the Gironde and Loire estuaries (to facilitate the use of imported iron ores), and an 'ore-field' phase of steel-making from 1878 to 1914 with development in Lorraine and western Normandy (Clout, 1977a, 476). Prior to the mid-nineteenth century more than half of the iron ore smelted in France had been in ubiquitous small charcoal-fired furnaces. In spite of the fact that in the period *c.* 1875–1914 French industrialization accelerated, and with it the transformation of the landscapes of the north and north-east in particular to those familiarly associated with the despoiled environments of industrialization elsewhere in Europe, the French experience did not match that of Britain, Belgium, Germany and the United States, preserving to a surprising extent its rural, peasant-based economic image. The social conditions of the industrial workforce and their attempts to assert their rights to form trade associations and unions is complex. From the 1860s, however, there was progress towards greater freedom for the industrial workforce, and in spite of the major and bloody setback to this cause during the Paris Commune of 1871, 13 years later freedom of association was granted by the Third Republic in a law of 1884, though peaceful trade unions had been tolerated after 1871 (Clapham, 1928, 270–1).

The German experience of industrialization was one of a late thrust from an essentially proto-industrial base towards rapid growth, characterized, according to Kemp (1969, 81), by 'a high concentration of economic power in the advanced industries, a close association between industry and the banks and the combination of an archaic, traditional institutional framework with the most developed forms of capitalism. It was a dynamic, not to say explosive, mixture'. In contrast to Britain and France, Germany's starting base for industrialization was in some respects less impressive, notably in terms of the problems posed by political fragmentation until unification in 1871, by a predominantly agrarian economy, and an underdeveloped transport network. Progress was helped, however, by the establishment of the free-trade area or 'Zollverein' in 1834, railway building from the 1840s, the increasing strength of the entrepreneurial middle classes after the failure of the revolution of 1848, and strong policies for economic development by Prussia, including the recruitment of foreign (particularly British) expertise and notably in the Ruhr.

In the eighteenth century there had been in Germany considerable encouragement of industry by the individual states, notably by Prussia in the case of Berlin and Silesia. In Solingen in the Sauerland, for example, the production of knives (the industry originally had used its special cutting steels for the production of swords) increased two-fold, and there were also increases in silk manufacture in Krefeld and cotton-weaving in Wuppertal. There is recognition that there had been further extensive industrial growth in Berlin in the 1830s and the Rhineland and Westphalia in the 1840s, but also that it is the period of the 1850s and after that marks the beginning of a period of rapid acceleration. Technological progress is chronologically marked by such advances as the use of the puddling process in the iron industry from 1826, the making of cast steel from 1830, and coke-smelting of iron ores from 1849. By about 1850 there were discernible shifts in the relative importance of the industrial regions of Germany, conspicuously the advance of the Ruhr beyond the production capacities of such areas as the Sauer and Siegerland. A major change in the coalfield areas was from the large number of adit mines to deeper pits in the concealed parts of the Ruhr, Silesian and Saar coalfields, from 1837, 1823, and 1840 respectively. Industrial growth in the Ruhr was one of the fastest in western Europe in the period from 1850 to 1914, based on high outputs of coal, especially once the 'hidden' field was exploited, and initially on blackband iron ores, though from about 1865 additional sources of iron ore were used, including Swedish ore. More efficent metallurgical production plants were created, using advanced techniques such as the Bessemer process (Figs 10.3 and 10.4). Expansion was on the basis of very large integrated iron and

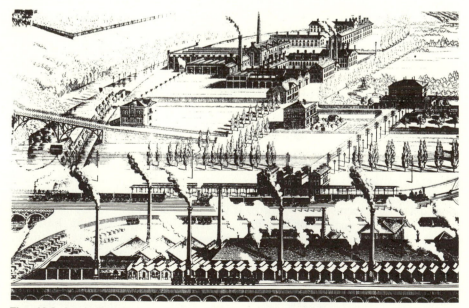

Fig. 10.3 *Iron-rolling factory, Hagen (Ruhr), c. 1860. Source:* Fragen an die Deutsche Geschichte *(1984, IV/102)*

Fig. 10.4 *Steel-making by the Bessemer process in the Ruhr, late nineteenth century. Source:* Fragen an die Deutsche Geschichte *(1984, IV/106)*

steelworks, including those of Thyssen at Hamborn, Krupp at Rheinhausen near Essen, and a group around Dortmund. Heavy industries also developed on: the Saar coalfield, expanding during the late nineteenth century, using the ores from Lorraine and Luxembourg, to become a very large industrial complex; in the region of Saxony and the Erzegebirge; and in Upper Silesia. There was extensive growth of textile industries in the Rhineland and Westphalia, and in the later nineteenth century came the important development of the electrical engineering and chemical industries.

In Germany the social consequences of the rapid industrial change were not greatly different in degree from those of Britain, though the organization of protest against poor working conditions and social provision did differ. The composition of the industrial labour force varied greatly between different industrial sectors. In the early phase of industrialization from the late eighteenth to the mid-nineteenth century the textile industry was the largest employer, and a significant feature was the high proportion of women and children—paid at lower rates than men—in the workforce. In this early phase miners were privileged workers, with defined working hours, wages, and conditions of employment, including compensation for accidents, and their organizations had a range of social functions and activities. They opposed the 1848 revolutionary activities and were generally conservative. After 1850 their privileged status was dissolved, and they slowly turned to socialist movements, though not to any significant extent until the end of the century (Sagarra,

1977, 360–1). By the end of the century the trade union movement had made relatively little headway, though after 1901 its growth was rapid, membership of trades unions reaching 1 million in 1902 and 3 million in 1909 (Clapham, 1928, 329). With the beginnings of growth to full industrialization from the 1850s, the conditions of the industrial labour force deteriorated. As Sagarra (1977, 366) reports, appalling conditions were found by Prussian government inspectors and county commissioners: 'The mill hands in his area, reported the Aachen factory inspector, lived almost exclusively on a diet of bread and so-called coffee water, varying this occasionally with potatoes and oil. The county commissioners for Silesia, where the weavers' revolt had taken place a decade previously, produced harrowing tales of near starvation among both the weavers and the factory workers in the province'.

The Russian experience

The Russian experience of modernization through industrial and urban development differed from that of much of the rest of Europe and of Asia.

By the mid-nineteenth century it was clear that Russia was falling behind the more advanced industrializing economies of western Europe and of the United States, symbolized by the defeat of Russia in the Crimean War of 1854–56 by an alliance of Britain, France, Sardinia and Turkey. Russia was a very late starter in the progress to modern industrialization. In spite of early attempts by Peter I (1689–1725) to initiate industrial development with the aid of external expertize—part of an enforced economic and cultural 'westernization'—and the rise in the number of Russian manufactories (many of them quite small workshops) during the reign of Catherine II (1762–96), by the middle of the nineteenth century there were about 10,000 manufacturing establishments employing a total of about 500,000 workers (Parker, 1968; Bater, 1983, 280). The obstacles to be overcome in order to modernize included the vast area of Russian territory and the problem of distance from markets; the feudal nature of Russian society (serfdom was not abolished until 1861) and the conservative nature of the autocracy towards the need for industrialization; together with technological backwardness and the lack of entrepreneurial skill. There were labour problems related to the deliberate control, for purposes of political stability, of migration of peasants from the countryside to the cities, but gradually the terms of labour employment and mobility were modified, and in the last half of the nineteenth century after the Crimean War a combination of state policies of railway construction, serf emancipation in 1861, and the Stolypin agrarian reforms of 1906–10, produced a three-fold increase in the number of factories and employees between 1850 and 1890, and by 1910 the growth of larger industrial establishments was indicated by the fact that over half the industrial workforce was employed in establishments of over 500 workers, though it also must be noted that by 1902 only 41 per cent of industrial employees were located in cities, the rest were in industrial establishments located in the countryside (Bater, 1983, 282).

The principal industries in Russia at the beginning of the nineteenth century were mining, textiles, metallurgy, engineering, and shipbuilding. The Urals was the most important mining region, with a wealth of minerals including iron, copper, coal, oil, salt, lead and silver, though other areas were opening up at this time, including the Donets Basin coalfield and the Baku oilfield. The main industry in the early nineteenth century was iron smelting and refining, using charcoal and iron ore and cheap servile labour, with the main ironworks being in northern forests and east of the Ural mountains. A major problem was the long distance to the ports from areas of iron production, which added to its sale price. Russia was one of the highest iron-producing regions in the world at the beginning of the nineteenth century (Pounds, 1990, 340–1). There were an estimated 1817 textile establishments in Russia in 1804, spread among the woollen cloth, linen, cotton, silk and leather sectors. Many of these were conducted on a domestic or cottage basis, especially the linen industry which was at its peak and shortly to decline. In contrast, the new cotton industry which had started in the mid-eighteenth century, accelerated steadily, both on the basis of state weaving and spinning factories, employing modern machines (and steam-power from 1805) and of domestic peasant production, especially in the region between Moscow and Vladimir (Parker, 1968, 168–70).

The dynamics of industrial change in Russia, as elsewhere, varied regionally. There were two sectors: the newer industrializing regions of the north, west and south of the Tsarist Empire, and the older industrial centres of the old core-regions of Russia: the Moscow-central Russian region, the Urals, and St Petersburg region, which exhibited both continuity with earlier activities and also new sectoral, technological and locational trends. An example of one of the newer regions was that around the major Baltic port of Riga, which had a long tradition of trading, developed at a meeting point of the rapidly developing West, especially Germany, and the underdeveloped Russian Empire in the east, the former providing capital and expertize, the latter the raw materials. Industries developing in the nineteenth century were closely linked to the use of primary materials coming from the Russian Empire and from abroad, and included paper-milling, cigar-making, sugar-refining, and textile factories. Later in the century newly founded merchant banks were part of an increasing group of financial institutions and individuals who promoted improved communication links, especially railways, ocean-going steamships, and both old-established and newer industries (railway rolling stock, electrical, chemical and rubber goods, especially footwear) (Blackwell, 1983, 398–400).

The Moscow-central Russian region was an old-established centre of production which underwent further changes in the nineteenth and early twentieth centuries. Although the older iron industry lost its predominance, there was a continued development of textiles in rural and urban areas, with Moscow itself experiencing major factory-based growth of woollen cloth manufacture by the 1820s, developing from urban domestic outworking, with the eastern and north-eastern suburbs dominated by textile production, and the western parts geared mainly to the production of machinery and leather goods (Blackwell, 1983, 415–16). In addition to the extensive urban development of industry in this region, there was also considerable development of rural industries, partly on account of the controls on peasant migration to the cities.

The Russian experience of industrialization was, by its own standards, quite dramatic, but the fact remains that on the eve of the First World War over 60 per cent of the population was still engaged in agriculture, the industrial per capita output was still behind that of the countries of western Europe, mechanization had still not reached some crucial industries, notably those producing consumer goods, and the Tsarist regime was nowhere near close enough to meeting the needs of the middle-class entrepreneurs in their attempts to drive business and industry forward (Kemp, 1969). The dramatically different means used in the post-revolutionary command economy to prioritize the development of strategic heavy industries were in some relative respects successful, but considerable and dreadful prices were to be paid in human and environmental terms.

The United States and Canada

The phases of industrial change in North America have a chronological semblance to those of parts of Europe, in that an economy related primarily to mercantile and commercial bases transformed to a highly capitalized industrial basis from the 1860s. A tripartite periodization of the phases of industrial development in the United States is possible, involving the colonial period, the period *c.* 1790–1860, and the period after 1860. In the colonial period the extent of industrial activity was small, with much manufactured material being imported from Britain, though there was production of household goods and craft products in the cities, and the extraction of natural resources such as pitch and tar for naval uses in North Carolina, timber extraction in New England, shipbuilding in Boston and Philadelphia, and ironworking, the latter expanding toward the close of the colonial period as a result of considerable increase in domestic demand. The production of naval stores (tar, pitch and turpentine) in North Carolina was a major activity in the eighteenth century, accounting in 1768 for about 60 per cent of all naval stores exported from North American colonies, and was based on the high-resin yielding longleaf pine of the sandhills and coastal plains of the southern seaboard. Key factors in production, especially in the Cape Fear region, were the existence of large land holdings and slave labour for extracting and making the naval stores (Merrens, 1964).

In the second, ante-bellum phase of industrial change the basis was laid for the later full development of manufacturing, in the sense that the dominant industries were the processing of iron, timber and wheat, and that there emerged a significant American manufacturing belt, described by Meyer (1990, 251) as a 'vast industrial landscape of about half a million square miles . . . occupied by discrete industrial cities, mines and lumber areas, separated by the dominant landscape of farms and forests. The belt can be thought of as a set of regional industrial systems, rather than as a uniform undifferentiated landscape', examples being Boston and Chicago and their smaller urban industrial satellites, and the chronology of the development of the belt reflected the westward movement of the settlement frontier, reaching the Middle West by 1860. Regional and local specialization of production was emerging, with, for example, Boston specializing in textiles and shoes for a national market. Iron production was still essentially based on the use of charcoal as a fuel, and the location mainly rural, declining from the 1840s when anthracite was first used for iron smelting in Pennsylvania (Meyer, 1990, 251). As with industrializing regions elsewhere in the world, an improved transport infrastructure was a key factor, involving the construction of turnpike roads (mainly from 1800 to 1830), canals (mainly from 1815 to 1844) including major constructions such as the Erie Canal joining the Hudson River with Lake Erie, and railroads, in regional systems before 1850 and longer-distance and transcontinental systems after about 1860. The link between railroad and industrial development became very strong in the third phase of industrialization after 1860, when the integration of much larger areas of space of the United States led to increased regional specialization of production. Technological changes in the production of iron and steel led to location shifts from rural areas to large urban industrial complexes and to large integrated units of production, concentrated in such places as Philadelphia, Pittsburgh, Chicago, eastern Ohio and western Pennsylvania. The factory or mill building and nearby workers' housing became a more familiar and ubiquitous part of the urban industrial landscape and of the daily life pattern of the growing industrial labour force, as for example in the textile towns of New England. As Meyer has indicated, by the late nineteenth century there was in the United States a core of manufacturing industry, mainly producing finished goods, and a periphery, including the South and the West, producing processed primary materials for the core regions, the critical link between the two being the railroad (Meyer, 1990, 259). The cutting and processing of timber was a major activity, and the Pacific coast lumber industry which had been active in western regional markets was serving national markets by the 1890s, and the western episodic and environmentally damaging mining booms, including the California Gold Rush of 1848, were another type of periphery activity.

In Canada the general sequence of industrial development is not dissimilar. The basis of the economy in the colonial period was essentially that of staple commodities for export such as fish and lumber in the Maritimes and wheat and furs from the St Lawrence region, in which the role of merchant traders steadily increased in importance, with Montreal's commercial interests in the staple trades central to the whole system. The staple theory of initiation of economic growth, that is the notion that demands from overseas markets, specifically in Europe, for basic primary materials such as fish, wheat, timber and partly processed mineral ores, creates a system of trade which facilitates the purchase and import of manufactured goods and provides a platform for further economic growth, has particular relevance to Canada, where the growth of modern manufacturing industry is late but rapid. Although it has been argued that this staple theory of growth has led to neglect of other aspects of the economy (Walker, 1980), it is true to say that the basis of industry prior to Confederation in 1867 was essentially small-scale and craft-related.

In the seventeenth century the French government had issued plans to broaden the Canadian economy, but these did not materialize, and in addition to flour-milling the main industries of French Canada and Acadia were the production of naval stores, shipbuilding, and some ironworking (Harris and Warkentin, 1974, 55–7). In areas of British Canada the position was similar: in the Atlantic region water-driven flour mills were ubiquitous, and in the coastal regions timber was sawn by water-powered mills both for local consumption and export, and in Nova Scotia and the Bay of Fundy shipbuilding developed in the eighteenth century, and a small number of iron-ore smelting furnaces were constructed. On the eve of Confederation, the Atlantic region had a small and inadequate base from which to advance to more intense manufacturing, in contrast to Ontario, where in addition to the many small scattered activities such as milling, blacksmithing, sawmilling, brewing and distilling, by the 1850s there were signs of modernization, including use of steam-power, specialist division of industrial labour, and the growth of agricultural engineering (Harris and Warkentin, 1974).

Major factors of growth in manufacturing industry in Canada after 1867 include: the raw material and energy resources; intensification of transportation networks, especially, roads, canals and railways; the activities of individual entrepreneurs and government; and the varied processes and strategies of financial investment. Water-power had been the basis of small-scale early industries such as milling and timber-processing, but gradually two other means of motive power were introduced: coal and hydro-electric power. Coal was imported from the United States, from the Appalachians to the lake ports of western Ontario such as Hamilton and Toronto, and its cost cheapened later when the Ontario government subsidized its purchase, to the advantage of the developing metallurgical industries. Hydro-electric power had been created in connection with the Lachine Canal project in Montreal in the 1840s, but its major use came from the 1890s when a small hydro-electric power station was opened at Niagara Falls. The widespread transmission of electricity at equal cost rates irrespective of distance from point of generation accelerated industrial development in southern Ontario, and, under a different system of management and pricing, in the St Maurice River valley of Quebec (Kerr, 1982, 86–7).

The intensification of manufacturing in the late nineteenth and twentieth centuries had a regional specificity, concentrated in southern Ontario and southern Quebec. In the Toronto urban industrial region there was by the 1880s a wide range of consumer goods industries such as textiles, boot and shoe manufacturing, and metallurgical industries and machinery. In Hamilton there were strong textile and metallurgical industries. In Quebec, the leading industrial centre was Montreal, which by the 1880s had become a major seaport and manufacturing city, with shipbuilding, engineering, and food-processing industries particularly notable. A major feature of the development of industry in Canada in the late nineteenth century was the policy of tariff protection from foreign competition, a policy growing in the nineteenth century but consolidated in national legislation of 1879. Between 1870 and 1915, the annual compound average rate of value of industrial output of Canada was 4.2 per cent, easily matching the output rates of other rapidly industrializing countries, and structural changes were occurring in the scale and constitution of manufacturing enterprises including mergers and combines, with 56 major company consolidations, and 3500 joint-stock company charters issued, in the period 1900–13. This policy not only aided the major industries of the heartland, but also facilitated growth of such ventures as cotton mills, sugar refineries, iron and steel plants in coastal and railway-linked settlements in smaller towns in the Maritimes, for example (Wynn, 1987, 393–4).

South Africa

Africa as a whole was subject to massive exploitation of resources and labour in the nineteenth and early twentieth centuries, being locked into a complex network of world colonial and trading systems, and the regional effects of these processes are reasonably clear (see Fig. 10.5).

An example of industrialization which affords strong contrast to the

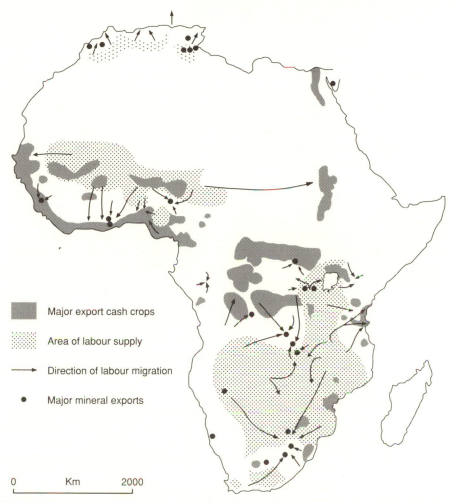

Fig. 10.5 *The African colonial economy, late nineteenth and early twentieth centuries. Source: Ade Ajayi and Crowder (1985, 65)*

examples considered above is that of South Africa, in which a colonial economy produced the worst possible social relations of extractive and manufacturing industry. Under colonial rule mining began in the 1850s, first with the development of copper deposits in Namaqualand, then with the discovery of diamonds in the Cape Colony in 1867, which led in turn to the diamond rush to the Vaal River valley from 1869 and the discovery of kimberlite pipes, in the vicinity of what was to become Kimberley (the first European type of industrial town in Africa), in the region to the south of the Vaal alluvial workings, and by 1877 the diamond industry had a labour force of 20,000. Initially fragmented and small scale in exploration unit size, the industry by 1889 was controlled, under the influence of Cecil Rhodes, by the De Beers Consolidated Mines Limited, which controlled prices of diamonds and the workforce, comprising a number of Europeans and a greater number of Africans, whose ranks were swelled by the increased numbers forced to look for paid labour as a result of the increase in colonial hegemony effected by the wars of 1877–85 (Christopher, 1984; 1988). The major mining developments in South Africa, however, resulted from the discovery of gold in the gold-bearing reefs of the Witwatersrand in 1886 in the southern Transvaal, and were exploited initially from shallow surface mines and shafts, but when the potential of this basic technology was exhausted major inputs of capital were invested to extract and process the ores. Increase in scale of gold mining required a major increase in the labour force, with very large numbers of Africans being added to the Europeans who had started the diggings. Changes of location occurred as old seams were exhausted and new ones opened up, such as the East Rand. Major urban mining-related settlements such as Johannesburg grew rapidly, Johannesburg having reached a population of 102,000 by 1896, half being European, the rest being male African migrants. The recruitment of African labour was controlled and accelerated by agencies such as the Witwatersrand Native Labour Association and the Native Recruiting Corporation, which was thus able to depress the wages of the labourers. The machinery for the operation of the goldfields was largely imported from Britain, Germany and America, and the coal used for power was from Boksburg and later southern Transvaal and Natal (Christopher, 1984, 113–5). If, as Crush (1986a, 3) contends, in the context of a 'people's' historical geography for South Africa, 'the task which confronts the historical geographer is to understand how South Africa's brutal landscapes were forged in subordination and struggle, and how the geography of privilege and deprivation has saturated the experience of both overlords and underlings in that society', then the questions that have to be addressed include those of working conditions, the processes of labour recruitment and exploitation, the nature of power, control and capitalization, the question of social deprivation and exploitation, and the strategies adopted by the exploited in their attempts to cope with discrimination, segregation and very low standards of living.

Crush's study of Swazi migrant workers in the Witwatersrand gold mines in the period 1886–1920 demonstrates three phases of the development of the notorious migrant labour system, and contests the conventional view that 'the incorporation of Swaziland into the South African migrant labour system proceeded smoothly and inevitably in response to the combined pressures of colonial coercion, land alienation and planned rural underdevelopment' (Crush, 1986b, 28). In the earliest phase of colonial administration—from 1895 when the country became a protectorate of the Kruger Republic—the lateness of colonial coercion, the productive independence of the Swazi homestead and the prevailing social relations (royal priority for labour for the army and agriculture) mitigated against the migration of Swazi labourers to the mines 350 miles or more to the east until 1898–99, as a result of the ecological effects of drought, locust swarms and rinderpest. These labourers experienced appalling working conditions and were subject to a range of illnesses and diseases. In the second phase, one of coerced and voluntary migration, from 1900 to 1910, migration began again after the Boer War, with Swaziland after 1902 under British control. Working and living conditions down the mines and in the residential compounds remained dangerous and squalid, with the combined effects of economic depression, colonial coercion and tax exertion producing a migration surge in 1907–08. Many of the migrants avoided the labour-recruiting agents and travelled independently to the mining regions. From 1910 to 1920 there was a third phase, involving dramatic acceleration in Swazi labour migration to the Rand gold mines and a change towards agent recruitment, and state intervention via the Native Labour Regulation Act of 1911 and the establishment of the Native Recruiting Corporation in 1912. Thus, in a short period of time the working conditions of labourers from Swaziland had changed from those of their own environment to that of the mining community, with all the massive disadvantages and deprivations that attended such conditions.

11

Historical Geographies of Trade, Transport and Communications

Introduction

The movement of goods and ideas is one of the most important and fundamental aspects of the geographies of the past, and its study requires attention to some very basic geographical traits and problems such as means and routes of communication, links between systems of production, changing technologies and changes in the control of space. A curious fact, however, is that the subject has not been widely addressed by geographers, the notable exceptions including Vance (1970; 1986; 1989) and Pounds (1973; 1974; 1979; 1985), the field largely having been dominated by economic historians, though there are some signs of a renewal of research by geographers. A wide range of scales can be involved in the study of the past geographies of trade and transport, from the movements of individuals and families within limited spaces and times to larger, global-scale movements of commodities and people within, for example, colonial empires.

The Evolution of Trading and Transportation Systems

'Trade' is a term used to denote the exchange of goods between countries, regions, or people, often of differing social classes. In the contemporary world its meaning is reasonably clear, but if one goes back in time one encounters a bewildering range of types of trade and hence a complex set of histories and geographies of trading systems. Primitive systems of change or exchange differ radically from those in advanced or late capitalism, for they symbolize cultural, religious, social and political reciprocity, frequently without reference to 'market' or monetary value of the goods exchanged. In capitalism, highly complex and large-scale processes of sale of commodities for profit, including labour, are effected through the mechanism of price-fixing markets which operate at a global scale and in which speculation and currency exchange rates play an important role. It is impossible to give a full account here of the processes of evolution and the resulting forms of trade and markets, but the following brief digest indicates some of their major features and changes through time, and the relations they have with transport systems. A useful model for an outline sequence of changes in exchange, trade and transport may be established by following the stages characterized by Dodgshon (1987) in his study of social evolution and spatial order in Europe, in which he adapts among others the models of Renfrew (1977) and Polanyi (1944; 1968; 1977). His basis for analysing the chronologies of social evolution and spatial order is a five-stage model, the stages being: hunter-gatherer bands; egalitarian tribes; chiefdoms; regulated or feudalized systems; and market-based systems. The systems of exchange and trade within each of these social orders differed, moving from reciprocal exchange, for example, of gifts and food through redistributive exchange, exchange via regulated markets (especially under the European feudal system) to the dramatically different price-fixing allocative markets of capitalism, increasingly evident from the late eighteenth century onwards. These stages are complex and neither ubiquitous nor chronologically discrete. They did not in many cases represent a spontaneous and natural evolution or progression from one stage to another, but sometimes a quite unpredicted change of direction.

Trade, whether it be local ritual gift, economic exchange or complex long-distance commerce organized by merchants, requires basic products for exchange or sale and a means of transportation from one place to another. The history of means of transportation is obviously a vital ingredient, starting with the domestication of what were to be key pack animals in the fourth and third centuries BC, such as the donkey and types of camel, and moving through to the use of wheeled vehicles on road systems and effective paddled and sailed vessels used on river systems, lakes and seas, and beyond to the great advances of the ages of discovery and subsequently of industrialization.

Trade in Early Societies: Modes and Media

The most common experience of movement of people and goods in different places over very long periods of time has been movement on foot and with pack animals along tracks and primitive roads and along waterways. Such systems were to be found in prehistoric societies and continue in the remoter parts of the world to the present day. They were extensively reported for most parts of the 'new worlds' at the time of European colonization from the late fourteenth to the early twentieth centuries. The fundamental components include human porterage, the use of animals for carriage of goods, movement along pathways or artificially improved road systems and along and across waterways, seas and lakes. The means of transport varied regionally and chronologically. The earliest form of transport of goods was by the human frame, with goods carried on the backs of males and females or by sticks or yokes over the shoulder or shoulders. The earliest use of an animal as a pack animal is that of the ass—about mid-fourth millenium BC—followed by the use of oxen (though these were primarily for traction of ploughs and carts), camels, and, in some regions, the horse. Simple sledges were the earliest form of land transport vehicle, and were used primarily in northern Europe in the coniferous forest zone but also elsewhere, for example in Mesopotamia. Tracks were commonly used in prehistoric times. Before the coming of wheeled vehicles trackways usually followed upland, dry routes, and where this was not possible the tracks were frequently raised or reinforced by brushwood (Cole, 1954). Evidence for the origin of wheeled carts dates back to about 3500 BC. The chronology of spread has been summarized by Childe (1954, 211):

> We find, then, wheeled vehicles in use in Sumer soon after 3500 BC; in Elam and probably as far up the Tigris as Assyria about 3000; on the steppes of central Asia and in the Indus valley soon after 2500; on the upper Euphrates just before or after 2250; in south Russia, and in Crete about 1800 (these all solid-wheeled); in Egypt and Palestine about 1600; in mainland Greece and Georgia about 1500; in China by 1300; in north Italy before 1000; in central and northern Europe a little after that date; and in Britain about 500 BC.

In some areas the used of wheeled vehicles was very much later: there was no use of wheeled carts in Latin America until the Spanish conquest from the late fifteenth century AD, and in parts of Africa there was no use in desert and forest regions. Wheeled carts or waggons for transport of goods were only effective where there were roads, and road systems with bridges were developed in many hearths of civilization in Asia, the Middle East and Europe from late prehistoric times, the oldest major system probably being that of China, though shorter stretches are to be found in the Middle East from the third millennium BC.

Boats and ships formed part of the transport systems of early societies. Digby (1954) has suggested four phases of development: the float, combined floats, shaped craft, and the true boat with increased hollowness, buoyancy and protection. The chronologies of transition through these phases varied from one location to another. One of the early forms of travel on water was the bark canoe, common in Palaeolithic times, and succeeded in the Neolithic by the dug-out canoe, characteristic obviously of forested areas. Further development from the canoe form was the construction of similar-shaped vessels from shaped and grooved planks of wood, and parallel sequences can be traced in more modern times in the ships and vessels of the Pacific, Latin America and the Indian Ocean. In Egypt reed rafts and canoes, propelled by paddles, existed from Neolithic times, and there is evidence from the third millennium BC of the use of sails on reed boats, which were used both on the Nile and for seagoing, the latter probably waterproofed with pitch. Wooden ships without keels and propelled by oars and sails existed in Egypt as early as *c*. 2600–2500 BC. On the rivers Tigris and Euphrates in Mesopotamia where there was no papyrus reed inflated skins were early used as floats, and subsequently skins were joined with a wooden framework to form a raft. Skin boats and circular coracles were also constructed. One of the major developments was the Aegean galley, originating in the dug-out canoe, but constructed with a keel and of flared planking (Digby, 1954). This was a fighting ship with a ram fixed to the bow, propelled by oars and perhaps two sails, initially at a single level but later in banks, and dates from about 3000 BC, being used, however, up to the early eighteenth century in the Mediterranean.

The nature of early voyages was influenced by the nature of the ships, their limited systems of navigation, and the environments in which they operated. The bulk of the voyages made in prehistoric and early historic times were coastal, coastal carriage of goods in ships dating from about 3500 BC, with transoceanic trading probably dating from the time of the Phoenicians in the first millennium BC, using a navigation system based on the stars.

Regional Histories of Early Transportation Systems

Each region has its own chronology of evolution of basic systems of transport and communication, and measures of similarity or dissimilarity of experience may best perhaps be derived from the study of different regional examples.

Latin America

In Latin America early modes of transport depended, as elsewhere, on the level of societal and economic development and on the nature of the environment. The most sophisticated transport and trade systems were those of the Aztec, Mayan and Inca civilizations. The trade and transport system of the Aztec tribute state in the eastern highlands of central Mexico was characterized by the use of extensive networks of pathways, carried across rivers by bridges, and by short-distance movement of tribute goods from within the empire, and longer-distance movement of luxury goods, such as cotton, feathers, gold, and precious stones to and from beyond the empire's borders, effected by a special class of merchants using human carriers as transport. The routes used were pathways running south and east from the Valley of Mexico, aimed at so-called ports of trade in the transition zones between highlands and lowlands, with other ports located on the Gulf of Mexico, the Gulf of Campeche and the Gulf of Honduras, and inland in the upper reaches of the Candelaria River (Rees, 1982, 90). The Mayan federation of small chiefdoms in the Yucatan Peninsula was by the eve of the European conquest an important trading influence, with its trading realm encompassing a large area from Tabasco to northern Honduras, including Nicaragua, highland Guatemala and highland Mexico, the primary exports being salt, cotton, cloth, slaves and honey, the imports including axes, bells, copper sheets and obsidian, the goods being moved primarily over land routes by human porterage (unpaid slaves) on foot trails through forests, sometimes on raised causeways or roads, but also via river and coastal travel using dug-out canoes (Rees, 1982, 91). In Andean America the major Incan Empire had an extensive and effective road system with the movement of goods, especially food, effected by llama pack trains. The roads were formally constructed, using a highly innovative and advanced set of engineering skills including excavation of rock faces and construction of ropeway suspension bridges, the raising of roadbeds bordered by stone walls. An efficient road network was crucial to the functioning of this extensive empire, and the major Inca highways ran the whole length of the empire by 1525. The network was influenced more by considerations of imperial control as well as by trade, whose pattern was of shorter-distance movement of necessities and longer-distance movement of luxuries. The overall pattern in pre-colonial Latin America, according to Rees, was one of '*internal* transport alignments serving regional or domestic stimuli. This geographical pattern was reversed by European colonization, with its *external* political and economic influences. For this reason there was only little accidental continuity between the routes of indigenous and colonial transportation in Latin America' (Rees 1982, 94).

Africa

The development of trading and transport systems in Africa is a complex and regionally varied story. As far as the means of transport are concerned, the primary means were, as in many other continents, animal and human.

In West Africa water transport was the cheapest means of carriage of heavy bulky commodities, with canoes, propelled by paddles and sometimes small sails, the most appropriate craft to overcome difficulties of river navigation such as rapids, flooding in the rainy season and lack of water in the dry season, but they were also employed on lakes. The main areas of commercial transport in West Africa were Lake Chad, the Niger (especially the central section), the Senegal, parts of the Volga, smaller forest rivers and coastal areas with sheltered estuaries. The scale of activity was substantial:

> The busiest inland waterway was the middle section of the Niger, which linked Timbuctu to the commercial and administrative centres of Djenne (250 miles upstream) and Gao (about the same distance downstream). Hundreds of craft were in use on this stretch of the river from the thirteenth century onwards and probably earlier. Some of these canoes carried twenty to thirty tons of merchandise, including foodstuffs as well as the more luxurious items of long-distance trade. Water transport enabled the middle Niger complex to become one of the great centres of pre-colonial trade in Africa (Hopkins, 1973, 72).

The means of transport in Africa was strongly influenced by the nature of the environment, notably topography, vegetation and climate, so that for example in West Africa pack animals were most important, notably camels in the desert areas of the north and donkeys elsewhere, together, of course, with human porterage. Wheeled transport was virtually non-existent.

Europe

Perhaps the best-known transport system of late prehistoric/early historic Europe is that of the Roman Empire. The city republic of Rome controlled the whole of Italy by 264 BC and the whole of the Mediterranean by 44 BC. The empire established under the rule of Octavian in 27 BC continued to expand to include much of western, central, and north-western Europe and Asia Minor, but the western part of the empire lapsed and fell in the fifth century AD. The enormous area covered by the whole of the empire at its maximum extent required sophisticated means of communication for troops, administrators and goods. A complex road system was constructed, primarily for movement of the military, though merchants could use them on payment of toll fees, and there were in addition public and private roads on the estates. As Smith (1967, 111) has indicated, the well-engineered roads of the Roman Empire were built over a long period of time and therefore not to a consistent major plan, but they do have spatially characteristic features such as the focal position of Rome in Italy and of Lyon in Gaul, and the radial pattern from military camps in the Rhône and Danube frontier areas. Pounds has shown that in spite of the extensive nature of the road system, it was not used for regular commerce, for 'The roads were built by the legions to satisfy military needs. Their layout was not adjusted to civilian needs, and, indeed, proved subsequently to be of small commercial value. Most roads available for local trade are unlikely to have been much more than tracks and the greatest use was in fact made of the river, especially in Gaul and the Rhineland' (Pounds, 1990, 66). The principal commodities traded and moved within the empire were bread grains, light manufactured goods, and luxury products, the latter used to pay for slaves, cattle and forest products from beyond the frontier (Pounds, 1990, 67).

With the fall of the western part of the Roman Empire and the Germanic invasions in the fifth century, and notably with the progress of the Muslim invaders along the southern shores of the Mediterranean, starting with invasion of Egypt in 640 and moving through North Africa in the seventh century, reaching southern Spain in 711, a new regime of trade and commerce was introduced to the Mediterranean, and with far-reaching effects on northern and western Europe.

Medieval Trading and Marketing Systems in Europe

A number of attempts have been made to produce chronologies of systems of exchange and marketing. Two of the best known are those of Pirenne and Polanyi. Pirenne, a Belgian economic historian, in a major study of the history of urbanization in medieval Europe—*Medieval Cities*—contends that there is conspicuous discontinuity of urban life in Europe during the Dark Ages, after the decline of the Roman Empire. Trade continued in the Mediterranean, this trade only being interrupted by the spread of Islamic power across the Mediterranean in the eighth and ninth centuries, giving rise to an internal European trading network and focus, under the feudal system.

Pirenne's thesis was that this change in trade-pattern effected a switch from major urban-based long-distance trade to shorter-distance commerce based on landed estates, reflecting a major phase of urban decay. Alternative views suggest a positive outcome from the Islamic conquest, namely a change from long-distance trade to a system of more local trading supported by an extensive and growing urban network and facilitated by improvements in land transport and ultimately by state support (Dodgshon, 1987, 204 *seq.*). Pounds' (1974) analysis of this transition in trading suggests a change in the location of economic activity as a result of the Muslim conquest of the Mediterranean, with a shift in focus from the Roman emphasis on the region of Languedoc to the Frankish region of northern France and the Low Countries, an important centre of activity by the Carolingian emperor and court, enhanced by the presence of many wealthy monasteries, and where the Frisians played an important role as traders.

From about the tenth century onwards in Europe there developed regional and international gatherings of merchants and their high-value commodities in particular places at regular intervals and times: these were known as fairs, centres of exchange of goods and of settlement of commercial debts. They seem to represent the solution to the special need of providing for the distribution and exchange of high-quality goods such as foodstuffs, wool, silk, cloth, and tapestries over long distances, and the fairs were often held at places which were at the intersections of major trading routes.

Trade in Asia

On and around the Indian Ocean, the main forms of trade were: seaborne trade by ships of various kinds, river transport, and land transport, especially via the caravan routes. Chaudhuri's (1985) masterly study of the trade and civilization on and around the Indian Ocean from the seventh century to 1750 places the commerce and transport systems of this major region in geographical, political, economic and cultural contexts. Climate and coastal configurations were naturally of great importance. The smoother coastlines of China and Africa's eastern seaboard facilitated the growth of port towns, in contrast to the reef-ridden coasts of the Red Sea and the hazardous and shifting estuaries of many of the major rivers of south Asia, though unloading offshore and transhipment of goods in lighter vessels was a partial solution to this latter problem. Some ports provided open access to the sea, such as Aden and Muscat, and the other major ports included Canton, Malacca, Calicut, Cambay and Hormuz. The goods traded through such ports, both for regional and longer-distance trade, often originated well inland, and were moved to (and imported goods from) the inland urban markets and the ports by river and road. Some idea of the kind of goods transported by Middle Eastern merchants is given in the account of trade in the Indian Ocean, the *Suma Oriental*, produced by the Portuguese Tomé Pires in 1512–15, incorporated by Chaudhuri in the following description:

> The description in the *Suma Oriental* of the Red Sea and East African trade of Cambay brings out the full extent of the intermediate role of the Indian port-city. The Cairene merchants brought to Gujarat through Aden the products of Italy, Greece and Syria as gold, silver mercury, vermilion, copper, rosewater, woollen cloths, glass beads, and weapons. Traders from Aden itself dealt in all these commodities and in addition brought madder, raisins, opium, and horses. The return cargo of the Middle Eastern merchants included the economic products of Gujarat and those of the Indonesian archipelago: rice and foodstuffs, cloves, nutmeg and mace, rare woods, Chinese porcelain, coarse pottery, indigo, carnelian beads, and above all cotton cloth (Chaudhuri, 1985, 109).

The major rivers involved in the transport of goods were the Tigris and Euphrates, Indus and Ganges, the Godavari and Krishna, the Mekong and the Yangtze. For drier areas without river networks the caravan routes of central and western Asia and Asia Minor were important, including the routes from the Gobi desert via Samarkhand to Baghdad, the nodal point of the caravans from Iran, India, central Asia and China, often travelled by enormous numbers of beasts of burden—caravans of up to 1000 camels (Chaudhuri, 1985, 169, 173). The donkey was the earliest of the pack animals, known to have been domesticated in Egypt by about 3000 BC (but more slowly elsewhere), and by virtue of greater speed, more tolerance of a wider range of fodder types and requirement of less water than cattle they facilitated longer-distance trade, as did the later domesticated Bactrian camel and the dromedary, the two-humped

Bactrian camel having been domesticated in central Asia *c.* 3–2000 BC and the one-humped dromedary in south Arabia about 2500 BC (Wagstaff, 1985, 86–7).

Merchant Capitalism

In the late fifteenth and early sixteenth centuries, early indications of a price revolution which were to develop fully by the end of the sixteenth century were observable in Europe, the product in part of the voyage of discovery to the West and to the Far East which also contributed to the creation of a capitalist world system of unequal exchange, in which one of the major driving forces was merchant capital. Although what have been described as petty forms of capitalism can be found throughout the whole of medieval Europe, the increase in the scale of trading and business in the sixteenth and seventeenth centuries was dramatic and produced what is seen as a commercial revolution, supported by encouragement, investment and force by the new mercantile states, so that

> Merchants involved in activities like cloth-making and metalworking began to build up larger, more elaborate networks of trade, linking together the labour of numerous scattered artisans and craftsmen into a single production system. Much of the capital involved in these burgeoning systems of trade comprised circulating rather than fixed capital, that is, raw materials and semi-finished goods—goods whose embodied capital was quickly returned for reinvestment—rather than equipment and plant. The trading companies created over the sixteenth and seventeenth centuries to deal in overseas trade (e.g. East India Company, 1600) created equally impressive aggregations of capital (Dodgshon, 1990, 259).

An important aspect of these trading networks established by the merchant capitalists of London, Amsterdam, Venice and Lisbon, for example, was the increasing incentive for and efficiency of maritime trade, and the beginnings of improvement in overland means of communication, though temptations to see too much innovation in this regard must be resisted: in the sixteenth and seventeenth centuries the bulk of transport of goods being traded was carried over short distances on the backs of people, haulage animals, on carts, and small boats and ships. Nevertheless with the opening up of all-sea routes to the New World, to the west of Europe and to Asia, changes were made to the nature of trading ships. The Spanish carrack, for example, a large three-masted trading vessel operating from north-west and southern Europe from the fourteenth to the end of the seventeenth century, was a strong sailing ship, the largest being about 1600 tons. In the sixteenth and early seventeenth centuries most of Portuguese and Spanish trade to the Americas, China and India was carried out in such vessels, which were ultimately succeeded by the galleon during the seventeenth century. The trade to the east was mainly carried out by East India trading companies established in all the main maritime states of Europe, and the size of the trading ships ('East Indiamen') increased beyond the size of warships, and they often carried guns themselves. In the seventeenth, eighteenth and nineteenth centuries they increased from three-masted to four- or five-masted ships, to accommodate the need for greater capacities for trade (Kemp, 1976). The profit to be made from long-distance trade was very substantial, and not usually, as in the case of short-distance overland trade, subject to the sharing of profit between many intermediaries involved in transport of goods from one place to another. Rapid expansion of trading routes across the major oceans of the world occurred in the eighteenth and nineteenth centuries, including the routes across the Pacific (Fig. 11.1).

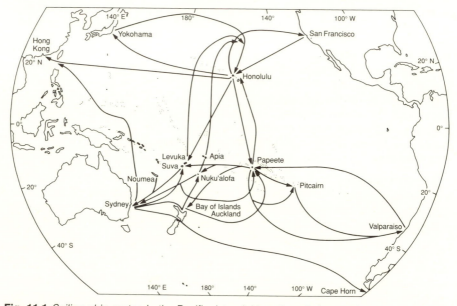

Fig. 11.1 *Sailing ship routes in the Pacific, late eighteenth and nineteenth centuries. Source:* Geographical Handbook Series, Pacific Islands, *vol. I (1945, 272)*

Overland transport was the principal means of conveying traded goods and information, sometimes in the hands of small commercial carriers, but mostly effected by individual peasants taking their goods to nearby markets. Goods transport along the major national and international overland routes (see Fig. 11.2) for example from north-west Europe to northern Italy, were handled by specialist large commercial carriers by the late seventeenth century, the larger firms being based in the Swiss cantons or in southern Germany, located at a critical logistical position for trans-Alpine trade, using large numbers of pack-mules (Braudel, 1982, 354). River transport in Europe was slow, subject to the problems of river flow regimes, obstacles such as mills, weirs and rocks and gravel banks, to large numbers of toll- and customs-points (of quite astonishing density in places), and even to river piracy on the larger rivers.

In North America in the mercantile era river transport was a medium of growing importance, serving the coastal colonies and trading ports, but similar problems of natural obstacles obtained as in Europe, including rapids and major falls on rivers such as the St Lawrence and the Ohio, though the amount of human interference with the movement of goods was less.

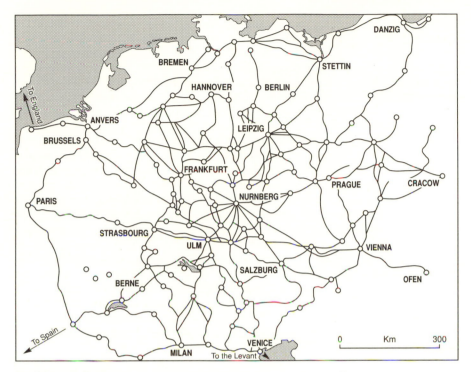

Fig. 11.2 *The German road system in the sixteenth century. Source: Thompson (1929, 90–1)*

Improved Waterways and Canals

One solution to the natural obstacles posed by unmodified river courses was the adoption of variations on a theme of controlling water flow, and 'stepping' and straightening steep and tortuous river courses. Navigations, such as the Naviglio Grande from Milan, were constructed in the late Middle Ages, and primitive forms of lock, improving on the 'stanch' (a wooden gate to control water flow, which developed into the much bigger and more powerful sluice gate) were developed in Holland and in Flanders in the fourteenth and early fifteenth centuries. The invention of the pound-lock in the fifteenth century and the advances of hydrology in the fifteenth and sixteenth centuries in the Low Countries and in Italy (especially the adoption of various techniques for straightening rivers and the cutting of artificial waterways), ushered the way for increases in the amounts of waterborne traffic in developed regions. In the Low Countries, Italy and China innovations in water transport were tied in with the advancement and increasing sophistication of drainage and irrigation schemes, the 'inter-city' canals or 'trekvaarten' of Holland being good examples, developed from the sixteenth century. Further development took the form, in particular circumstances of physical geography, of the watershed canal, which linked river systems across a dividing watershed, early examples being the Canal de Briare linking the Loire to the Seine via the Loin, constructed between 1604 and 1632, and the Canal des Deux Mers (now the

Canal du Midi), linking the Mediterranean with the Atlantic, constructed between 1667 and 1681. The construction of a major network of canals in France dates from the seventeenth century and effected a major network by the early nineteenth century (Vance, 1986). There were parallel developments in the Low Countries and in Italy in the early modern period, but the major factor influencing the development of the modern canal, from the eighteenth century onwards, was industrialization and the need for inexpensive transport of low-cost raw materials such as coal and iron ore.

One of the earliest industrializing countries in Europe was Britain, which also, like France had the advantage of political unity in the eighteenth century. Navigation schemes had been introduced in the seventeenth century, but in the eighteenth century the needs of provincial towns for better trading communications, especially with the major ports and with London, was met by major capital investment in canals (even though about 800 miles of rivers had been improved for navigation), the familiar chronology of construction including the Sankey Brook Navigation of 1757, the Bridgewater canal completed in 1765, ultimately linking the River Mersey at Runcorn to Manchester. The Trent and Mersey canal which opened in 1766 was the first one to cross a watershed in England, and intensification of construction took place during the period of 'canal mania' from 1792 to 1795, when there were 51 Acts of Parliament passed to enable the construction of canals, involving expenditure of £7.5 million, investment in which came from both local and nation-wide sources (Moyes, 1978, 411–12).

In North America the use of rivers for transport of people and goods was of importance for indigene and settler alike, but river improvement began with the early European colonists, including improvements on the lower St Lawrence. The independence of the United States in 1783 and the creation of a Federal government in 1791 necessitated a reorientation of trade and witnessed the continued geographical expansion of settlement and resource-use westwards. The improvement of inland waterway transportation was a key to local and national development, and a number of short canal cuts were made in New England in the late eighteenth century. The rectification of problems in the existing drainage systems which posed barriers to economic development, in relation to the non-major river location of many growing commercial cities at the coast, for example, plus the increasing continentality of American development, and the need to have easier transport systems for coal, led to a major era of canal development in the nineteenth century, initially within the area to the east of the Appalachians but quickly crossing watersheds, with the construction between 1819 and 1825 of the Erie canal across the Appalachian watershed (Vance, 1986).

In Europe and in North America there were parallel attempts at road improvement at the time of the initiation of industrialization, including the 'routes royales' of France and the new turnpike roads in Britain and in North America, the latter cheaper in construction than canals, and more substantial in total mileage constructed.

Models and Studies of Sea Transport and Port Development

A most interesting study of the development of ports and trading systems is to be found in Layton's work on trade in Upper Norrland in northern Sweden from the mid-eighteenth to the mid-twentieth century (Layton, 1981), with particular reference to the development of the port system. He identifies five stages in the development of the ports of this region: (1) 1750–85; (2) 1785–1855; (3a) 1855–85; (3b) 1885–1925; (4) 1925–50; and (5) 1950–75. Stages 1, 2 and 3a are characterized by diffusion of ports, stages 3b to 5 by selective concentration of growth.

Broader issues are raised in the comparison made by Layton in his study with broader models of port and transport development, especially those of Taafe, Morrill and Gould (1963) and Vance (1970). The Taafe, Morrill and Gould model of transport development comprised six stages: scattered ports; initial inland penetration and port concentration; the development of feeder networks; the initial interconnection of networks; complete interconnection; and finally the growth of high-priority routes. This model was based on empirical investigations of the experiences of Ghana and Nigeria in the late nineteenth and the twentieth centuries in a context of colonial introductions of industrial and transport technologies. Layton's model for port development in Upper Norrland—his Bottenhamn model, of long-term seaward port migration—differs in that the experiences incorporated are more typically European and having a much longer time-base than the more colonial models of Africa and Australasia for example, though there are similarities to models of the New World experience, especially North America, on account of northern Sweden's colonial character. The Bottenhamn model has five stages of port morphology and functional evolution: initial church settlement (probably medieval); old town; new town; industrial quays; and modern outport. It has similarities with Pounds' (1947a) port–outport model, and Bird's (1963) Anyport model, and seems to have broader possibilities of application, for as Layton (1981, 315) suggests in his summary 'Port models at the local and regional levels and for different parts of the world are likely to be interrelated and demonstrate similar processes because of the rapid diffusion of innovations in marine technology'.

Railways

The form of transport which is most generally viewed as the symbol of the capitalist industrial age is the railway, which not only transformed the speed of transport of goods and people but also radically affected notions of space (including the identity and associations of places) and time. Reflecting rapidly increasing needs for speedier and cheaper movement of heavy goods such as coal, iron, steel, and bricks, the combination of steam-driven engines and fixed iron rails effected a transport revolution from the late eighteenth century onwards, though the origins of the system date from the plateways, wagon-ways and the 'railroads' and 'railways' of the industrializing regions of Britain such as north-east England, Shropshire and south Wales, which had developed over the previous two centuries. What characterized the new railway system was the application of locomotive steam-power, in contrast to the human and animal propulsion of the earlier fixed trackway systems. The history of railway technology is complex, but generally the formative stage in Britain is thought to have been initiated by the opening of the 25-mile main track of the Stockton and Darlington Railway, in September 1825, engineered by George Stephenson and promoted by Edward Pease (a banker from Darlington), for the purpose of moving coal from the Durham coalfield, though some would argue that the first real railway was the Liverpool and Manchester, opened in September 1830, for this was the first railway to depend entirely on steam-power for locomotion. Thereafter in Britain a major network was built up in a relatively short period, the major expansion being in the period 1844–60. Thrift has described the 'mania' for railway construction in the period 1844–47 as

> fuelled by cheap money, by a fear that railway promotion would soon be controlled by Parliament, by rising earnings and by evidence of latent demand. Most 'mania' lines have some economic or geographical justification although some lines were constructed for which little reason existed. By 1860 the basic network that exists today had already been built. The introduction of cheap passenger fares revolutionized the amount of rail travel, evidenced in the contrast between the 30 million journeys by rail in 1845 and the 336.5 million in 1870 (Thrift, 1990, 463).

By mid-century freight rates and times were reducing, and an assessment of the wider effects of the railways on the British economy has to incorporate such features as the railway companies as mobilizers of capital, as markets for raw materials, as employers of large numbers of workers, skilled and unskilled, and their effects on the landscape, especially in towns.

Vance (1986) has suggested that there were four main stages of railway development in Britain: the first, characterized by the meeting of a specialized local need, mainly the transport of minerals; the second, differing in that railway systems constructed were for both passengers and freight and also that they connected major provincial cities with London, via trunk lines; the third involved the development of trunk-line networks not involving London; and the fourth, the connection of these regional networks with London.

The second major adoption of the railway came in North America, for the first rail line in the United States (Quincy, Massachusetts) opened in 1826. Vance (1986) takes the view that there was little interconnection between the early development of the railway systems in Britain and in North America, contrasting the long-established economies and settlement pattern of Britain with the more recent development of advanced economy in the United States and the legacy of a settlement pattern which reflected colonial experience. The main British contribution to an otherwise independent development of the North American network was 'its demonstration of the viability of the form rather than any direct contribution of genetic material' (Vance, 1986, 267).

The initial context for railway development was the problem of depression in the immediate aftermath of the war of 1812 and the need for the colonial ports to rectify the disadvantages of their coastal geographical locations with regard to the advancement of trade with the interior, which was accommodated initially by the building of short railways inland. Some such links were initiated in the 1830s, the first being the Baltimore and Ohio, construction of which commenced in 1828 and was completed to the Ohio River in 1852. The first phase, that of the building of short experimental lines, has been labelled the 'phase of the misplaced city' in American railway development, and was followed by: a second phase of short line construction to connect adjacent cities; a third phase involving the completion of the building of five trans-Appalachian routes in 1851–52; a fourth phase involving the creation of subcontinental systems; and a fifth which included the building of trans-continental systems (Vance, 1986). The impetus for the construction of the transcontinental railways came from a mixture of factors, including the increased potential for American Pacific and Asian trade, the Californian Gold Rush and the acquisition by the United States of the southern part of the Oregon County and the south-west of the United States, and Congress authorized the Pacific Railroad survey of 1854, which was to investigate six potential routes. The survey indicated that three of the six parallel routes might be feasible—along the 32nd, 35th and 41st parallels—and eventually the 41st parallel route was chosen, and the Union Pacific/Central Pacific 'Overland' route, from Omaha via Ogden to Oakland, was completed in May 1869. In all seven major transcontinental railways were built.

The effects of the railways on the economy and settlement geography of the United States were extensive. As Brown (1948, 349) has put it: 'The expanding network of iron rails (not steel until the 1870s) was in part the effect and in part the cause of industrial changes of the time. It contributed to the transformation of small towns to commercial and industrial cities, and opened up resources that had been of little significance. Changes wrought by the railroads included also the development of great inland cities such as Chicago, the extension of agriculture into vast areas of land inaccessible by water, and an enormous increase in movement of persons and freight from place to place'. Figure 11.3 shows the progress made in railroad development in the United States to 1860, and the use of the overland mail routes for communication with the West.

The Canadian experience was not vastly different from that of the United States. The earlier lines of the 1830s, especially those of the Maritimes, covered short distances, with longer lines such as the Grand Trunk Railway between Montreal and Toronto being constructed in the 1850s, but the rail network remained regional and close to the American border (reflecting the distribution of population) until the 1870s, when the newly confederated Canada (1867) looked for stronger links with the West, resulting in the completion of the Canadian Pacific Railway in 1885.

The chronology and effects of railway development in continental Europe varied widely, and can only be touched on briefly here. The earliest lines were built in south Germany and Belgium in 1835. Belgium expanded her network rapidly, with a network covering the northern plain completed within 10 years, but thereafter followed a quiescent period, rapid growth only being resumed in the 1870s and 1880s.

The German experience affords an interesting example of the influence of changing territorial patterns, especially before unification into one territory in 1871, on the development of transport networks. As in most industrializing countries, the era of the railway proper was preceded by a period of wagonways and plateways, wooden rails being used from the sixteenth century and iron plateways from the eighteenth century.

Interest in steam-powered rail systems was stimulated by the early English railways, and the potential for an all-German system proposed, but not immediately realized, by the economist List in 1833. The first line to be built was the short three-mile railway between Nuremberg and Fürth, opened in

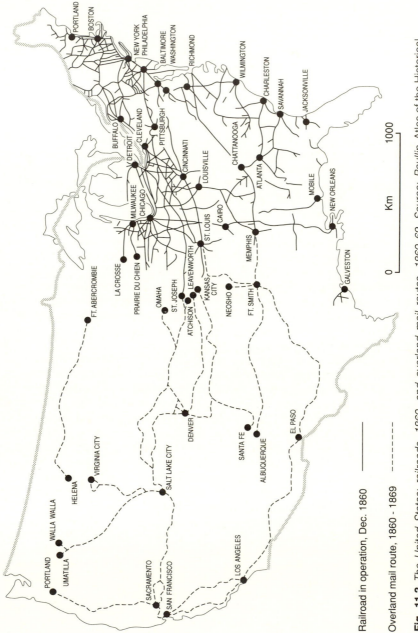

Fig. 11.3 *The United States: railroads, 1860, and overland mail routes, 1860–69. Source: Paullin, Atlas of the Historical Geography of the United States (1932, Plate 139B)*

Railroad in operation, Dec. 1860 ————

Overland mail route, 1860 - 1869 - - - - - - -

1835, using an English locomotive and German rails, and was followed by constructions between Dresden and Leipzig, Braunschweig and Wolfenbüttel, Berlin to Potsdam, Leipzig to Magdeburg, and Mannheim to Basel. By 1845 the length of railways in Germany was 1250 miles, most of it owned by private companies and one-quarter by the states. By 1855 the length had increased to 5300 miles (Mellor, 1979, 12–13). During the period up to unification there were difficulties of constructing railway routes which ran across different states, but with unification this problem largely disappeared, and the economic incentives for the exploitation of Germany's industrial resources led to a rapid expansion of the network, notably in the Ruhr region, and to an increase in goods traffic. From 1865 to 1914 the length of railway routes increased by 24,500 miles, much of it by the multiplication of existing lines. Considerable influence on routes was exerted by the military, anxious to use the railway for strategic purposes, and evidenced by the construction of such routes as those from central Germany to the Rhine and from Berlin to Schönberg. In the aftermath of unification there was also a move from private to state railways, which also enabled a standardization of equipment. After the First World War rapid progress was made toward the development of a national railway system, the Deutsche Reichsbahn. Within a broader context, Mellor (1979) has compared the German with the British experience, and suggested that the main contrasts were in relation to: the much later industrial development and upsurge of population growth in Germany (c. 1870–1914), the existence of fewer and more widely scattered coalfields in Germany, the particularism and parochialism of the German states' railway policy, and the different commercial philosophies of the two countries, with Britain favouring controlled private companies and Germany seeking state control. The development of the French railway network was again preceded by wagonways and tramways, with the first railway route, between Paris and Saint-Germain, opened in 1837. Initially a series of short lines were constructed by 33 private companies, but under the Second Empire the private lines were bought by the state, the length of track increased from 1800 to 9715 miles (2915–15,544 km) in the period 1850–70 (Pounds, 1985, 454). A further period of accelerated construction was from 1879 to 1910.

Elsewhere in Europe the system of the Netherlands was later than that of Belgium and Germany, that of Switzerland, the Hapsburg lands and Poland roughly similar to that of Germany, while the Balkans was the latest region of Europe to develop a railway network, with Spain, Italy and the Scandinavian states also being slower in this regard, though for different reasons (Pounds, 1985).

The growing imperial influence of Europe overseas in the late nineteenth and early twentieth centuries effected an interesting transfer of railway expertise and technology to the distance colonies and also to non-colonial states seeking to improve their infrastructures. Christopher (1984, 74–5) states that

> Colonial and metropolitan governments were particularly enamoured with the construction of railways. Lines were viewed not only as a means of transport but also demonstrated the technological skills of the colonial power and appealed to the humanitarian movements in the metropoles. The problems of transportation, especially porterage, were emphasized. The system drained labour from the routes as some were forcibly recruited and

others fled to avoid empressment, and it acted as corridors along which human and animal diseases were transmitted. . . . Railway construction often had to be viewed in terms of prestige rather than profit.

The motives for colonial railway construction were both economic and strategic, with the economic motive, especially the need to transport goods from hinterlands to ports, the more important. The cost of railway construction was high, and in consequence narrow gauges were often used, and the cost also reduced by land-grants by governments to the railway companies. The commonest type of railway was a short single line connecting areas of agriculture or mining to a port, as opposed to a regional network or long-distance route. Christopher (1984) has suggested that the chronology of railway development in colonial Africa involved an initial phase in the 1850s of construction of lines facilitating more rapid connections between Europe and India by linking steamer services through, for example, the lines from Alexandria to Cairo and Cairo to Suez. This was followed in 1860s by short-line port-linked railways in the Cape Colony, Natal and Algeria. Later in the nineteenth century, with improved transport technology, evidenced by trans-North American railways and the Suez Canal (1869), longer-distance railways into the interior of Africa were planned and, in some cases, realized. Ambitious but only partially successful schemes included the successful French plan for a trans-Saharan route and the British plan for a Cape to Cairo railway, posited mainly by interests in South Africa, but which was never fully realized. The majority of railway building in the later nineteenth century was, on the whole, less ambitious than the grander schemes, and conspicuously through the economic expansion of North and South Africa and the export lines of tropical Africa. The major regional systems by 1911 were those of Algeria and Tunisia, South Africa (over half the total railway length of Africa, stimulated by the new gold and diamond mining discoveries in the Witwatersrand and at Kimberley), French West Africa, and German South-West Africa (Christopher, 1984, 76–7). In tropical and equatorial Africa, the economic bases for railway development were thought to be smaller, resulting initially in the construction of light railways, but the systems of these regions expanded in the late nineteenth and early twentieth centuries with an intensification of the awareness of politicians of their economic potential, especially in British colonial East Africa and in the German colonies. The railways of the colonies were constructed in different gauges, resulting in conspicuous problems, for example between the states of Australia and between feeder lines and main lines in Algeria and South Africa, in the movement of goods from one region to another.

A major colonial railway system was that of India, which had a strong strategic input. Planned from the early 1840s, the earliest line to open was one in Bombay in 1853, then in Calcutta in 1854 and Madras in 1856. The prime factor was the need to link the interior with the coast after the rising of 1857, albeit at very considerable cost given the nature of the terrain. Acceleration of construction was greatest in the 1890s and 1900s, and after 1870 the British system was added to by the linking networks developed by the Indian states, and also used for relief of the famine of 1874–79. The effects of the growth of railways on landscape and economy was profound: 69,000 km/43,125 miles of line constructed by 1936; 750,000 people employed by the 1920s; major workshops constructed at Byculla, Howrah and Jamalpur; major engineering feats accomplished including the Darjeeling Railway's steep ascent of part of the Himalayas; and the use of elaborate architectural styles for major stations, including the use by William Stevens for the Bombay Victoria terminus of the Great Indian Peninsula Railway of what has been termed 'an exciting and essentially Victorian blend of Venetian-Gothic design and Indo-Saracencic motifs, which epitomized the search for a new Anglo-Indian Imperial style' (Christopher 1988, 54–6).

In China railway development came late, the way for western influences to penetrate the long-isolated country being facilitated by the wars of 1840–42 and 1856–60 with Britain, the Taiping Rebellion, the 1894 war with Japan, and the Boxer uprising. The success of the first, narrow-gauge railway, between Woo-sung and Shanghai (1876), built with foreign capital, was short-lived, being destroyed in 1877 as a result of the xenophobia of the Imperial court and peasant opposition based on the belief that railways, telegraph and mining systems disturbed the spirits of wind and water ('feng shui') in the land. The major phase of railway construction came between 1900 and 1920, when 9600 km/6000 miles of track was built, reflecting in part the scramble by European states to obtain footholds within China. Most of the railways were built by foreign investment and expertise, notably from Belgium, Japan, Russia and Britain (Tregear, 1976, 184–6).

The development of railway systems in Latin America in the nineteenth and early twentieth centuries was strongly conditioned by the fact that notwith-standing the new independence of the countries of Latin America in the period *c.* 1810–90 the economy remained essentially neo-colonial, and was strongly tied to the aggressive trade and capital investment policies of Britain, Germany, France and the United States. The initiation of the railways derives in part from the declining quality of road transport in the first half of the nineteenth century and the consquent difficulty and cost for overseas companies attempting to export basic raw materials, so that the early enterprises were mainly coastal in location. The first railway was built in Havana in Cuba in 1837 to facilitate sugar and coffee cultivation, but the first line on mainland Latin America was constructed in 1851 between Lima and the port of Callao. The lines built in the 1850s were short and essentially for historically important peripheral cities and ports (Rees, 1982, 124). From the 1860s onwards there was penetration into the interior using the new engineering technologies necessary to combat major topographical problems, examples being the Mexican Railway reaching a height of 8250 ft en route from Mexico City and Veracruz (1873), and the Mollendo–Arequipa–Puno railway in Peru (1868–77) ascending 14,850 ft from the coast into the Andes. Further extensions took place in the 1870s and 1880s. According to Rees (1982, 124–5):

> The 1870s and 1880s saw the railroads of Mexico, Central America, Brazil, Uruguay, Argentina, Chile and Peru relatively well developed. The 1880s also saw the beginnings of railroad penetration in Bolivia, Ecuador, and Colombia, although it was another two decades before these railroads were well established, perhaps reflecting the even more severe engineering problems set against the slower development of an incentive for communications. Finally, some countries, such as Venezuela, Paraguay, and the Guiana colonies, experienced very little railroad construction at all.

Rees suggests three categories of Latin American railway: the first built to extract a particular raw material or improve an existing routeway, and dominated by traffic from the interior, as in Mexico; the second was the type connecting the Atlantic and Pacific oceans, both in Central and South America, including the Buenos Aires to Valparaiso route; and the third, the 'speculative' railway, seeking to open up pioneer territory, such as the Madeira–Mamoré route through the Amazon rainforest and interior Bolivia.

The Movement of Ideas and Information

In addition to the study of means of transportation and of goods and people transported, the movement of information and ideas—some pertaining to trade, some not—is beginning to attract the attention of historical geographers, and is certain to be further researched in the future. An interesting example is Thrift's study of changes in transport and communication in England and Wales in the period 1730–1914, which emphasizes the inseparability of transport and communication, and their integral importance in people's lives. More rapid development of commerce in the late seventeenth and early eighteenth centuries promoted the increasing use of mail, the Post Office being founded in 1660, and the need for more political and cultural material and information in an increasingly literate society was met by an increase in books, magazines and newspapers, the number of newspapers in Britain increasing from 61 in 1782 to 369 by 1833 (Thrift, 1990, 469). In 1839 the telegraph was used for the first time. It was organized between 1840 and 1870 by the Electric Telegraph Company, and from 1870 by the Post Office, though it was not until after 1885 that it ceased largely to be an urban-based system and became more generally available to the populace outside the main urban areas. The telephone was developed in the late nineteenth and early twentieth centuries through private companies, and was taken over by the Post Office in 1911, the year when major expansion began. Other important technical innovations around this time were the photographic camera, the phonograph, the magic lantern, kinetoscope and cinemograph, and later the wireless, and the broadening of experience for increasing numbers of people through these media was also paralleled by the widening of horizons through cheaper rail travel, working-class holidays, and the availability of affordable bicycles (Thrift, 1990, 471–7).

Effective systems of communication were not only essential for the maintenance and advancement of economic, social and political systems and the enhancement of individual life-styles in individual countries, they were vitally important, for example, in the control of and contact with colonial and imperial territories. Colonial governments in the British Empire were heavily dependent on the mail services operated by steamship, with inland communication by coach and courier, later by railway. An imperial postal system operated from the late 1890s, with large post offices in most cities of the Empire (Christopher, 1988, 60–3). The added speed of communication by telegraph made it of particular significance, in both civil and strategic matters, effected overseas by the laying of submarine cables. Christopher shows the extent and accelerating use of this means of communication with the following facts: that in 1929 when the Cable and Wireless Company was created, in which the British telegraph lines were grouped, it controlled half the world's mileage of cable, that is 164,400 nautical miles; that the number of Colonial Office telegrams increased from 800 in 1870 to 10,000 in 1900; and that in 1929 the Cable and Wireless Company was responsible for 253 cable and wireless stations around the world, with over 8000 operators (Christopher, 1988, 63–6).

References

ADE AJAYI, J.F. and CROWDER, M. 1985: *Historical Atlas of Africa*. London: Longman.

AMOROS, C. and VAN URK, G. 1989: Palaeoecological analyses of large rivers: some principles and methods. In Petts, G.E., Möller, H. and Roux, A.L. (eds), *Historical change of large rivers: Western Europe* (Chichester: John Wiley), 143–65.

ANDREWS, J.H. 1961: *Ireland in Maps*. Dublin.

ANDREWS, J.H. 1962: Ireland in maps: a bibliographical postscript. *Irish Geography* 4, 234–43.

ANDREWS, J.H. 1985: *Plantation Acres. An Historical Study of the Irish Land Surveyor*. Omagh, Co. Tyrone: Ulster Historical Foundation.

AUSTIN, D. 1985: Doubts about morphogenesis. *Journal of Historical Geography* 11, 201–9.

BAIGENT, E. 1990: Swedish cadastral mapping 1628–1700: a neglected legacy. *The Geographical Journal* 156, 62–9.

BAKER, A.R.H. (ed.) 1972: *Progress in historical geography*. Newton Abbot: David and Charles.

BAKER, A.R.H. 1975: *Historical Geography and Geographical Change*. London: Macmillan.

BAKER, A.R.H. 1979: Historical geography: a new beginning? *Progress in Human Geography* 3, 560–70.

BAKER, A.R.H. 1980: Ideological change and settlement continuity in the French countryside during the nineteenth century: the development of agricultural syndicalism in Loir-et-Cher during the late nineteenth century. *Journal of Historical Geography* 6, 163–77.

BAKER, A.R.H. 1981: An historico-geographical perspective on time and space and on period and place. *Progress in Human Geography* 5, 439–43.

BAKER, A.R.H. 1983: Conference report. IGU working group on historical changes in spatial organisation: Warsaw symposium. *Journal of Historical Geography* 9, 307–8.

BAKER, A.R.H. 1984a: Reflections on the relations of historical geography and the *Annales* school of history. In Baker, A.R.H. and Gregory, D. (eds), *Explorations in historical geography* (Cambridge: Cambridge University Press), 1–27.

BAKER, A.R.H. 1984b: Fraternity in the forest: the creation, control and collapse of the woodcutters' unions in Loir-et-Cher 1852–1914. *Journal of Historical Geography* 10, 157–73.

BAKER, A.R.H. 1986: The infancy of France's first agricultural syndicate: the Syndicat des Agriculteurs de Loir-et-Cher 1881–1914. *Agricultural History Review* 34, 45–59.

BAKER, A.R.H. 1988: Historical geography and the study of the European rural landscape. *Geografiska Annaler* 70B, 1, 5–16.

BAKER, A.R.H. 1990: Fire-fighting fraternities? The corps de sapeurs-pompiers in Loir-et-Cher during the nineteenth century. *Journal of Historical Geography* 16, 121–39.

BAKER, A.R.H. and BUTLIN, R.A. 1973: Introduction: materials and methods. Chapter 1 of Baker, A.R.H. and Butlin, R.A. (eds), *Studies of field systems in the British Isles* (Cambridge: Cambridge University Press), 1–40.

BAKER, A.R.H., HAMSHERE, J.D. and LANGTON, J. (eds) 1970: *Geographical interpretations of historical sources*. Newton Abbot: David and Charles.

BAKER, J.N.L. 1935: The last hundred years of historical geography. *History* NS 21, 193–207.

BAKER, J.N.L. 1951–52: The development of historical geography in Britain during the last hundred years. *Advancement of Science* 8, 406–12.

BAKER, J.N.L. 1963a: *The History of Geography*. Oxford: Blackwell.

BAKER, J.N.L. 1963b: The history of geography in Oxford. Reprinted in *The history of geography. Papers by J.N.L. Baker* (Oxford: Blackwell), 119–29.

BARENDS, S., HAARTSEN, A.J., RENES, J. and STOL, T. 1988: Nederlandse cultuurlandschappen. *Historisch-Geographisch Tijdschrift*, 2–4.

BARENDS, S., HAARTSEN, A.J., RENES, J. and STOL, T. (eds) 1991: *Het Nederlandse landschap. Een historisch-geographische benadering*. Utrecht: Matrijs.

BARRELL, J. 1982: Geographies of Hardy's Wessex. *Journal of Historical Geography* 8, 347–61.

BARROWS, H.H. 1923: Geography as human ecology. *Annals, Association of American Geographers* 13, 1–14.

BATER, J.H. 1983: The industrialization of Moscow and St Petersburg. In Bater, J.H. and French, R.A. (eds), *Studies in Russian historical geography* (London: Academic Press), 279–303.

BECKETT, J.V. 1989: *A History of Laxton. England's Last Open-Field Village*. Oxford: Basil Blackwell.

BECKINSALE, R.P. 1981: W.M. Davis and American Geography (1880–1934). In Blouet, B.W. (ed.), *The origins of academic geography in the United States* (Hamden, Connecticut: Archon Books), 107–22.

BEN-ARIEH, J. 1984: *Jerusalem in the 19th Century. The Old City*. Jerusalem: Yad Izhak Ben Zvi Institute; New York: St Martin's Press.

BEN-ARIEH, J. 1989: Perceptions and images of the Holy Land. In Kark, R. (ed.), *The land that became Israel. Studies in historical geography* (Jerusalem: The Magnes Press, Hebrew University), 37–53.

BENITEZ, L.R. 1992: La geografia en el proyecto nacional de Mecixco independiente, 1824–1835. La fundacion del Instituto Nacional de Geografia y Estadistica. *Interciencia* 17, 155–60.

BENTLEY, P. 1966: *The English Regional Novel*. New York: Haskell House.

BERDOULAY, V.R.H. 1977: Louis-Auguste Himly 1823–1906. *Geographers. Bio-bibliographical Studies* 1, 43–8.

BERDOULAY, V.R.H. 1981: *La Formation de l'École Française de Géographie (1870–1914). Comité des Travaux Historiques et Scientifiques, Mémoires de la Section de Géographie*. Paris: Bibliothèque Nationale.

BERESFORD, M.W. 1957: *History on the Ground: Six Studies in Maps and Landscapes*. London: Lutterworth.

BERESFORD, M.W. and HURST, J. (eds), 1971: *Deserted Medieval Villages*. London: Lutterworth.

BERG, M., HUDSON, P., and SONNENSCHER, M. (eds), 1983: *Manufacture in Town and Country Before the Factory*. Cambridge: Cambridge University Press.

BILLINGE, M. 1977: In search of negativism: phenomenology and historical geography. *Journal of Historical Geography* 3, 55–68.

BILLINGE, M. 1982: Reconstructing societies in the past: the collective biography of local communities. In Baker, A.R.H. and Billinge, M. (eds), *Explorations in historical geography* (Cambridge: Cambridge University Press), 19–32.

BILLINGE, M. 1984: Hegemony, class and power in late Georgian and early Victorian England: towards a cultural geography. In Baker, A.R.H. and Gregory, D. (eds), *Explorations in historical geography. Interpretative essays* (Cambridge: Cambridge University Press), 28–67.

BIRD, J.H. 1963: *The Major Seaports of the United Kingdom.* London: Hutchinson.

BIRKS, H.J.B. and BIRKS, H.H. (1980): *Quaternary Palaeoecology.* London: Edward Arnold.

BLACKWELL, W.L. 1983: The historical geography of industry in Russia during the nineteenth century. In Bater, J.H. and French, R.A. (eds), *Studies in Russian historical geography* (London: Academic Press), 387–422.

BLOUET, B.W. (ed.) 1981: *The origins of academic geography in the United States.* Hamden, Connecticut: Archon Books.

BLOUET, B.W. and BLOUET, O.M. (eds) 1982: *Latin America. An Introductory Survey.* New York: John Wiley.

BORSAY, P. (ed.) 1990: *The Eighteenth Century Town. A Reader in English Urban History 1688–1820.* London: Longman.

BOWDEN, M.J. 1969: The perception of the western interior of the United States, 1800–1870: a problem in historical geosophy. *Proceedings, Association of American Geographers* 1, 16–21.

BOWEN, E.G. 1932: Early Christianity in the British Isles. A study in historical geography. *Geography* 17, 267–76.

BOYER, J.-C. 1978: Formes traditionelles et formes nouvelles de la géographie historique: leur place dans la recherche en géographie. *Comité des Travaux Historiques et Scientifiques. Bulletin de la Section de Géographie* 82, 55–63. Paris: Bibliothèque Nationale.

BRADLEY, R.S. and JONES, P.D. (eds) 1992: *Climate since AD 1500.* London: Routledge.

BRAGA, G. and GERVASONI, S. 1989: Evolution of the Po River: an example of the application of historic maps. In Petts, G.E., Möller, H. and Roux, A.L. (eds), *Historical change of large alluvial rivers: Western Europe* (London: Wiley), 113–26.

BRAUDEL, F. 1972: *The Mediterranean and the Mediterranean world in the age of Philip II*, vol. I. London: Collins. Originally published in 1949 as *La Méditerranée et le Monde Méditerranéen à l'Époque de Philippe II.* Paris: Armand Colin.

BRAUDEL, F. 1982: *Civilization and Capitalism 15th–18th Century. Vol. II. The Wheels of Commerce.* London: Collins.

BRAVARD, J.-P. and BETHEMONT, J. 1989: Cartography of rivers in France. In Petts, G.E., Möller, H. and Roux, A.L. (eds): *Historical change of large alluvial rivers: Western Europe* (London: Wiley), 95–112.

BROC, N. 1970: Histoire de la Géographie et nationalisme en France sous la Troisième République, 1871–1914. *L'Information Historique* 32, 20–6.

BROC, N. 1974a: *La géographie des philosophes. Géographes et voyageurs français au XVIIe siècle.* Revised edition. Paris: Éditions Orphrys.

BROC, N. 1974b: L'établissement de la géographie en France: diffusion, institutions, projets (1870–1890). *Annales de Géographie* 83, 459, 545–68.

BROC, N. 1979: Histoire et historiens de la géographie. Notes bio-bibliographiques (milieu du XVIIIe siècle-1914), *Comité Nationale des Travaux Historiques et Scientifiques. Bulletin de la Section de Géographie* 84, 71–116. Paris.

BROWN, R.H. 1948: *Historical Geography of the United States.* Orlando: Harcourt Brace Jovanovich.

BUCHANAN, R.H., BUTLIN, R.A. and McCOURT, D. (eds) 1976: *Fields, Farms and Settlement in Europe.* Holywood, Co. Down: Ulster Folk and Transport Museum.

BUCHANAN, R.H., JONES, E. and McCOURT, D. (eds) 1971: *Man and his Habitat. Essays presented to Emyr Estyn Evans.* London: Routledge and Kegan Paul.

BULLOCK, A.L.C. 1977: Hegemony. In Bullock, A. and Stalybrass, O. (eds), *The

Fontana dictionary of modern thought (London: Fontana/Collins), 279.

BUTLIN, R.A. 1976: Land and people, *c.* 1600. In Moody, T.W., Martin, F.X. and Byrne, F.J. (eds), *A new history of Ireland*, vol. III (Oxford: Clarendon Press), 142–67.

BUTLIN, R.A. 1986: Early industrialization in Europe: concepts and problems. *Geographical Journal* 152, 1–8.

BUTLIN, R.A. 1987: Theory and methodology in historical geography. In Pacione, M. (ed.), *Historical geography: progress and prospect* (London: Croom Helm), 16–45.

BUTLIN, R.A. 1988: George Adam Smith and the historical geography of the Holy Land: contents, contexts and connections. *Journal of Historical Geography* 14, 381–404.

BUTLIN, R.A. 1990a: A short chapter in French historical geography: the *Bulletin du Comité Français de Géographie Historique et d'Histoire de la Géographie*, 1935–1938. *Journal of Historical Geography* 16, 438–55.

BUTLIN, R.A. 1990b: Drainage and land use in the Fenlands and fen-edge of northeast Cambridgeshire in the seventeenth and eightcenth centuries. In Cosgrove, D. and Petts, G. (eds), *Water, engineering and landscape* (London: Bellhaven Press), 54-76.

BUTLIN, R.A. 1990c: Regions in England and Wales, *c.* 1600–1914. In Dodgshon, R.A. and Butlin, R.A. (eds), *An historical geography of England and Wales* (2nd edition, London: Academic Press), 223–54.

BUTLIN, R.A. 1992: Ideological contexts and the reconstruction of Biblical landscapes in the seventeenth and eighteenth centuries: Dr Edward Wells and the historical geography of the Holy Land. In Baker, A.R.H. and Biger, G. (eds), *Ideology and landscape in historical perspective* (Cambridge: Cambridge University Press), 31–62.

BUTZER, K.W. 1982: *Archaeology as Human Ecology.* Cambridge: Cambridge University Press.

BUTZER, K.W. 1989: Cultural ecology. In Gaile, G.L. and Willmott, C.J. (eds), *Geography in America* (Columbus: Merrill Publishing Co.), 192–208.

BUTZER, K.W. 1990: The Indian legacy in the American landscape. In Conzen, M. (ed.), *The making of the American landscape* (Boston: Unwin Hyman), 27–50.

BYLUND, E. 1960: Theoretical considerations regarding the distribution of settlement in inner north Sweden. *Geografiska Annaler* 52, 225–31.

CABRERA, L.L.-O. 1992: Medio siglo de actividades cientificas de la Sociedad Geografica de Lima. *Interciencia* 17, 147–54.

CALDWELL, J.C. 1987: Population. In Vamplew, W. (ed.), *Australians. Historical statistics* (Cambridge: Cambridge University Press), 23–41.

CAMPBELL, E.M.J. 1987: Geography at Birkbeck College, University of London, with particular reference to J.F. Unstead and E.G.R. Taylor. In Steel, R.W. (ed.), *British Geography* (Cambridge: Cambridge University Press), 45–57.

CANNADINE, D. 1984: The past and the present in the English Industrial Revolution 1880–1980. *Past and Present* 103, 131–72.

CAPPON, L.J. (ed.) 1976: *Atlas of early American history.* Princeton: Princeton University Press.

CARRIER, E.H. 1925: *Historical Geography of England and Wales (South Britain).* London: George Allen and Unwin.

CARTER, H. 1983: *An Introduction to Urban Historical Geography.* London: Edward Arnold.

CARTER, H. and LEWIS, C.R. 1990: *An Urban Geography of England and Wales in the Nineteenth Century.* London: Edward Arnold.

CATCHPOLE, A.J.W. 1992: Hudson's Bay Company ships' log-books as sources of sea ice data, 1751–1870. In Bradley, R.S. and Jones, P.D. (eds), *Climate since AD 1500* (London: Routledge), 17–39.

CERTEAU, M. de, 1988: *The Practice of Everyday Life.* Berkeley: University of California Press.

CHALKLIN, C.W. 1974: *The Provincial Towns of Georgian England: a Study of the Building Process*. London: Edward Arnold.

CHAPMAN, J. 1987: The extent and nature of parliamentary enclosure. *Agricultural History Review* 35, 25–35.

CHAPMAN, J. and HARRIS, T.M. 1982: The accuracy of the enclosure estimates: some evidence from northern England. *Journal of Historical Geography* 8, 261–4.

CHARLESWORTH, A. 1979: *Social protest in a rural society: the spatial diffusion of the Captain Swing disturbances 1830–31*. Norwich: Historical Geography Research Series, 1.

CHARLESWORTH, A. 1986: Labour protest 1780–1850. In Langton, J. and Morris, R.J. (eds), *Atlas of industrializing Britain* (London: Methuen), 185–9.

CHAUDHURI, K.N. 1985: *Trade and Civilisation in the Indian Ocean. An Economic History from the Rise of Islam to 1750*. Cambridge: Cambridge University Press.

CHAUDHURI, K.N. 1990: *Asia Before Europe. Economy and Civilisation of the Indian Ocean from the Rise of Islam to 1750*. Cambridge: Cambridge University Press.

CHILDE, V.G. 1954: Rotary motion. In Singer, C., Holmyard, E.J. and Hall, A.R. (eds), *A history of technology. Vol. I. From early times to fall of ancient empires* (Oxford: Clarendon Press), 187–215.

CHRISTOPHER, A.J. 1983: From Flint to Soweto: reflections on the origins of the apartheid city. *Area* 15, 145–9.

CHRISTOPHER, A.J. 1984: *Colonial Africa*. Beckenham, Kent, and Canberra: Croom Helm.

CHRISTOPHER, A.J. 1988: *The British Empire at its Zenith*. Beckenham, Kent: Croom Helm.

CLAPHAM, J.H. 1926–1938: *An Economic History of Modern Britain*. 3 vols, Cambridge: Cambridge University Press.

CLAPHAM, J.H. 1928: *The Economic Development of France and Germany 1815–1914*. 3rd edition. Cambridge: Cambridge University Press.

CLARK, A.H. 1949: *The Invasion of New Zealand by People, Plants and Animals*. New Brunswick, NJ: Rutgers University Press.

CLARK, A.H. 1954: Historical geography. In James, P.E. and Jones, C.F. (eds), *American geography: inventory and prospect* (Syracuse, New York: Syracuse University Press), 71–105.

CLARK, A.H. 1956: The modification of mid-latitude grasslands and forests by man. In Thomas, W.L. Jr, (ed.), *Man's role in changing the face of the earth* (Chicago: Chicago University Press), 721–62.

CLARK, A.H. 1959: *Three Centuries and the Island*. Toronto: University of Toronto Press.

CLARK, A.H. 1968: *Acadia: The Geography of Early Nova Scotia to 1760*. Madison: University of Wisconsin Press.

CLARK, A.H. 1972: Historical geography in North America. In Baker, A.R.H. (ed.), *Progress in historical geography* (Newton Abbot: David and Charles), 129–43.

CLARK, A.H. 1975: First things first. In Ehrenberg, R.E. (ed.), *Pattern and process. Research in historical geography* (Washington, DC: Howard University Press), 9–24.

CLARKE, C. and LANGTON, J. 1990: Introduction. In Clarke, C. and Langton, J. (eds), *Peasantry and progress: rural culture and the modern world*, Research paper 45 (School of Geography, University of Oxford), 5–12.

CLARKE, R.L. 1975: Some sources in the national archives for studies of Afro-American population: growth and movement. In Ehrenberg, R.E. (ed.), *Pattern and process in historical geography* (Washington, DC: Howard University Press), 73–80.

CLARKSON, L.A. 1985: *Proto-industrialization: The First Phase of Industrialization?* London: Macmillan.

CLAVAL, P. 1981: Géographie historique. *Annales de Géographie* 90, 669–71.

CLAVAL, P. 1984: The historical dimension in French geography. *Journal of Historical Geography* 10, 229–45.

CLIFF, A.D., HAGGETT, P., ORD, J.K. and VERSEY, G.R. 1981: *Spatial Diffusion. An Historical Geography of Epidemics in an Island Community.* Cambridge: Cambridge University Press.

CLIFF, A.D., HAGGETT, P. and GRAHAM, R. 1983: Reconstruction of diffusion processes at local scales: the 1846, 1882 and 1904 measles epidemics in northwest Iceland. *Journal of Historical Geography* 9, 347–68.

CLINE, H.F. 1964: The *Relationes Geográficos* of the Spanish Indies, 1577–1586. *Hispanic American Historical Review* 44, 341–74.

CLOUT, H.D. (ed.), 1977a: *Themes in the Historical Geography of France.* London: Academic Press.

CLOUT, H.D. 1977b: Agricultural change in the eighteenth and nineteenth centuries. In Clout, H.D. (ed.), *Themes in the historical geography of France* (London: Academic Press), 407–46.

CLOUT, H.D. 1980: *Agriculture in France on the Eve of the Railway Age.* London: Croom Helm.

CLOUT, H.D. and PHILLIPS, A.D.M. 1972: Fertilisants minéraux en France au XIXe siècle. *Études Rurales* 45, 9–28.

CLOUT, H.D. and SUTTON, K. 1969: The cadastre as a source for French rural studies. *Agricultural History* 13, 215–23.

COHEN, A. 1973: *Palestine in the 18th Century. Patterns of Government and Administration.* Jerusalem: The Magnes Press.

COLE, J.P. and KING, C.A.M. 1968: *Quantitative Geography.* London: Wiley.

COLE, S.M. 1954: Land transport without wheels. Roads and bridges. In Singer, C., Holmyard, E.J. and Hall, A.R. (eds), *A History of Technology. Vol. I. From Early Times to Fall of Ancient Empires* (Oxford: Clarendon Press), 704–15.

COLEMAN, D.C. 1983: Proto-industrialization: a concept too many. *Economic History Review* (2nd series) 36, 435–48.

COLSON, J., MIDDLETON, R. and WARDLEY, P. 1992: Annual review of information technology developments for economic and social historians, 1991. *Economic History Review* 45, 378–412.

CONZEN, M.P. (ed.) 1990a: *The Making of the American Landscape.* Boston: Unwin Hyman.

CONZEN, M.P. 1990b: Town-plan analysis in an American setting: cadastral processes in Boston and Omaha, 1630–1930. In Slater, T.R. (ed.), *The built form of western cities* (Leicester and London: Leicester University Press), 142–70.

COPPOCK, J.T. 1956: The statistical assessment of British agriculture. *Agricultural History Review* 4, 4–21 and 66–79.

COPPOCK, J.T. 1984: Mapping the agricultural returns: a neglected tool of historical geography. In Reed, M. (ed.), *Discovering past landscapes* (London: Croom Helm), 8–55.

CORBRIDGE, S. 1987: Industrialisation, internal colonialism and ethnoregionalism: the Jharkhand, India, 1880–1980. *Journal of Historical Geography* 13, 249–66.

CORNISH, V. 1915: Notes on the historical and physical geography of war. *Geographical Journal* 45, 371–84.

CORNISH, V. 1923: *The Great Capitals. An Historical Geography.* London: Methuen.

COSGROVE, D. 1984: *Social Formation and Symbolic Landscape.* London: Croom Helm.

COSGROVE, D. 1985: Prospect, perspective and the evolution of the landscape idea. *Transactions, Institute of British Geographers* NS 1, 45–62.

COSGROVE, D. 1988: The geometry of landscape: practical and speculative arts in sixteenth-century Venetian land territories. In Cosgrove, D. and Daniels, S. (eds), *The iconography of landscape: essays on the symbolic representation, design and use of past environments* (Cambridge: Cambridge University Press), 254–76.

COSGROVE, D. 1990: Platonism and practicality: hydrology, engineering and landscape in sixteenth-century Venice. In Cosgrove, D. and Petts, G. (eds), *Water, engineering and landscape* (London: Bellhaven Press), 35–53.

CRAFTS, N.F.R. 1985: *British Economic Growth During the Industrial Revolution.* Oxford: Clarendon Press.

CRAWFORD, O.G.S. 1922: Prehistoric geography. *Geographical Review* 12, 257–63.

CRONE, G.R. 1978: *Maps and Their Makers.* 5th edition. Folkestone: William Dawson.

CRUSH, J. 1986a: Towards a people's historical geography for South Africa. *Journal of Historical Geography* 12, 2–3.

CRUSH, J. 1986b: Swazi migrant workers and the Witwatersrand gold mines 1886–1920. *Journal of Historical Geography* 12, 27–40.

CUMBERLAND, K.B. and WHITELAW, J.S. 1970: *New Zealand.* London: Longman.

CURSCHMANN, F. 1916: Die Entwicklung der historisch-geographischen Forschung in Deutschland durch zwei Jahrhunderte. *Archiv für Kulturgeschichte* 12, 128–63, 285–325.

DAINVILLE, F. de 1940: *La Géographie des Humanistes.* Paris: Beauchesne et Fils.

DANIELS, S. 1982a: The political landscape. In Carter, G., Goode, P. and Laurie, K. (eds), *Humphrey Repton landscape gardener 1752–1818* (Norwich: Sainsbury Centre for Visual Arts), 110–27.

DANIELS, S. 1982b: Humphrey Repton and the morality of landscape. In Gold, J.R. and Burgess, J. (eds), *Valued environments* (London: Allen and Unwin), 124–44.

DANIELS, S. 1985: Arguments for a humanistic geography. In Johnston, R. (ed.), *The future of geography* (London, Methuen), 143–58.

DANIELS, S. and COSGROVE, D. 1988: Introduction: iconography and landscape. In Cosgrove, D. and Daniels, S. (eds), *The iconography of landscape* (Cambridge: Cambridge University Press), 1–10.

DANIELS, S. and SEYMOUR, S. 1990: Landscape design and the idea of improvement 1730–1914. In Dodgshon, R.A. and Butlin, R.A. (eds), *An historical geography of England and Wales* (2nd edition, London: Academic Press), 487–520.

DARBY, H.C. 1931: The role of the Fenland in English history. In Quicke, F. (ed.), *Congrès Internationale de Géographie historique, Tome II, Mémoires* (Brussels), 62–5.

DARBY, H.C. 1932: The medieval sea state. *Scottish Geographical Magazine* 48, 136–9.

DARBY, H.C. (ed.) 1936: *An Historical Geography of England before AD 1800.* Cambridge: Cambridge University Press.

DARBY, H.C. 1940a: *The Medieval Fenland.* Cambridge: Cambridge University Press.

DARBY, H.C. 1940b: *The Draining of the Fens.* Cambridge: Cambridge University Press.

DARBY, H.C. 1948: The regional geography of Thomas Hardy's Wessex. *Geographical Review* 38, 426–43.

DARBY, H.C. 1951: The changing English landscape. *Geographical Journal* 117, 377–98.

DARBY, H.C. 1953: On the relations of geography and history. *Transactions, Institute of British Geographers* 19, 1–11.

DARBY, H.C. 1954: Some early ideas on the agricultural regions of England. *Agricultural History Review* 11, 30–47.

DARBY, H.C. 1956: The clearing of the woodland in Europe. In Thomas, W.L. Jr (ed.),

Man's role in changing the face of the earth (Chicago: Chicago University Press), 183–216.

DARBY, H.C. 1962: Historical geography. In Finberg, H.P.R. (ed.), *Approaches to History* (London: Routledge and Kegan Paul), 127–56.

DARBY, H.C. (ed.) 1973a: *A New Historical Geography of England.* Cambridge: Cambridge University Press.

DARBY, H.C. 1973b: Domesday England. In Darby, H.C. (ed.), *A new historical geography of England* (Cambridge: Cambridge University Press), 39–74.

DARBY, H.C. 1977: *Domesday England.* Cambridge: Cambridge University Press.

DARBY, H.C. 1979: Some reflections on historical geography. *Historical Geography* 9, 9–14.

DARBY, H.C. 1983: Historical geography in Britain, 1920–1980: continuity and change. *Transactions, Institute of British Geographers* NS 8, 421–8.

DATOO, B.A. 1979: Population change in eastern Africa, AD 1500. In Udo, R.K. (ed.), *Population education source book for sub-Saharan Africa* (Nairobi: Heinemann), 41–8.

DAUNTON, M.J. 1983: *House and Home in the Victorian City.* London: Edward Arnold.

DAVIS, M.B. 1976: Erosion rates and land-use history in Southern Michigan. *Environmental Conservation* 3, 139–48.

DELANO SMITH, C. 1987: Maps in sixteenth-century Bibles. *The Map Collector* 19, 2–14.

DELANO SMITH, C. 1990: Maps as art *and* science: maps in sixteenth-century Bibles. *Imago Mundi* 42, 1–19.

DELANO SMITH, C. and PARRY, M. (eds), 1981: *Consequences of Climatic Change.* Nottingham: Department of Geography, University of Nottingham.

DEMANGEON, A. 1928: *La Géographie de l'habitat rurale.* Report of the Commission on types of rural settlement, International Geographical Union, Cambridge, 41–80.

DEMANGEON, A. 1939: Types de villages en France. *Annales de Géographie* 48, 1–21.

DENECKE, D. 1976: Innovation and diffusion of the potato in central Europe in the seventeenth and eighteenth centuries. In Buchanan, R.H., Butlin, R.A. and McCourt, D. (eds), *Fields, farms and settlement in Europe* (Holywood, Co. Down: Ulster Folk and Transport Museum), 60–96.

DENNIS, R. 1987: Faith in the city. *Journal of Historical Geography* 13, 210–16.

DENNIS, R. 1988: By the waters of Babylon. *Journal of Historical Geography* 14, 307–8.

DENNIS, R. 1990: The social geography of towns and cities 1730–1914. In Dodgshon, R.A. and Butlin, R.A. (eds), *An historical geography of England and Wales*, 2nd edition (London: Academic Press), 429–51.

DESREUMAUX, A. and SCHMIDT, F. (eds), 1988: *Moïse Géographe. Recherches sur les Représentations Juives et Chrétiennes de l'Espace.* Paris: Librairie philosophique J. Vrin.

DIARRA, S. 1981: Historical geography: physical aspects. In Ki-Zerbo, J. (ed.) *General history of Africa vol. I. Methodology and African prehistory* (London: Heinemann), 348–58.

DICKINSON, R.E. 1939: Landscape and society. *Scottish Geographical Magazine* 55, 1–15.

DICKINSON, R.E. 1969: *The Makers of Modern Geography.* London: Routledge and Kegan Paul.

DIGBY, A. 1954: Boats and ships. In Singer, C., Holmyard, E.J. and Hall, A.R. (eds), *A history of technology. Vol. I. From early times to fall of ancient empires* (Oxford: Clarendon Press), 730–43.

DIGBY, A. 1982: *The Poor Law in Nineteenth-Century England and Wales*. London: The Historical Association.

DION, R. 1934: *Le Val de Loire. Étude de Géographie Régionale*. Tours: Arrault.

DIXON, R. and MUTHESIUS, S. 1978: *Victorian Architecture*. London: Thames and Hudson.

DOBSON, M. 1987: *A chronology of epidemic disease and mortality in southeast England, 1601–1800*, Historical Geography Research Series, Number 19, London: Historical Geography Research Group.

DODGSHON, R.A. 1978: The early Middle Ages. In Dodgshon, R.A. and Butlin, R.A. (eds), *An historical geography of England and Wales*, 1st edition, (London: Academic Press), 81–118.

DODGSHON, R.A. 1980: *The Origin of British Field Systems: An Interpretation*. London: Academic Press.

DODGSHON, R.A. 1987: *The European Past. Social Evolution and Spatial Order*. London: Macmillan.

DODGSHON, R.A. 1988: The ecological basis of Highland peasant farming. In Birks, H.H., Birks, H.J.B., Kaland, P.E. and Moe, D. (eds), *The cultural landscape—past, present and future* (Cambridge: Cambridge University Press), 139–51.

DODGSHON, R.A. 1990: The changing evaluation of space 1500–1914. In Dodgshon, R.A. and Butlin, R.A. (eds), *An historical geography of England and Wales*, 2nd edition (London: Academic Press), 255–83.

DODGSHON, R.A. and BUTLIN, R.A. (eds), 1990: *An historical geography of England and Wales*. 2nd edition. London: Academic Press.

DODGSHON, R.A. 1992: The role of Europe in the early modern world-system: parasitic or generative? *Political Geography* 11, 396–400.

DOMOSH, M. 1987: Imagining New York's first skyscrapers, 1875–1910. *Journal of Historical Geography* 13, 233–48.

DONKIN, R.A. 1973: Changes in the early middle ages. In Darby, H.C. (ed.), *A new historical geography of England* (Cambridge: Cambridge University Press), 75–135.

DONKIN, R.A. 1977: Spanish Red: an ethnogeographical study of cochineal and the opuntia cactus. *Transactions of the American Philosophical Society* 67, Part 5.

DONKIN, R.A. 1985: The peccary—with observations on the introduction of pigs to the New World. *Transactions of the American Philosophical Society* 75, Part 5.

DRAKAKIS-SMITH, D. 1983: Advance Australia fair: internal colonialism in the Antipodes. In Drakakis-Smith, D. and Williams, S.W. (eds), *Internal colonialism. Essays around a theme*. Monograph No. 3, Developing Areas Study Group, Institute of British Geographers (Edinburgh: University of Edinburgh, Department of Geography), 81–103.

DRAKAKIS-SMITH, D. and WILLIAMS, S.W. (eds), *Internal colonialism. Essays around a theme*. Monograph No. 3, Developing Areas Study Group, Institute of British Geographers. Edinburgh: University of Edinburgh, Department of Geography.

DRIVER, F. 1988: The historicity of human geography. *Progress in Human Geography* 12, 497–506.

DRIVER, F. 1990: Discipline without frontiers? Representations of the Mettray reformatory colony in Britain, 1840–1880. *Journal of Historical Sociology* 3, 272–93.

DRIVER, F. 1992: Geography's empire: histories of geographical knowledge. *Environment and Planning, D. Society and Space* 10, 23–40.

DUNBAR, G.S. 1981: Credentialism and careerism in American geography, 1890–1915. In Blouet, B.W. (ed.), *The origins of academic geography in the United States* (Hamden, Connecticut: Archon Books), 71–88.

DUNCAN, J.S. 1985: Individual action and political power: a structuration perspective. In Johnston, R.J. (ed.), *The future of geography* (London: Edward Arnold), 174–89.

DUNFORD, M. and PERRONS A.C. 1983: *The Arena of Capital*. London: Macmillan.

EARLE, C. 1992: *Geographical Enquiry and American Historical Problems*. Stanford: Stanford University Press.

EAST, W.G. 1933: A note on historical geography. *Geography* 102, 18, 282–92.

EAST, W.G. 1935: *An Historical Geography of Europe*. London: Methuen.

EAST, W.G. 1938: *The Geography Behind History*. London: Nelson.

EDWARDS, C.R. 1975: The Relationes de Yucatán as sources for historical geography. *Journal of Historical Geography* 1, 245–58.

ELLIOTT, J. 1990: The mechanical conservation of soil in Rhodesia/Zimbabwe. In Cosgrove, D. and Petts, G. (eds), *Water, engineering and landscape* (London: Bellhaven Press), 115–28.

EVANS, B. 1990: Migration processes in Upper Peru in the seventeenth century. In Robinson, D.J. (ed.), *Migration in colonial Spanish America* (Cambridge: Cambridge University Press), 62–85.

EVANS, E.E. 1951: *Mourne Country: Life and Landscape in South Down*. Dundalk: Dundalgan Press.

EVANS, E.E. 1957: *Irish Folk Ways*. London: Routledge Kegan Paul.

EVANS, E.E. 1959: Rural settlement in Ireland and western Britain. *Advancement of Science* 15, 333–45.

EVANS, E.E. 1973: *The Personality of Ireland. Habitat, Heritage and History*. Cambridge: Cambridge University Press.

FAEGRI, K. and IVERSEN, J. 1975: *Textbook of Pollen Analysis*. 3rd edition. Oxford: Blackwell.

FAIRGRIEVE, Mr 1921: contribution to discussion listed as 'The content of historical geography'. *The Geographical Teacher* 11, 1921, 40–3.

FEHN, K. 1975: Historische geographie. Eigenständige wissenschaft und teilwissenschaft der gesamtgeographie. *Sonderdruck aus den Mitteilungen der Geographischen Gesellschaft in München* 61, 35–51.

FEHN, K. 1982: Die historische geographie in Deutschland. *Erdkunde* 36, 65–70.

FEHN, K., BRANDT, K., DENECKE, D. and IRSIGLER, F. 1988: *Genetische Siedlungsforschung in Mitteleuropa und sienen Nachbarräumen*. 2 vols. Bonn: Verlag Siedlungsforschung.

FIELDHOUSE, D.K. 1982: *The Colonial Empires*. 2nd edition. London: Macmillan.

FIGUEROA, S.F.M. de 1992: Asociativismo cientifico en Brasil: el Instituto Historico y Geografico Brasilera como espacio institucional para las ciencias naturales durante el siglo XIX. *Interciencia* 17, 141–6.

FINK, C. 1991: *Marc Bloch. A Life in History*. Cambridge: Cambridge University Press, Canto edition.

FINLAY, R. 1981: *Parish registers. An introduction*. Historical Geography Research Series, No. 7. Norwich: Geobooks.

FLENLEY, J.R. 1979: *The Equatorial Rain Forest: A Geological History*. London: Butterworth.

FOGELVIK, S., GERGER, T. and HOPPE, G. 1981: *Man, Landscape and Society. An Information System*. Stockholm: Almqvist and Wiksell International.

FOORD, J. and GREGSON, N. 1986: Patriarchy: towards a reconceptualization. *Antipode* 18, 186–211.

FOX, C. 1932: *The Personality of Britain*. Cardiff: National Museum of Wales.

FOX, R. 1980: The savant confronts his peers: scientific societies in France, 1815–1914. In Fox, R. and Weitz, G. (eds), *The organisation of science and technology in France 1808–1914* (Cambridge: Cambridge University Press), 241–82.

FRANDSEN, K.-E. 1985: Danish field systems in the seventeenth century. *Scandinavian Journal of History* 8, 293–317.

FRASER, N. 1989: *Unruly Practices: Power, Discourse and Gender in Contemporary Social Theory.* Cambridge: Polity Press.

FREEMAN, E.A. 1881: *The Historical Geography of Europe.* London: Longmans, Green, and Co.

FRENCH, R.A. 1964: The reclamation of swamp in pre-revolutionary Russia. *Transactions, Institute of British Geographers* 34, 175–88.

FRENCH, R.A. 1983a: Introduction. In Bater, J.H. and French, R.A. (eds), *Studies in Russian historical geography*, vol. I (London and New York: Academic Press), 13–21.

FRENCH, R.A. 1983b: The early and medieval Russian town. In Bater, J.H. and French, R.A. (eds), *Studies in Russian historical geography*, vol. 2 (London: Academic Press), 249–77.

FRIEDMAN, D. 1988: *Florentine New Towns. Urban Design in the Late Middle Ages.* Cambridge, Mass.: MIT Press.

FRIIS, H. 1940a: *A Series of Population Maps of the Colonies and the United States, 1625–1790.* New York: American Geographical Society, Publication No. 3.

FRIIS, H. 1940b: A series of population maps of the Colonies and the United States. *Geographical Review* 30, 463–70.

FUKUYAMA, F. 1989: The end of history? *The National Interest* (Summer), 3–18.

FURBANK, P.N. 1992: *Diderot.* London: Secker and Warburg.

GANN, L.H. and DUIGNAN, P. 1977: *The Rulers of German Africa 1884–1914.* Stanford: Stanford University Press.

GATES, P.W. 1960: *The Farmer's Age: Agriculture, 1815–1860. Economic History of the United States, vol. III.* New York: Harper and Row.

GEORGE, H.B. 1924: *A Historical Geography of the British Empire.* 7th edition. London: Methuen.

GERHARD, P. 1972: *A Guide to the Historical Geography of New Spain.* Cambridge: Cambridge University Press.

GIBSON, J.R. (ed.) 1978: *European Settlement and Development in North America. Essays on Geographical Change in Honour and Memory of Andrew Hill Clark.* Toronto: University of Toronto Press.

GIEDION, S. 1954: *Space, Time and Architecture.* 3rd edition. Cambridge, Mass.: MIT Press.

GILBERT, E.W. 1932: What is historical geography? *Scottish Geographical Magazine* 48, 129–35.

GILBERT, E.W. 1960: The idea of the region. *Geography* 45, 157–75.

GLASSCOCK, R.E. 1973: England circa 1334. In Darby, H.C. (ed.), *A new historical geography of England* (Cambridge: Cambridge University Press), 136–85.

GLASSCOCK, R.E. 1975: *The Lay Subsidy of 1334. British Academy Records of Social and Economic History*, New Series, II. London: The British Academy.

GLASSCOCK, R.E. 1978: Darby's Domesday geography. *Journal of Historical Geography* 4, 395–7.

GOBLET, Y.-M. 1935: Géographie historique et histoire de la géographie. *Bulletin du Comité Français de Géographie Historique et d'Histoire de la Géographie* 1, 10–17.

GOBLET, Y.-M. 1955: *Political Geography and the World Map.* London: George Philip and Son.

GOODMAN, D.S.G. 1983: Guizhou and the People's Republic of China: the development of an internal colony. In Drakakis-Smith, D. and Williams, S.W. (eds), *Internal colonialism. Essays around a theme.* Monograph No. 3, Developing Areas Study Group, Institute of British Geographers (Edinburgh: University of Edinburgh, Department of Geography), 107–24.

GOSAL, G.S. 1984: Population geography in India. In Clarke, J.I. (ed.), *Geography and population. Approaches and applications* (London: Pergamon), 203–14.

GOTTSHALK, M.K.E. 1971: *Stormvloeden en Rivieroverstromingen in Nederland. I. De Periode voor 1400.* Assen.

GOTTSHALK, M.K.E. 1975: *Stormvloeden en Rivieroverstromingen in Nederland. II. De Periode 1400–1600*. Assen.

GOTTSHALK, M.K.E. 1977: *Stormvloeden en Rivieroverstromingen in Nederland. III. De Periode 1600–1700*. Assen/Amsterdam.

GOUDIE, A.S. 1976: Geography and prehistory, a survey of the literature with a select bibliography. *Journal of Historical Geography* 2, 197–205.

GOUDIE, A.S. 1990: *The Human Impact on the Natural Environment*. Oxford: Blackwell.

GOUROU, P. 1982: Roger Dion, 1896–1981. *Journal of Historical Geography* 8, 182–4.

GRADMANN, R. 1898: *Das Pflanzenleben der Schwäbischen Alb mit Berücksichtigung der agrenzenden Gebiete Suddeutschlands*. Tübingen: Verlag d. Schwab.

GRADMANN, R. 1901: Das Mitteleuropäische Landschaftsbild nach seiner geschichtlichen Entwicklung. *Geographische Zeitschrift* 7, 361–77, 435–47.

GRADMANN, R. 1931: *Süddeutschland*, 2 vols. Stuttgart: J. Engelhorns.

GRADMANN, R. 1934: Palästinas urlandschaft. *Zeitschrift des Deutschen Palästina-Vereins* 57, 161–85.

GRAHAM, B. 1988: The town in the Norman colonisations of the British Isles. In Denecke, D. and Shaw, G. (eds), *Urban historical geography* (Cambridge: Cambridge University Press), 37–52.

GRANTHAM, G., 1989: Agrarian organization in the century of industrialization: Europe, Russia, and North America. In Grantham, G. and Leonard, C.S. (eds), *Agrarian organization in the century of industrialization: Europe, Russia, and North America. Research in economic history*. Supplement 5. Part A (Greenwich, Connecticut: JAI Press), 1–29.

GREEN, C. McL. 1957: *American Cities in the Growth of the Nation*. New York: Harper and Row.

GREGORY, D. 1976: Re-thinking historical geography. *Area* 8, 295–8.

GREGORY, D. 1978: The discourse of the past: phenomenology, structuralism and historical geography. *Journal of Historical Geography* 4, 161–73.

GREGORY, D. 1981a: Historical geography. In Johnston, R.J. *et al.* (ed.), *The dictionary of human geography* (Oxford: Blackwell), 146–50.

GREGORY, D. 1981b: Human agency and human geography. *Transactions, Institute of British Geographers* 6, 1–18.

GREGORY, D. 1982a: Action and structure in historical geography. In Baker, A.R.H. and Billinge, M. (eds), *Period and place* (Cambridge: Cambridge University Press), 244–50.

GREGORY, D. 1982b: *Regional Transformation and Industrial Revolution. A Geography of the West Yorkshire Woollen Industry*. London: Macmillan.

GREGORY, D. 1985: Suspended animation: the stasis of diffusion theory. In Gregory, D. and Urry, J. (eds), *Social relations and spatial structures* (London: Hutchinson), 296–336.

GREGORY, D. 1986a: Urban origins. In Johnston, R.J., Gregory, D. and Smith, D.M. (eds), *The dictionary of human geography*, 2nd edition (Oxford, Blackwell), 511–12.

GREGORY, D. 1986b: Diffusion. In Johnston, R.J., Gregory, D. and Smith, D.M. (eds), *The dictionary of human geography*. 2nd edition (Oxford: Blackwell), 106–9.

GREGORY, D. 1986c: Time-geography. In Johnston, R.J., Gregory, D. and Smith, D.M. (eds), *The dictionary of human geography*. 2nd edition (Oxford: Blackwell), 485–7.

GREGORY, D. 1990: 'A new and differing face in many places': three geographies of industrialization. In Dodgshon, R.A. and Butlin, R.A. (eds), *An historical geography of England and Wales*, 2nd edition (London: Academic Press), 352–99.

GREGORY, D. and URRY, J. (eds) 1985: *Social Relations and Spatial Structures*. London: Macmillan.

GREGORY, K.J. (ed.) 1977: *River Channel Changes*. Chichester: John Wiley.

GREGORY, K.J. (ed.) 1983: *Background to Palaeohydrology*. Chichester: John Wiley.

GRIGG, D. 1967: The changing agricultural geography of England: a commentary on the sources available for the reconstruction of the agricultural geography of England, 1770–1850. *Transactions, Institute of British Geographers* 41, 73–96.

GRIGG, D.B. 1974: *The Agricultural Systems of the World. An Evolutionary Approach*. Cambridge: Cambridge University Press.

GROVE, J.M. and BATTAGEL, A. 1981: Tax records as an index of Little Ice Age environmental and economic deterioration, from Sunnjord Fogderi, western Norway 1667–1815. In Delano Smith, C. and Parry, M. (eds), *Consequences of climatic change* (Nottingham: Department of Geography, University of Nottingham), 70–87.

GROVE, R.H. 1990: Colonial conservation, ecological hegemony and popular resistance: towards a global synthesis. In MacKenzie, J.M. (ed.), *Imperialism and the natural world* (Manchester: Manchester University Press), 15–50.

GROVES, P.A. 1974: The 'hidden' population: Washington alley dwellers in the late nineteenth century. *Professional Geographer* 3, 270–6.

GROVES, P.A. and MULLER, E.K. 1975: The evolution of black residential areas in late-nineteenth century cities. *Journal of Historical Geography* 1, 169–91.

GUELKE, L. 1974: An idealist alternative in human geography. *Annals, Association of American Geographers* 64, 193–202.

GUELKE, L. 1975: On re-thinking historical geography. *Area* 7, 135–8.

GUELKE, L. 1982: *Historical Understanding in Geography: An Idealist Approach*. Cambridge: Cambridge University Press.

GULLICKSON, G.L. 1983: Agriculture and cottage industry: re-defining the causes of proto-industrialization. *Journal of Economic History* 43, 831–50.

HÄGERSTRAND, T. 1952: *Innovationsförloppet ur korologisk synpunkt*. Lund: Gleerup. Translated 1968 by Pred, A., as *Innovation diffusion as a spatial process*. Chicago: Chicago University Press.

HALLEWAS, D.P. and VAN REGTEREN ALTINA, J.F. 1980: Bewoningsgeshiednis en landschapsontwikkeling rond de Maasmond. In Verhulst, A. and Gottshalk, M.K.E. (eds), *Transgressies en occupatiegeschiednis in de kustgebieden van Nederland en België* (Ghent: Belgisch Centrum voor Landelijke Geschiednis), 155–207.

HAMILTON, W.B. 1974: *Local History in Atlantic Canada*. Toronto: The Macmillan Company of Canada.

HAMSHERE, J.D. 1982: A computer-assisted study of Domesday Warwickshire. In Slater, T.R. and Jarvis, P.J. (eds), *Field and Forest* (Norwich: Geobooks), 105–24.

HAMSHERE, J.D. 1987: Data sources in historical geography. In Pacione, M. (ed.), *Historical geography: progress and prospect* (London: Croom Helm), 46–69.

HAR-EL, M. 1977: *This is Jerusalem*. Jerusalem: Kiryat-Sefer Ltd.

HARDY, D. 1988: Historical geography and heritage studies. *Area* 20, 333–8.

HARLEY, J.B. 1972: *Maps for the Local Historian. A Guide to the British Sources*. London: Bedford Square Press of the National Council of Social Service.

HARLEY, J.B. 1973a: Change in historical geography: a qualitative impression of quantitative methods. *Area* 5, 69–74.

HARLEY, J.B. 1973b: England *c.* 1850. In Darby, H.C. (ed.), *A new historical geography of England* (Cambridge: Cambridge University Press), 527–94.

HARLEY, J.B. 1982: Historical geography and its evidence: reflections on modelling sources. In Baker, A.R.H. and Billinge, M. (eds), *Period and place. Research methods in historical geography* (Cambridge: Cambridge University Press), 261–73.

HARLEY, J.B. 1988a: Maps, knowledge, and power. In Cosgrove, D. and Daniels, S. (eds), *The iconography of landscape* (Cambridge: Cambridge University Press), 277–312.

HARLEY, J.B. 1988b: Silences and secrecy: the hidden agenda of cartography in early modern Europe. *Imago Mundi* 40, 57–76.

HARLEY, J.B. 1989a: Historical geography and the cartographic illusion. *Journal of Historical Geography* 15, 1, 80–91.

HARLEY, J.B. 1989b: Why cartography needs its history. *The American Cartographer* 16, 5–15.

HARLEY, J.B. 1989c: Deconstructing the map, *Cartographica* 26, 1–20.

HARLEY, J.B. and WOODWARD, D. 1987: *The History of Cartography, vol. 1, Cartography in Prehistoric, Ancient and Medieval Europe and the Mediterranean.* Chicago: Chicago University Press.

HARRIS, D.R. 1965: Plants, animals and man in the outer Leeward Islands, West Indies. *University of California Publications in Geography* 18, 1–184.

HARRIS, D.R. 1967: New light on plant domestication and the origins of agriculture: a review. *Geographical Review* 57, 90–107.

HARRIS, D.R. 1971: The ecology of swidden cultivation in the upper Orinoco rain forest, Venezuela. *Geographical Review* 61, 475–95.

HARRIS, D.R. 1984: Ethnohistorical evidence for the exploitation of wild grasses and forbs: its scope and archaeological implications. In Zeist, W. van and Casparie, W.A. (eds), *Plants and ancient man* (Rotterdam: A. A. Balkema), 63–9.

HARRIS, R.C. 1967: Historical geography in Canada. *Canadian Geographer* 11, 235–50.

HARRIS, R.C. 1976: Andrew Hill Clark, 1911–1975. *Journal of Historical Geography* 2, 1–2.

HARRIS, R.C. 1978: The historical mind and the practice of geography. In Ley, D. and Samuels, M.S. (eds), *Humanistic geography* (London: Croom Helm), 123–37.

HARRIS, R.C. (ed.) 1988: *Historical atlas of Canada. Vol. I. From the beginning to 1800.* Toronto: University of Toronto Press.

HARRIS, R.C. 1990: French landscapes in North America. In Conzen, M.P. (ed.), The making of the American landscape (Boston: Unwin Hyman), 63–79.

HARRIS, R.C. and GUELKE, L. 1977: Land and society in early Canada and South Africa. *Journal of Historical Geography* 3, 135–53.

HARRIS, R.C. and WARKENTIN, J. 1974: *Canada Before Confederation.* New York: Oxford University Press.

HARTSHORNE, R. 1939: *The Nature of Geography: A Survey of Current Thought in the Light of the Past.* Lancaster, Pa: Association of American Geographers.

HARVEY, D. 1981: Marxist geography. In Johnston, R.J. et al. (ed.), *The dictionary of human geography* (Oxford: Blackwell), 209–12.

HARVEY, D. 1983: *The Limits to Capital.* Oxford: Blackwell.

HARVEY, D. 1985a: *The Urbanization of Capital. Studies in the History and Theory of Capitalist Urbanization.* Oxford: Blackwell.

HARVEY, D. 1985b: The geography of capitalist accumulation: toward a reconstruction of the Marxian theory. Chapter 2 of Harvey, D., *The urbanization of capital* (Oxford: Blackwell), 32–61.

HARVEY, D. 1985c: *Consciousness and the Urban Experience. Studies in the History and Theory of Capitalist Urbanization.* Oxford: Blackwell.

HARVEY, D. 1985d: The geopolitics of capitalism. In Gregory, D. and Urry, J. (eds), *Social relations and spatial structures* (London: Macmillan), 128–63.

HARVEY, D. 1987: The representation of urban life. *Journal of Historical Geography* 13, 317–21.

HARVEY, D. 1988: The production of value in historical geography. *Journal of Historical Geography* 14, 305–8.

HARVEY, D. 1989: *The Condition of Postmodernity.* Oxford: Blackwell.

HEATHCOTE, R.L. 1975: *Australia.* London: Longman.

HEATHCOTE, R.L. and McCASKILL, M. 1972: Historical geography in Australia and New Zealand. In Baker, A.R.H. (ed.), *Progress in historical geography* (Newton Abbot: David and Charles), 145–67.

HECHTER, M. 1975: *Internal Colonialism: the Celtic Fringe in British National Development, 1536–1966.* London: Routledge and Kegan Paul.

HEFFERNAN, M.J. 1988: A French colonial controversy: Captain Roudaire and the Saharan Sea, 1872–83. *The Maghreb Review* 13, 145–60.

HEFFERNAN, M.J. 1991: The desert in French orientalist painting during the nineteenth century. *Landscape Research* 16, 37–42.

HELMFRID, S. (ed.) 1961a: *Morphogenesis of the agrarian cultural landscape.* Papers of the Vadstena symposium of the XIXth International Geographical Congress. *Geografiska Annaler* 43, 1–328.

HELMFRID, S. 1961b: The Storskifte, Enskifte and Lagaskifte in Sweden—general features. *Geografiska Annaler* 43, 114–29.

HENDERSON, H.O. 1952: Agriculture in England and Wales in 1801. *Geographical Journal* 118, 338–45.

HENRY, L. 1965: The population of France in the eighteenth century. In Glass, D.V. and Eversley, D.E.C. (eds), *Population in history* (London: Edward Arnold), 434–56.

HETTNER, A. 1922: Zur Stellung der historischen geographie. *Geographischer Anzeiger* 23, 93–4.

HEWES, L. and FRANDSON, P.E. 1952: Occupying the wet prairie: the role of artificial drainage in Story County, Iowa. *Annals of the Association of American Geographers* 42, 24–50.

HILLIARD, S. 1990: Plantation and the moulding of the Southern landscape. In Conzen, M.P. (ed.), *The making of the American landscape* (Boston: Unwin Hyman), 104–26.

HODGES, R. 1982: *Dark Age Economics: the Origins of Towns and Trade AD 600–1000.* London: Duckworth.

HOOKE, J.M. and KAIN, R.J.P. 1982: *Historical Change and the Physical Environment: a Guide to Sources and Techniques.* London: Butterworth.

HOPKINS, A.G. 1973: *An Economic History of West Africa.* London: Longman.

HOPPE, G. and LANGTON, J. 1986: Time-geography and economic development: the changing structure of livelihood positions on arable farms in nineteenth-century Sweden. *Geografiska Annaler* 68B, 115–37.

HOPPIT, J. 1987: Understanding the Industrial Revolution. *The Historical Journal* 30, 211–24.

HOSKINS, W.G. 1955: *The Making of the English Landscape.* London: Hodder and Stoughton.

HOURANI, A. 1991: *A History of the Arab Peoples.* London: Faber.

HOUSTON, J.M. 1968: The foundation of colonial towns in Hispanic America. In Beckinsale, R.P. and Houston, J.M. (eds), *Urbanization and its problems* (Oxford: Oxford University Press), 352–90.

HOUSTON, R. and SNELL, K.D.M. 1984: Proto-industrialization? Cottage industry, social change and industrial revolution. *Historical Journal* 27, 473–92.

HUDSON, J.C. 1990: Settlement of the American grassland. In Conzen, M.P. (ed.), *The making of the American landscape* (Boston: Unwin Hyman), 169–85.

HUDSON, P. 1986: *The Genesis of Industrial Capital: a Study of the West Riding Wool Textile Industry c. 1750–1850.* Cambridge: Cambridge University Press.

HUDSON, P. 1989: The regional perspective. In Hudson, P. (ed.), *Regions and industries. A perspective on the Industrial Revolution in Britain* (Cambridge: Cambridge University Press), 5–38.

HUGGETT, F.E. 1975: *The Land Question in Europe.* London: Thames and Hudson.

HUNT, E.K. and SHERMAN, J. 1972: *Economics. An Introduction to Traditional and Radical Views.* 2nd edition. New York: Harper and Row.

HUNT, J.D. 1986: *Garden and Grove. The Italian Renaissance Garden in the English Imagination: 1600–1750.* London: Dent.

JÄGER, H. 1969: *Historische Geographie.* Braunschweig: Georg Westermann.

JÄGER, H. 1979: Wüstungsforschung in Geographischer und historischer Sicht. *Geschichtswissenschaft und Archäologie, Vorträge und Forschungen* 22, 193–240.

JÄGER, H. 1987: *Entwicklungsprobleme Europäischer Kulturlandschaften. Eine Einführung.* Darmstadt: Wissenschaftliche Buchgesellschaft.

JAKLE, J.A. 1971: Time, space, and the geographic past: a prospectus for historical geography. *American Historical Review* 76, 1084–1103.

JARVIS, P.J. 1979: Plant introductions to England and their role in horticultural and sylvicultural innovation, 1500–1900. In Fox, H.S.A. and Butlin, R.A. (eds), *Change in the Countryside.* (London: Institute of British Geographers), 145–64.

JOHNSON, H.B. 1957: Rational and ecological aspects of the Quarter Section. *Geographical Review* 47, 330–48.

JOHNSON, H.B. 1975: The United States land survey as a principle of order. In Ehrenberg, R.E. (ed.), *Pattern and process. Research in historical geography* (Washington, DC: Howard University Press), 114–30.

JOHNSTON, R.J. 1986: Space. In Johnston, R.J., Gregory, D. and Smith, D. (eds), *The dictionary of human geography*, 2nd edition (Oxford: Blackwell), 443–4.

JONES, E.L. 1968: Agricultural origins of industry. *Past and Present* 40, 58–71.

JONES, E.L. 1981: *The European Miracle. Environments, Economies and Geopolitics in the History of Europe and Asia.* 1st edition. Cambridge: Cambridge University Press.

JONES, G.R.J. 1961: Early territorial organization in England and Wales. *Geografiska Annaler* 43, 174–81.

JONES, G.R.J. 1971: The multiple estate as a model framework for tracing early stages in the evolution of rural settlement. In Dussart, F. (ed.), *L'habitat et les paysages ruraux d'Europe* (Liège: University of Liège), 251–67.

JONES, G.R.J. 1972: Post-Roman Wales. In Finberg, H.P.R. (ed.), *The agrarian history of England and Wales*, 1–ii (Cambridge: Cambridge University Press), 281–332.

JONES, G.R.J. 1973: Field systems of North Wales. In Baker, A.R.H. and Butlin, R.A. (eds), *Studies of field systems in the British Isles* (Cambridge: Cambridge University Press), 430–79.

JONES, G.R.J. 1976: Multiple estates and early settlement. In Sawyer, P.H. (ed.), *Medieval settlement* (London: Edward Arnold), 15–40.

JONES, G.R.J. 1985: Multiple estates perceived. *Journal of Historical Geography* 11, 352–63.

JONES, G.R.J. 1989: The Dark Ages. In Owen, D.H. (ed.), *Settlement and society in Wales* (Cardiff: University of Wales Press), 185–7.

JONES, L.R. 1925: Geography and the university. *Economica*, Old Series, 241–57.

JONES HUGHES, T. 1965: Society and settlement in nineteenth-century Ireland. *Irish Geography* 5, 79–96.

JONES HUGHES, T. 1981: Village and town in nineteenth-century Ireland. *Irish Geography* 14, 99–106.

JONES HUGHES, T. 1986: The estate system of landholding in nineteenth-century Ireland. In Nolan, W. (ed.), *The shaping of Ireland* (Cork: The Mercier Press), 137–50.

JOYCE, P. 1991: History and post-modernism. *Past and Present* 133, 204–9.

KAIN, R.J.P. 1984: The tithe files of mid-nineteenth-century England and Wales. In Reed, M. (ed.), *Discovering past landscapes* (London: Croom Helm), 56–84.

KAIN, R.J.P. 1986: *An Atlas and Index of the Tithe Files of Mid-Nineteenth-Century England and Wales.* Cambridge: Cambridge University Press.

KAIN, R.J.P. and PRINCE, H.C. 1985: *The Tithe Surveys of England and Wales.* Cambridge: Cambridge University Press.

KARK, R. 1990: *Jaffa. A City in Evolution, 1799–1917*. Jerusalem: Izhak Ben-Zvi Press.

KATZ, Y. 1986: Ideology and urban development: Zionism and the origins of Tel-Aviv, 1906–1914. *Journal of Historical Geography* 12, 402–24.

KAY, J. 1991: Landscapes of women and men: rethinking the regional historical geography of the United States and Canada. *Journal of Historical Geography* 17, 435–52.

KAY, J. and BROWN, C.J. 1985: Mormon beliefs about land and natural resources 1847–1877. *Journal of Historical Geography* 11, 253–67.

KEARNS, G. 1984: Closed space and political practice: Frederick Jackson Turner and Halford Mackinder. *Environment and Planning, D. Society and Space* 2, 23–34.

KEARNS, G. 1985a: Halford John Mackinder 1861–1947. *Geographers Biobibliographical Studies* 9, 71–3.

KEARNS, G. 1985b: *Urban Epidemics and Historical Geography: Cholera in London, 1848–9*. Historical geography research series. Geo Books: Norwich.

KEARNS, G. 1985c: *Aspects of Cholera, Society and Space in Nineteenth-Century England and Wales*. Ph.D. Thesis, University of Cambridge.

KEARNS, G. 1991: Historical geography. *Progress in Human Geography* 15, 47–56.

KELLY, C. 1991: History and post-modernism. *Past and Present* 133, 209–13.

KELTIE, J.S. 1885: *Geographical education*. Report to the council of the Royal Geographical Society. London: John Murray.

KEMP, P. 1976: *The Oxford Companion to Ships and the Sea*. Oxford: Oxford University Press.

KEMP, T. 1969: *Industrialization in Nineteenth-Century Europe*. London: Longman.

KERMACK, W.R. 1919: Notes on the historical geography of the Dardanelles. *Scottish Geographical Magazine* 25, 241–8.

KERR, D. 1982: The emergence of the industrial heartland *c.* 1750–1950. In McCann, L.D. (ed.), *Heartland and hinterland. A geography of Canada* (Scarborough, Ontario: Prentice-Hall), 65–94.

KESWICK, M. 1986: China. In Jellicoe, G., Jellicoe, S., Goode, P. and Lancaster, M. (eds), *The Oxford companion to gardens* (Oxford: Oxford University Press), 111–16.

KNIFFEN, F. 1965: Folk housing: key to diffusion. *Annals, Association of American Geographers* 55, 549–77.

KNOX, J.C. 1972: Valley alluviation in southwestern Wisconsin. *Annals, Association of American Geographers* 62, 401–10.

KOELSCH, W. (ed.) 1962: *Lectures on the Historical Geography of the United States as given in 1933 by Harlan H. Barrows*. Chicago: Department of Geography, University of Chicago. Research paper No. 77.

KOFMAN, E. and PEAKE, L. 1990: Into the 1990s: a gengered agenda for political geography. *Political Geography Quarterly* 9, 313–36.

KOELSCH, W. 1969: The historical geography of Harlan H. Barrows. *Annals, Association of American Geographers* 59, 632–51.

KONVITZ, J.W. 1987: *Cartography in France 1660–1848. Science, Engineering, and Statecraft*. Chicago: University of Chicago Press.

KORNHAUSER, D. 1976: *Urban Japan: its Foundations and Growth*. London: Longman.

KÖTZSCHE, R. 1906: Quellen und Grundbegriffe der historischen Geographie Deutschlands und seiner Nachbarländer. *Grundriss der Geschichtswissenschaft* 1, 397–449.

KRIEDTE, P. 1983: *Peasants, Landlords and Merchant Capitalists. Europe and the World Economy, 1500–1800*. Leamington Spa: Berg Publishers.

KRIEDTE, P., MEDICK, H. and SCHLUMBOHM, J. (eds), 1981: *Industrialization before Industrialization*. Cambridge: Cambridge University Press.

LAMB, H.H. 1977: *Climate, Past, Present, and Future. Vol. 2. Climatic History and the Future*. London: Methuen.

LAMB, H.H. 1980: Climatic fluctuations in historical times and their connexion with transgressions of the sea, storm floods and other coastal changes. In Verhulst, A. and Gottshalk, M.K.E. (eds), *Transgressies en occupatiegeschiednis in de kustgebieden van Nederland en België* (Ghent: Belgisch Centrum voor Landelijke Geschiednis), 251–90.

LAMBIN, D.A. 1986: The United States. In Jellicoe, G., Jellicoe, S., Goode, P. and Lancaster, M. (eds), *The Oxford companion to gardens* (Oxford: Oxford University Press), 572–5.

LANGTON, J. 1972: Potentialities and problems of adopting a systems approach to the study of change in human geography. *Progress in Geography* 4, 127–79.

LANGTON, J. 1984: The industrial revolution and the regional geography of England. *Transactions, Institute of British Geographers*, New Series 9, 145–67.

LANGTON, J. 1986: Habitat, economy and society revisited: peasant ecotypes and economic development in Sweden. *Cambria* 13, 5–24.

LANGTON, J. 1988: The two traditions of geography, historical geography and the study of landscapes. *Geografiska Annaler* 70B, 17–26.

LANGTON, J. and HOPPE, G. 1983: *Town and Country in the Development of Early Modern Western Europe*. Norwich: Geobooks. Historical Geography Research Series, No. 11.

LANGTON, J. and MORRIS, R.J. 1986: *Atlas of Industrializing Britain*. London: Methuen.

LAWTON, R. (ed.) 1978: *The Census and Social Structure*. London: Cass.

LAWTON, R. 1987: Peopling the past. *Transactions, Institute of British Geographers* NS 12, 259–83.

LAWTON, R. 1989: Introduction: aspects of the development and role of great cities in the Western World in the nineteenth and twentieth centuries. In Lawton, R. (ed.), *The rise and fall of great cities* (London: Bellhaven Press), 1–19.

LAWTON, R. 1990: Population and society. In Dodgshon, R.A. and Butlin, R.A. (eds), *An historical geography of England and Wales*, 2nd edition (London: Academic Press), 285–316.

LAWTON, R. and POOLEY, C. 1992: Urbanization and urban life from the 1830s to the 1890s. In Lawton, R. and Pooley, C. (eds), *Britain 1740–1950. An historical geography* (London: Edward Arnold), 195–221.

LAXTON, P. 1986: Textiles. In Langton, J. and Morris, R.J. (eds), *Atlas of industrializing Britain* (London: Methuen), 106–13.

LAYTON, I.G. 1981: *The evolution of Upper Norrland's ports and loading places 1750–1976*. Geographical Reports No. 6. Umeå: Department of Geography, University of Umeå.

LEE, C. 1986: Services. In Langton, J. and Morris, R.J. (eds), *Atlas of industrializing Britain* (London: Methuen), 140–3.

LE ROY LADURIE, E. 1972: *Times of Feast, Times of Famine*. London: Allen Unwin.

LEHRMAN, J. 1986: Gardens of Islam. In Jellicoe, G., Jellicoe, S., Goode, P. and Lancaster, M. (eds), *The Oxford companion to gardens* (Oxford: Oxford University Press), 277–80.

LEMON, J.T. 1972: *The Best Poor Man's Country. A Geographical Study of Early Southeastern Pennsylvania*. Baltimore: The Johns Hopkins Press.

LENZ, K. and FRICKER, W. 1969: Der Beitrag Friedrich Magers zur historischen Geographie und Kulturlandschaftsgenese, Eine Würdigung zu seinem 85. Geburtstag. *Berichte zur deutschen Landeskunde* 43, 213–20.

LEWIS, G.M. 1966: Changing emphases in the descriptions of the natural environment of the American Great Plains region. *Annals, Association of American Geographers* 56, 33–51.

LEWIS, P.F. 1979: Axioms for reading the landscape. In Meinig, D.W. (ed.), *The interpretation of ordinary landscapes* (New York: Oxford University Press), 11–32.

LLEWELLYN, B. 1989: *The Orient Observed. Images of the Middle East from the Searight Collection*. London: The Victoria and Albert Museum.

LOBB, C.G. 1982: Agriculture. In Blouet, B.W. and Blouet, O.M. (eds), *Latin America. An introductory survey* (New York: John Wiley), 150–83.

LOWENTHAL, D. 1985: *The Past is a Foreign Country*. Cambridge: Cambridge University Press.

LOWTHER, G.R. 1959: Idealist history and historical geography. *The Canadian Geographer* 14, 30–6.

LUCAS, C.P. 1897: *A Historical Geography of the British colonies. Vol. IV. South and East Africa. Part I. Historical*. Oxford: Clarendon Press.

LUCAS, C.P. 1906: *A Historical Geography of the British Colonies. Vol. I. The Mediterranean and Eastern Colonies*. 2nd edition. Revised by Stubbs, R.E.. Oxford: Clarendon Press.

LYONS, F.S.L. 1973: *Ireland since the Famine*. Revised edition. London: Fontana/Collins.

MABIN, A. 1986a: Labour, capital, class struggle and the origins of residential segregation in Kimberley, 1880–1920. *Journal of Historical Geography* 12, 4–26.

MABIN, A. 1986b: At the cutting edge: the new African history and its implications for African historical geography. *Journal of Historical Geography* 12, 74–80.

MACKENZIE, J.M. (ed.) 1990: *Imperialism and the Natural World*. Manchester: Manchester University Press.

MACKINDER, H.J. 1915: *Britain and the British Seas*. 2nd edition. Oxford: Clarendon Press.

MAGNUSSON, L. and ISACSON, M. 1982: Proto-industrialization in Sweden: smithcraft in Eskiltuna and southern Dalecarlia. *Scandinavian Economic History Review* 30, 73–99.

MANN, M. 1986: *The Sources of Social Power. Vol. I. A History of Power from the Beginning to AD 1760*. Cambridge: Cambridge University Press.

MATTHEWS, E. 1983: Global vegetation and land use: new high resolution data bases for climatic studies. *Journal of Climate and Applied Meteorology* 22, 474–87.

MEAD, W.R. 1981: *An Historical Geography of Scandinavia*. London: Academic Press.

MEDICK, H. 1976: The proto-industrial family economy: the structural function of household and family during the transition from peasant society to industrial capitalism. *Social History* 3, 291–315.

MEINIG, D.W. 1963: *On the Margins of the Good Earth. The South Australian Wheat Frontier 1869–1884*. London: John Murray. Monograph series of the Association of American Geographers.

MEINIG, D.W. 1968: *The Great Columbia Plain: a Historical Geography*. Washington, DC: University of Washington Press.

MEINIG, D.W. 1971: *Southwest. Three Peoples in Geographical Change*. New York: Oxford University Press.

MEINIG, D.W. 1978a: Prologue: Andrew Hill Clark, historical geographer. In Gibson, J.R. (ed.), *European settlement and development in North America: essays on geographical change in honour and memory of Andrew Hill Clark* (Toronto and Buffalo: University of Toronto Press), 2–26.

MEINIG, D.W. 1978b: The continuous shaping of America: a prospectus for geographers and historians. *American Historical Review* 83, 1186–1205.

MEINIG, D.W. (ed.) 1979a: *The Interpretation of Ordinary Landscapes*. New York: Oxford University Press.

MEINIG, D.W. 1979b: Symbolic landscapes. Some idealizations of American communities. In Meinig, D.W. (ed.), *The interpretation of ordinary landscapes* (New York: Oxford University Press), 164–92.

MEINIG, D.W. 1986: *The Shaping of America. A Geographical Perspective on 500 Years of History. Vol. 1: Atlantic America, 1492–1800.* New Haven and London: Yale University Press.

MEITZEN, A. 1895: *Siedlung und Agrarwesen der Westgermanen und Ostgermanen, der Kelten, Römer, Finnen und Slawen.* 3 vols and atlas. Berlin.

MELLOR, R.H. 1979: *German railways: a study in the historical geography of transport.* Aberdeen: Department of Geography, O'Dell memorial monograph No. 8.

MENDELS, F.F. 1972: Proto-industrialization: the first phase of the industrialization process. *Journal of Economic History,* 32, 241–61.

MERRENS, H.R. 1964: *Colonial North Carolina in the Eighteenth Century. A Study in Historical Geography.* Chapel Hill: The University of North Carolina Press.

MERRENS, H.R. 1965: Historical geography and early American history. *William and Mary Quarterly* 22, 529–48.

MERTZ, J.T. 1904: *A History of European Scientific Thought in the Nineteenth Century.* London: Blackwood.

MEYER, D.R. 1990: The new industrial order. In Conzen, M.P. (ed.), *The making of the American landscape* (Boston: Unwin Hyman), 249–68.

MILES, L.J. 1982: *Ralph Hall Brown: gentlescholar of historical geography.* Ph.D. dissertation, University of Oklahoma, Graduate College, Norman, Oklahoma.

MILLER, G. and GERGER, T. 1985: *Social Change in Swedish 19th Century Agrarian Society.* Stockholm: Almqvist and Wiksell International.

MILLS, D. and PEARCE, C. 1989: *People and places in the Victorian census. A review and bibliography of publications based substantially on the manuscript census enumerators' books, 1841–1911.* Historical geography research series, No. 23. Cheltenham: Historical Geography Research Group.

MILWARD, A.S. and SAUL, S.B. 1979: *The Economic Development of Continental Europe 1780–1870.* 2nd edition. London: Allen and Unwin.

MITCHELL, J.B. 1954: *Historical Geography.* London: The English Universities Press.

MITCHELL, R.D. 1977: *Commercialism and Frontier: Perspectives on the Early Shenandoah Valley.* Charlottesville: University Press of Virginia.

MORRIS, J.E. *et al.* 1932: What is historical geography? *Geography* No. 95, 17, 39–45.

MOYES, A. 1978: Transport 1730–1900. In Dodgshon, R.A. and Butlin, R.A. (eds), *An historical geography of England and Wales* (London: Academic Press), 401–29.

MULLER, E.K. 1990: The Americanization of the city. In Conzen, M.P. (ed.), *The making of the American landscape* (Boston: Unwin Hyman), 269–92.

MYRES, J.L. 1921: Contribution to discussion listed as 'The content of historical geography'. *The Geographical Teacher* No. 65, 11, 1921, 40–3.

NEWCOMB, R.M. 1979: *Planning the Past.* Folkestone: Dawson.

NITZ, H.-J. 1976: Konvergenz und Evolution in der Entstehung ländlicher Siedlungs-formen. *Tagungsbericht und wissenschaftliche Abhandlungen. 40 Deutscher Geo-graphentag Innsbruck 1975.* Wiesbaden: Franz Steiner Verlag, 208–77.

NITZ, H.-J. 1984: Siedlungsgeographie als historisch-gesellschaftswissenschaftslich prozessforschung. *Geographische Rundschau* 36, 162–9.

NORWOOD, V. and MONK, J. (eds), 1987: *The Desert is No Lady: Southwestern Landscapes in Women's Writing and Art.* New Haven and London: Yale University Press.

OLDFIELD, F. 1983: The role of magnetic studies in palaeohydrology. In Gregory, K. (ed.), *Background to palaeohydrology* (Chichester: John Wiley), 141–65.

OGILVIE, A.G. 1952: The time-element in geography. *Transactions, Institute of British Geographers* 18, 1–16.

OLWIG, K. 1984: *Nature's Ideological Landscape: a Literary and Geographical*

Perspective on the Development and Preservation of Denmark's Jutland Heath. London: Allen and Unwin.

ORWIN, C.S. and ORWIN, C.S. 1938: *The Open Fields.* Oxford: Oxford University Press.

OSBORNE, B.S. 1988: The iconography of nationhood in Canadian art. In Cosgrove, D. and Daniels, S. (eds), *The iconography of landscape* (Cambridge: Cambridge University Press), 162–78.

OVERTON, M. 1977: Computer analysis of an inconsistent data source: the case of the probate inventories. *Journal of Historical Geography* 4, 317–26.

OVERTON, M. 1984a: Probate inventories and the reconstruction of agricultural landscapes. In Reed, M. (ed.), *Discovering past landscapes* (London: Croom Helm), 167–94.

OVERTON, M. 1984b: Agricultural revolution? Development of the agrarian economy in early modern England. In Baker, A.R.H. and Gregory, D. (eds), *Explorations in historical geography* (Cambridge: Cambridge University Press), 118–39.

OVERTON, M. 1985: The diffusion of agricultural innovations in early modern England: turnips and clover in Norfolk and Suffolk 1580–1740. *Transactions, Institute of British Geographers* NS 10, 205–22.

PACIONE, M. 1987: *Historical Geography: Progress and Prospect.* London: Croom Helm.

PALMER, J.J.N. 1986: Computerizing Domesday Book. *Transactions, Institute of British Geographers* NS 11, 279–89.

PARKER, G. 1991: Y.-M. Goblet. *Geographers Biobibliographical Studies* 13, 39–44.

PARKER, W.H. 1968: *An Historical Geography of Russia.* London: University of London Press.

PARKER, W.N. 1979: Industry. In Burke, P. (ed.), *The new Cambridge modern history, XIII Companion volume* (Cambridge: Cambridge University Press), 43–79.

PARRY, M. 1981: Evaluating the impact of climatic change. In Delano Smith, C. and Parry, M. (eds), *Consequences of climatic change* (Nottingham: Department of Geography, University of Nottingham), 3–16.

PAULLIN, C.O. 1932: *Atlas of the Historical Geography of the United States.* Washington: Carnegie Institution and New York: American Geographical Society.

PAWSON, E. 1990: British expansion overseas *c.* 1730–1914. In Dodgshon, R.A. and Butlin, R.A. (eds), *An historical geography of England and Wales.* 2nd edition. London: Academic Press, 521–44.

PÉGUY, C.-P. 1986: L'univers géographique de Fernand Braudel. *Éspace Temps* 34/5, 77–82.

PERLIN, F. 1983: Proto-industrialisation and pre-colonial south Asia. *Past and Present* 98, 30–95.

PETTS, G.E. 1989: Historical analysis of fluvial hydrosystems. In Petts, G.E., Möller, H. and Roux, A.L. (eds), *Historical change of large alluvial rivers: Western Europe* (Chichester: John Wiley), 1–18.

PHILLIPS, A.D.M. 1989: *The Underdraining of Farmland in England during the Nineteenth Century.* Cambridge: Cambridge University Press.

PHILO, C. 1987: Fit localities for an asylum: the historical geography of the nineteenth-century mad-business in England as viewed through the pages of the *Asylum Journal. Journal of Historical Geography* 13, 398–415.

PHILO, C. 1989: Thoughts, words, and 'creative locational acts'. Chapter 11 of Boal, F.W. and Livingstone, D.N. (eds), *The behavioural environment* (London: Routledge), 205–34.

PIRENNE, H. 1925: *Medieval Cities.* Princeton: Princeton University Press.

PIRENNE, H. 1956: *Medieval Cities.* (Revised translation). New York: Doubleday and Company, Anchor Books.

PITTE, J.-R. 1983: *Histoire du Paysage Français.* 2 vols. Paris: Tallandier.

PLANHOL, X. de, 1961: Les nouveaux villages d'Algérie. *Geografiska Annaler* 43, 243–51.

PLANHOL, X. de, 1988: *Géographie Historique de la France*. Paris: Librairie Arthème Fayard.

POLANYI, K. 1944: *The Great Transformation: the Political and Economic Origins of Our Time*. New York: Rinehart and Co.

POLANYI, K. 1968: *Primitive, Archaic and Modern Economies*. Boston: Beacon Press.

POLANYI, K. 1977: *The Livelihood of Man*. Pearson, H.W. (ed.). New York and London: Academic Press.

POLLARD, S. 1981: *Peaceful conquest. The industrialization of Europe 1760–1970*. Oxford: Oxford University Press.

POTTER, J. 1965: The growth of population in America, 1700–1860. In Glass, D.V. and Eversley, D.E.C. (eds), *Population in history. Essays in historical demography* (London: Edward Arnold), 631–92.

POUNDS, N.J.G. 1947a: Ports and outports in north-west Europe. *Geographical Journal* 109, 216–28.

POUNDS, N.J.G. 1947b: *An Historical and Political Geography of Europe*. London: Harrap.

POUNDS, N.J.G. 1973: *An Historical Geography of Europe, 450 BC to 1330 AD*. Cambridge: Cambridge University Press.

POUNDS, N.J.G. 1974: *An Economic History of Medieval Europe*. London: Longman.

POUNDS, N.J.G. 1979: *An Historical Geography of Europe, 1500–1840*. Cambridge: Cambridge University Press.

POUNDS, N.J.G. 1985: *An Historical Geography of Europe, 1800–1914*. Cambridge: Cambridge University Press. Citations are from 1988 paperback edition.

POUNDS, N.J.G. 1990: *An Historical Geography of Europe*. Cambridge: Cambridge University Press.

POWELL, J.M. 1970: *the Public Lands of Australia Felix*. Melbourne: Oxford University Press.

POWELL, J.M. 1977: *Mirrors of the New World. Images and Image-makers in the Settlement Process*. Folkestone: Dawson, Archon Books.

POWELL, J.M. 1981: Wide angles and convergences: recent historical-geographical interaction in Australia. *Journal of Historical Geography* 7, 407–13.

POWELL, J.M. 1988: *An Historical Geography of Modern Australia*. Cambridge: Cambridge University Press.

PRED, A. 1981: Production, family, and free-time projects: a time-geographic perspective on the individual and societal change in nineteenth-century US cities. *Journal of Historical Geography* 7, 1, 1–36.

PRED, A. 1985: The social becomes the spatial, the spatial becomes the social: enclosures, social change and the becoming of places in the Swedish province of Skåne. In Gregory, D. and Urry, J. (eds), *Social relations and spatial structures* (London: Macmillan), 337–65.

PRED, A. 1986: *Place, Practice and Structure. Social and Spatial Transformation in Southern Sweden: 1750–1850*. Cambridge: Polity Press.

PRINCE, H.C. 1971: Real, imagined, and abstract worlds of the past. *Progress in Geography* 3, 4–86.

PRINCE, H.C. 1978: Time and historical geography. In Carlstein, C., Parkes, D. and Thrift, N. (eds), *Making sense of time* (London: Edward Arnold), 17–37.

PRINCE, H.C. 1980: Historical geography in 1980. In Brown, E.H. (ed.), *Geography, yesterday and tomorrow* (Oxford: Oxford University Press), 229–50.

PRINCE, H.C. 1988: Art and agrarian change, 1710–1815. In Cosgrove, D. and Daniels, S. (eds), *The iconography of landscape* (Cambridge: Cambridge University Press), 98–118.

PURVIS, M. 1986: Popular institutions. In Langton, J. and Morris, R.J. (eds), *Atlas of industrializing Britain* (London: Methuen), 194–7.

QUICKE, F. (ed.) 1931: *1er Congrès Internationale de Géographie Historique.* 2 vols. Brussels: Librairie Falk Fib.

RADFORD, J.P. 1979: Race, residence, and ideology: Charleston, South Carolina in the mid-nineteenth century. In Ward, D. (ed.), *Geographic perspectives on America's past. Readings in the historical geography of the United States* (New York: Oxford University Press), 344–55.

RAMSAY, W.M. 1890: *The Historical Geography of Asia Minor.* London: John Murray.

RAPOPORT, A. 1969: *House Form and Culture.* Englewood Cliffs, New Jersey: Prentice-Hall.

REDFIELD, R. 1956: *The Little Community and Peasant Society and Culture.* Chicago: Chicago

REES, P.W. 1982: Transportation. In Blouet, B.W. and Blouet, O.M. (eds), *Latin America. An introductory survey* (New York: John Wiley), 87–149.

RENFREW, C. 1977: Space, time and polity. In Friedman, J. and Rowlands, M.J. (eds), *The evolution of social systems* (London: Duckworth), 89–112.

REVILL, G. 1989: *Paternalism, community and corporate culture: a study of the Derby headquarters of the Midland Railway Company and its workforce, 1840–1900,* Ph.D. thesis, Loughborough University of Technology.

REYNOLDS, H. 1982: *The Other Side of the Frontier. Aboriginal Resistance to the European Invasion of Australia.* Harmondsworth: Penguin Books.

ROAF, M. 1990: *Cultural Atlas of Mesopotamia and the Near East.* Oxford: Facts on File.

ROBERTS, B.K. 1987: *The Making of the English Village.* London: Longman.

ROBERTS, N. 1989: *The Holocene. An Environmental History.* Oxford: Blackwell.

ROBINSON, D.J. (ed.) 1990: *Migration in Colonial Spanish America.* Cambridge: Cambridge University Press.

ROBINSON, D.J. 1972: Historical geography in Latin America. In Baker, A.R.H. (ed.), *Progress in historical geography* (Newton Abbot: David and Charles), 168–86.

ROBINSON, J.L. 1967: Growth and trends in geography in Canadian universities. *Canadian Geographer* XI, 1967, 216–29.

RODGERS, H.B. 1960: The Lancashire cotton industry in 1840. *Transactions, Institute of British Geographers* 28, 135–53.

RODRIGUE, C.M. 1990: Women and the land: a review of *The desert is no lady* and a discussion of women in the west. *Historical Geography* 20, 21–3.

ROGERS, J.D. 1911: *A Historical Geography of the British Colonies. Vol. V. Canada—Part III Geographical.* Oxford: Clarendon Press.

RONAN, C.A. 1983: *The Cambridge Illustrated History of the World's Science.* Cambridge: Cambridge University Press.

ROSE, G. and OGBORN, M. 1988: Feminism and historical geography. *Journal of Historical Geography* 14, 405–9.

ROXBY, P.M. 1909–10: Historical geography of East Anglia. *Geographical Teacher* 128–44.

ROXBY, P.M. 1933: Foreword. To Wilcox, H.A., *The woodlands and marshlands of England.* University Press of Liverpool. London: Hodder and Stoughton.

RUGG, D.S. 1981: The Mid-West as a hearth area in American academic geography. In Blouet, B.W. (ed.), 1981: *The origins of academic geography in the United States* (Hamden, Connecticut: Archon Books), 175–91.

SACK, R.D. 1986: *Human Territoriality: Its Theory and History.* Cambridge: Cambridge University Press.

SAGARRA, E. 1977: *A Social History of Germany 1648–1914.* London: Methuen.

SAHLINS, P. 1990: Natural frontiers revisited: France's boundaries since the seventeenth century. *American Historical Review* 95, 1423–51.

SAID, E. 1978: *Orientalism*. London: Routledge.

SAID, E. 1985: Opponents, audiences, constituencies and community. In Foster, H. (ed.), *Postmodern culture* (London: Pluto Press), 135–59.

SAID, E. 1989: Representing the colonized: anthropology's interlocutors. *Critical Enquiry* 15, 205–25.

SAID, E. 1990: Narrative, geography and interpretation. *New Left Review* 180, 81–97.

SAMUEL, R. 1981: *People's History and Socialist Theory*. London: Routledge.

SARGENT, C. 1982: The Latin American city. In Blouet, B.W. and Blouet, O.M. (eds), *Latin America. An introductory survey* (New York: Wiley), 201–49.

SAUER, C.O. 1925: The morphology of landscape. *University of California Publications in Geography* 2, 19–54.

SAUER, C.O. 1939: *Man and Nature: Early America Before the Days of the White Men*. New York: Scribner's.

SAUER, C.O. 1941a: Foreword to historical geography. *Annals of the Association of American Geographers* 31, 1–24.

SAUER, C.O. 1941b: The personality of Mexico. *Geographical Review* 31, 353–64.

SAUER, C.O. 1944: A geographic sketch of early man in America. Geographical Review 34, 529–73.

SAUER, C.O. 1952: *Agricultural Origins and Dispersals*. New York: American Geographical Society.

SAUER, C.O. 1963: The morphology of landscape. 1925 article reprinted in Leighly, J. (ed.), *Land and life: a selection from the writings of Carl Ortwin Sauer*. Berkeley: University of California Press, 315–50.

SAUER, C.O. 1966: *The Early Spanish Main*. Berkeley and Los Angeles: The University of California Press.

SCHAFER, J. 1921–22: The microscopic method applied to history. *Minnesota History Bulletin* 4, 3–20.

SCHÖN, L. 1982: Proto-industrialisation and factories: textiles in Sweden in the mid-nineteenth century. *Scandinavian Economic History Review* 30, 57–71.

SCHRÖDER, K.H. 1977: *Geographie an der Universität Tübingen 1512–1977*. Tübingen: Geographisches Institut der Universität Tübingen.

SCHWARZ, G. 1959: *Allgemeine Siedlungsgeographie*, Berlin.

SCHWARTZ, G. 1986: Joseph Franz Maria Partsch, 1851–1925. *Geographers Bio-bibliographical Studies* 10, 125–33.

SENDA, M. 1982: Progress in Japanese historical geography. *Journal of Historical Geography* 8, 170–81.

SHANIN, T. (ed.) 1971: *Peasants and Peasant Societies*. Harmondsworth: Penguin.

SHAW, G. 1986: Retail patterns. In Langton, J. and Morris, R.J. (eds), *Atlas of industrializing Britain* (London: Methuen), 180–4.

SHAW, G. 1989: Industrialization, urban growth and the city economy. In Lawton, R. (ed.), *The rise and fall of great cities* (London: Bellhaven), 55–79.

SHEAIL, J. 1978: Rabbits and agriculture in postmedieval England. *Journal of Historical Geography* 4, 343–55.

SIMMS, A., 1976: Deserted medieval villages and fields in Germany. A survey of the literature with a select bibliography. *Historical Geography* 2, 223–38.

SIMMS, A. 1982: Die historische geographie in Gross Brittanien; a personal view. *Erdkunde* 36, 71–8.

SINGER, C., HOLMYARD, E.J. and HALL, A.R. (eds) 1954: *A history of technology. Vol. I. From early times to fall of ancient empires*. Oxford: Clarendon Press.

SLATER, T. and JARVIS, P. (eds) 1982: *Field and forest. An historical geography of Warwickshire and Worcestershire*. Norwich: GeoBooks.

SJOBERG, G. 1960: *The Pre-industrial City: Past and Present*. Glencoe: Free Press.

SMITH, C.T. 1967: *An Historical Geography of Western Europe Before 1800*. London: Longmans.

SMITH, D.M. 1963: The British hosiery industry at the middle of the nineteenth century. *Transactions, Institute of British Geographers* NS 32, 125–42.

SMITH, G.A. 1894: *The Historical Geography of the Holy Land*. London: Hodder and Stoughton.

SMITH, G.A. 1907–8: *Jerusalem*. 2 vols. London: Hodder and Stoughton.

SMITH, G.A. 1915: *The Atlas of the Historical Geography of the Holy Land*. London: Hodder and Stoughton.

SMITH, G.A 1966: *The Historical Geography of the Holy Land*. Reprint for the Fontana Library of the 25th edition of 1931. London: Collins.

SMITH, J.F. 1975: Settlement on the public domain as reflected in Federal records. Suggested research approaches. In Ehrenberg, R.E. (ed.), *Pattern and process. Research in historical geography* (Washington, DC: Howard University Press), 290–304.

SMITH, R.M. 1990: Geographical aspects of population change in England 1500–1730. In Dodgshon, R.A. and Butlin, R.A. (eds), *An historical geography of England and Wales*, 2nd edition (London: Academic Press), 151–75.

SMITH, W. 1949: *An economic geography of Great Britain*. London: Methuen.

SMYTH, W.J. and WHELAN, K. (eds), 1988: *Common Ground. Essays on the Historical Geography of Ireland Presented to T. Jones Hughes*. Cork: Cork University Press.

SOUTHALL, H. 1986: Unionization. In Langton, J. and Morris, R.J. (eds), *Atlas of industrializing Britain* (London: Methuen), 189–93.

SPATE, O.H.K. 1979: *The Pacific since Magellan: I. The Spanish Lake*. London: Croom Helm.

SPATE, O.H.K. 1983: *The Pacific since Magellan: II. Monopolists and Freebooters*. London: Croom Helm.

SPIEGEL, G.M. 1992: History and post-modernism. *Past and Present* 135, 194–208.

STANLEY, A.P. 1856: *Sinai and Palestine. In Connection with their History*. London: John Murray.

STARKEL, L., GREGORY, K.J. and THORNES, J.B. (eds) 1991: *Temperate palaeohy-drology. Fluvial processes in the temperate zone during the last 15,000 years*. Chichester: John Wiley.

STEPHENS, N. and GLASSCOCK, R.E. (eds), 1970: *Irish geographical studies in honour of E. Estyn Evans*. Belfast: Queen's University, Department of Geography.

STONE, L. 1991: History and post-modernism, *Past and Present*, 131, 217–18.

STONE, L. 1992: History and post-modernism. *Past and Present* 135, 189–94.

SUTTON, K. 1984: Reclamation of wasteland during the eighteenth and nineteenth centuries. In Clout, H.D. (ed.), *Themes in the historical geography of France* (London: Academic Press), 247–300.

SZULC, H. 1978: Regular green villages in Pomerania. *Geographia Polonica* 38, 265–70.

SZULC, H. 1988a: *Morfogenetyczne typy osiedli wiejskich na Pomorzu Zachodnim*. Warsaw: Instytut Geografii i Przestrzennego Zagospodarowania, Polska Akademia Nauk.

SZULC, H. 1988b: The origin, evolution and distribution of open fields in Poland: a case study of Pomerania. *Geografiska Annaler* 70B, 179–96.

TAAFE, E.J., MORILL, R.J. and GOULD, P.R. 1963: Transport expansion in underdeveloped countries: a comparative analysis. *Geographical review* 53, 503–29.

TAYLOR, P.J. 1985: *Political Geography. World Economy, Nation-state, and Locality*. London: Longman.

THIRSK, J. 1961: Industries in the countryside. In Fisher, F.J. (ed.), *Essays in the economic and social history of Tudor and Stuart England* (Cambridge: Cambridge University Press), 70–88.

THIRSK, J. 1987: *England's Agricultural Regions and Agrarian History, 1500–1750.* London: Macmillan.

THOMAS, C. 1985: Landscape with figures: in the steps of E.G. Bowen. *Cambria* 12, 15–31.

THOMPSON, E.P. 1968: *The Making of the English Working Class.* Harmondsworth: Pelican Books.

THOMPSON, J.M. 1929: *An Historical Geography of Europe 1800–1889.* Oxford: Clarendon Press.

THORNES, J.B. 1987: The palaeo-ecology of erosion. In Wagstaff, J.M. (ed.), *Landscape and Culture* (Blackwell, Oxford), 37–55.

THORPE, H. 1954: Lichfield: a study of its growth and function. *Collections for a history of Staffordshire 1950 and 1951,* 137–212.

THRIFT, N. 1983: On the determination of social action in space and time. *Environment and Planning. D. Society and Space* 1, 23–57.

THRIFT, N. 1990: Transport and communication 1730–1914. In Dodgshon, R.A. and Butlin, R.A. (eds), *An historical geography of England and Wales*, 2nd edition (London: Academic Press), 453–86.

THRIFT, N. and PRED, A. 1981: Time-geography: a new beginning. *Progress in Human Geography* 5, 277–86.

TOZER, H.F. 1935: *A History of Ancient Geography.* 2nd edition. Cambridge: Cambridge University Press.

TRANTER, N.L. 1985: *Population and Society 1750–1940.* London: Longman.

TREADGOLD, D.W. 1982: Russian expansion in the light of Turner's study of the American frontier. *Agricultural History* 26, 147–52.

TREGEAR, T.R. 1976: *China. A Geographical Survey.* London and Sydney: Hodder and Stoughton.

TRISTRAM, H.B. 1872: *Bible Places, or, The Topography of the Holy Land.* London: Society for Promoting Christian Knowledge.

TUAN, Yi-Fu 1970: *China.* London: Longman.

TUCKER, R.P. 1988: The depletion of India's forests under British imperialism: planters, foresters and peasants in Assam and Kerala. In Worster, D. (ed.), *The ends of the earth* (Cambridge, Cambridge University Press), 118–40.

TURNER, F.J. 1894: The significance of the frontier in American history. Originally published in the Annual Report of the American Historical Association for 1893 (Washington, DC 1894) and reprinted in Turner, F.J. (ed.), *The frontier in American history* (New York: Holt, Rinehart and Wilson), 243–68.

TURNER, M. 1980: *English Parliamentary Enclosure.* Folkestone: Dawson.

TURNER, M. 1981: Arable in England and Wales: estimates from the 1801 crop return. *Journal of Historical Geography* 7, 291–302.

TURNER, M. 1984: *Enclosures in Britain 1750–1830.* London: Macmillan.

UHLIG, H. 1961: Old hamlets with infield and outfield systems in Western and Central Europe. In Helmfrid, S. (ed.), *Morphogenesis of the agrarian cultural landscape, Geografiska Annaler* 43, 285–312.

UHLIG, H. and LIENAU, C. 1972: *Die Siedlungen des Ländlichen Raumes.* Giessen: Lenz Verlag.

UNWIN, P.T.H. 1990: Towns and trade 1066–1500. In Dodgshon, R.A. and Butlin, R.A. (eds), *An historical geography of England and Wales*, 2nd edition (London: Academic Press), 123–50.

UZOIGWE, G.N. 1988: The results of the Berlin West Africa conference: an assessment. In Förster, S., Mommsen, W.J. and Robinson, R. (eds), *Bismarck, Europe, and Africa. The Berlin Africa conference 1884–1885 and the onset of partition* (Oxford: The German Historical Institute, London, and Oxford University Press), 541–52.

VAMPLEW, W. 1986: Sport. In Langton, J. and Morris, R.J. (eds), *Atlas of industrializing Britain* (London: Methuen), 198–201.

VANCE, J.E. Jr 1970: *The Merchant's World: The Geography of Wholesaling.* Englewood Cliffs, New Jersey: Prentice-Hall.

VANCE, J.E. Jr 1986: *Capturing the Horizon: The Historical Geography of Transportation since the Transportation Revolution of the Sixteenth Century.* New York: Harper and Row.

VANCE, J.E. Jr 1989: Transportation and the geographical expression of capitalism. In Genovese, E.D. and Hochberg, L. (eds), *Geographical perspectives in history* (Oxford: Blackwell), 118–43.

VERHULST, A. 1980: Die historische geografie in Belgie en Haar ontwikkeling sedert 1930. In Mertens, J. (ed.), *Bronnen voor de historische geografie van België* (Brussels: Algemeen Rijksarchief en Rijksarchief in de provinciën), 21–33.

VERHULST, A. 1989: The origins of towns in the Low Countries and the Pirenne thesis. *Past and Present* 122, 3–35.

VERHULST, A. and GOTTSHALK, M.K.E. (eds), 1980: *Transgressies en Occupatie-geschiedenis in de kustgebieden van Nederland en België.* Ghent: Belgisch Centruum voor Landelijke Geschiednis.

VERLEY, P. 1991: La révolution anglaise: une révision (note critique). *Annales E.S.C.* 3, 735–55.

WACKER, P.O. 1975: Patterns and problems in the historical geography of the Afro-American population of New Jersey, 1726–1860. In Ehrenberg, R.E. (ed.), *Pattern and process in historical geography* (Washington, DC: Howard University Press), 25–72.

WAGSTAFF, J.M. 1985: *The Evolution of Middle Eastern Landscapes.* London and Sydney: Croom Helm.

WAGSTAFF, J.M. (ed.) 1987: *Landscape and Culture. Geographical and Archaeological Perspectives.* Oxford: Blackwell.

WALKER, D.F. 1980: *Canada's Industrial Space-Economy.* London: Bell and Hyman.

WALLERSTEIN, I. 1974: *The Modern World-System I: Capitalist Agriculture and the Origins of the European World-Economy in the Sixteenth Century.* London: Academic Press.

WALLERSTEIN, I. 1980: *The Modern World-System II: Mercantilism and the Consolidation of the European World-Economy, 1600–1750.* London: Academic Press.

WALLERSTEIN, I. 1989: *The Modern World-System III: the Second Era of Great Expansion of the Capitalist World-Economy, 1730–1840s.* London: Academic Press.

WALSH, M. 1981: *The American Frontier Revisited.* London: Macmillan.

WALTON, J.R. 1987: Agriculture and rural society. In Pacione, M. (ed.), *Historical geography. Progress and prospect* (London: Croom Helm), 123–57.

WALTON, J.K. 1989: Proto-industrialisation and the first industrial revolution: the case of Lancashire. In Hudson, P. (ed.), *Regions and industries* (Cambridge: Cambridge University Press), 41–68.

WARD, D. 1971: *Cities and Immigrants. A Geography of Change in Nineteenth-Century America.* London: Oxford University Press.

WARD, D. 1978: The early Victorian city in England and America: on the parallel development of an urban image. In Gibson, J.R. (ed.), *European settlement and development in North America. Essays on geographical change in honour and memory of Andrew Hill Clark* (Toronto: Toronto University Press), 170–89.

WARD, D. (ed.) 1979a: *Geographic perspectives on America's Past. Readings in the Historical Geography of the United States.* New York: Oxford University Press.

WARD, D. 1979b: The internal spatial differentiation of immigrant residential districts. In Ward, D. (ed.), *Geographic perspectives on America's past. Readings in the historical geography of the United States* (New York: Oxford University Press), 335–43.

WARD, D. 1980: Environs and neighbours in the Two Nations: residential differentiation in mid-nineteenth century Leeds. *Journal of Historical Geography* 6, 133–62.

WATTS, D. 1987: *The West Indies: Patterns of Development, Culture and Environmental Change Since 1492.* Cambridge: Cambridge University Press.

WELLS, E. 1701: *A Treatise of Antient and Modern Geography.* Oxford.

WELLS, E. 1708: *An Historical Geography of the New Testament.* London.

WELLS, E. 1710, 1711, 1712: *An Historical Geography of the Old Testament.* 3 vols. London.

WESSELING, H.L. 1988: The Berlin Conference and the expansion of Europe: a conclusion. In Förster, S., Mommsen, W.J. and Robinson, R. (eds), *Bismarck, Europe, and Africa. The Berlin Africa conference 1884–1885 and the onset of partition* (London: The German Historical Institute; Oxford University Press), 527–40.

WEST, R.C. 1982: Aboriginal and colonial geography of Latin America. In Blouet, B.W. and Blouet, O.M. (eds), *Latin America: an introductory survey* (New York: John Wiley), 34–86.

WESTLAKE, J. 1894: *International Law.* Cambridge: Cambridge University Press.

WHEATLEY, P. 1971: *The Pivot of the Four Quarters. A Preliminary Enquiry into the Origins and Character of the Ancient Chinese City.* Edinburgh: Edinburgh University Press.

WHITEHAND, J.W.R. 1972: Building cycles and the spatial pattern of urban growth. *Transactions, Institute of British Geographers* 56, 39–55.

WHITEHAND, J.W.R. 1987: Urban morphology. In Pacione, M. (ed.), *Historical geography. Progress and prospect* (London: Croom Helm), 250–76.

WHITEHAND, J.W.R. 1988: Recent developments in urban morphology. In Denecke, D. and Shaw, G. (eds), *Urban historical geography* (Cambridge: Cambridge University Press), 285–96.

WHITTINGTON, G. and GIBSON, A.J.S 1986: The military survey of Scotland 1747–1755: a critique. *Historical Geography Research Series*, 18. Norwich: Geobooks.

WHITTLESEY, D. 1929: Sequent occupance. *Annals of the association of American Geographers* 19, 162–5.

WHYTE, I.D. and WHYTE, K.A. 1981: Sources for Scottish historical geography. An introductory guide. *Historical Geography Research Series*, 6. Norwich: Geobooks.

WILCOX, H.A. 1933: *The Woodlands and Marshlands of England.* University Press of Liverpool. London: Hodder and Stoughton.

WILLIAMS, M. 1983: 'The apple of my eye': Carl Sauer and historical geography. *Journal of Historical Geography* 9, 1–28.

WILLIAMS, M. 1989: Deforestation: past and present. *Progress in Human Geography* 13, 176–207.

WILLIAMS, R. 1973: *The Country and the City.* London: Palladin.

WILLIAMS, S.W. 1983: The theory of internal colonialism: an examination. In Drakakis-Smith, D. and Williams, S.W. (eds), *Internal colonialism. Essays around a theme.* Monograph No. 3, Developing Areas Study Group, Institute of British Geographers (Edinburgh: University of Edinburgh, Department of Geography).

WILLIGAN, J.D. and LYNCH, K.A. 1982: *Sources and Methods of Historical Demography.* New York: Academic Press.

WINSOR, R.A. 1987: Environmental imagery of the wet prairie of east central Illinois, 1820–1920. *Journal of Historical Geography* 13, 375–97.

WISHART, D.J. 1979: *The Fur Trade of the American West, 1807–1840.* London: Croom Helm.

WITHERS, C.W.J. 1988: *Gaelic Scotland. The Transformation of a Cultural Region.* London: Routledge.

WITTFOGEL, K. 1956: The hydraulic civilizations. In Thomas, J.L. Jr (ed.), *Man's role in changing the face of the earth* (Chicago: University of Chicago Press), 152–64.

WITTFOGEL, K. 1957: *Oriental Despotism*. New Haven: Yale University Press.

WOLF, E.R. 1982: *Europe and the People Without History*. Berkeley and Los Angeles: University of California Press.

WOODS, R. 1979: *Population Analysis in Geography*. London: Longman.

WRIGHT, P. 1985: *On Living in an Old Country*. London: Verso.

WRIGLEY, E.A. 1988: *Continuity, Chance and Change. The Characters of the Industrial Revolution in England*. Cambridge: Cambridge University Press.

WRIGLEY, E.A. and SCHOFIELD, R.S. 1981: *The Population History of England 1541–1871: A Reconstruction*. London: Edward Arnold.

WYCKOFF, W.K. 1990: Landscapes of private power and wealth. In Conzen, M.P. (ed.), *The making of the American landscape* (Boston: Unwin Hyman), 335–54.

WYNN, G. 1977: Discovering the Antipodes, a review of historical geography in Australia and New Zealand, 1969–1975, with a bibliography. *Journal of Historical Geography* 3, 251–66.

WYNN, G. 1987: Forging a Canadian nation. In Mitchell, R.D. and Groves, P.A. (eds), *North America. The historical geography of a changing continent* (Totowa, New Jersey: Rowman and Littlefield), 373–409.

YATES, E.M. 1960: History in a map. *Geographical Journal* 126, 1, 32–51.

ZELINSKY, W. 1973a: *The Cultural Geography of the United States*. Englewood Cliffs, New Jersey: Prentice-Hall.

ZELINSKY, W. 1973b: The strange case of the missing female geographer. *The Professional Geographer* 25, 101–5.

ZIMMERN, A.E. 1911: *The Greek Commonwealth*. Oxford: Clarendon Press.

Index